Palestine, Taiwan, and Western Sahara

Palestine, Taiwan, and Western Sahara

Statehood, Sovereignty, and the International System

Edited by Sabella Ogbobode Abidde

LEXINGTON BOOKS
Lanham • Boulder • New York • London

Published by Lexington Books
An imprint of The Rowman & Littlefield Publishing Group, Inc.
4501 Forbes Boulevard, Suite 200, Lanham, Maryland 20706
www.rowman.com

86-90 Paul Street, London EC2A 4NE

British Library Cataloguing in Publication Information Available

Library of Congress Cataloging-in-Publication Data

Names: Abidde, Sabella Ogbobode, 1962- editor.
Title: Palestine, Taiwan, and Western Sahara : statehood, sovereignty, and the international system / edited by Sabella Ogbobode Abidde.
Description: Lanham, Maryland : Lexington Books, 2023. | Includes bibliographical references and index. | Summary: "An examination of the undercurrents of statehood and sovereign integrity vis-à-vis the State of Palestine, Taiwan, and Western Sahara; and examines why the international system is convoluted and often powerless in effecting the principles of self-determination. This denial of collective aspiration continues to be a source of regional and global insight"-- Provided by publisher.
Identifiers: LCCN 2023014535 (print) | LCCN 2023014536 (ebook) | ISBN 9781666932003 (cloth) | ISBN 9781666932010 (ebook)
Subjects: LCSH: Sovereignty. | State, The. | Palestine--International status. | Taiwan--International status. | Western Sahara--International status.
Classification: LCC JZ4034 .P35 2023 (print) | LCC JZ4034 (ebook) | DDC 320.1/50951249--dc23/eng/20230419
LC record available at https://lccn.loc.gov/2023014535
LC ebook record available at https://lccn.loc.gov/2023014536

Contents

Preface

Within African studies, there seems to be a limited number of academic writings—especially books—that deal with the issue of statehood: how and under what condition does a political entity gain statehood or become a nation-state. And indeed, much of the available literature, it seems, was produced or is being produced by scholars in the areas of international relations and international law. Otherwise, such and related books deal mostly with issues relating to state formation, power and authority, governance and leadership, public institutions, military rule, maladministration, etc.

The dearth of literature on how political entities become a nation-state could be because most African countries—during and after colonialism—didn't bother with that question. They didn't because statehood was a forgone conclusion just before or right after the colonizer officially vacated a country. Within a decade or so, many of the independent countries had to grapple with ethnicity, weak states, overbearing military, religious and ethnic conflicts, and ethnonationalism (wherein ethnic group seeks their own independence or self-determination).

This book came about because of this understanding. But beyond that—and especially since my scholarship centers on different regions of the world—I deemed it necessary, as a first step, to examine the situation in Palestine, Taiwan, and Western Sahara. The next volume would concentrate on other entities in Africa: Southern Cameroon, Tigray, Biafra, and Somaliland.

All the aforementioned entities, along with Kosovo and a few others around the world, are variously referred to either as quasi-states; ambiguous states; non-recognized states; state-like entities; or contested states. These are entities that have a geographical space with citizens and have a functioning government that carries out the duties and responsibilities of a government, and also can participate in regional and international affairs. Essentially, they have established de *facto control* over their territory but want *de jure recognition.*

The national aspiration of these contested states, therefore, is to be seated among sovereign equals and have a complete engagement with the United Nations member states and multitudes of intergovernmental agencies that makes up the international community.

The State of Palestine is "governed" by three competing political authorities: The Palestine Liberation Organization (PLO); the Palestinian National Authority (PNA) and Hamas. Nonetheless, Palestine is currently a UN observer state that is recognized by 138 UN member states. Its full independence has been in limbo for decades mainly due to the objection of the State of Israel. Until 1971, Taiwan, officially the Republic of China (ROC), was the assumed representative of the people and government of China. And since the end of the Chinese Civil War in 1949, which forced the losing side (the Kuomintang) to berth in Taiwan, Mainland China, officially the People's Republic of China (PRC) has claimed it as one of its provinces.

More than seven decades later, the contest and contestation between the ROC and the PRC have not been settled. And as of the spring of 2023, only a dozen or so countries around the world consider Taiwan a nation-state and instead adhere to the "One China" policy. The Organization of African Unity (OAU) and its successor, the African Union (AU), consider Western Sahara a sovereign nation-state (to the objection of Morocco), which has claimed it since 1957. As of 2023, Morocco occupies and has administrative control over some percent of the country. Western Sahara is an anomaly insofar as colonialism and decolonization in Africa are concerned because of the failure of the AU to rid the continent of the last vestiges of inhumanity.

In 1998, the then-secretary-general of the United Nations (UN), Kofi Annan, asserted that the struggle for independence, for the right of a people to be a master of its own destiny, is the struggle for human rights. Believing this to be true, then, where does that leave the Palestinians, the Taiwanese, and the Saharawi people who have for decades been clamoring for independence and statehood?

It is hoped that more scholars will examine and reexamine the issue of statehood especially as it concerned the remaining dozen or so contested states around the world.

Sabella Ogbobode Abidde, PhD
Alabama State University
Montgomery, Alabama
Spring 2023

Acknowledgments

Writing a book can be tough, yet exciting. It can be stressful yet rewarding. Either way, it can be lonely and isolating. Edited collections are especially so because it is impossible to be fully in control of the enterprise. One must deal with issues such as multiple and or excessive demands in terms of extension of manuscript submission. And of course, some contributors do unilaterally decide on a different topic or veer off the thrust of their initial abstract. One of the most perplexing sources of annoyance are contributors who, after several months of engagement, decide not to finish or submit their chapters. In other words, anything can happen to aggravate, frustrate or discourage an editor.

All the aforementioned scenarios were part of the experience of putting this volume together. Nonetheless, it was still a joy that this volume was published. It was joyful because of the efforts and contributions of those scholars who made the final product possible. Thank you, thank you, and thank you so very much!

I am also indebted to Ms. Sydney Wedbush, who signed off on the project. Sydney is ever so patient, responsive, thoughtful, and kind. I am also grateful to Mr. Joseph C. Parry and Ms. Emilia Rivera and their team of professionals for bringing this book to fruition. Thank you! I would also like to thank the anonymous reviewers, the copy editor, and the production staff at Lexington Books. And of course, Ms. Felica Kemp (formerly the administrative secretary in the Department of History and Political Science, ASU). Thank you!

Federica Stagni would like to thank Donatella della Porta and Lorenzo Bosi for their constant support and trust in this work, despite the risks and difficulties that such research could entail also for their positions. I would also like to thank Benoit Challand for introducing me to the study of Settler Colonialism, and Florian Car for reading the very first draft of this work and helping me edit it. Without Florian continuous help and support over these years, particularly during the period of fieldwork, this work would have not taken the shape it has now.

List of Abbreviations

AL	African League
AL	Arab League
ALA	Arab Liberation Army
ARPS	Aborigines Rights Protection Society
AU	African Union
AWAM	Association of West African Merchants
BMAs	British Mandate Authorities
CERD	Committee on the Elimination of Racial Discrimination
CJEU	Court of Justice of the European Union
CPP	Convention People's Party's
CTS	Consolidated Treaty Series
DFNS	Democratic Federation of Northern Syria
DPP	Democratic Progressive Party
EEC	European Economic Community
EMGF	East Mediterranean Gas Forum
EU	European Union
Frente POLISARIO	Frente Popular de Liberación de Saguía el Harma y Río de Oro
GB	Great Britain
GCYM	Gold Coast Youth Movement
Hamas	Harakat al-Muqaawama al-'Islamiyya
ICC	International Criminal Court
ICERD	International Convention on the Elimination of All Forms of
ICJ	International Court of Justice
IDF	Israeli Defence Forces
IGO	Intergovernmental organization

ILM	International Legal Materials
INTERPOL	International Criminal Police Organization
IO	International organization
IPU	Inter-Parliamentary Union
IRA	Irish Republican Army
IRM	Islamic Resistant Movement
KDP	Kurdistan Democratic Party
KMT	Kuomintang Party (Nationalists in Taiwan/China
LAS	League of Arab States
LNTS	League of Nations Treaty Series
MAL	Moroccan Army of Liberation
MB	Muslim Brotherhood
MINURSO	United Nations Mission for the Referendum in Western Sahara
NATO	North Atlantic Treaty Organization
NCBWA	National Congress of British West Africa
NSGT	Non-Self-Governing Territory
NYM	Nigeria Youth Movement
OAS	Organization of American States
OAU	Organization of African Unity
OIC	Organization of Islamic Cooperation
OPCW	Organization for the Prohibition of Chemical Weapons
PA	Palestinian Authority
PE	Personal Envoy of the Secretary General for Western Sahara
PEA	Protest Event Analysis
PF	Polisario Front
PFLP	Popular Front for Liberation of Palestine
PFLP–GC	Popular Front for Liberation of Palestine - General Command
PLC	Palestinian Legislative Council
PLO	Palestinian Liberation Organization
PNA	Palestinian National Authority
POS	Political Opportunity Structure
PRC	People's Republic of China
PUK	Patriotic Union of Kurdistan

RIAA	Reports of International Arbitral Awards
ROC	Republic of China (Taiwan)
SADR	Sahrawi Arab Democratic Republic (Western Sahara)
SLPP	Sierra Leone People's Party
SOP	State of Palestine
SRSG	Special Representative of the Secretary General
SU	Soviet Union
TRC	Taiwan Relations Act
UDI	Unilateral declaration of independence
UGCC	United Gold Coast Convention
UN	United Nations
UNCTAD	United Nations Conference on Trade and Development
UNESCO	United Nations Educational, Scientific and Cultural Organization
UNGA	United Nations General Assembly
UNIDO	United Nations Industrial Development Organization
UNO	United Nations Organisation
UNSC	United Nations Security Council
UNTAG	United Nations Transition Assistance Group in Namibia
UNTS	United Nations Treaty Series
UPU	Universal Postal Union
US	United States
USA	United States of America
USSR	United Soviet Socialists Republics
WASU	West African Students Union
WAYL	West African Youth League
WHO	World Health Organization
WTO	World Trade Organization
WWI	First World War

Introduction

Statehood, Sovereignty, and the International System

Sabella Ogbobode Abidde

Since the twentieth century at least, the creation and recognition of new states has been one of the most difficult aspects of international law and international relations. Yet many groups and state-like entities have devoted a lot of resources to achieving independent statehood. This is so because with statehood comes many benefits and privileges which include the sole authority within the territory, rights and protection in international affairs, and membership in the United Nations (UN) and other intergovernmental organizations. Though the emergence of new states has been met with considerable opposition, the twentieth century witnessed the emergence of some 150 new states mostly brought about because of global wars, decolonization, ethnic conflicts, and civil wars (Visoka, Newman, and Doyle, 2020).

Insofar as state creation is concerned, there are two dominant theories: the Declaratory theory, the Constitutive theory; and the hybrid approach to state creation and recognition (Nicholson and Grant, 2020). According to Nicholson and Grant, the *declaratory theory* is a theory of how states come into being and that there is a general rule of international law under which an entity becomes a state by meeting the criteria of effectiveness which are formulated from Article 1 of Montevideo Convention of 1933, viz: a permanent population; a defined territory; a government; and the capacity of the government to enter into relations with the other states (pp. 25–26). Over the years, however, a fourth prerequisite has become germane: the prospective states must be recognized by many of the existing nation-states and admitted into the family of nations as represented by the UN.

The *constitutive theory*, meanwhile, strongly opposes the idea that there is a legal duty to recognize new entities. Constitutive theorists and thinkers argue that the legal existence of new entities derives solely from the will of those that are already established. In other words, the constitutive view holds that recognition is a precondition to the existence, legitimacy, and associated legal rights. In this conception, recognition is a matter of sovereign consent and is based on the mutuality of recognition. Because there is no duty to recognize, states are free to recognize new entities entirely at their own discretion (Meachum, 2022). Essentially, criteria such as territory, population, and government are not necessary; however, recognizing states may take them into account (ibid., Nicholson and Grant). Nicholson and Grant went on to assert that the

> Adherents of the traditional or pure constitutive theory have declined . . . 'Constitutivist' in truth takes elements from both of the traditional theories. The approaches can be classified into two broad families: those in which recognition and the criteria for statehood both play necessary roles in constituting statehood, and those in which the criteria suffice on their own but, in particular circumstances, recognition may also suffice (p. 29).

Nonetheless, since the UN was created after the Second World War, one of the primary criteria for the establishment of a new state has been international recognition by member states of the organization. It is where issues relating to statehood, self-rule, and related matters are discussed and often adjudicated. Indeed, it is almost inconceivable for a state to gain statehood without going through the "UN process." Ultimately, a political entity or states-like asking for statehood must have broad international support and recognition—without which full membership of the UN may be impossible. It is for these reasons that Palestine, Taiwan, and Western Sahara do not wear the toga of a State even though nearly all the conditions recognized and recommended within all applicable theories have been met. This is so because the process for granting statehood is a political act and not a legal necessity. The prevailing political condition at the international level makes it difficult for the abovementioned political entities to achieve statehood.

THEMATIC THREADS AND METHODOLOGICAL PRINCIPLES

There are at least four (4) *thematic threads* that connect the three political entities in question. First, as opposed to most of the member states of the UN opposing their sovereignty and statehood, what we have here is *single-state opposition*. That's to say that each of the contested states—Palestine, Taiwan, and Western Sahara—each has one major opposition to their sovereignty: Israel; China; and Morocco. In the case of Palestine, Israel and the United

States (US) are in concert insofar as the opposition to Palestinian Statehood is concerned.

Second, the three political entities have *mixed levels of recognition*. Palestine, for example, had its observer status upgraded to "non-member observer state" status in the UN thereby conferring on it the de facto recognition of a sovereign state. This was done in 2012. Three years later, the International Criminal Court (ICJ) announced that Palestine should be considered a "state." Governments around the world have taken a similar stance. Shortly, thereafter, the Vatican announced it was shifting recognition and conferring recognition of statehood. Taiwan, on the other hand, is recognized by some fifteen (15) countries, while Western Sahara is recognized by forty-one (41) UN member states.

What if Palestine, Taiwan, and Western Sahara unilaterally declare their independence? In the summer of 2010 for instance, ICJ ruled, regarding Kosovo, that some political entities could unilaterally declare independence (ICJ, 2010; Nte, 2023). However, such a move on the part of Palestine, Taiwan, and Western Sahara may cause commotion within the international system. For instance, a UDI may cause China to militarily invade Taiwan. How the governments of Israel/the US and Morocco would react is also predictable. The fourth thematic thread goes to the heart of the raison d'être of the United Nations: "The maintenance of international peace and security." What's the point of the UN if it cannot solve/resolve three of the major contestations of the twentieth and twenty-first centuries?

While one concedes that many hot spots around the world command the UN's resources; the Israeli-Palestinian conflict and the Morocco-Western Sahara conflict have resulted in exorbitant economic costs and unconscionable human suffering. Left unsettled, the predicted conflict between the People's Republic of China (PRC/China) and the Republic of China (ROC/Taiwan) has the potential to destabilize East Asia and beyond. The political and economic consequences of such a conflict would, indeed, reverberate around the world.

Each of the thirteen scholars had the leeway to apply theoretical and conceptual frameworks that apply to their chapter. But beyond that, there is an overarching methodological tool that broadly applies to this volume: comparative-historical analysis. While each of the political entities has its unique internal composition and dynamics, they share strands of history and historical experiences in terms of their struggle for statehood and territorial sovereignty.

Comparative-historical analysis has been used by scholars in the social sciences—especially political science and sociology—to trace and survey historical paths as well as to, for instance, identify historical prerequisites that gave rise to nation-states. This method is particularly useful because it is a tool with which we can compare the similarity and or otherwise of the political antecedents, current conditions, and aspirations of the three political entities in question.

THE PROJECT: AIM AND STRUCTURE

Palestine, Taiwan, and Western Sahara are all ambiguous, restricted, contested states. In the case of Palestine, unless the United States/Israel acquiesce to statehood, the Palestinians are likely to remain in limbo for many decades to come. Although the Palestinians could force the issue on the UN; whether they would succeed is debatable. In dealing with China, Taiwan is limited to four options: acquiesce to China's demand to join the mainland as a province; maintain the ongoing status quo; engage in a unilateral declaration of independence (UDI) or be granted statehood at the UN to the protest and displeasure of Beijing. An inkling of the latter two options is likely to compel China to invade Taiwan.

The Western Sahara situation, in many ways, is akin to what we have between China and Taiwan: unless Morocco agrees to the collective demand of the Sahrawi Arab Democratic Republic, things are likely to remain the way they are for the foreseeable future. Western Sahara's situation is compounded by the lack of political will and moral leadership on the continent and by the African Union (AU).

What we have here is the unrealized and seemingly unrealizable dream of three contested states in search of territorial sovereignty, statehood, and political legitimacy. The aim of this volume is therefore threefold: First, to examine the undercurrents of statehood and independence; (b) to examine why the named political entities should or should not be granted independence and international recognition; (c) to examine why the international system is convoluted and often powerless in effecting the wishes of most of the member states of the UN. Under these objects, scholars from diverse but complementary disciplines are assembled to examine the foretasted issues.

And so in chapter 1—*International Law and the Politics of State Recognition: A Comparative Study of the Palestinian, Western Sarahan, and Tiawanese Struggle for Statehood*—Priye Torulagha asserts that the efficacy of international law is always a subject of intense debate among scholars, lawyers, international relations experts, and diplomats because it operates in an environment dominated by sovereign states whose main goal is to enhance their national interests. Hence, the process of gaining statehood through diplomatic recognition is heart-wrenching due to the indeterminate nature of international law. Torulagha then explores the issues of the recognition of Western Sahara (Sahrawi Arab Democratic Republic), the State of Palestine, and the Republic of China; and identifies the types of diplomatic recognition and the conditions in international law that a political community must meet to achieve independence; determines whether the three political communities meet the conditions for gaining recognition; and explores the influence of international politics on state recognition. He posits that the fact that international law stipulates that political communities seeking independence must meet Montevidio's four conditions does not mean that independence or sovereignty could be gained. Consequently, Western Sahara, the State of Palestine, and the Republic of China have struggled for decades to gain statehood without succeeding. The difficulty is prompted by the fact that the decision to offer diplomatic recognition is based mostly on national interest and not necessarily on the conditions stipulated in international law.

Gbensuglo Alidu Bukari, in chapter 2—*The Undercurrents of Political Economy of Nationalism*—contributes to the wealth of knowledge and scholarly debate in the political economy of nationalism. He began with a set of questions, i.e., how, and when did sovereignty of nation-states as a legal and political concept come into being; and how does nationalism animate the sovereign power of Westphalia nation-states? Bukari provides answers to these conceptual questions by interrogating how nationalism is credited with being a major contributor to the birth and growth of nation-states as we know them. His chapter also contributes to the theoretical and conceptual clarity of political economy nationalism. It further accentuates the real and perceived political economy factors of nationalism. He concluded that nationalism is a phenomenon of rising expectations of the nation-states wherein people make ever-increasing demands for more economic, social and political benefits. Nationalism should therefore deliver a state with organized forces supreme in its territory, and pursue a conscious policy of aggrandizement in its relations with other states. It should have the right and obligation to regulate and control all other institutions of society and to direct on lines overly set by the interest of the state itself. Thus, the state should have all-inclusive characteristics with the overarching organizational authority to hold it together.

In chapter 3—*U.S. Recognition of the Illegal Israel and Moroccan Annexations of Occupied Territories*—Stephen Zunes proclaims that the United States is the only country in the world to have formally recognized Morocco's annexation of Western Sahara and Israel's annexations of the Golan Heights and its settlement blocs in the West Bank, placing the United States well outside international legal norms that prohibit the expansion of territory by force. Though these recognitions took place during the Trump administration, they have not been subsequently reversed and are in many respects the culmination of decades of bipartisan support for the Moroccan and Israeli occupations which have sometimes strongly implied recognition of sovereignty by the occupying powers. Zumes also opines that due to the broader international legal implications, U.S. policy impacts not just those suffering under foreign belligerent occupation but establishes dangerous precedents that undermine the United Nations Charter and weaken Western resolve against Russian irredentism in Ukraine. He concludes that as with the former Indonesian occupation of East Timor, the best hope for a just resolution may be through global civil society pressuring the United States and other Western powers to end their support for the Israeli and Moroccan occupations and allowing for self-determination consistent with international law.

In chapter 4—*Comparing Hamas and Irgun in the Struggles for Independence: A Continuation of the Same Terrorist Strategy by Different Actors?*—Lawrence Mhandara states that the Palestinian and Israeli struggles for self-determination and independence are colored with narratives that are more reflective of each other. In particular, both peoples believe they have been victims of historical injustices and claim the same territory which has been a salient feature in their counterclaims. Mhandara examines the strategy of the Irgun (National Military Organization) in the pre-1948 period and juxtaposes it with Hamas' contemporary resistance formula. Resistance movements in both nations have engaged in acts of terrorism in the pursuit of national self-determination and independence. Yet when one is exposed to the question of terrorism in the context of the protracted Palestinian struggle for independence, Hamas has been subjected to unfavorable stereotypes or projected as a profane movement compared to the Irgun's struggle for Jewish independence. Mhandara further argues that it is ahistorical to discount how the same strategy of terrorism was employed by the Jewish groups in the voyage towards the establishment of the state of Israel in 1948. Based on the conceptual framework of 'costly signaling,' similarities are ascertained between Irgun's strategies and tactics before 1948 and the Hamas' strategy and tactics in their search for the elusive Palestinian independence. Evidence shows that the Irgun and Hamas have employed similar terrorist strategies—attrition, intimidation, spoiling, and outbidding—validating the view that the two movements embraced the same strategy at different intervals. Indeed, comparing the two group's *modus operandi*, a compelling conclusion is that Hamas is continuing with the same rewarding terrorist strategies in a different epoch just as Irgun.

In chapter 5—*The State of Palestine as a Sovereign Actor in the International Community: Implications for Its Legal Status*—Konstantinos Magliveras and Gino Naldi contend that presently, 139 states have recognized the State of Palestine, but none of the G7 countries, which has so far prevented its accession to the United Nations, an act that would have allowed its universal acceptance as an independent, sovereign state. At the same time, the State of Palestine seeks to engage with the international community as an equal member not only to strengthen its position but also to uphold its rights and to challenge the legitimacy of acts taken by third states against its interests. After offering an overview of the unresolved question of Palestine's international legal status, which goes back to 1916, Magliveras and Naldi analyze the three pillars on which its diplomatic strategy for active participation in the international arena has been based, a strategy which does not always have the desired results: (a) accession to a large number of multilateral treaties as well as participation in negotiating new treaties; (b) membership in international organizations and institutions; and (c) recourse to international courts and quasi-judicial bodies.

Federica Stagni, in chapter 6, *The State of Palestine: Between Abstraction and Reality*, addresses the issue of Palestinian statehood from an analysis of a social movement campaign. Given that Israel is a full-fledged and powerful state, she would never give up on its claim to Palestinian lands despite the inalienable Palestinian right to self-determination, as claimed by the United Nations. Hence, one of the questions is "how is the settler colonial framework reconcilable with a reality of the relentless occupation of the Palestinian land that does not provide space for the creation of an independent Palestinian state; and how can the Palestinian Authority be reframed, being a de facto subcontractor of the Israeli Defence Force in the West Bank, and the Hamas hegemony on an isolated unliveable enclave?" Stagni addresses these questions starting with an analysis of a social movement campaign that has seen the cooperation of different activist organizations from the two different national groups that try to implement concrete acts of prefigurative politics, to make the one-state solution the only feasible anti-colonial option. Although they are a minority of activists, they overtly embrace an anti-colonial discourse that seeks to address the root of the conflict recognizing its settler-colonial nature. And after a first historical introduction to the Palestinian context, she reviews those works that have examined the Palestinian context through the lenses of settler colonialism. Then, a critique of the dichotomy created by such an approach, which sees the colonized and the colonizers as inevitably competing entities are considered. Stagni concludes by arguing that any type of future arrangement for Palestine needs to include the settler-colonial responsibility that Israel holds towards Palestinians, but with a closer look at the reality on the ground, going over the dichotomy created by such an approach to envisage a unique state in which Israeli and Palestinians have equal rights.

In chapter 7—*Toward a Global Agenda: Resolving the Israeli–Palestinian Conflict*—Idowu Johnson wrote that among the key issues in contemporary international political debates is the protractedness of the Isreali-Palestinian conflict. The conflict can be regarded as the lengthiest in recorded human history. The complexities of the conflict have led to serious acrimonious, hateful, and belligerent aspirations between the two countries. To be sure, the two countries are caught in a web of extreme complexities on how best to resolve the aged-long conflict. Johnson utilizes descriptive and qualitative research methods by relying on secondary materials to analyze the trend in the Israeli-Palestinian conflict. He asserts that the conflict transcended the initial grapple over a geographical entity to which both sides largely lay claims and were willing to sacrifice their last blood in the protection of their national interest. He then argues that the conflict has a global outlook, judging from the interference and interest of several powerful states of the world (Britain and the United States), which directly or indirectly shapes their perception and reaction towards the conflict. Furthermore, the global dynamism of the conflict defined in terms of religious, national, and ideological interests has made the conflict an enduring one. The conflict however raises global concern as many states supporting either Israel or Palestine are now at war, which polarizes the international system. Despite several peace initiatives by international organizations, the conflict is unabated. This however implies global peace and security. In resolving the conflict, Johnson concludes that a global peaceful settlement framework should be designed and signed by all member states of the UN.

Dean Karalekas, in chapter 8, *Kurdayeti and Taiwan Rentong: Identity and Nation Building in Under-Recognized States*, declares that the disparate, largely unrecognized nations of Taiwan and Kurdistan share remarkable similarities in how they have conducted their respective nation-building projects. Kurdayeti became a potent political force after the fall of the Persian and Ottoman empires, though the Kurds were denied participation in this process. In Taiwan, on the other hand, centuries of colonization led rise to the emergence of a Taiwanese consciousness with different customs, practices, and belief systems from those in China. According to Karalekas, the national symbols, celebrations, and a rich localized tradition of literature all contribute to making newly constructed traditions feel primordial and inspire the same loyalty and patriotism so necessary to building a nation. This is especially true when, as both Kurdistan and Taiwan are, the imagined community is under intense existential threat from hostile external forces, and risks being subsumed by the tyranny of a foreign other. Situated on different continents and having different languages and cultural influences, both share certain remarkable similarities: They both represent nationhood projects predicated on an ethnic identity that is distinct from the one in which they risk being subsumed; they both employ the concept of "imagined community" in order to establish unity among their members; and they both, unlike the powers that surround them in their respective regions, demonstrate a propensity to cherish universal values such as respect for human rights and the dignity of the individual.

In chapter 9—*Taiwan in United States Domestic Politics and Foreign Policy Agenda*—Felix Kumah-Abiwu contends that the relations between the United States and Taiwan did not only change in 1979 after the diplomatic recognition of China by the U.S., but the geopolitics of the region and the Taiwan sovereignty question on the "one-China policy" where China maintains the principle of one China with Taiwan as part of its territory, while Taiwan also seeks to gain independence as a sovereign country has positioned Taiwan in U.S. domestic politics and foreign policy agenda for several decades. To further enhance our understanding of the strong unofficial relations between the United States and Taiwan and to unpack the emerging debates on the relevance of the U.S. policy of strategic ambiguity, Kumah-Abiwu draws on relevant works from the extant literature to explore these issues. He argues that Taiwan appears to have continued to successfully capture the attention of the U.S. political elites and policymakers for three reasons. First, because of the volatile nature of the Taiwan sovereignty question between China and Taiwan. Second, the U.S. foreign/security objective of maintaining peace and stability in the region where the United States has vital interests. Third, the strong economic ties between the United States and Taiwan and the U.S. support Taiwan's democratic practices and values. He concludes by advancing the argument that a likely conflict-related deteriorating situation between China and Taiwan will shape the response or behavior of the United States toward the region.

In chapter 10—The Sahrawi Arab Democratic Republic—A State That Never Was?—Gino Naldi and Cristiano d'Orsi argue that when the former Spanish colony of Western Sahara was proclaimed as an independent State in 1976, its independence was recognized by a significant number of States from the Global South. In 1982 the SADR was admitted to membership of the OAU. In an article published in 1985 (*Indian Journal of International Law*) the present author argued that a presumption of statehood existed in favor of the SADR. This contention was based on the view that at the time the SADR satisfied in the main the criteria of statehood but that any deficiencies, e.g., lack of control over part of the territory, could be counterbalanced by the principle of self-determination; Western Sahara was a victim of a forcible denial of the right of the people to self-determination, a right that had been explicitly recognized by the ICJ in the *Western Sahara Case*. Furthermore, the ousting of the occupying forces by the Polisario Front seemed imminent. All these developments were evidential factors supportive of statehood. However, since then the cause of the SADR has gone into reverse. Morocco has secured control over large swathes of the territory, including most major areas of habitation and its natural resources, and the Polisario Front has been largely neutered as a military threat. However, the current UN position favors a political solution based on compromise providing for self-determination. Many States have withdrawn their recognition of the SADR. Western Sahara remains listed as a non-self-governing territory by the UN Special Committee of twenty-four. The UK, like many other Western States, regards the status of Western Sahara as undetermined, and in 2020 the Trump administration recognized Moroccan sovereignty over Western Sahara. According to Naldi and d'Orsi, the resolution of the dispute over Western Sahara must conform with the right of self-determination and, in principle, calls for a more resolute approach from the UN.

In chapter 11—*The Sahrawi Arab Democratic Republic: The Case for Independence)*—J.J.P. Smith contends with the viability and apparent necessity of creating a Sahrawi state. The Sahrawi people's journey to an emergent statehood is first canvassed. Sahrawi *political independence* is arguably well-established, needing only culmination through an act of self-determination and wider recognition among states. Smith argues that a principal area of inquiry is what can be called the *internal*, namely, the right of the Sahrawi people to make an elective choice of their status, including one of international legal personality. The analysis considers the political landscape, starting with the Sahrawi aspiration to create for themselves a nation-state, before turning to the viability of a prospective state. The conditions for a democratic, capably governed, and economically successful state are explored. The second area of inquiry is what can be called the external associative, reviewing the utility and apparent obligation for the organized international community to accept and even support the creation of a Sahrawi state. The role and implications for the African Union are of particular interest. A third area of inquiry is the importance of realizing the goals of the post-colonial order to ensure sufficient political independence of non-self-governing peoples so that they are capable of choosing Westphalian statehood. This involves assuring the rule of law, especially the right to self-determination standing at the apex of the international human rights order. For a Western Sahara in Africa, the significance of such a vindication is greater. Achieving a Sahrawi state marks a new beginning for an African polity.

And in chapter 12—*Western Sahara Peace Process, 1975–2008: An Overview*—Meriem Naili asserts that a failed decolonization process of the Non-Self-Governing Territory of Western Sahara has resulted in a self-determination conflict that has become frozen over the past few decades. At the time Staffan de Mistura was appointed personal envoy to the secretary-general for Western Sahara (PE) in October 2021, the position had been vacant for over two years and the people of Western Sahara are yet to express their right to self-determination today. The UN Mission for the Referendum in Western Sahara (MINURSO) arguably stands as an exception in modern peacekeeping. All documents bear witness to the deadlock that the negotiation process has reached. The diverging interpretations by the parties to its mandate are unambiguous and are regarded as a continuous major challenge to the mission's operations. Naili further discusses the various phases in the peace process since the rendering of the International Court of Justice Advisory Opinion in 1975 to the Manhasset negotiations in 2007–2008 and its consequent crystallization. It firstly identifies a significant involvement on the part of the UN and other regional organizations in the mid-1880s resulting in the deployment of MINURSO in 1991. It also highlights the many challenges encountered in the process leading up to the appointment of James Baker as PE in 1997. Finally, Naili discusses Baker's resignation in 2004 and the Moroccan proposal for Autonomy in 2007 marking the breakpoint in the peace process in the conflict over Western Sahara.

In the concluding chapter, Sabella Abidde opined that justice—as opposed to the tenets of international law, international relations, or politics—is the best way to approach the issue of statehood insofar as contested states are concerned. And that the UN, the AU, and all the member-states of both organizations must do the right things for the Palestinians, Taiwanese, and the Sahrawi Arab Democratic Republic if there is to be a decrease in regional and global conflicts and insecurity. After all, there can be no enduring peace in an atmosphere of colonialism, suppression, and injustice. Denying people their right to self-rule, territorial sovereignty, or statehood is unjust and a catalyst for intermittent or prolonged violent conflicts.

REFERENCES

International Court of Justice (ICJ). (2010, July 22). *"Accordance with international law of the unilateral declaration of independence in respect of Kosovo."* http://www.icj-cij.org/docket/files/141/15987.pdf. Retrieved January 1, 2023.

Meachum, M. S. (2022). Joining the Club? The Politics of Government Recognition. *Questions in Politics*, *IX*, 1–16.

Nicholson, R., & Grant, T. D. (2020). Theories of State Recognition. In G. Visoka, J. Doyle, & E. Newman (Eds.), *Routledge Handbook of State Recognition* (pp. 25–36). essay, Routledge.

Nte T.U. (2023) The Burden of Recognition in the Unilateral Declaration of Independence by Kosovo, Global Journal of Political Science and Administration, Vol. 11, No. 1, pp.1–19

Visoka, G., Newman, E., & Doyle, J. (2020). Introduction: statehood and recognition in world politics. In G. Visoka, E. Newman, & J. Doyle (Eds.), *Routledge Handbook of State Recognition* (pp. 1–21). Introduction, Routledge.

I

Nationalism and Nation-States in Recent Times

1

International Law and the Politics of Recognition

A Comparative Study of the Palestinian, Western Saharan, and Taiwanese Struggle for Statehood

Priye S. Torulagha

INTRODUCTION

The efficacy of international law is always a subject of intense debate. The debate is prompted by the fact that international law operates in an environment dominated by sovereign states that work fastidiously to ensure their national interests. Hence, while some scholars, jurists, and diplomats believe that international law is an effective means to establish a universalized standard of behavior among states, others believe that due to the chaotic nature of international politics and sovereignty, international law is ineffective and unreliable for establishing a universalized standard of behavior (Wolfe, 2002). The doubters emphasize that powerful military and economic states rarely abide by international law as they pursue and reinforce their geopolitical interests while less powerful states are subjected to it. They also note that less powerful states that are aligned with the most powerful states can also ignore or violate international law with little or no penalty. As a result, if two political communities seek statehood at the same time, they might end up with two different results with one gaining sovereignty while the other is denied the status, even though both met the conditions for attaining independence.

This buttresses the argument by those who doubt the efficacy of international law since states are driven primarily by national interest (Goldstein,

2005). National interest is perpetrated through the principle of expediency, which seems to be an overriding consideration, despite the existence of other doctrines of recognition, such as the Tobar, Estrada, belligerency, and insurgency. Thus, the politics of state recognition mitigate international law in such a manner that it is a grueling exercise to achieve sovereignty.

The purpose here is to accomplish the following goals: (1) explore the issues pertaining to the recognition of Western Sahara (Sahrawi Arab Democratic Republic), State of Palestine (SOP), and Republic of China (Taiwan), (2) identify the types of diplomatic recognition and the conditions in international law that a political community must meet to achieve independence, (3) determine whether the three political communities meet the conditions to gain independence, and (4) explore the influence of international politics on state recognition. For the purpose of this chapter, Western Sahara and Sahrawi Arab Democratic Republic (SADR) and Republic of China (ROC), and Taiwan are used interchangeably.

EXPLORATION OF THE ISSUES PERTAINING TO STATEHOOD AND RECOGNITION

In this section, the historical sources of the Sahrawi, Palestinian, and Taiwanese efforts to gain independence are explored.

Western Sahara/Sahrawi Arab Democratic Republic (SADR)

As the name indicates, Western Sahara is a geographic area located between the Atlantic Ocean and the coastal plains that border Morocco on the north, Algeria by the northeast, and Mauritania by the east and south of Northwest Africa. The Western Saharan issue began when in 1884, following the Berlin Conference to divide Africa into European spheres of control, Spain colonized an area stretching from Cape Bojador to Cape Blanc to create a protectorate (d'Origny, 2005). This led to resistance organized by Ma al-Ayn, the politico-religious head of Tindouf and Smara in 1910 against the French, with Moroccan assistance. The indigenous (Sahrawis) resistance against Spanish and French forces continued until 1934 when both countries put down the resistance. Later, Spain incorporated the districts of Sagula el-Hamra and the Rio de Oro with the protectorate to establish a province in 1958. The Sahrawis rebelled against the colonization by launching attacks against Spanish forces. In attempting to extend its colonial influence in North Africa, France also intervened in the territory. Morocco became actively involved in the Western Saharan conflict when the Moroccan Army of Liberation initiated the Ifni War in 1956. However, Spanish forces were able to gain control with the assistance of the French after two years of skirmishes (Ifni War, 2022). Despite gaining control, resistance continued in various forms in the territory.

As the territorial dispute remained unresolved, Sahrawi students in various universities in Morocco formed the Popular Front for the Liberation of Sagua e-Hamra and Rio de Oro on May 10, 1973. Known as the Polisario Front (PF), the movement, made up of both men and women, sought assistance from various Arab countries but received most from Libya and Mauritania. The PF relocated to the territory and launched a war of liberation (Morris, 2013). In 1974, under the dictatorship of Francisco Franco, Spain carried out a census of the territory to conduct a referendum to determine self-determination for Western Sahara. The referendum could not take place, instead, Spain signed the Madrid Accords with Morocco and Mauritania on November 14, 1975, in which it decided to hand over the territory to the two countries (UN, 1975). Thereafter, Spanish forces withdrew from the region.

Following the Spanish withdrawal, Morocco and Mauritania annexed the territory in 1976. They argued that Western Sahara was part of their territories before Spain colonized the area. Hence, Morocco took two-thirds of the northern region while Mauritania took control of a portion of the southern region (World Population Review, 2022). While Morocco insisted on the ownership of the territory, the ICJ indicated in a legal opinion that Morocco had no right to claim Western Sahara as its territory (d'Origny, 2008). The annexation led to the Western Saharan War in which the Polisario Front, supported by Algeria and Libya, fought against Morocco and Mauritania starting in 1975. While the battle raged on, the PF declared the establishment of the Sahrawi Arab Democratic Republic (SADR), in conformity with the resolution of the United Nations in February 1976 (Gonzalez, 2016). In response, some countries recognized SADR as an independent state. In 1979, Mauritania withdrew from the contested region, leaving Morocco to continue the war with the PF. The United Nations also reacted to the Moroccan annexation by passing a General Assembly Resolution 34/37, which affirmed the right of the Sahrawi people to self-determination in 1979. Morocco and PF agreed on an UN-brokered ceasefire in the same year even though most of the territory was under Moroccan control while the PF controlled about twenty percent of the territory. The Western Sahara War between the PF and Morocco has claimed thousands of lives while hundreds of thousands live in refugee camps.

Several efforts have been made to end the conflict, including a plan to conduct a referendum, the Houston Agreement, a UN plan to find a common agreement between the Polisario and Morocco, the Baker Plan which proposed self-determination for the Sahrawi people, the Moroccan plan of 2006 which called for the autonomy for Western Sahara, and the 2007 United

Nations Security Council Resolution 1754, which encouraged direct negotiation between the PF and Morocco without preconditions. The conflict has not been resolved, hence, the Sahrawis have not gained full independence as Morocco continues to maintain its grip on most of the disputed territory.

The Israeli-Palestinian Conflict and the Struggle for Palestinian Statehood

The conflict between the Israelis and Palestinians is traceable to the late nineteen century. While the Trans-Jordanian region, including Palestine, was under the Ottoman Empire, with the area dominated by the Palestinians and most of the Jews living outside the territory, the Jews in the First Zionist Congress of 1897, declared their intention to establish a homeland in Palestine just as the Arabs too wanted to establish a state of their own in the same territory. During the First World War, Britain liberated the territory from the Ottoman Empire and was mandated to administer it through the League of Nations Mandate for Palestine and Transjordan in April 1920, following the San Remos conference. Arthur James Balfour, the British Foreign Minister made the Balfour Declaration on November 2, 1917, by indicating British support for the establishment of a Jewish homeland in Palestine. The declaration angered the Arabs who felt that Britain did not consult or negotiate with them before making the declaration in support of a Jewish homeland (Neal, 1995).

The struggle to control the territory turned into a sectarian conflict between the Arabs and Jews. The conflict escalated after the Franco–Syrian War of the 1920s into a wider regional conflict during the 1930s and 1940s. Palestinian nationalism increased following the return of Palestinians led by Haj Amin al-Hussein from Damascus to establish a homeland for Palestinians (Avraham, 2002). The violent riots that followed resulted in the deaths of many Jews in Hebron and Safed and the subsequent evacuation of the Jews from Hebron and Gaza. The Jews responded by forming a paramilitary force known as the Haganah. Sheikh Izaddin al Qassam from Syria established the Black Hand militant group which launched the 1936 Arab revolt. The revolt lasted from 1936 to 1939 during which the British managed to expel some leaders of the group. The revolt led to the establishment of the Peel Commission, which initiated a plan to partition Palestine into two. The Palestinians rejected the plan while Chaim Weizmann and David Ben-Gurion, the two main Jewish leaders, accepted the plan even though other Jewish leaders rejected it (Morris, 20029).

During the Second World War, Palestine experienced a temporary de-escalation of sectarian conflicts between the Arabs and Jews. However, the end of the Second World War was characterized by an increase in tension as many Jewish survivors of the Nazi holocaust migrated to Palestine, both officially and unofficially. At this time, Jewish militancy was being directed against the British presence in the territory. Perhaps, to reduce tension, the United Nations General Assembly adopted Resolution 181 (II) on November 29, 1947, which recommended the partitioning of Palestine into two states, one for the Arabs and the other for the Jews (Baum, 2015). The resolution led to Palestinian riots that culminated in a civil war. Jewish militias led by Haganah, Irgun, and Lehi and backed by veterans of the Second World war gained a military advantage over the volunteered Arab Liberation Army and the Palestinian Arab Army of the Holy War, which was commanded by Abd al-Qadir al Husayni and Hasan Salama.

On May 14, 1948, the Jews declared the establishment of the State of Israel. The declaration led to the Arab-Israeli War of 1948, in which the Arab League intervened militarily by sending forces into Palestine. Due to military successes in the war, Israel gained a territorial advantage over the Arabs. However, Jordan annexed the West Bank and Egypt took control of the Gaza Strip (Gelvin, 2014). In the Suez Crisis or Second Arab-Israeli War, which lasted from October 29 to November 7, 1956, Israel briefly occupied the Gaza Strip and exiled the All-Palestinian Government before withdrawing.

In 1964, under the leadership of Yasser Arafat, the Palestinians established the Palestinian Liberation Organization (PLO) to continue the struggle against Israel and the establishment of a State of Palestine. Three years later, the Six-Day War erupted on June 5, 1967, and Israel gained control of both the West Bank and the Gaza Strip. This forced the PLO to move and set up its headquarters in Jordan. However, following a clash between the PLO and Jordanian military forces in 1970, the PLO was again forced to move to Southern Lebanon to set up a base. The PLO used its base in South Lebanon to launch attacks against Israel and participated in the internal Lebanese Civil War. However, the Palestinian killing of some Israelis which was referred to as the "Coastal Road massacre" led to the Israeli invasion and momentary occupation of Southern Lebanon. The situation worsens when the PLO attempted to assassinate an Israeli diplomat, resulting in a full-scale Israeli invasion of Lebanon in 1982. The invasion culminated in the capture of Beirut and some parts of Lebanon. The PLO was forced again to move its headquarters to Tunisia. However, due to escalating clashes with Iranian-backed Shia militias, including Hezbollah, Israeli forces withdrew from most of Lebanon and occupied a tiny strip of land in Southern Lebanon in 1985.

An international effort to resolve the Israeli - Palestinian conflict led to the conveyance of the Oslo Accord in Norway in 1993. The accord allowed the PLO to return to take control of the West Bank and Gaza Strip and established the Palestinian National Authority (PNA). The accord had significant support among Palestinians and Israelis, but it also galvanized Hamas and

Palestinian Islamic jihad to oppose the effort. In Israel, some right-wing elements and religious fundamentalists opposed the accord, so much so that Yigal Amir, a law student assassinated Israeli Prime Minister Yitzhak Rabin on November 4, 1995. The assassination changed the political dynamics as subsequent Israeli governments became cautious in responding to the accord (Avraham, 2002).

Despite the setback, President Bill Clinton of the United States of America initiated the Camp David Summit in 2000. Chairman Yasser Arafat of the Palestinian National Authority and Prime Minister Ehud Barak of Israel attended. The Israeli government submitted a six-point program as a basis for negotiation, including (1) a nonmilitarized Palestinian state, the ceding of 69 Jewish settlements in the West Bank to Israel, (3) no right of return for Palestinians, (4) no Palestinian sovereignty over the Temple Mount and core sections of East Jerusalem, (5) Israeli control of the Jordanian valley. Chairman Arafat rejected the Israeli proposal (Malley and Agha, 2001). President Bill Clinton released his plan for resolving the conflict. The plan included (1) the establishment of a sovereign Palestine state in 94 to 96 percent of the West Bank, and Gaza Strip plus a 1 to 3 percent land swap, (2) Arab areas of Jerusalem to remain under Palestinian control, and Jewish areas to remain under Israel, (3) the splitting of the holy sites with Palestinians having control over the Temple Mount/Noble Sanctuary while Israel would have possession of the Western wall, the right of return for Palestinians, and (5) financial compensation, (6) the Israeli acknowledgment of the suffering of the Palestinian people, (7) a non-militarized Palestinian state, and (8) an international force to provide border security. The Israeli and Palestinian teams accepted the Clinton proposals (Pressman, 2023).

The Camp David Proposal was followed by the Taba Summit which took place on January 2001 in Egypt. Both sides agreed to remove the temporary Israeli-controlled areas. However, the negotiation did not go far as Ariel Sharon of the Likud Party won the election and became prime minister of Israel. Despite the setback, a peace plan known as the "Road Map for Peace" was initiated by the European Union, Russia, the United States, and the United Nations on September 17, 2002. The plan did not attempt to solve the thorny issues but called for the stoppage of Israeli construction of settlements in the West Bank and for both sides to stop violence (Levinson, 2015). While this plan did not go far in galvanizing both sides to agree, the Arabs, led by Saudi Arabia also offered a peace plan to resolve both the Arab-Israeli and Israeli-Palestinian issues. The Arab plan called for (1) a two-state solution with borders based on the United Nations recommendation following the six-day war in 1967, (2) the normalization of relations with Israel based on Israeli withdrawal of its forces from all occupied territories, (3) the return of Golan Height, (4) the Israeli recognition of Palestinian State with East

Jerusalem as its capital, (5) a just solution to the Palestinian refugee problem (*Guardian*, 2002). The Israeli government accepted some points and made reservations about other points.

Thus, despite several efforts to resolve the Arab—Israeli and Israeli—Palestinian conflicts, some fundamental issues remain. They include (1) security, (2) borders of the proposed two states, (3) the status of Jerusalem, (4) holy sites, (5) Israeli settlements, (6) water rights, and (7) Palestinian freedom of movement (World Bank Technical Team, 2007). These issues remained unresolved as hardliners, particularly religiously motivated elements on both sides make it difficult to compromise. On the Israeli side, hardline religious ideologues do not want Israel to compromise and hand over any land in the occupied areas to the Palestinians. On the Palestinian side, Hamas and Islamic Jihad have ideological differences with the Fatah and this impedes a good working relationship that is necessary to pursue a common goal (Berger and Khoury, 2018).

The lack of progress in the peace process led to a series of Palestinian uprisings known as the Intifada. The Palestinian effort to negotiate with Israel to resolve the issues is complicated by the electoral victory of Hamas in the Gaza Strip in 2006. Hamas refused to accept prior Israeli—Palestinian agreements including recognizing the right of Israel to exist and agree not to instigate violence (Erlanger, 2006). Since Hamas controls Gaza Strip and Fatah controls the West Bank, the Palestinians seem divided in pursuing a common goal, to a certain degree (Oren, 2007).

The Republic of China (Taiwan) Issues

Before 1895, Taiwan was part of mainland China but due to the resistance of the indigenous population, only about 45 percent of the territory was under China's administration. In the conflict over the sovereignty of Korea, China under the Qing Dynasty and Japan fought the first Sino-Japanese War, resulting in Japanese victory. In the Treaty of Shimonoseki of 1895, imperial China ceded the islands of Taiwan and Penghu in perpetuity to Japan. With the collapse of the Qing Dynasty, the Republic of China (ROC) was established in 1912, thereby ending the imperial period of China. While under Japanese control, the Taiwanese formed the Formosa Resistance Movement which resisted Japanese occupation but were defeated resulting in five decades of Japanese control.

A second Sino-Japanese War erupted when Japan invaded China as part of its expansion program in 1937. The war continued until the end of the Second World War in August 1945 when Japan surrendered. Taiwan was given back to China following the General Order of No. 1 in October 1945. Japan formally renounced its sovereignty over Taiwan in the Treaty of San

Francisco, effective April 28, 1952 (Peter, 2007). Thus, before October 1949, there was only one Republic of China (ROC) led by Chiang Kai-Shek and the Kuomintang (Nationalists Party). The political dynamics changed completely when the Chinese Communists led by Mao Zedong won the civil war against the ruling Kuomintang party and formed the People's Republic of China (PRC). President Chiang Kai-Shek and the Nationalists moved to the Island of Taiwan and continue to operate as the Republic of China (ROC). Suddenly, two governments claimed to represent China with the PRC on the mainland and the ROC in Taiwan. While in Taiwan, the Nationalists (Kuomintang) continue to maintain the position that the ROC was the sole government of China. At the same time, the PRC also claimed to be the sole government of China. During the 1950s, 1960s, and early 1970s, the ROC (Taiwan) had an advantage over the PRC since it was generally regarded as the legitimate government of China. Hence, it held the China seat, both in the General Assembly and in the Security Council of the United Nations. The United States and its Western allies supported the ROC as part of the Cold War strategy to keep Communist China out of the UN.

in August 1945 when Japan surrendered. Taiwan was given back to China following the General Order of No. 1 in October 1945. Japan formally renounced its sovereignty over Taiwan in the Treaty of San Francisco, effective April 28, 1952 (Peter, 2007).

in August 1945 when Japan surrendered. Taiwan was given back to China following the General Order of No. 1 in October 1945. Japan formally renounced its sovereignty over Taiwan in the Treaty of San Francisco, effective April 28, 1952 (Peter, 2007).

It should be noted that it was the ROC, under the Kuomintang Party in Taiwan which insisted on the One-China principle by maintaining that it was the only legitimate government of China and there could be no other China. The strategy was designed to delegitimize the PRC and prevent it from being recognized (Wong, 2000). This position was reinforced by the United States whose foreign policy supported the full recognition of the government in Taiwan from 1950 to 1971. As a result, the PRC could not gain a seat at the UN since every country has one seat and the ROC was already occupying the China seat. However, as many colonial territories in Africa, the Middle East, and Asia gained independence, they changed the political dynamics by recognizing the PRC since it supported liberation wars in many former colonies. Eventually, in October 1971, the UN General Assembly passed Resolution 2758 in October 1971, which expelled the ROC (Taiwan) from the United Nations and replaced it with the PRC. The ROC also lost membership in major international organizations, including the International Court of Justice (Lee, 2012). However, the US Congress passed Taiwan's Relations Act, which guarantees US military assistance and support if attacked by the PRC (Columbia University, 2022).

Having been replaced by the UN, the ROC worked hard to gain recognition from several sovereign states. In addition, it amended its constitution in 1991 under the leadership of President Lee Teng-hui to indicate that the One-China applied only to Taiwan. This was intended to separate Taiwan from China to create an independent path. However, in 1999, the Taiwanese government under the Kuomintang (KMT) negotiated with China and agreed again with the One-China principle for both mainland and Taiwan but disagreed on which government should represent China (Brookings, 2017). It should be noted that the Kuomintang administration ruled Taiwan under martial law until the 1990s when the society was transformed into a democracy and adopted a free economic enterprise system. With a population of 23.57 million people, Taiwan is a buoyant nation with a high standard of living. It is one of the Asian tigers but its effort to gain sovereignty is indeterminate.

DIPLOMATIC RECOGNITION AND CONDITIONS IN INTERNATIONAL LAW TO ACHIEVE INDEPENDENCE

Under international law, any political community that wishes to gain independence must do so by being recognized by other sovereign states who are members of the United Nations. This is necessary for the political entity to avail itself of the rights, duties, and obligations of international law as well as become a member of the international community. There are two major ways in which recognition can take place: (1) De facto Recognition and (2) De jure recognition. De facto recognition takes place when a political community is given temporary recognition since it already exists as a functioning entity. A de jure recognition takes place when a political community meets all the requirements that warrant full legal recognition. Legal recognition is essential for statehood since it is irrevocable. Sometimes, conditional recognition may be given to a political community instead of meeting all the requirements for statehood (Verna, 2012).

To achieve full recognition, based on the Montevideo Convention of 1933, a political community must meet four conditions by having, (1) an indigenous population, (2) a defined territory, (3) an autonomous government, and (4) the capacity to establish relations with other sovereign states in the global community (Wolfe, 2002). If a political community meets the conditions for recognition, a sovereign state may choose to recognize it through official declaration (expressed) recognition or through indirect (implicit) recognition by signing treaties or doing business with it. However, the process of recognizing a political community may also involve order considerations such as the Tobar and Estrada doctrines. The Tobar Doctrine was enunciated by Carlos Tobar y Borgono (1884–1923), an Ecuadorian diplomat and jurist who insisted that diplomatic recognition should not be accorded to any government that came into power through military coups or force of arms to avoid the forceful overthrow of democratically elected governments. On the other hand, the Estrada Doctrine was developed by Mexico's foreign minister, Genaro Estrada in 1936, when he insisted in a press conference that it was a violation of the sovereignty of Mexico for other states to determine the legitimacy of Mexico's government following a military coup staged by Gen. Victoriano Huerto. He argued that such action constitutes an interference in the internal affairs of the country (Wolfe, 2002). States may consider these doctrines in deciding to recognize a new state.

DETERMINING WHETHER THE FOUR CONDITIONS IN INTERNATIONAL LAW ARE MET FOR GAINING INDEPENDENCE

The purpose of this section is to apply the four Montevideo conditions above to the Western Sahara, which is also known as the Sahrawi Arab Democratic Republic (SADR), State of Palestine (SOP), and the Republic of China (Taiwan) to determine whether they meet the conditions for international diplomatic recognition.

Having an Indigenous Population

The requirement for the presence of an indigenous population is very important for the granting of statehood through diplomatic recognition. In 2021, it was estimated that there were 621,000 Sahrawis. Of this number, about 170,000 lived in refugee camps in Algeria, about 200,000 in the southern part of Morocco, and about 30,000 lived in the free zone (Cortugo, 2020). Others live in various parts of the world. However, the situation in the WS/SADR is complicated by the fact that Morocco and the PF disagreed about the Sahrawis who should vote in a referendum to decide the fate of the territory. The PF insisted that only Sahrawis who remained in the territory after Spanish occupation should be allowed to vote while Morocco argued that Sahrawis who continue to live in the territory, as well as those who flee the territory in the nineteen century and continue to live in Morocco, should also be allowed to vote in the referendum. In the Houston Agreement of September 28, 1997, both sides agreed with a UN compilation that 80,000 Sahrawis are eligible to vote in a referendum to determine the status of the territory. Unfortunately, after the agreement on the number of eligible voters, a referendum has not been carried out and the Sahrawis are still waiting (D'Origny, 2002). The restlessness even resulted in the Intifada uprisings which took place in the territory.

In 2019, the UN estimated the Palestinian population at 4.8 million with 1.8 million in Gaza Strip and 2.9 million in the West Bank. In addition, there were 5.6 million refugees in various places (UN, 2022). The Palestinian Bureau of Statistics estimated that at the end of 2021, there were 14 million Palestinians worldwide, including 3.2 million in the West Bank and East Jerusalem, 2.1 million in Gaza Strip, 1.7 million in Israel, and over 7 million overseas (Xinhua, 2021). There is a general agreement on the Palestinian population through UN resolutions.

However, the population issue is being complicated by Israel's building of Jewish settlements in East Jerusalem and the West Bank. Thus, the presence of Jewish settlers contributes to the prolongation of the unresolved population issue. In addition, the split between Hamas and Fatah divides the Palestinian population into two camps: those who support Fatah and the Palestinian National Authority (PNA) and those who support Hamas and the Islamic Jihad, as indicated above.

Of the three political communities that are seeking independence, Taiwan has the largest population with about 23.57 million people, as per 2020 estimates. Of this number, 98 percent are Han Chinese who speak Mandarin. About 12 percent of them are known as the Waishengren because they arrived from Mainland China after the Chinese Civil War to join their kin who moved to Taiwan in the seventeenth century (World Population Review, 2022). Apart from the Han Chinese, 2 percent of the population are aboriginal Austronesian Taiwanese. They constitute the sixteen officially recognized ethnic groups and the unrecognized groups in Taiwan's plains, thus making the indigenous population about 800,000 people (Hattaway, 2000 and Blust, 1999).

The Taiwanese seek independence, but the members of the Kuomintang (KMT) party still seem to have a strong attachment to the principle of One-China while members of the Democratic Progressive Party (DRP) are committed to Taiwan's independence. The KMT position seems to reinforce the PRC view that there is only one China. In fact, President Lee Teng-hui agreed with the PRC in the "1992 Consensus" that there is only one sovereign China state comprising both the mainland and Taiwan. This was confirmed by former President Ma Ting-jeou in an interview (Brookings, 2017). The difference in perception regarding the One-China principle between the KMT and the DPP slightly divides the population regarding sovereignty for Taiwan.

Having a Defined Territory

The issue of a defined territory is also complicated and contributes to the three nations not having gained full independence. The Sahrawis have a defined territory after the Spanish left the area following the Madrid Accord on November 14, 1975. However, Morocco and Mauritania took possession of the territory. This culminated in the PF declaring the territory as the Sahrawi Arab Democratic Republic (SADR) in February 1976 and waging a sixteen-year war against Morocco and Mauritania to liberate the territory. France, too, intervened in 1977, hoping to extend its territorial influence in North Africa. After a series of military confrontations between the forces of PF, Morocco, and Mauritania, the latter withdrew its territorial claims in 1979 but Morocco insisted that the territory belongs to it. This is even though the International Court of Justice (ICJ) had made a legal opinion that denied Moroccan claims, and this was backed by a United Nations resolution supporting the right of the Sahrawi people to self-determination (Zunes, 2008).

Despite numerous peace efforts to end the conflict, Morocco still holds about 80 percent while the PF holds about 20 percent of the territory. Morocco refers to the zone it controls as the Southern Province while the zone controlled by the PF is referred to as the Sahrawi Arab Democratic Republic (SADR). In place of self-determination, Morocco proposes autonomy rather than independence for SADR. UNGA Resolutions 22/29 of 1966 and UNGA Resolution 34/37 of 1979 support self-determination for Western Sahara.

On the Palestinian matter, the territorial situation is complicated by Israeli settlements which tend to upset the general agreement for a two-state solution. As of 2020, Israel had about 132 Jewish settlements and 124 outposts with a population of 430,000 Jews in the West Bank (BBC News, 2020). If the settlements in East Jerusalem are added, the total number increases, thereby, breaking up the Palestinian territory into scattered enclaves. During the Camp David Accord, Israel submitted a plan that tended to whittle away the UN General Assembly's Resolution 181 (II), which partitioned the territory into two. It also threatened the agreement that a Palestinian state would include East Jerusalem, West Bank, and Gaza. Apart from Israeli settlements, within the Palestinian camp, the Fatah and Hamas, and Islamic Jihad seem to have divided the territory into two camps (BBC News, 2021). While Fatah which produces the Palestinian National Authority (PNA) government seems to be flexible and willing to make a deal acceptable to Israel, Hamas which controls Gaza Strip is ideologically committed to an Islamist position, thereby making it difficult for both sides to develop a common plan.

Taiwan has no issue with a defined territory, but it should be noted that the island was a Japanese colony from 1895 to 1945. China ceded the island to Japan in perpetuity following the first Sino-Japanese War of 1895 in which

Japan won. Having ceded the island, Taiwan technically became a colony of Japan even though Japan regarded it as part of its sovereign territory. There has been a debate as to whether Japan gave up its sovereignty, thereby providing Taiwan an opportunity to seek independence like other colonies in the world (US Department of State, 1971). As indicated above, it was the Republic of China under Chiang Kai-Shek which instituted the One-China policy to prevent the People's Republic of China from gaining a seat at the United Nations. The situation turned around when the ROC was replaced by the PRC in 1971. Thus, Taiwan has no territorial problem, nevertheless, it is considered part of China under the One-China principle, which is agreed to by the world community, including the United States that affirmed it in the Shanghai Communique of 1972 (PBS, American Experience, n.d.). It appears that the members of the Kuomintang who left China to settle in Taiwan following the Communists' victory continue to believe in one China, as demonstrated by the "1992 Consensus" agreement between PRC and ROC. On the other hand, the Democratic Progressive Party (DPP) has insisted that Taiwan is not part of China and should be treated as a separate political entity.

Having An Autonomous Government

Any political community that seeks independence must have an autonomous government that is accepted by most of the population. This implies that the political community or nation must have the capability to run the affairs of the territory and provide services to the citizens. In the case of Western Sahara, the Polisario Front has been running its affairs since it came into existence as a liberation force in 1973. In addition, following the declaration of independence as the Sahrawi Arab Democratic Republic (SADR) in 1976, the PF has served as the legitimate government of the Sahrawi people and is recognized as the legitimate representative of the Sahrawi people by the United Nations (Chograni, 2021). Even though it is regarded as a non-self-governing territory by the United Nations, it is recognized by several countries, including Algeria and the African Union (AU). Likewise, even though it controls only about 20 percent of the territory, the SADR is viewed as an autonomous government that has been responsible for pursuing the struggle for independence. Thus, a sizable number of Sahrawis leave outside the territory with a considerable number in Algeria, Morocco, and Mauritania.

The Palestinian situation is increasingly trickier in terms of defining an autonomous government. Before Hamas took over of Gaza Strip on June 7, 2007 (BBC News, 2021), the Palestinian Liberation Organization (PLO), which was established in 1964 stood as the primary government for running the affairs of the Palestinians even though other organizations existed. In fact, through Resolution 3210 (XXIX), passed on October 14, 1974, the UN

General Assembly recognized the PLO as the representative of the Palestinian people. Consequently, for decades, the PLO led by Yasser Arafat served as the autonomous governmental entity in negotiating the Israeli/Palestinian matter. Hence, it represented the Palestinians in the Oslo Accord of 1993, the Camp David Summit of 2000, the Taba Summit of 2001, the Road Map for Peace in 2002, and the Arab Peace Initiative in 2002. It is accepted not only by the Palestinians but also by regional organizations such as the Arab League (AL), African Union (AU), Organization of American States (OAS, and the European Union (EU) as the legitimate representative of the Palestinian people. The split between Fatah and Hamas seems to divide the population into two as those in Gaza increasingly come under the leadership of Hamas while those in the West Bank come under the authority of the Palestinian National Authority.

The status of the Republic of China (Taiwan) is very complex. During the 1950s and 1960s, the ROC gained more diplomatic recognition than the PRC and exchanged ambassadors with several countries in the world. The ROC situation changed when it was replaced by the PRC in 1971 following UN Resolution 2758. Despite being expelled from the United Nations; it continues to claim as representing China but operates as an autonomous country because many sovereign states broke diplomatic relations with it while recognizing the PRC as the sole government of China. Nonetheless, it continues to maintain diplomatic relations with about fifteen members of the United Nations (World Population Review, 2022). Thus, there is no question that Taiwan has an autonomous democratic government that is supported by most of the citizens. It is one of the most successful economic players in the world, however, it is trapped by the One-China policy which means that there can be only one China.

Thus, of the three political communities, Taiwan has the most recognizable autonomous government and has operated like an independent state for decades. However, Taiwan's internal politics is dominated by the KMT and the Democratic Progressive Party (DPP). The KMT seems to have an attachment to a One China principle, hence, is not definitive in its position. On the other hand, the Democratic Progressive Party (DPP) originally argued for the separation of Taiwan from China by adopting the One-China, One-Taiwan principle but it had to tone down its position and took a middle-of-the-road stance to win votes among those who believe in One-China. The change in tactics forced many independent-minded Taiwanese to leave the DPP and formed the Taiwan Independence Party (TIP) which is committed to Taiwan's independence (Wang, 2000).

The Capacity to Establish Relations with Other Sovereign States

Of the four conditions that must be met for a political community to achieve sovereignty, the fourth condition, which is the "capacity to establish relations with other sovereign states" is the trickiest. The capacity to establish relations with other states is a vague requirement in international law due to a lack of specificity in the number of states in that relations could be established to determine whether a threshold has been met or not.

For instance, Western Sahara received recognition from about eighty-four UN member states when it declared its independence in 1976. However, due to the chaotic and fluid nature of global politics, many withdrew or froze their recognition. Liberia was the most recent country to do so in August 2020. Even then, about thirty-one countries continue to maintain diplomatic relations with WS/SADR. In addition, the SADR is a member of about eighteen international organizations, including the African Union (AU), the Women's International Democratic Federation, and the World Federation of Trade Unions. It is a participating non-member of about ten international organizations, including the African Union—European Union Summit, the Andean Community of Nations, Ibero- American Summit, the New Asian—African Strategic Partnership, the on-Aligned Movement, Permanent Conference of Political Parties of Latin American and the Caribbean (COPPPAL) (Sahara Press Service, 2012). Western Sahara is a signatory to about seventeen international treaties and or conventions. Despite this vigorous effort to establish relations with sovereign states and participate in international organizations, it is still not allowed to gain sovereignty and become a member of the United Nations.

The United Nations General Assembly on November 22, 1974, passed Resolution 3236 which recognized the right of the Palestinian people to self-determination, national independence, and sovereignty. It also accepted the Palestine Liberation Organization (PLO) as the sole legitimate representative of the Palestinian people as indicated above. In the quest for statehood, the Palestinian National Council (PNC) declared the independence of the State of Palestine on November 15, 1988, in Algeria. As soon as the declaration was made, about fifty-five states, including China, India, the Soviet Union, Greece, Sri Lanka, Yugoslavia, and many African states recognized it as an independent state within two weeks of the declaration (Tessler, 2009). By July 31, 2019, one hundred and thirty-eight (138) states, which is about 71.5 of the 193 member states of the United Nations had recognized the State of Palestine (World Population Review, 2021). The 138 number of recognitions is not far from that of the State of Israel which received recognition from 164 states to achieve its sovereignty.

Even before the diplomatic recognition, the State of Palestine had been a non-member of the United Nations. In addition, it is a signatory to several multilateral treaties, including (1) the Convention Respecting the Laws and Customs of War on Land, (2) the Treaty on the Non-Proliferation of nuclear weapons, (3) the Geneva Convention and Protocols, (4) Vienna Convention on Diplomatic Relations Statue of the International Criminal Court, and so forth. Yet, it is still not fully accepted as a full member of the United Nations. Even UN Resolution 3236 does not seem to matter much.

Of the three political communities, Taiwan's political path is completely different from those of the other two in terms of establishing relations with other sovereign states. As indicated repeatedly above, before October 1949, there was only the Republic of China (ROC) and led by Chiang Kai-Shek and the Nationalists. The ROC represented China at the United Nations and the Security Council since it was a founding member of the UN. It had full diplomatic relations with other sovereign states.

The ROC (Taiwan) was expelled and replaced by the PRC at the UN in 1971. The replacement resulted in the termination of diplomatic recognition for the ROC. Hence, today, only about 15 sovereign states continue to recognize Taiwan as an independent state (O'Connor, 2019). Most of them are small countries in the Pacific, Caribbean, and Central and South America. On the other hand, all the large and powerful states, including the United States, Russia, Germany, Britain, France, Brazil, India, and so forth, have terminated their diplomatic recognition of ROC. In Africa, only Eswatini, former Swaziland continues to maintain diplomatic relations with it. In addition, the ROC maintains unofficial relations with about 58 countries, and possibly with the European Union. It is very active in seeking to establish relations with many countries as possible, hence it has about thirty-one diplomatic networks with about 110 offices around the world (van der Wees, 2021).

Taiwan's desire for independence is hampered by the fact that it was responsible for initiating the One-China principle. The policy created the view in the world that there can be only one China and not two. This position turned against its interest when it was expelled and replaced by the PRC in 1971. On realizing that the One-China policy was antithetical to its strategic interest, it changed course and adopted a Two-China policy in the 1990s. Unfortunately, the damage had been done since the UN had accepted a One-China policy. Therefore, it is understandable why the PRC insists that there can be only one China.

THE INFLUENCE OF INTERNATIONAL POLITICS ON STATE RECOGNITION

Indeed, the fourth condition, "an ability to establish relations with other sovereign states," is the most challenging requirement because even after a political community might have met the conditions for statehood, there is no guarantee that it would gain sovereignty. A major reason is the lack of specification on the number of states that diplomatic relations is required to meet an acceptable threshold for recognition. Moreover, the chaotic and contradictory manner in which sovereign states advance their national interests mitigates international law. For instance, while SW/SADR was negotiating with Morocco to resolve the territorial issue, in February 2019, the European Union passed the Sustainable Fisheries Partnership Agreement and negotiated with Morocco to allow European fishing vessels to fish in Moroccan waters, including the disputed Sahrawi territorial seacoast. The EU's action necessitated the PF to file a case in the European Court of Justice (ECJ) to challenge the decision. By implication, the EU technically recognized the right of Morocco over Western Sahara and ignored the rights of Sahrawis. The United States, too, tends to approach the Sahrawi issue from two opposing perspectives. For instance, the George Bush Jr. administration supported the Moroccan position that Western Sahara is part of Morocco. On the other hand, the Barack Obama administration took a more neutral view by encouraging the disputants to resolve the matter amicably. The Donald Trump administration counteracted the Obama position and sided with Morocco (*World Tribune*, 2009). The United States commits totally to Israel's sovereignty while its support for a Palestinian state seems circumstantial.

On the other hand, it agrees with the One-China policy on Taiwan while providing security for the island. Surprisingly, the Arab League, which emphatically supports Palestinian independence, seems less enthusiastic about supporting SADR, hence it supports a Moroccan map that includes Western Sahara (Ganot, 2021). This could be prompted by the fact that Morocco is an influential member of the organization. On the other hand, the African Union (AU) seems committed to the independence of SADR and Palestinian statehood while it supports the One-China policy, and so is the Organization of American States (OAS). Russia and China support the establishment of a Palestinian State while they are circumstantial in their actions toward Western Sahara with Russia tilting closer to Morocco.

It is an understatement to note that international law is confusing. For instance, the Tobar Doctrine, as described above, maintains that no government that came into power by insurrection or military intervention should be recognized. On the other hand, the Estrada Doctrine insists that no other state should be able to determine the legitimacy of government in another sovereign state. This means that some states could render diplomatic recognition based on the Tobar Doctrine while some states may do so by adhering to the Estrada Doctrine.

Thus, on the issue of state recognition, just as international law appears to be ineffective in some cases, so is the United Nations. The reason is that the UN was established to ensure peace and security after the bloody Second World War that claimed over 50 million lives. Therefore, the primary purpose of the UN is (1) maintaining international peace and security, (2) developing friendly relations among nations, (3) and promoting social progress, better living standards, and human rights.

It was these noble goals as embedded in various articles of the UN Charter and the General Assembly Resolution 1541 of 1960 that provided the momentum for the decolonization of the world to reduce conflict, oppression, and injustice (UN, 2022). It passed Resolutions 22/29 and 34/37 to support independence for Western Sahara. The UN also passed Resolution 181 (1) to partition Palestine into two states, yet nothing has happened. Thus, the current UN system is antithetical to the goals of the organization in the sense that since it was established in 1948, only five countries in the Security Council are permanent members with veto powers. On the other hand, Africa and South America have no country with veto power while the largest continent (Asia) has only China. Moreover, India with 1.4 billion people is not a permanent member of the UNSC. Thus, the UN cannot be an effective tool for ensuring peace and security, as far as Africa, Asia, and South America are not represented as permanent members of the UNSC. The imbalance affects the politics of state recognition in the sense that political communities that have strong backing from one or two permanent members of the UNSC are most likely to sail through the recognition tussle to gain sovereignty. On the other hand, communities with little or no backing from one or two permanent members of the UNSC are likely to meet a political brick wall.

CONCLUSION

Having examined the four conditions necessary for the attainment of statehood under the Montevideo Convention of international law and applying them to the Western Sahara/SADR, State of Palestine, and ROC (Taiwan), it is appropriate to draw some inferences. First, international law is defective in resolving disputes concerning state recognition due to the chaotic nature of international politics and state sovereignty. Hence, the three political communities are victims of ineffective international law and the structural imbalance in the Security Council system of the United Nations. Second, the UN needs to put pressure on the major actors on the Sahrawi issue so that a referendum is conducted to determine the status of SADR. Third, as Israel continues to build settlements in the West Bank and the Palestinians (Fatah and Hamas) are not in unison, a two-state solution as recommended by the UN and the Oslo Accord is eroding and incrementally being replaced by a possible one-state solution. In this case, both the Jews (Israelis) and Arabs

(Palestinians) could end up becoming members of a single state. In such a development, the notion of a purely Jewish or Palestinian state might be replaced by a binational state. Fourth, since the idea of a One-China policy was originally initiated by the Republic of China and the world community agreed with the policy, Taiwan's desire for independence is compromised. Therefore, the only option left for both China and Taiwan is to continue to negotiate and find a peaceful means to resolve the matter, as recommended by the United States in the Starr Memorandum of July 12, 1971.

Based on the inferences drawn above, it is recommended that: (1) in any given territorial dispute in which the indigenous population is seeking independence, it should be a codified requirement of international law that a referendum must be automatically conducted to allow people to decide whether they want independence or not in a disputed territory; (2) the global community must specify the minimum number of sovereign states an independent-seeking political community should establish relations with to gain full international recognition; and (3) to create continental equality at the UNSC to facilitate the process of state recognition, it is time to include two states each from Africa, Asia, and Central and South America, as permanent members with veto powers in the Security Council.

REFERENCES

Asia for Educators)2022). "U.S.–China Relations since 1949." Columbia University. http://afe.easia.columbia.edu/special/china_1950_us_china.htm (Accessed January 10, 2022).

Avraham, Sela. "*Arab–Israeli Conflict*." In The Continuum Political Encyclopedia of the Middle East 2nd ed., edited by Sela Avraham. New York: Continuum, 2002.

Baum, Noa. "Historical Timeline for Israel/Palestine." *Middle East Facts*. January 9, 2015. http://middleeastfacts2015.blogspot.com/2015/01/historical-time-line-for-israelpalestine.html.

BBC News. "Explainer: Israel, Annexation and the West Bank." June 25, 2020. https://bbc.com/news/world-middle-east-52756427.

BBC News. "Israeli-Palestinian Conflict: Life in Gaza Strip." May 20, 2021. https://www.bbc.com/news/world-middle-east-20415675.

Berger, Yotam and Jack Khoury. "How Many Palestinians Live in Gaza and the West Bank? It's Complicated." *Haaretz*. March 28, 2018. https://www.haaretz.com/israel-news/how-many-palestinians-live-in-gaza-and-the-west-bank-it-s-complicated-1.5956630.

Brookings, "Former Taiwan President Ma on One China, the 1992 Consensus and Taiwan's Future." March 16, 2017, https://www.brookings.edu/blog/order-from-chaos/2017/03/16/former-taiwan-president-ma-on-one-china-the-1992-consensus-and-taiwans-future/.

Blust, Robert. "Subgrouping, circularity and extinction: Some issues in Austronesian comparative linguistics." In Selected Papers From the 8th International

Conference on Austronesian Linguistics, edited by Zeitoun, E., and P. J.-K. Li, International Conference on Austronesian Linguistics. 1999. Taipei, Taiwan: Academica Sinica. http://language.psy.auckland.ac.nz/austronesian/language.php?id=280 (accessed July 2013).

Chograni, Houda. "The Polisario Front, Morocco, and the Western Sahara Conflict." *The Arab Center*. June 22, 2021. https://arabcenterdc.org/resource/the-polisario-front-morocco-and-the-western-sahara-conflict/.

Cortugo, Ferdinando. "The Saharawi People of Western Sahara are Still Waiting for a Homeland: Tensions are now Rising Among the Young." *Geographical*. July 17, 2020. https://geographical.co.uk/people/the-refugee-crisis/item/3731-the-saharawi-people-of-western-sahara-are-still-waiting-for-a-homeland-tensions-are-now-rising-among-the-young.

D'Origny, Gilonne. "Africa's Last Colony." November 15, 2008. *Forbes*. https://www.forbes.com/2008/11/14/western-sahara-morocco-co-oped-cx_gd_1115dorigny.html?sh=412ab0b614ec.

Erlanger, Steven. "Hama's Leader Faults Israeli Sanction Plan. *New York Times*, 18 February 2006. https://www.nytimes.com/2006/02/18/world/middleeast/hamas-leader-faults-israeli-sanction-plan.html.

Ganot, Steven. "Algeria Angry after Arab League Endorses Moroccan Map Including Western Sahara." *Middle East Daily News*. December 28, 2021. https://themedialine.org/mideast-daily-news/algeria-angry-after-arab-league-endorses-moroccan-map-including-western-sahara/.

Gelvin, James. *History of the Israeli-Palestinian Conflict: One Hundred Years of War*, 3rd ed. Cambridge University Press, 2014.

Gonzalez, Eduardo. "Western Sahara and Spain's Exit: 40 Years in the International Limbo." *The Diplomat*. February 29, 2016. https://thediplomatinspain.com/en/2016/02/western-sahara-and-spains-exit-40-years-in-the-international-limbo/.

Hattaway, Paul. *Operation China, Introducing all the Peoples of China*. Pasadena, CA: William Carey Publishing, 2000.

Krauss, Joseph and Mohammed Daraghmeh. "New Data Shows Israeli Settlement Surge in East Jerusalem." *AP*. June 12, 2019. https://apnews.com/article/israel-donald-trump-ap-top-news-international-news-jerusalem-98e4ad57e0784e05b9fdde2e0ffd7439.

Lee, Wei-chine. "Diplomatic Impetus and Altruistic Impulse: NGOs and the Expansion of Taiwan's International Space." *Brookings*. July 16, 2012. https://www.brookings.edu/opinions/diplomatic-impetus-and-altruistic-impulse-ngos-and-the-expansion-of-taiwans-international-space/.

Levinson, Chaim. "Israel moves to Green Light 2,200 New Settlement Units, Recognize Outposts." *Haaretz*. November 15, 2015. https://www.haaretz.com/israel-news/.premium-israel-moves-to-green-light-2-200-new-settlement-units-1.5419087.

Loveday, Morris. "Women on Frontline in Struggle for Western Sahara." *The Guardian*. July 16, 2013. https://www.theguardian.com/world/2013/jul/16/women-western-sahara-independence-morroco.

Malley, Robert, and Hussein Agha (9 August 2001). "Camp David: The Tragedy of Errors." *New York Review of Books*. August 9, 2001. https://www.nybooks.com/articles/2001/08/09/camp-david-the-tragedy-of-errors/.

Morris, Benny. *One state: Resolving the Israeli/Palestine Conflict*. Yale University Press, 2009.

Neal, Lorena S. "The Roots of the Israeli-Palestinian Conflict: 1882–1914." *Honors Projects 27, Digital Commons, Illinois Western University*. May 1995. https://digitalcommons.iwu.edu/cgi/viewcontent.cgi?article=1026&context=history_honproj.

O'Connor, Tom. 20 September 2019, "Which Countries still recognize Taiwan? Two More Nations Switch to China in Less than a Week." *Newsweek*. September 20, 2019. https://www.newsweek.com/who-recognizes-taiwan-two-change-china-1460559 (Accessed September 5, 2021).

Oren, Michael B. 2007, *Power, Faith, and Fantasy: America in the Middle East, 1776 to the Present*. W. W. Norton & Company,2007.

Organization of American States. "A-40: Convention on the Rights and Duties of States in Multilateral Treaties. December 26, 1933. https://www.oas.org/juridico/english/sigs/a-40.html.

PBS. "Shanghai Communique Issued." American Experience. https://www.pbs.org/wgbh/americanexperience/features/china-communique/ (Accessed March 13, 2022).

Peter, Chen C. "Japan's Surrender: 14 August 1945–2 September 145." World *War II Data Base*. May 2007. https://ww2db.com/battle_spec.php?battle_id=13 (Accessed November 24, 2022).

Pressman, Jeremy. (Fall 2003). "Visions in Collusion: What Happened at Camp David and Taba." *International Security* Vol 28 No. 2. (Fall 2003), 5–43. https://muse.jhu.edu/article/50967 (Accessed October 7, 2021).

Roberts, Adam. "United Nations and International Security." In *International Politics: Enduring Concepts and Contemporary Issues*, edited by Robert J. Art and Robert Jervis. Longman, 2003.

Sahara Press Service. "Saharawi Representation to Mexico to Attend COPPPAL–ICAPP Meeting." October 15, 2012. Archived from original on December 24, 2013. https://web.archive.org/web/20131224092314/http://www.spsrasd.info/en/content/saharawi-representation-mexico-attends-copppal-icapp-meeting (January 19, 2022).

Tessler, Mark, *A History of the Israeli-Palestinian Conflict*. Indiana University Press, 2009.

The Guardian. "The Arab Peace Initiative: Full Text." March 28, 2002. https://www.theguardian.com/world/2002/mar/28/israel7.

United Nations. "The United Nations and Decolonization." https://www.un.org/dppa/decolonization/en/about (Accessed February 17, 2022).

United Nations. "The Question of Palestine." https://www.un.org/unispal/in-facts-and-figures/ (Accessed February 16, 2022).

United Nations "Declaration of Principles on Western Sahara by Spain, Morocco and Mauritania." *Treaty Series*. November 19, 1975. https://peacemaker

.un.org/sites/peacemaker.un.org/files/MA-MR-ES_751114_DeclarationPrinciples OnWesternSahara_0.pdf.

US Department of State. "Starr Memorandum." July 13, 1971. https://www .taiwanbasic.com/wash/rethinking/starr-pages.htm.

Verma, S. K. *Introduction to Public International Law*, 2nd ed. Satyam Law International, October 12, 2012.

Wang, T. Y. "one China, One Taiwan: An Analysis of the Democratic Progressive Party's China Policy." February 2000. *Journal of Asian and African Studies* 35 (1) (February 2000): 159–82.

Wees, Gerrit van der, "Is Taiwan's International Space Expanding or Contracting*? The Diplomat*. December 14, 2021, https://thediplomat.com/2021/12 /is-taiwans-international-space-expanding-or-contracting/.

Wolfe, James. *Modern International Law: An Introduction to the Law of Nations*. Upper Saddle River, New Jersey: Prentice-Hall, 2002.

Wong, Timothy Ka-ying. "Changing Taiwan's Foreign Policy from One China to Two States." *Asian Perspective*, Vol 24, No1, (2000) 5 – 45, https://www.jstor.org/stable /42704247 (Accessed October 10, 2021).

World Bank Technical Team. "Movement and Access Restrictions in the West Bank: Uncertainty and Inefficiency in the Palestinian Economy." May 9, 2007. http://ftp.miftah.org/Doc/Reports/2007/WestBankrestrictions9Mayfinal[1] .pdf.

World Population Review. "Countries That Recognize Palestine 2021." https: //worldpopulationreview.com/country-rankings/countries-that-recognize -palestine (Accessed February 22, 2022).

World Population Review. "Western Sahara Population Live." February 14, 2022. https: //worldpopulationreview.com/countries/western-sahara-population (Accessed February 15, 2022).

World Population Review. "Taiwan Population 2022 (Live)." https://www.google .com/search?q=population+of+taiwan&rlz=1C1CHBF_enUS964US964&oq= &aqs=chrome.1.69i59i450l8.442581887j0j15&sourceid=chrome& (Accessed February 16, 2022).

World Population Review. " Countries that Recognize Taiwan 2022." https:// worldpopulationreview.com/country-rankings/countries-that-recognize-taiwan. (Accessed February 27, 2022).

World Tribune. "Obama Reverses Bush-backed Morocco Plan in Favor of Polisario State." July 9, 2009. https://www.worldtribune.com/worldtribune/WTARC/2009/ af_morocco0547_07_09.html.

Xinhua. December 31, 2021 "Palestinian Population Amounts to 14 mln by end of 2021: Report." December 31, 2021. http://www.xinhuanet.com/english /20211231/df86c0b9cb574ff7afaaad8057b215fc/c.html.

Zunes, Stephen. "Western Sahara: Self-Determination and International Law." *Middle East Institute*. April 2, 2008. https://www.mei.edu/publications/western -sahara-self-determination-and-international-law.

2

The Undercurrents of Political Economy of Nationalism

Gbensuglo Alidu Bukari

INTRODUCTION

The struggle and the debate surrounding the phenomenon of 'Nationalism' are underpinned by 'Politics' and 'Economics of the nation-state. A nation is an appropriate unit of political rule and has sacrosanct rights to political and economic independence, and self-determination (Rousseau, 1913). Historically, conscious resistance and struggle for these inviolable rights of nation-states were demonstrated by the tempo of nationalism (Gellner, 1983; Alter, 1989; Kellas, 1991; Brown, 1995; Brown, 2000; Heywood, 2007). Heywood (2007, p. 6) for instance argued that 'Nationalism' has in many ways 'dwarfed' the more precise and systematic political ideologies in the world. It contributes to the outbreak of many wars and successful revolutions, and these have defined the new world order of contemporary times. Consequently, nationalism gave birth to new nation-states, disintegrates empires and redrew national and international borders, reshaped the existing regimes, and above all granted them independent sovereignty (Gellner, 1983; Anderson, 1984; Brown, 2000; Heywood, 2007). However, the new nation-states are increasingly beset by both political and economic pressures in contemporary times due to population growth rates and globalization.

Conceptually, there is an established relationship between politics, economics, and nationalism, at least in the modern world, that is reciprocal. On one hand, politics and economics determine the nature of nationalism and channel it in a direction intended to serve the interests of citizens in a polity (Aristotle, 1948; Anderson, 1983; Alter, 1989). Also, the exercise of political power in all its forms is a major determinant of the nature of political and economic systems in the new nation-states (Brown, 1995). On the other hand, nationalist activities tend to influence the political and economic independence, and self-determination of a sovereign nation, and seek to also ensure redistribution of political power and wealth; transform the power relationships among groups in a nation (Aristotle, 1948; Anderson, 1983; Alter, 1989). Hence, the main objective of nationalism is to transform the political system and establish a new sovereign nation-state, thereby giving rise to a new structure of economic and political relationships. Accordingly, the dynamics of international politics, diplomacy, and power relations in the new world order, particularly after World War II and the subsequent end of the Cold War ending the bipolar world is largely a function of reciprocal interaction between politics and economics in the new nation-states (Brown, 1995).

Arguably, there is not much scholarly discussion on the subject matter of politics and economics of nationalism. Though debates and discussions on nationalism have received a lot of scholarly attention, much of the discussions and analyses concentrated on explaining the evolution, principles, and effects of nationalism on political independence and self-determination of the new nation-states in general (Alter, 1989; Anderson, 1983; Brown, 2000; Balaam & Veseth, 2001). The available literature failed to adequately address the undercurrents of nationalism, that would provoke a political-economic argument. There is also a limited theoretical and conceptual clarification of the concept of 'Nationalism.' This is the gap that underpins the interest and relevance of this article. The article is expected to accentuate the real and perceived political and economic factors of nationalism to contribute to the wealth of knowledge, and scholarly debate in the political economy of nationalism lexicon.

The most obvious questions are: how and when did the sovereignty of nation-states as a legal and political concept come into being in the first place? And how does nationalism stimulate the sovereign power of Westphalia nation-states? This chapter provides answers to these conceptual questions by interrogating how nationalism is credited with being a major contributor to the birth and growth of the nation-states as we know them today. When connected to anti-colonialism, nationalism is accredited with being the major force in the proliferation of the new nation-states following the end of World War II in 1945. The rest of the chapter is as follows: The next section is the theoretical issues of nationalism, followed by the conceptual issues of nationalism. It then problematizes the political economy of nationalism and interrogates the legal, political, and economics of Westphalia nation-states in the new world order. The last section is the concluding remarks followed by the references.

THEORETICAL ISSUES OF NATIONALISM

In this article, the concept of 'Nationalism' (struggle for the sovereignty of nation-states) is discussed within the theoretical framework lens of political economy. In literature, theories or models propounded to explain the sovereign power of Westphalia nation-states are relatively scarce. However, earlier scholars laid some theoretical foundations of 'Nationalism.' For instance, earlier scholars such as Loke (1965), Bodin (1962), Hobbes (1968), Rousseau (1913), Bentham (1948), Gellner (1983), and others have propounded theories on sovereignty in an attempt to strengthen the authority of kings, and to bring about law and order as well as unity in the nation-state. These theories were propounded based on the series of religious and civil wars that vacillated Europe in the sixteenth and seventeenth centuries, especially over the question of 'who; should 'wield final authority' in a state (Berger, 1981; Anderson, 1983; Gellner, 1983; Alter, 1989; Kellas, 1991). These theories stimulate scholarly discussions and debates surrounding the phenomenon of nationalism and have received varied views from different schools of thought. First, one school of thought understands nationalism as a vehicle through which national independence or unity can be achieved. Second, another school of thought perceives nationalism as an irrational and reactionary tool used by nationalists to lunch aggression and pursue policies of expansion or annexation or war against others in the name of a nation. Some scholars have described nationalism as either progressive and reactionary, democratic and authoritarian, liberating and oppressive, or left-wing and right-wing (Alter, 1989; Kellas, 1991; Brown, 1995; Brown, 2000; Heywood, 2007). For this conceptualization, Heywood (2007 p115) said:

> Perhaps it is better to view nationalism not as a single or coherent political phenomenon, but as a series of nations. That is, as a complex of traditions that share but one characteristic each in its own particular way, acknowledge bs the central political importance of the nation.

Other scholars conceptualized nationalism from the perspective of 'circumstances' and 'political cause.' For instance, if the nationalist struggle is against foreign domination or anti-colonialism, then nationalism should be conceived as a 'liberating force linked to goals of liberty, justice, and democracy' (Brown, 2000). Also, it could be seen as a vehicle for racism and xenophobia when the movement is a 'product of social dislocation and for demographic change' (Keith, 1993). Besides, the conception of nationalism is also shaped by perspectives clouded by contemporary political ideals making the term 'Nationalism' a cross-cutting ideology. This gave birth to the manifestations or theories of the political economy of nationalism as; the theory of liberalism, conservatism theory, expansionism theory, and theory of anti-colonialism (Gellner, 1983; Alter, 1989; Kellas, 1991; Brown, 1995; Brown, 2000; Heywood, 2007).

The liberal theory of nationalism is underpropped by the assumption that man is naturally divided into a collection of nations with unique identities. It links the idea of the nation with credence in popular sovereignty. Accordingly, the assumption of liberal conception of nationalism is its commitment to the principle of independence and self-determination for a sovereign nation-state. It consequently proclaims that every nation has a right to freedom and self-determination and that all nations are equal. National self-determination in this case refers to 'the principle that the nation is a sovereign entity, and self-determination implies both national independence and democratic rule' (Gellner, 1983; Heywood, 2007 p116). Also, in Mills (1951, p. 392) words:

> When the sentiment of nationality in any force is a *prima facie case* for uniting all members of nationality under one government, and a government to themselves apart. This is merely saying that the question of government should be de ide by the governed.

Nationalism, based on this conception, is a means of enlarging political freedom, and also a vehicle for securing stable democratic nation-states based on mutual respect for national rights and characteristics. However, the conception of liberal nationalism is not only to the sovereignty of the nation-state but also seeks to promote and protect individual rights and equality in a sovereign nation (Alter, 1989; Kellas, 1991; Brown, 2000; Heywood, 2007). This is now widely accepted as 'fundamental human rights' under the principle of 'Universalism' concept (a principle that believes individuals everywhere on the planet earth have equal status and entitlements). This principle of liberalism rather provoked a debate that says placing a premium on 'individualism' means violating 'national sovereignty.' But liberals' position is that 'a world of only sovereign nation-states may degenerate into an international state of nature and that national sovereignty may be used a cloak for expansionism and conquest' (Heywood, 2007, p. 117). However, the liberal conception of nationalism has been criticized. First, the universal principle of nationalism is seen as problematic and fails to appreciate the emotional power of nationalism. It is argued that emotional power can be used to persuade people to fight, kill, and die for their countries. Also, the principle of nation-state construction is a misguided one, as it can be used as 'ethnic cleansing' or invade others in the name of a nation (Alter, 1989; Kellas, 1991; Brown, 2000; Heywood, 2007).

Conservatism theory relates more to social cohesion and public order on the principle of 'National Patriotism' rather than the 'Universal

Self-Determination' espoused by liberalism. Conservative nationalism is reinforced by the assumption that a nation is an organic entity, and security and identity of membership are through the national community. Hence, conservative nationalism develops in an established nation-state, rather than a process of nation-building. However, Heywood (2007, p. 119) argued that:

> Although conservative nationalism had been linked to military adventure and expansion, its distinctive character is that it is 'inward-looking and insular.' If conservative governments have used foreign policy as a device to stoke up public favor, this is an act of political opportunism rather than because conservative nationalism is relentlessly aggressive or inherently materialistic.

Also, the conservative conception of nationalism has been criticized for being an elite manipulation or ruling-class ideology. Based on this, the nation is considered as invented and defined by the political leadership and ruling elites of the conservative class with a view to manufacturing consent and political engineering passivity. Conservative nationalism has also been criticized for the promotion of intolerance and bigotry in an established nation-state (Gellner, 1983; Alter, 1989; Kellas, 1991, Brown, 2000; Heywood, 2007).

The expansionist theory of the political economy of nationalism is aggressive and militaristic. It is the opposite of the principle of equality and self-determination of the nation-state. It is a militate and intense form of nationalism, often associated with political dictators. The fundamental principle of expansionist nationalism is the 'idea of national rebirth or regeneration' (Gellner, 1983; Alter, 1989; Heywood, 2007). This form of nationalism involves re-establishing and re-gaining national glory through militarisation. It is the quest for expansion or search for colonies, often referred to as 'pan-nationalism' (Gellner, 1983; Alter, 1989; Kellas, 1991, Brown, 2000; Heywood, 2007, p. 121).

Anti-colonialism theory of nationalism is used to explain the form of nationalism in the developing world including Africa and was waged against the European powers and expansionist activities. For instance, in Africa and Asia, anti-colonialism was shaped by the desire for liberation from colonialism marked by nationalist movements and protests against the foreign rule (Gellner, 1983; Alter, 1989; Kellas, 1991; Brown, 1995; Brown, 2000; Heywood, 2007). Colonialism is the theory or practice of establishing control over a foreign territory and turning it into a colony, and it is a particular form of imperialism (Heywood, 2007, p. 122). Therefore, the anti-colonialism movement was inspired by political independence and self-determination. This was also linked to social development in all colonies, and the aim of national liberation movements and activities had economic as well as political dimensions (Alter, 1989; Brown, 1995; Brown, 2000; Heywood, 2007).

CONCEPTUAL ISSUES OF NATIONALISM

Theoretically, the state is an institution through which the process of politics and economics are organized and formalized (Leftwich, 2004; Heywood, 2007). Thus, political and economic systems exist in a nation-state. Therefore, a nation or state exists primarily to secure the welfare of its citizens. Conceptually, politics is conceived as the art of influencing, manipulating, and controlling groups to advance the purposes and interests of some against the opposition of others. in a state (Leftwich, 2004; Heywood, 2007). The process by which these purposes and interests are advanced depends on the political system operating in the group. Such systems can vary, in the extremes, from one person deciding for the entire group to each member of the group voting in each decision. In a modern political system, these extremes are rarely encountered. Most often, the political system will be a combination of several forms which correspond more or less to the theoretical form of government (Leftwich, 2004; Heywood, 2007). Nationalism is defined as a state of mind in which the supreme loyalty of the individual is due to the nation-state' (Berger, 1981; Anderson, 1983; Gellner, 1983; Alter, 1989; Kellas, 1991). It is a conscious resistance and struggle against foreign domination and rule, and for the establishment of autonomous rule or self-government. Based on this definition, reference is often made to certain concepts which underpin the conceptual explanation of nationalism, and their meanings must be clearly understood to appreciate the concept of nationalism.

First nationalism will be better understood if the man and nature of society are defined. A society is a group of people with some degree of shared values, beliefs, or goals, sufficient to cause a self-conscious awareness of the group. The boundaries of any society are determined by the extent of interaction and by the relative degree of shared values and beliefs. Clans, tribes, and nations are thus all societies. Most societies are usually, but not necessarily, territorially bound and persist beyond the life span of any individual members. The distinctive pattern of shared values, beliefs, norms of interaction, and organization are generally referred to as the "social institutions" of a specified society. Thus, to understand nationalism, it is essential to be aware of the inherent nature of man to live in groups. That is families, clans, tribes, and nations. All these groups fundamentally reflect certain social patterns and have an inevitable necessity for societal interdependence. Hence, in this context, the interdependence of the family is analogous to the independence of tribes within a nation or a state. Patterns of social interdependence are affected by the diversity of human values and preferences. The basic assumptions of society and state (Alter, 1989; Brown, 1995; Brown, 2000; Heywood, 2007) are:

i. Human needs are nearly universal (what these specific needs are less important at this point than is the idea that people seek essentially the same kinds of need fulfillment.
ii. Man, living in a society is the architect of his social institutions, social institutions which function to meet human needs.
iii. The difference in such essential and universal institutions are government and economic systems therefore lie not so much in the needs they meet as in the form they take.
iv. The form or structure of all social institutions is determined by the human (cultural) context within which they exist. Hence, comparative analysis of social structure requires; a knowledge of the basic function served by the social institutions and an understanding of some of the human factors which shape the form of the institutions;
v. Some of these human factors which require particular emphasis are culture, religion, ideology, and the nature of nationalism.

Also, culture as a concept of nationalism refers to the whole complex of knowledge, belief, art, morals, law, customs, and any other capabilities and habits acquired by man as a member of society. The concept embraces not only the specific characteristics of the social institutions of a given society but also those processes of change and accommodation which produce variation in those institutions through time. Thus, the concept can be used to refer to a specific pattern of social institutions in a particular society, at a particular time, and to the processes which produce a change in social institutions. For example, one can refer to the 'Culture' of ancient Greece and to the effects of Western culture on developing" societies.

The concept of 'Nation' stems from the Latin verb *nasci*, 'to be born,' and originally meant a group of people born in the same location, whether that location was thought of as a few dozen or many thousands of square miles. In modern usage the term nation has come to refer to a central political concept—a human group bound together by a common loyalty to the group as a whole over any conflicting loyalties. As Mill (1951) succinctly put it:

> A portion of mankind may be said to constitute a nation if they are united among themselves by common sympathies which do not exist between them and any other which make them cooperate with each other more willingly than with other people, desire to be under the same government, and desire that it should be governed by themselves exclusively.

In short, the term 'nation' may be simply thought of as a type of human society whose cohesiveness derives in large part from their common territorial or ethnic origins. The nation can also be an imagined community, and this should include the dead and the unborn who are supposed to be bound together by ties of kinship, language, custom, and shared myths and beliefs. We can also have a nation without a state (like the case of the Kurds) or states that comprise many nations (such as the former USSR and Yugoslavia) and a nation divided between several states (as in the case of the Italians and Germans) before the unification of the two Germanys and two Koreas of more recent history (Brown, 1995; Brown, 2000; Heywood, 2007). Thus, for the purpose, of this article, the concept of 'nation' is used to refer to a group of people who tend to have such common characteristics as language, ethnic origins, or religious beliefs which produce a unique and cohesive feeling of a common bond.

When a nation geographically coincides with a state, we call the result a 'nation-state.' It is a compliment, in a sense, because such coincidence represents a relatively high order of political development and sophistication. The French people are a nation. France is a state and its government is sovereign. Thus, France is a nation-state. The Gypsies and the Moshie peoples can be considered nations. These two socio-ethnic groups have a unique feeling of a common bond, but they do not have a territory that they can call their own. They can be called nations, but not nation-states. There can be more than one nation within a state. The United Kingdom has a government that is sovereign and recognized, but there are at least four nations within that state - the English, Scottish, Welsh, and Irish. The opposite condition exists in North and South Korea. The Korean people—a nation—occupy the entire peninsula, but they are divided into two states.

When equated to nationhood, nationalism is credited with being a major contributor to the birth and growth of the nation-state as we know it. When equated to anti-colonialism, it is credited with being the major force in the proliferation of new states following World War II. Nationalism has exhibited the potential of both constrictive and destructive in altering the former world order (with some help through the weakening of Europe by both world wars). It aided in the creation of a new order based on twice the number of states, and it can contribute to the cohesiveness and strength of these new states. On the one hand, nationalism of radical or dissident variety further fragments the world by breaking up otherwise viable states. This was recently demonstrated unsuccessfully with the Biafran separatist movement in Nigeria, and successfully with the creation of Bangladesh out of the former east wing of Pakistan. Nationalism is further described as 'an old force in a new setting.' It can have a variety of effects depending on how national boundaries relate to state boundaries. It can force the creation of new states, foster the maturity of existing states, fragment both older and newly created states, cause interstate conflict and contribute to social unrest in mature states.

State involves machinery, agencies, jurisdiction, powers, and rights. Here we refer to the common concept of the territorial state. This term refers to the geographic entities seen on maps, coupled with the governments that represent those physical areas. For a state to exist, three fundamental conditions must be fulfilled. First, there must be an identifiable territory, second, there must be a politically organized group of people within the territory; and, third, there must be a government to which all people of the state, both domestically and internationally belong. When these conditions exist, that geopolitical entity is called a 'state,' and the government of that state is said to be 'sovereign' over the territory and its people. This provoked the traditional definition of the concept 'Sovereignty' as 'the total of authority in a state unrestrained by law' (Dicey, 1939). Sovereignty also connotes absolute and unlimited power; sovereignty can either imply supreme legal authority or unchallengeable legal political power (Heywood, 2007, p. 131). Hobbes (1968) and Bodin (1962) were concerned with the principle of sovereignty, and that it is the basis of all political regimes. Whiles Hobbes described sovereignty as a 'monopoly of coercive power,' Bodin described sovereignty as the 'absolute power in a state' or the most 'high and perpetual power,' a 'power that alone could guarantee orderly rule' (Heywood, 2007, p. 28). The traditional concept of sovereignty as the sum total of authority in a state, unrestrained by law has the features being the existence of absolute, perpetual, unlimited, determinable, inalienable, indivisible, and comprehensive power in a state (Dicey, 1939; Heywood, 2007) as follows:

i. Absolute sovereign power means that power is not subject to a legal limit. It is supreme;
ii. Perpetual sovereign power means that the exercise of the power is permanent, continuous, or constant.
iii. Unlimited sovereign power means that the exercise of that power has no end or barrier; It stretches everywhere in a state.
iv. Determinable means the real source of power in a state can be identified.
v. Inalienable means the sovereign power cannot be transferred;
vi. Indivisible means that no authority or person can share power with the sovereign; and
vii. Comprehensive means that laws and orders of the sovereign affect every person or organization in the state.

The classical conceptualization of sovereignty is unworkable, hence the categorizing definition of the concept, resulting in Dicey (1939) revision of the traditional definition of sovereignty into political and legal forms. Political sovereignty is considered the source of the sovereignty or political power in a state. It relates to the right that individuals have in participating in the process of government. This includes the right to vote and to be voted for, and the right to criticize the system of administration in a state. It is also connected with the right of a citizen to be educated on his or her political rights. Legal sovereignty refers to the recognized institutions and bodies established by law for the administration of the state. These include the Legislature, the Executive and the Judiciary, the Constitution itself, and the Ombudsman among others in a democratic state. The concept of sovereignty usually refers to a government's recognized right and responsibility to:

i. Control a clear preponderance of force (power) within the state. No force within the state can challenge its right to rule with any hope of success).
ii. Recognize no higher decision-making body than itself within the territory. (Alabama claims to be a sovereign state, but it is not sovereign because it recognizes the right of the United States government to overrule its decisions).
iii. Possess the ultimate authority over the affairs of the people in the territory. (No external agency will be allowed to overrule the decisions made by the government concerning its internal affairs).

However, sovereignty is not an either/or argument. Some governments are more sovereign than others. The degree of sovereignty depends on the extent to which the government exercises the rights and responsibilities set forth above. Sometimes the government's sovereignty is challenged from within. In Nigeria during the Ibo nation's attempt to create the state of Biafra, the sovereignty of the Nigerian government over the territory and people of that area was challenged and it took a thirty-month bloody civil war to restore the sovereignty. During the American Civil War, the Federal Government's sovereignty over the territory and people of the Confederacy was challenged over the territory and people of the government's sovereignty over the Confederate South. Occasionally, outside forces challenge a government's sovereignty. Shortly after the invasion of Czechoslovakia in 1968, the Soviet Union proclaimed what some call the 'Doctrine of Limited Sovereignty' for the states of Eastern Europe (Heywood, 2007). This doctrine states essentially that, as far as the Soviet Union is concerned, these states are sovereign unless the Soviet Union decides that their actions constitute a threat to the greater good of the 'Socialist Commonwealth.' In that case, the Soviet Union reserved the right to interfere as it saw fit to remove the threat. Of course, this worried these and other states considerably. It severely reduced the degree to which they were sovereign because the Soviet Union had the power to enforce such a doctrine. Therefore, the state is a political and administrative unit, claiming the 'monopoly of the legitimate use of force' over all the inhabitants of a given territory (Heywood, 2007).

THE UNDERCURRENTS OF NATIONALISM

This chapter teases out the legal, political, and economics of Westphalia nation-states in the new world order. Perhaps, human institutions like states or nations can be compared and examined based on the structure and function of those institutions. An institution can be examined in two ways; we may ask, what structures perform such and function in a particular society? or, conversely, we may ask, what function does such a structure perform for the society it serves? For example, a useful way of questioning the rationale of nationalism is to ask, what function does that state establishment serve in its society? Conversely, a useful way of comparing economic systems in a state is to ask, what structures perform basic economic functions of allocating scarce resources? If that structure is the government as opposed to a free-market structure of private firms and consumer groups, you may deduce something of the relative efficiency, flexibility, and freedom of the economic system in question. These two criteria, the structure and the function of nation-states are useful tools for examining the undercurrents of nationalism.

Self-determination is worth considering as a key undercurrent of nationalism. The fight for identity and self-rule by nationalists underpins the nationalist struggle for a sovereign nation-state. In this regard, there is a relationship between self-identity (self-determination) and governance ideal. The nationalists' struggle against the occupation and dominance of powerful states underprops the rationale and relevance of nationalism which is 'the hope to liberate people and governance ideal' from the oppressed. For instance, many of the nationalist movements and activities in Africa were against European occupation and rule, and many of the African nationalists initially preferred communism but later embraced the liberal form of democracy. Nationalism's focus is therefore on 'universal humanity' with the belief that 'identity and self-determination' is the ideal form of democracy and governance.

Also, when the collective identity of people increased, then nationalism grow. In this case, nationalism can be seen as a sense of collective identity (collective feelings), and a nation is a group of people bound together by nationalism. The first nationalistic political activity is the effort to create a state, and self-determination is the rallying cry under which the state is created. When the state is created, it reinforces the collective identity, and thus empowers the nation. The second political activity is the desire to be self-contained, and self-determination and irredentism share the goal of identifying the state with the nation. The basis of nationalism, therefore, lies in the common identity and sovereignty of the nation-state.

Besides, nationalism is a strong state-building force. For instance, many of the new states resulted from the reaction of colonialism in the Third World. However, the processes of state and nation-building are often characterized by violence. Thus, implicit in nationalism is the nation-building process and of nations for the state-building process. But it should however be noted that sometimes, nation-state is used interchangeably with country or state. Nation reinforces states when territorial boundaries coincide with the loyalty and commitment of nations to their states constituting a source of political power. Nations can also undercut and could destroy states in a manner that makes nations the global political actors. To understand the dynamics of such far-reaching changes in contemporary geopolitics, and place them in perspective, new analytical approaches are needed. As Schumpeter (1951, p. 211) puts it, "nationalism is affirmative awareness of national character, together with an aggressive spirit of superiority. It arose from the autocratic state." Also, the element of what Orwell (1945, p. 412) calls 'competitive prestige,' inseparably associated with the idea of nationalism, appears to have played a major role in the drive for national unification.

CONCLUDING REMARKS

The politics and economics debate of nationalism has now graduated from the fight for national independence to the struggle for national liberation (because of the neo-colonial forces of imperialism). The idea of potential new markets becoming economically self-reliant is triggering delinks from the Western economies. The world now is witnessing a new form of nationalism which is the radical shift of the center of gravity of world politics away from Western Europe and the United States of America (USA) toward China and lately Russia (Russia in Africa) with the strategy of national liberation being adapted to suit the social, political, and economic conditions of third world countries that have to bear the brunt of imperialism, and its local allies for far- too long. Nationalism can also be seen as the response of the diverse local cultures and peoples to modernization within a colonial framework. The existence of high religious and indigenous kingdoms triggered the growth of nationalist ideology. More, importantly, unity stimulates the struggle and the concerted resistance against colonialism and foreign occupation. In the process, many independent new states have emerged. However, the problems of nationalism in the world today fall into three categories:

i. Movements for autonomy and even secession by ethnically or culturally distinct regions in advanced industrial countries, such as Quebec in Canada, the Basques and the Catalans in Spain, and Northern Ireland, Scotland, and Wales in Great Britain, Ukraine;
ii. The breakup of the former Soviet Union, Yugoslavia, and Czechoslovakia into component republics based on distinct ethnic and cultural identities and emerging economic and political issues.
iii. Ethnic tensions and clashes in developing countries, military coups, and civil wars in immediate post-colonial Africa, and the upsurge of the new wave of military interventions and unconstitutional order in Africa (Sudan, Chad, Mali, Burkina Faso, Guinea, Ivory Coast).

The conclusion is that nationalism is a phenomenon of rising expectations of the nation-state wherein people make ever-increasing demands for more economic, social, and political benefits. It is a relatively recent phenomenon, contributing to major social, economic, and political changes after World War II. In the centuries before, societies stratified, and the poor were generally resigned to their lot. But, with nationalism catapulted by war, technology advanced rapidly, industries expanded, and modern communication has been in both the old and the new states emerged. Many young men from the developing areas fought on the side of Europeans and Americans in Europe and Asia. They saw and briefly enjoyed some of the material benefits of twentieth-century progress. They returned home knowing that a better life existed and they wanted their share of it. Not long afterward radio became readily accessible, and the message of affluence was spread to areas hitherto uninformed. This was the genesis of what has come to be called 'rising expectations' that underpin the nationalism of nation-states. However, new governments frequently experience serious difficulties in attempting to keep pace with these growing demands. They allocate funds to satisfy initial expectations. Yet, paradoxically, popular demands rise rather than decline. Fearing overthrow in reprisal for failure to respond, governments are often drawn into over-committing their scarce resources. In the face of inflation and a mounting debt burden, demands continue to increase. It is a never-ending spiral, frequently leading developing countries to economic collapse and political chaos. In developed areas, such problems manifest themselves in social protest, activism, and inflation.

The phenomenon of nationalism (rising expectations) usually follows a certain pattern. People first demand a greater share of material benefits, more food, better housing, and an income sufficient to provide for their basic needs. This is the case in less developed countries today. Once reasonably satisfied with their material environment, people shift their demands to the more intangible benefits like learning, social and political participation, leisure, and a sense of identity and dignity. This is the case today among the relatively developed states. Therefore, the state should have all-inclusive and pluralistic characteristics and overarching organizational authority to hold it together. Nationalism should deliver a state with organized forces supreme in its territory and pursue a conscious policy of aggrandizement in its relations with other states. It should have the right and obligation to regulate and control all other institutions of society and to direct on lines overly set by the interest of the state itself.

REFERENCES

Dulley, S. (1983). *The Political Economy of Nationalism*. Oxford: Oxford University Press.

Alter, P. (1983). *Nationalism*. London: Edward Arnold.

Anderson, B. (1983). *Imagined communities: reflections on origins and spread of nationalism*. London: Verso.

Aristotle (1984). *Politics*. Oxford: Clarendon Press.

Balaam, D. N & Veseth, M. (2001). *International political economy*. London: Palgrave.

Ball, A. & Peters, G. (2005). Modern Politics and Government. Basingstoke and New York: Palgrave Macmillan.

Barker, I. (1988). *Politics of humans: Research on American leadership*. Durham, NC: Duke University Press.

Barry, N. P (1987). *The new right*. London: Croom Helm.

Bauman, Z. (2004). *Identity*. Cambridge: Polity Press.

Beetham, D. (1991). *The legitimation of power*. Basingstoke: Macmillan.

Bell, D. (1960). *The end of ideology: on the exhaustion of political ideas in the 1950s*. New York: Free Press.

Bentham, J. ([1776] 1948). *Fragments on government and an introduction to the principles of law and legislation*. Oxford: Blackwell.

Berger, S. (1981). *Organizing interest in Western Europe: pluralism, corporatism and the transformation of politics*. New York; Cambridge University Press.

Bertsch, G., Clarke, R. & Wood, D. (1992). *Comparing political system: power and policy in three worlds (4th ed)*. New York: Macmillan.

Birch, A. H. (1972). *Representation*. London: Macmillan; New York: Praeger.

Birch, A. H. (2000). *The concepts and theories of democracy*. London: Routledge.

Bodin, J. ([1576] 1962). *The six books of commonwealth*. Cambridge, MA: Harvard University Press.

Brown, D. (2000). *Contemporary nationalism*. London and New York: Routledge.

Brown, M. B. (1995). *Models in political economy: a guide to the arguments (2nd ed.)*. Harmondsworth: Penguin.

Connolly, W. (1984). *Legitimacy and the state*. Oxford: Blackwell.

Cooper, R. (2004). *The breaking of nations: order and chaos in the twenty-first century*. London: Atlantic Books.

Dicey, A. V. ([1885] 1939). *Introduction to the study of the law of the constitution.* London: Macmillan.

Easton, D. (1979). *A framework for political analysis (2nd ed.).* Chicago: University of Chicago Press.

Gellner, E. (1983). *Nations and Nationalism.* Ithaca, New York: Cornell University Press.

Gibbins, J. (1989). Contemporary political culture; politics in a post-modern age. London: Sage.

Gill, S. & Law, D (1988). *The Global Political Economy: Perspective, Problems and Policies.* Brighton: Harvester Wheatsheaf.

Ginsberg, B. (1982). The Consequences of consent. Reading MA: Addison-Wesley.

Graham, B. D. (1993). Representations and party politics: a comparative perspective. Oxford: Blackwell.

Habermas, J. (1973). *Legimation crisis.* Boston: Beacon.

Hearn, F. (2006). *Rethinking nationalism: a critical introduction.* Basingstoke and New York: Palgrave Macmillan.

Hobbes, T. ([1665]1968). *Leviathan.* Harmondsworth: Penguin.

Hobsbawm, E. (1993). Nations and Nationalism since 1780. (2nd ed.). Cambridge: Cambridge University Press.

Hogwood, B & Gunn, I (1984). *Policy analysis for the real world.* Oxford University Press.

Keating, M. (1988). *State and regional nationalism: territorial politics and the European state.* London and New York: Harvester Wheatsheaf.

Keith, M. (1993). *Race riots and policing.* London: UCL Press.

Kellas, M. (1991). *The politics of nationalism and ethnicity.* London: Macmillan.

Kennedy, P (1989). *The rise and fall of the great powers.* London: Fontana.

Le Grand, I. (1982). *The strategy of equality: redistribution and social services.* London: Allen and Unwin.

Leftwich, A (2004). *What is politics? The activity and its study.* Cambridge: Polity.

Lenin. V. I ([1902] 1970). *Imperialism. The Highest stage of capitalism.* Moscow: Progress.

Lock, J ([1690] 1965). *Two treaties of government.* New York: New American Library.

Mill, J.S. ([1859]). *On liberty.* Harmondsworth: Penguin.

Mill, J.S. ([1861] 1951). Considerations on Representative Government in H. B. Acton (ed) *Utilitarianism, Liberty and Representative Government.* London: Dent.

Mills, C. W. (1956). *The power elite.* New York: Oxford University Press.

Morgenthau, H. (1948). *Politics amongst nations. the struggle for power and peace.* New York: Knop.

Orwell, G. (1945). Notes on nationalism in collected essays: Journalism and Letters. Penguin Books.

Ohmae, K. (1989). *Borderless world and strategy in the interlinked economy.* London: Harper Collins.

Olson, M. (1982). *The rise and decline of nations.* Newhaven. CT: Yale University Press.

Poggi, G. (1990). *The state*. Cambridge: Polity Press.

Przeworski, A. (1991). *Democracy and the market political and economic reforms in Eastern Europe and Latin America.* Cambridge and New York: Cambridge University Press.

Rousseau, J.J ([1762]1913). *The social contract.* London: Dent.

Sen, A. (2006). *Identity and violence.* New York: W.W Norton.

Schumpeter, J (1951). The Sociology of Imperialism in *The Economics and Sociology of Capitalism.* Princeton University Press.

Timuss, R. M. (1968). *Essays on the welfare state.* London: Allen and Unwin.

3

U.S. Recognition of the Illegal Israeli and Moroccan Annexations of Occupied Territories

Stephen Zunes

INTRODUCTION

U.S. support for allied governments engaged in repressive and illegal actions has long been a subject of controversy, including backing the Israeli occupation of Palestinian and Syrian territory seized by force in 1967 and the Moroccan occupation of Western Sahara, seized by force in 1975.

Both Palestine and Western Sahara are predominantly Arab Muslim nations from which much of their populations have lived in the squalor of refugee camps for decades in exile from their homeland. Most of the remaining Palestinian and Sahrawi populations suffer under foreign military occupation, with a smaller number living as a minority within the legally recognized territory of the occupier. Outside of four small Druze villages, the Syrian population of the Israeli-occupied Golan were expelled and have been unable to return. The occupying powers violate a series of UN Security Council resolutions, have illegally brought in hundreds of hundreds of settlers into their occupied territories, routinely violate provisions of the Fourth Geneva Convention and other international human rights standards, have built a heavily fortified separation barrier deep inside their occupied territories, and continue to defy landmark advisory opinions of the International Court of Justice. And both occupying powers are considered to be close allies of the United States, receiving substantial military, economic and diplomatic support to maintain their occupation and colonization of their conquered territories.

The inadmissibility of any country expanding its territory by force is a longstanding principle of the international legal order, enshrined in the United Nations Charter and U.N. Security Council resolutions, and repeatedly confirmed by the International Court of Justice. Russia's annexation of Ukraine's Crimean Peninsula in 2014 and its efforts to forcibly seize Ukraine's Donbas region and other parts of Ukraine in 2022 have brought this issue to the forefront of global attention. However, despite the United States taking a lead in mobilizing a tough international response to Russian aggression, the United States remains the only country in the world to formally recognize Morocco's annexation of Western Sahara and some parts of Israel's annexations of occupied Arab lands.

This chapter looks at U.S. recognition of these illegal annexations, which—while formally taking place under the Trump administration—are the result of decades of bipartisan support for the expansionist ambitions of these two U.S. allies and have not been reversed by the Biden administration.

U.S. RECOGNITION OF SYRIA'S GOLAN HEIGHTS AS PART OF ISRAEL

In March 2019, the United States became the first and only country to formally recognized Israel's annexation of the Golan Heights (Cheslow, 2019). Following its conquest of the Golan region in June 1967, Israeli forces drove out most of its residents in what has accurately been called ethnic cleansing (Pessah, 2019). The Druze inhabitants of the four remaining villages have suffered under years of Israeli military occupation and largely remain loyal to Syria. Protests immediately broke out following Trump's announcement (France 24 News, 2019). When Israel tried to impose its laws on the region in 1981, the Syrian Druze engaged in a successful nonviolent resistance campaign, blocking Israeli efforts to force them to carry Israeli ID cards, conscript them into the Israeli military, and other efforts to incorporate them into Israel (Kennedy, 1984).

In response to Israel's attempted annexation, the U.N. Security Council in 1981 unanimously adopted, without objections from the United States, resolution 497, which declared that "the Israeli decision to impose its laws, jurisdiction, and administration in the occupied Syrian Golan Heights is null and void and without international legal effect" (UNHCR, 1981). The United States, however, blocked any effort to enforce this and related resolutions. Subsequently, the Israeli government has been building settlements in the fertile highlands and growing Golan's Jewish population to some twenty-six thousand people (Hubbard, 2019), in violation of international law and U.N. Security Council resolutions, which prohibit occupying powers from settling civilians onto territories seized by military force. Again, however, the United States has blocked enforcement of these resolutions and Israeli colonization has therefore continued unabated. (UNSCR, 1980).

Due to the ongoing Syrian civil war and war crimes by the Assad regime, few are suggesting an immediate return of the Golan to Syria. However, several other options are available, including handing over the territory to the United Nations administration, as took place following the Indonesian withdrawal from occupied East Timor in 1999 (UN 2001). However, the U.S. position—in the words of then–Secretary of State Mike Pompeo when he became the first high-ranking U.S. official to visit the Israeli-occupied territory—is that the Golan Heights are "a central part of Israel" (Knell, 2020).

International reaction to Trump's decision was overwhelmingly negative (Holmes, 2019). The French foreign ministry noted how "The recognition of Israeli sovereignty over the Golan, occupied territory, would be contrary to international law, in particular, the obligation for states not to recognize an illegal situation" (Irish, 2019). The German government condemned the "unilateral steps" taken by Washington, D.C., observing that, "If national borders should be changed, it must be done through peaceful means between all those involved" (Nasr, 2019). Former U.S. deputy assistant secretary of state for Near Eastern affairs Tamara Cofman Wittes noted in a tweet that the decision "yanks the rug out from under U.S. policy opposing Russia's annexation of Crimea, as well as U.S. views on other disputed territories." (Borger, 2019) She added, "If Washington stops upholding the core international principle opposing the acquisition of territory by force, we should expect more states to seize territory they covet from their neighbors" (Wittes and Goldenberg, 2019).

Despite Trump's claim that Israeli control of the Golan Heights is vital for Israeli security, there is a growing awareness within Israel that it is far less important to hold the high ground in an era when the principal threats to Israel's security come in the form of suicide bombers and long-range missiles. Israeli army chief Lt. Gen Moshe Yaalon observed in 2004 that Israel could cede the Golan Heights in return for peace and more successfully defend Israel's internationally recognized border (Plushnick-Masti, 2004).

Trump's decision to recognize Israeli sovereignty over the Syrian Golan was built on policy failures of previous administrations. Israel and Syria came close to a peace agreement in early 2000 when Israeli Prime Minister Ehud Barak agreed to withdraw from Syrian territory in return for the Syrian government agreeing to strict security guarantees, normalized relations, the demilitarization of the Golan, and the end of support for radical anti-Israel groups. A dispute regarding the exact demarcation of the border, constituting no more than a few hundred meters, prevented a final settlement (Zunes and Yackley, 2002). With the death of Syrian president Hafez al-Assad later that year and the coming to power of the rightwing Likud Bloc in the subsequent Israeli election, talks were indefinitely suspended. Assad's successor, Bashar al-Assad, called for the resumption of talks where they left off, but both Israel and the United States rejected the proposal. A 2003 resolution supported by an overwhelming bipartisan majority of Congress insisted that Syria instead enter new talks "unconditionally" (U.S. House of Representatives, 2003) effectively rejecting the position of the more moderate Israeli government of former Prime Minister Barak and instead embracing the rejectionist position of the subsequent right-wing Prime Minister Ehud Olmert.

In 2006, several prominent members of the Israeli cabinet—including Defense Minister Amir Peretz and Internal Security Minister Avid Dichter—called on their government to resume negotiations with Syria. Although Foreign Minister Tzipi Livni appointed a senior aide to prepare for possible talks, such initiatives did not get any support from Washington. According to the *Jewish Daily Forward*, it appeared that "Israel would be prepared to open a channel with Syria but does not want to upset the Bush administration" (Popper, 2006). Indeed, when Israeli officials asked Secretary of State Condoleezza Rice about pursuing exploratory talks with Syria, her answer, according to the Israeli newspaper *Haaretz*, was, "don't even think about it" (Brilliant, 2007). Similarly, the Israeli daily *Yedioth Ahronoth* reported that Israeli government officials "understood from President Bush that the United States would not take kindly to reopening a dialogue between Israel and Syria" (Nir, 2006). U.S. pressure succeeded. Israeli Prime Minister Ehud Olmert reportedly expressed concern that it would be inappropriate to counter President Bush's "clear position on this issue," whom he described as "Israel's most important ally" (Nir, 2007). Similarly, Israeli Vice Premier Shimon Peres was quoted as saying, "The worst thing we could do is contradict the United States, which opposes negotiating with Syria" (Zunes, 2013). Interior Minister Ronni Baron told a television reporter, "When the question on the agenda is the political legacy of Israel's greatest friend, President Bush, do we really need now to enter into negotiations with Syria?" (Nir, 2007).

The failure of the United States to help bring peace between Syria and Israel when it was possible led to the U.S. and Israeli governments believing they could get away with this dangerous defiance of international legal norms and worsen an already difficult situation regarding Israel, Syria, and its neighbors.

U.S. recognition of West Bank Settlements as Part of Israel

In March 2019, the State Department announced that not only would the United States no longer refer to the Golan Heights as occupied territory, but the United States would also no longer use that term in reference to the West Bank either (Jones, 2019). Then, in November 2020, Secretary of State Mike Pompeo announced that the United States was recognizing illegal Israeli settlements constructed in the occupied West Bank as somehow legal and part of Israel. The illegality of Israel's settlements in the West Bank is clear: Article 49 of the Fourth Geneva Convention—to which both Israel and the United States are signatories—prohibits any occupying power from transferring "parts of its own civilian population into the territory it occupies" (United Nations, 1949). United Nations Security Council resolutions 446, 452, 465, 471, and 2334 have explicitly recognized the application of the Fourth Geneva Convention to Israeli-occupied territories, as does a landmark 2004 decision by the International Court of Justice (ICJ, 2004).

The Nixon, Ford, and Carter administrations all recognized the illegality of these settlements when Israel's colonization drive began in the 1970s. In 1978, the U.S. State Department issued a formal finding that they were indeed a clear-cut violation of international law (Hansel, 1978). In 2019, however, the Trump administration revoked this longstanding ruling and declared that the United States now considered the settlements legal (Higgins, 2019).

During his trip to the region in November 2020, Pompeo made U.S. recognition of Israeli sovereignty of the areas of the West Bank colonized by Israeli official policy as he became the highest-ranking U.S. official to visit one of these illegal settlements, crossing into the occupied West Bank to visit the Psagot Winery built on confiscated private Palestinian land and funded by American donors to the Trump campaign. While there, he sampled a red blend named after him, declaring that his visit was a "simple recognition of this as part of Israel" and "a recognition of the reality" (Liebermann, Hansler, and Atwood, 2020).

This "reality" of facts on the ground cited by Pompeo was made possible by both Republican and Democratic administrations' acquiescence, despite occasional expressions of disapproval, to Israel's settlement expansion, as well as a series of bipartisan congressional resolutions (Zunes, 2011). Indeed, the trend toward U.S. acceptance of Israel's colonization drive has been moving forward for decades.

The Reagan administration was the first to stop referring to the settlements as illegal but still opposed their expansion. In 1991, President George H.W. Bush insisted on a settlement freeze as a condition for granting a controversial $10 billion loan guarantee to Israel. In response, leading members of Congress—as well as then-Arkansas governor Bill Clinton and most other candidates for the 1992 Democratic presidential nomination—attacked Bush from the right by calling on the president to grant the loan guarantee unconditionally. He eventually capitulated, though insisting that the United States cut the amount of the loan guarantee granted in $2 billion increments over the subsequent five years by the equivalent amount Israel paid for settlement construction (Zunes, 2001).

It was under the Clinton administration that U.S. support for Israeli settlements became apparent, increasing aid to Israel by roughly the same amount deducted from the loan guarantee, thereby using taxpayer dollars to subsidize the settlements' expansion and undermining efforts by Israeli peace activists and the international community to freeze settlement expansion (Zunes, 2011). When the Oslo Accords were signed in September 1993 and the Palestinians pressed to address the settlements issue immediately, Clinton insisted that it be delayed as a "final status issue" to be dealt with later in the talks following security and redeployment issues, thereby enabling Israel to create "facts on the ground" by building more and more settlements, even as the peace process slowly moved forward (Zunes, 2017). To the shock of much of the international community, the Clinton administration also insisted that the Fourth Geneva Convention and the four U.N. Security Council resolutions addressing the settlements issue were suddenly no longer relevant, vetoing two otherwise unanimous new resolutions calling on Israel to cease its settlement activities. In 1998, the Clinton administration and Congress approved additional aid to Israel to build "bypass roads" and security enhancements for Israeli settlers in the occupied territories (Zunes, 2009).

Clinton and Israeli Prime Minister Ehud Barak's proposed boundaries of a future Palestinian state, unveiled at the July 2000 Camp David Summit, excluded most of the new and expanded settlement blocs developed during the previous years by incorporating them into an enlarged Israel, dividing the Palestinian West Bank into four noncontiguous regions (Zunes, 2001). The Palestinians recognized that such a fractured mini-state would be unviable and therefore rejected the proposal, leading Clinton and a bipartisan majority of Congress to blame the Palestinians for the failure of the talks. This failure by the United States to demand that Israel live up to its international legal obligations and cease its settlements expansion was therefore largely responsible for the collapse of the peace process and the rise of Palestinian groups like Hamas (Zunes, 2007).

George W. Bush's support for right-wing Israeli Prime Minister Ariel Sharon's 2004 "convergence plan"—which would have incorporated virtually all West Bank settlements into Israel and left the Palestinians with even less territory than in the Camp David proposal four years earlier—was endorsed by a broad bipartisan majority in Congress, including Chuck Schumer, John Kerry, Hillary Clinton and Joe Biden (Zunes, 2005). The Trump administration's proposal for Israeli-Palestinian peace, which also received bipartisan support, also would have allowed Israel to annex the illegal settlements on West Bank land.

In response to an International Court of Justice (ICJ) ruling against Israel building a security barrier deep into occupied Palestinian territory in order to incorporate the settlements into Israel, a large bipartisan majority in Congress (including the aforementioned senators) voted in favor of a resolution condemning the World Court for its opposition to what the resolution described as "the security fence being constructed by Israel to prevent Palestinian terrorists from entering Israel" (Zunes, 2005). However, the ICJ ruling explicitly defended the right of Israel to build such a barrier along its internationally recognized border to prevent terrorists from entering Israel; it only opposed its construction deep inside the Israeli-occupied West Bank to protect illegal Israeli settlements. In saying that entering settlement enclaves was "entering Israel," Congress was effectively agreeing with Pompeo that the West Bank settlements were indeed part of Israel. (While Pompeo was the first sitting secretary of state to visit a settlement, Hillary Clinton had visited a West Bank settlement before she took that post while she was a U.S. senator. During that visit, she insisted it was in Israel. Earlier, she had categorically stated that she had no intention of visiting "Palestinian areas" during her trip, even though the settlement was in the West Bank on land seized from a Christian Palestinian family that had been farming the land for generations.)

Obama was more critical of the settlements but was reluctant to explicitly call them illegal. In 2011, in his administration's only U.N. Security Council veto, the United States blocked an otherwise-unanimous resolution reiterating the illegality of the settlements and calling for a construction freeze. In December 2016, just weeks before Obama was to leave office, he had the United States abstain on a similar resolution calling on Israel to stop expanding its illegal settlements in the occupied West Bank. In reaction, a Congressional resolution was passed by a large bipartisan majority criticizing Obama's failure to veto the resolution in language that effectively insisted that the United Nations stay out of questions of international humanitarian law in occupied territories and that the decision as to whether expand these illegal settlements should instead be left to the voluntary compliance of the occupying power (Zunes, 2017).

Following his visit to Psagot, Pompeo declared that the United States would require goods imported from areas "where Israel exercises the relevant authorities" to be marked as "Made in Israel" or a "Product of Israel." (Pompeo, 2020) This runs counter to the policies of virtually the entire international community, including the European Union (EU), which recognizes that the settlements are outside Israel's borders. (The EU has a similar policy in regard to Moroccan-occupied Western Sahara.) Pompeo condemned what he called "pernicious EU labeling efforts," saying, "The U.S. stands with Israel and will not tolerate any form of delegitimization (Krauss, 2020)," thereby underscoring Washington's longstanding insistence that failure to recognize illegal Israeli irredentism means delegitimizing Israel's existence as a state.

As far back as 2015, a bipartisan majority of Congress passed a trade bill that formally defined "Israel" as including the occupied territories (US Congress, H.R.2146). It was attached to the "fast track" legislation to pave the way for the Trans-Pacific Partnership, the free trade agreement that was a priority for President Obama, in order to force him to pressure potential U.S. trading partners to no longer boycott products made in illegal settlements or discourage their companies from supporting the Israeli occupation. This followed a letter sent by Senator Ben Cardin (D-MD), the then-ranking member on the Senate Foreign Relations Committee and the de facto foreign policy spokesperson for Senate Democrats, to the chief U.S. trade representative calling on him to try to block European governments from "differentiating between pre-and post-1967 Israel" because there should be "no differentiation" between "Israel or territories controlled by Israel." In a signing statement, Obama declared that he would not abide by that section of the legislation. The State Department also rejected the pro-settlements language, observing how "every U.S. administration since 1967—Democrat and Republican alike—has opposed Israeli settlement activity beyond the 1967 lines" (Americans for Peace Now, 2015).

While it is easy to see Pompeo's announcements as simply another one of the Trump administration's renunciations of longstanding international norms or an embrace of the agenda of right-wing evangelical Christians, support for the Israeli colonization of occupied Palestinian territory has been ongoing for years. It has been endorsed by Republicans and Democrats alike, including Joe Biden and Kamala Harris when they were senators. These policies make a viable two-state solution impossible by dividing Palestinian-populated areas of the West Bank into multiple non-contiguous canons, creating an apartheid-like situation on the West Bank of exclusively Jewish towns and roads while the Palestinian majority is squeezed into increasingly small enclaves. It is also an effective renunciation of some of the most basic principles of international law established after World War II, enshrined in the UN Charter and other international legal statutes, prohibiting the expansion of any nation's territory by military force and forbidding the colonization of one nation by another.

U.S. RECOGNITION OF MOROCCO'S ANNEXATION OF WESTERN SAHARA

As controversial as the Trump administration's recognition of Israel's annexation of Syria's Golan Heights and the recognition of illegal Israeli settlements in the West Bank as part of Israel were, the United States did not question the existence of Syria as a state and Washington has remained open to the possibility of a Palestinian ministate alongside Israel. However, in December 2020, the Trump administration had the United States become the only major country to formally recognize Morocco's illegal annexation of the entire country of Western Sahara. (White House, 2020)[1] Blindsided by the decision, senior officials in the State Department suggested to their staff that the United States could simultaneously recognize Moroccan sovereignty over Western Sahara and continue to push within the United Nations for a negotiated political solution that would provide for self-determination. Arguments such as this not only implied that the United States was willing to derecognize Morocco's annexation of Western Sahara (should negotiations lead to that outcome), but they also failed to recognize the extent to which Trump's proclamation would embolden Morocco to reject any peace process that was not premised on Moroccan sovereignty over Western Sahara. Over a decade of bipartisan U.S. praise lavished on Morocco's dubious 2007 autonomy proposal as "serious, realistic, and credible" had only served to justify Rabat's campaign to stall and subvert negotiations with the Polisario since 2009. In recognizing Morocco's claim on Western Sahara, the Trump administration had seemingly driven the final nail into the coffin of the UN peace process.

The announcement in the final six weeks of the Trump presidency of U.S. recognition of the annexation of an entire country is a particularly dangerous precedent. As with his earlier recognition of Israel's conquests, Trump was effectively renouncing longstanding international legal principles forbidding the expansion of territory by force in favor of the right of conquest. And, since Western Sahara is a full member state of the African Union, Trump was essentially endorsing the conquest of one recognized African state by another, not only damaging the U.S. reputation on the continent but potentially leading other countries to believe they could also get away with territorial expansion with the support of the world's most powerful nation. It was the prohibition of such territorial conquests enshrined in the UN Charter that the United States insisted had to be upheld by launching the Gulf War in 1991, reversing Iraq's conquest of Kuwait. Now, the United States is essentially saying that an Arab country invading and annexing its small southern neighbor based on dubious historical claims was legitimate after all.

As with Israel and Palestine, U.S. policy toward Morocco and Western Sahara had been one of longstanding bipartisan backing of the occupation through blocking effective action by the United Nations, providing arms to the occupying power, and insisting that there be a negotiated settlement between the two parties regardless of the asymmetry in power between the occupier and those under occupation, effectively enabling the occupying power to further consolidate its control and continue its colonization. Since the early 2000s, bipartisan majorities in Congress and successive administrations have endorsed Morocco's so-called autonomy plan which is quite limited in scope and would fail to meet the international standard for autonomy. It does not allow the Sahrawis the option of independence—to which they are entitled as a U.N.-recognized non-self-governing territory according to international law, a series of U.N. resolutions, and a landmark World Court ruling.

However, until Trump's announcement, previous administrations recognized the dangerous legal precedent of formal recognition, making Trump's announcement the most dramatic shift in policy towards Western Sahara in forty-five years. Going well beyond the Bush and Obama administration's encouragement of the Moroccan autonomy plan to be considered as one viable option towards a peace settlement, the Trump administration declared that it was "the only basis for a just and lasting solution" (White House, 2020). And rather than maintaining the longstanding view that any solution had to be acceptable to both parties, Trump was essentially insisting that the people of Western Sahara simply had to accept their incorporation into Morocco.

Human Rights Watch, Amnesty International, and other reputable investigative groups have documented widespread arrests, the torture of dissidents, and violent suppression of peaceful protests by Moroccan authorities in Western Sahara. Freedom House, in its survey of 210 countries, has ranked Moroccan-occupied Western Sahara as having the worst record on political rights in the world save for Syria (Repucci and Slipowitz, 2021). This raises serious questions regarding how much "autonomy" would mean in practice as well as whether the Biden administration's rhetoric in support of human rights and democracy is at all sincere. Sahrawi women are particularly visible in the leadership of the nonviolent resistance movement in the occupied territories and have been specifically targeted for sexual abuse by Moroccan occupation forces. Indeed, the Biden administration's apparent belief that Western Sahara should be governed by a foreign, autocratic, right-wing monarchy instead of a relatively progressive and secular republic says a lot about its priorities.

In the weeks that followed Trump's proclamation, several Western countries and the United Nations were forced to reaffirm their neutrality on the question of Western Sahara, and even France, Morocco's most important ally, refrained from likewise offering to recognize Morocco's claim. Germany, having called for a UN Security Council meeting on recent developments in Western Sahara, questioned whether or not the United States could continue to serve as the "penholder" (the drafter of Council resolutions on an issue), as such a role "has to come with a strong commitment to resolving an issue, it has to be equitable, it has to be evenhanded, it has to have a legitimate interest of all parties in mind and it has to act within the framework of international law" (Heusgen, 2020). There was additional international criticism as well, including from UN Secretary-General Antonio Guterres, who reaffirmed that "the solution of Western Sahara does not depend on recognitions by individual states, but depends on the implementation of the Security Council resolutions, of which we are the guardians" (Guterres, 2021).

Both Americans who served as UN Personal Envoys to Western Sahara, James Baker and Christopher Ross, broke their silence and criticized Trump's move as entirely inconsistent with the search for peace and American values (Baker III, 2020). Former National Security Advisor John Bolton and other formal senior U.S. officials did so as well (Bolton, 2020). In the US Congress, even some of Israel's strongest supporters, such as Senate Armed Services Committee chair James Inhofe (Inhofe, 2020), a Republican, and House Foreign Affairs Committee Chairman Eliot Engel (Engel, 2020), a Democrat, while welcoming the news of Morocco's recognition of Israel, criticized the dangerous precedent set by President Trump in recognizing Moroccan sovereignty over Western Sahara. Yet, the Biden administration has refused to reverse Trump's decision.

The Sahrawis have fought for their national rights primarily by legal and diplomatic means, not through violence. Unlike the Palestinians and several other peoples engaged in national liberation struggles, the Sahrawis have never committed acts of terrorism. Even during their armed struggle against the occupation, Polisario forces restricted their attacks exclusively toward Moroccan and other occupation forces, never toward civilians.

Approximately one-third of the Sahrawi population lives in exile in the desert of western Algeria in refugee camps under the Polisario administration. The 175,000 Sahrawis living in these desert camps have developed a remarkably progressive political and social system governed by participatory democracy and collective economic enterprises within a limited market economy in the camps. Though devoutly Muslim, Sahrawi women are unveiled, enjoy equal rights with men regarding divorce, inheritance, and other legal matters, and hold major leadership positions in the Polisario's administration, including several cabinet ministers. In short, this is the very kind of governance the United States claims it seeks to establish throughout the Arab and Islamic world. In reality, however, the U.S. government is actively preventing the Sahrawis from establishing such a democratic system outside these refugee camps by supporting the occupation of their country by an autocratic monarchy.

The Sahrawi Arab Democratic Republic has been recognized at one time or another as an independent country by 84 governments. The SADR has been a full member state of the African Union (formerly known as the Organization for African Unity) since 1984 and most of the international community recognizes Western Sahara as Africa's last colony. By contrast, with only a few exceptions, the Arab states—despite their outspoken opposition to the Israeli occupation of Palestinian and Syrian land—have supported Morocco's occupation of Western Sahara.

BUILDING AN ANTI-OCCUPATION MOVEMENT

Israel and Morocco are unique among the world's occupying powers. Russia's 2014 annexation of Crimea were also illegitimate and received worldwide condemnation, and Turkey remains in violation of a series of UN Security Council resolutions regarding its 1974 invasion of Cyprus and its establishment of an independent state of ethnic Turks, At least in those cases, the vast majority of the peoples native to those territories were of the same ethnicity as their conqueror. Likewise, there are other occupied nations whose peoples arguably deserve statehood, such as Tibet and Chechnya, but these nations are legally recognized by the international community as part of the sovereign territory of their occupiers.

Western Sahara and the remaining territories still held by Israel since the June 1967 war are the only lands recognized by the United Nations as being illegitimately under the rule of a foreign power against the will of the subjected population. (The only other cases in recent years have been East Timor, which finally won independence in 2002 following a quarter century of brutal Indonesian occupation; Namibia, which became free from control by the then-white minority ruled South Africa in 1990; and Kuwait, which was liberated from six months under Iraqi occupation by a massive U.S.-led military operation in February 1991.)

The strong U.S. support for the Israeli occupation has often been blamed on the influence of the "Israel Lobby." However, the fact that the United States has also been willing to support the Moroccan occupation (and previous occupations by Indonesia and apartheid South Africa) despite the absence of a similarly strong domestic constituency favoring the occupying powers would seem to indicate that there is a broader U.S. policy at work that effectively undermines the UN Charter's prohibition against the expansion of territory by force. By rejecting law-based responses to irredentist efforts by U.S. allies, Washington has effectively endorsed the right of conquest.

When U.S. foreign policy has contradicted widely-perceived values—such as human rights and international law—popular movements have sometimes arisen to pressure Washington to change its policy. Unfortunately, efforts to end U.S. support for the Israeli occupation have been hampered by powerful constituencies with an ideological commitment to Israel, and efforts to end U.S. support for the Moroccan occupation have been hampered by the fact that few people are even aware of it. However, there are few indications that a majority of Americans actually believe the United States should recognize illegal territorial conquests, even if done by U.S. allies. A well-organized campaign could reverse U.S. policy.

The end of South Africa's occupation of Namibia and the end of apartheid in South Africa itself owes much to the work of activists in the United States and elsewhere, who campaigned for sanctions against the white minority regime. Audie Klotz has argued that although many international relations theorists "emphasize the difficulties of coordinating multilateral policies and the primacy of material interests," normative values manifested on a global scale were what led to South Africa's diplomatic, cultural, and economic isolation. "The loose coalition of governments, nongovernmental organizations, and individuals that made up the transnational anti-apartheid movement" successfully "globalized" their concerns as an influential political force, which could be replicated elsewhere. Most realist perspectives see little chance of Morocco or Israel rescinding their annexations and ending their occupation, but Klotz notes how "norms constrain states' behavior through reputation and group membership, and that norms constitute states' definitions of their own identities and interests." She reminds readers of how the history of decolonization "demonstrates the power of weak and non-state actors to transform both global norms and the distribution of social power in the international system" (Klotz, 1995).

Increasingly, nongovernmental actors are playing an important role in mobilizing social movements to force governments and international organizations to increase their efforts to resolve conflicts (Moser-Puangsuwan and Weber, 2000). According to Eileen Babbitt, in her study of mediating rights-based conflicts, the first criterion in such situations should be to establish the view that international norms are at stake. Although such norms in relation to the Moroccan and Israeli occupations have long been reiterated, these norms have become increasingly marginalized in "peace processes" dominated by powerful nations allied with the occupiers. Babbitt also notes, however, that human rights norms have more potency than they did several decades ago and have played a major role in the resolution of longstanding conflicts. Resolution to these conflicts came not simply from the parties' greater willingness to compromise, but from increased internal and international pressure on the more powerful side to negotiate a settlement based on international norms (Babbitt, 2006).

Neither Israel nor Morocco has the incentive to rescind their annexations, end their occupations, and allow for self-determination as long as they have the support of the United States, the world's most powerful nation. Changing U.S. policy, therefore, is a critical step towards resolving these conflicts and defending the post-World War II international legal order.

One of the major accusations leveled against those working to end Israel's policies of occupation and colonization is somehow "anti-Israel," based on the argument that if you oppose Israel's occupation, annexation, and colonization of territories seized by military force, it must be based on ideological opposition to Israel and Zionism, thereby raising the specter of anti-Semitism. Even those who do not oppose Israel's existence as a Jewish state are accused of unfairly singling out Israel for criticism. If those involved in the various campaigns to end Israel's occupation and end unconditional U.S. support for the Israeli government were also willing to address Morocco's occupation and unconditional U.S. support for the Moroccan government, it would not only provide badly needed additional support for Western Sahara self-determination but would focus attention on issues human rights and international law rather than ideological debates around Zionism.

Imagine, for example, if a divestment campaign included not just Caterpillar, Motorola, and other American companies backing the Israeli occupation and colonization of the West Bank, but also companies supporting the Moroccan occupation. Or a campaign for conditioning U.S. military aid to Israel on the Israeli government ending its occupation also demanding the same regarding U.S. military aid to Morocco. Rather than provoking divisive and polarizing arguments along the false dichotomy of "pro-Israel" versus "pro-Palestine," the debate on college campuses and within labor unions, Christian denominations, and other institutions could instead center on the real issues: the right of self-determination, the repressive nature of foreign military occupation and colonization, and the illegitimacy of invading and annexing neighboring lands. Rather than solely targeting the world's only Jewish state, such an anti-occupation movement would target an Arab Muslim country as well.

There is a sizable movement in Europe supporting the Sahrawis' right to national self-determination, often working in conjunction with those supporting the Palestinians, yet there is relatively little activism on Western Sahara here in the United States. This can change, however: In the mid-1990s, there was relatively little activism regarding East Timor either. Working in conjunction with fellow peace and human rights activists in Canada, Great Britain, and Australia, however, supporters of East Timorese self-determination eventually forced the United States and these other governments to end their support for the Indonesian occupation. As a result, East Timor is now free.

A similar campaign may be the best hope for the people of Moroccan and Israeli-occupied territories and the best hope to save the vitally important post-World War II principles enshrined in the United Nations Charter. Increased activism in support of the Sahrawis' right to self-determination will also enhance the struggle for Israeli-Palestinian peace by helping to redirect the debate from bitter ideological disputes unique to that conflict to the defense of universal moral and legal principles. Focusing on the United States' role in maintaining the Moroccan occupation will also further expose the false claims of Washington that its Middle East policy is based upon supporting freedom and democracy and upholding the rule of law.

What is at stake in regard to the Israeli and Moroccan occupations is which principle will prevail in the 21st century: the right of self-determination, or the right of conquest? The answer could determine the fate not just of these occupied territories, but of the entire international legal order for many decades to come.

REFERENCES

Americans for Peace Now, *APN slams Bush for pressuring Israel to avoid peace talks*. (2006, October 6). Retrieved September 18, 2022, from http://archive.peacenow.org/entries/archive3058.

Babbitt, E. (2006). Mediating rights-based conflicts: Making self-determination negotiable. *International Negotiation*, *11*(1), 185–208. https://doi.org/10.1163/157180606777835757.

Baker, III, J. A. (2020, December 18). *Opinion | trump's recognition of Western Sahara is a serious blow to diplomacy and international law*. Washington Post. Retrieved August 27, 2022, from https://www.washingtonpost.com/opinions/2020/12/17/james-baker-trump-morocco-western-sahara-abraham-accords/.

Bolton, J. (2020, December 15). *Biden must reverse course on Western Sahara*. Foreign Policy. Retrieved July 21, 2022, from https://foreignpolicy.com/2020/12/15/biden-reverse-course-western-sahara/.

Borger, Julian (2019, March 21) *Trump says US will recognize Israel's sovereignty over Golan Heights*, from: https://www.theguardian.com/us-news/2019/mar/21/trump-us-golan-heights-israel-sovereignty.

Brilliant, J. (2007, February 23). *Analysis: U.S. nixes Israel-Syria talks*. Retrieved August 21, 2022, from https://www.upi.com/Analysis-US-nixes-Israel-Syria-talks/28231172253756/.

Cheslow, D. (2019, March 21). *President Trump backs Israeli sovereignty claim over Golan Heights*. Retrieved August 21, 2022, from https://www.npr.org/2019/03/21/705583795/president-trump-backs-israeli-sovereignty-claim-over-golan-heights.

France 24. (2019, March 23). *Golan Druze protest Trump pledge to Israel*. Retrieved August 19, 2022, from https://www.france24.com/en/20190323-golan-druze-protest-trump-pledge-israel.

Hansell, H. J. (n.d.). *Letter of the State Department Legal Advisor, Mr. Herbert J. Hansell, Concerning the Legality of Israeli Settlements in the Occupied Territories*. Retrieved September 21, 2023, from https://www.hlrn.org/img/documents/USSDLegalAdvisorHansell_ltr.pdf.

Heusgen, C. (2020, December 21). *Statement by Ambassador Christoph Heusgen in the Security Council VTC Consultations on Western Sahara, December 21, 2020*. Permanent Mission of the Federal Republic of Germany to the United Nations.

Retrieved October 7, 2022, from https://new-york-un.diplo.de/un-en/news-corner/-/2430402.

Higgins, E. (2019, November 19). *'Naked violation' of human rights: Global condemnation over new US position on Israeli occupation*. Common Dreams. Retrieved July 12, 2022, from https://www.commondreams.org/news/2019/11/19/naked-violation-human-rights-global-condemnation-over-new-us-position-israeli.

Holmes, O. (2019, March 22). *Trump provokes global anger by recognizing Israel's claim to Golan Heights*. Retrieved September 11, 2022, from https://www.theguardian.com/world/2019/mar/22/trump-provokes-global-anger-by-recognising-israels-claim-to-golan-heights.

House Foreign Affairs Committee. (n.d.). *Engel Statement on Morocco-Israel announcement*. Retrieved August 9, 2022, from https://foreignaffairs.house.gov/2020/12/engel-statement-on-morocco-israel-announcement.

Hubbard, B. (2019, March 22). *The Golan Heights was once an Arab rallying cry. Not anymore*. Retrieved October 18, 2022, from https://www.nytimes.com/2019/03/22/world/middleeast/golan-heights-israel-syria.html.

International Court of Justice. (2004, July 9). *Legal Consequences of the Construction of a Wall in the Occupied Palestinian Territory (Request for advisory opinion)*. Retrieved September 19, 2022, from https://www.icj-cij.org/public/files/case-related/131/1677.pdf.

Irish, J. (2019, March 22). *Responding to Trump, France Says Israeli Sovereignty Over Golan Breaks International Law*. Retrieved September 19, 2022, from https://www.usnews.com/news/world/articles/2019-03-22/responding-to-trump-france-says-israeli-sovereignty-over-golan-breaks-international-law.

Jones, E. (2019, March 14). *US State Dept. no longer calling Golan, Gaza, West Bank 'occupied territory.'* CBN News. Retrieved July 30, 2022, from https://www1.cbn.com/cbnnews/israel/2019/march/us-state-depart-no-longer-calling-golan-gaza-west-bank-occupied-territory.

Kennedy, R. S. (1984). The Druze of the Golan: A case of non-violent resistance. *Journal of Palestine Studies*, *13*(2), 48–64. https://doi.org/10.2307/2536896.

Klotz, A. (1999). *Norms in international relations the struggle against apartheid*. Cornell University Press.

Knell, Y. (2020, November 19). *Pompeo makes unprecedented visits to Israeli settlements in West Bank and Golan*. Retrieved July 18, 2022, from https://www.bbc.com/news/world-middle-east-54999008.

Krauss, J. (2020, November 19). *Pompeo is 1st top US diplomat to visit an Israeli settlement*. AP NEWS. Retrieved August 21, 2022, from https://apnews.com/article/race-and-ethnicity-israel-boycotts-west-bank-jerusalem-38f09415fb4990ebdcbfea15dccff514.

Levine, M. (2020, December 10). *Inhofe slams Trump Administration on Western Sahara policy*. POLITICO. Retrieved January 29, 2022, from https://www.politico.com/news/2020/12/10/inhofe-slams-trump-administration-on-western-sahara-policy-444459.

Liebermann, O., Hansler, J., & Atwood, K. (2020, November 19). *Pompeo's West Bank Trip would be unthinkable for any other US secretary of State. but not him |*

CNN politics. CNN. Retrieved August 21, 2022, from https://www.cnn.com/2020/11/19/politics/mike-pompeo-israel-west-bank-visit-intl/index.html.

Moser-Puangsuwan, Y., & Weber, T. (2000). *Nonviolent intervention across borders: A recurrent vision*. The University of Hawaii Press.

Nasr, J. (2019, March 22). *Germany Rejects Trump's Call to Recognize Golan Heights as Israeli*. Retrieved July 18, 2022, from https://www.usnews.com/news/world/articles/2019-03-22/germany-rejects-trumps-call-to-recognize-golan-heights-as-israeli.

Nir, O. (2006, Oct. 18) "America impedes peace in Mideast," *Baltimore Sun* https://www.baltimoresun.com/news/bs-xpm-2006-10-19-0610190056-story.html.

Nir, O (2007, January 9) "U.S. Should Encourage Peace Talks Between Israel and Syria," *Mifta*

http://www.miftah.org/PrinterF.cfm?DocId=12381.

Nir, O. (2012, January 21). *U.S. should encourage peace talks between Israel and Syria*. Retrieved July 29, 2022, from https://www.sfgate.com/opinion/openforum/article/U-S-should-encourage-peace-talks-between-Israel-2659883.php.

Pessah, T. (2019, March 26). *Talk of Golan annexation leaves out those expelled from it*. Retrieved August 21, 2022, from https://972mag.com/talk-of-golan-annexation-leaves-out-those-expelled-from-it/140692/.

Pompeo, M. (2020, November 19) *Making of Country of Origin*, Department of State Press Statement.

Popper, Nathaniel (2006, August 25) *Calls for Talks With Syria Increase in U.S., Israel,* in *Forward* https://forward.com/israel/1443/calls-for-talks-with-syria-increase-in-us-israel/.

Plushnick-Masti, R. (2004, August 14). *Israel could cede Golan Heights, army chief says*. Retrieved August 21, 2022, from http://www.boston.com/news/world/middleeast/articles/2004/08/14/israel_could_cede_golan_heights_army_chief_says/.

Press release: APN Welcomes Administration's clarification on U.S. policy re: Settlements. APN. (2015, July 1). Retrieved October 21, 2022, from http://peacenow.org/entry.php?id=12425.

Repucci, S., & Slipowitz, A. (n.d.). *Democracy under siege*. Freedom House. Retrieved September 21, 2022, from https://freedomhouse.org/report/freedom-world/2021/democracy-under-siege.

Resolution 471 - Territories occupied by Israel. (1980, May). Retrieved October 21, 2022, from http://unscr.com/en/resolutions/doc/471.

Text - H.R.2146–114th congress (2015–2016): Defending public safety . . . (n.d.). Retrieved September 21, 2022, from https://www.congress.gov/bill/114th-congress/house-bill/2146/text.

United Nations High Commissioner for Refugees. (1982, December 17). *Security Council resolution 497 (1981) [israel-syrian arab republic]*. Retrieved August 20, 2022, from http://www.refworld.org/cgi-bin/texis/vtx/rwmain?docid=3b00f15734.

United Nations Transitional Administration in East Timor. (2001). Retrieved August 28, 2022, from https://peacekeeping.un.org/mission/past/etimor/etimor.htm.

United Nations. (2020, December 12). *Press conference by secretary-general António Guterres at United Nations Headquarters | UN Press*. United Nations. Retrieved July 18, 2022, from https://www.un.org/press/en/2020/sgsm20499.doc.htm.

United Nations. (1949, August 12) *IV Geneva Convention Relative to the Protection of Civilian Persons in Time of War*, https://www.un.org/en/genocideprevention/documents/atrocity-crimes/Doc.33_GC-IV-EN.pdf.

United States House of Representatives, H.R.1828 - *Syria Accountability and Lebanese Sovereignty Restoration Act of 2003*, 108th Congress https://www.congress.gov/bill/108th-congress/house-bill/1828.

White House, "Proclamation on Recognizing the Sovereignty Of The Kingdom Of Morocco Over Western Sahara," 10 December 2020.

Wittes, T. C., & Goldenberg, I. (2019, March 22). *Trump's Golan Fiasco*. Retrieved August 27, 2022, from https://www.politico.com/magazine/story/2019/03/22/trumps-golan-fiasco-226102?cid=apn.

Zunes, S. (2001). The United States and the breakdown of the Israeli-Palestinian peace process. *Middle East Policy*, *8*(4), 66–85. https://doi.org/10.1111/j.1475–4967.2001.tb00009.x.

Zunes, S. (2005). The United States Reaction to the International Court of Justice Ruling on Israel's Separation Barrier. *Middle East Policy*, XII (1).

Zunes, S. (2007). The Rise of Hamas, *Foreign Policy in Focus,* June 22, 2007.

Zunes, S. (2009). How Clinton and the Democrats Made Possible Israel's Settlements Expansion. *San Francisco, Alternet*.

Zunes, S. (2011, May 25). *How Clinton and the Democrats made possible Israel's settlements expansion*. HuffPost. Retrieved September 23, 2022, from https://www.huffpost.com/entry/how-clinton-and-the-democ_b_212292.

Zunes, S. (2013, May 13). *Israel, Syria and the United States*. Retrieved September 21, 2022, from https://truthout.org/articles/israel-syria-and-the-united-states/.

Zunes, S. (2014, May 8). *Congress overwhelmingly endorses Ariel Sharon's annexation plans*. Institute for Policy Studies. Retrieved September 10, 2022, from https://ips-dc.org/congress_overwhelmingly_endorses_ariel_sharons_annexation_plans/.

Zunes, S. (2017). The United States and Israeli violations of international humanitarian law. In A. Chase (Ed.), *Handbook on Human Rights and the Middle East and North Africa* (pp. 142–155). essay, Routledge.

Zunes, S. (2021, March 3). *Once again, Democrats are blowing it on Middle East Peace*. Foreign Policy in Focus. Retrieved September 23, 2022, from https://fpif.org/democrats-blowing-middle-east-peace/.

Zunes, S., & Yackley, J. (2002.). The Peace Process Between Israel and Syria. *Foreign Policy in Focus Policy Brief.* Vol. 7, No. 5, https://fpif.org/the_peace_process_between_israel_and_syria/.

NOTES

1. Eight poor conservative African countries (apparently motivated by economic incentives) and the United Arab Emirates have opened consulates in the

Moroccan-occupied Western Saharan city of Dahkla. Such a move implies recognition, but none of these governments has made a formal announcement comparable to that of the United States. Since recognizing Morocco's annexation, the United States has opened a consulate in Dahkla as well despite the absence of many U.S. citizens or discernable U.S. interests in the area.

4

Comparing Hamas and Irgun in the Struggles for Independence

A Continuation of the Same Terrorist Strategies by Different Actors?

Lawrence Mhandara

INTRODUCTION

This chapter contemplates the strategy of Irgun (National Military Organization) in the pre-1948 period with a view to juxtaposing it with the contemporary resistance formula of the Gaza-born Harakat al-Muqaawama al-ʾIslamiyya (the Islamic Resistance Movement), commonly known by the acronym Hamas. The Palestinian and Israeli struggles for self-determination and independence are colored with narratives that are more reflective of each other. In particular, both peoples deeply believe they have been victims of historical injustices and claim the same territory, which has been a salient feature in their counterclaims. Beyond that, resistance movements in both nations have engaged in acts of terrorism in the pursuit of national self-determination and independence. A quick review of the literature on terrorism in the Middle East reveals two broad methodological strands. The first group of studies examines, separately, the motivations to engage in terrorism and the tactics of Irgun and Hamas. The second set of studies analyses the attacks instigated by Hamas and also the counter-terrorism strategies employed by Israel and the West in the region. Precisely, there is a dearth of literature specifically dedicated to a comparison of the terror groups in Israel and Palestine, from both a contemporary and historical point of view. The imposing discourses on terrorism in the context of the protracted Palestinian struggle for statehood and independence reveal the proclivity to subject the Hamas organization to unfavorable reviews, and stereotypes or to project it as a profane movement compared to their equals in the Jewish struggle for independence.

In this chapter, we attempt to challenge such ideologically influenced moral relativism that is selectively and frequently assigned to Palestine movements and their suspect backers, but not to the Jewish groups. We posit that it is ahistorical to discount how the same strategy of terrorism was employed by the Jewish groups in the voyage towards the establishment of the state of Israel in 1948. Continuities and discontinuities are ascertained between Irgun's strategies and tactics before 1948 as they sought to deliver an independent state for the Jews and the Hamas' strategies and tactics in the search for the elusive Palestinian independence. Guided by Kydd and Walter's (2006) framework—costly signaling—for understanding terrorism, the chapter uses a comparative approach predicated on discourse analysis and meta-analysis of data on the aspirations, motivations, strategies, and tactics of the two resistance movements. The aim is to participate in the academic project to revive the debate about the role of revolutionary terrorism in the making of contemporary states while escaping the incarcerating trap of moral relativism in examining the struggles for independence in Israel and Palestine by radical groups.

The chapter is divided into three parts. The first section provides the birth and growth of Irgun and Hamas, examining their aims and doctrines. The next section is conceptual and mainly serves the purpose of showing the author's hypothesis that the aims, doctrine, strategies, and tactics of Irgun and Hamas do not in any way circumscribe analogies. The implications of the findings are discussed in the concluding section.

BACKGROUND: GESTATION AND BIRTH OF IRGUN AND HAMAS

The struggle for independence and statehood in Israel and Palestine has been entangled with the developments and shifts in international politics in the post-World War I (WWI) milieu. Renton (2013) heralds that the promotion of Wilsonian ideals after the war was a major catalyst in the growth of anti-colonial nationalism in Asia and North Africa in the twentieth century. In the last two years of the war, Woodrow Wilson's calls for the self-determination of oppressed nations and an end to secret diplomacy and annexation were disseminated widely and became the catchphrases of international politics. As a result, among the small nationalist elites that had sprung up across the European empires in Asia and North Africa, the war gave rise to millenarian expectations of a post-colonial order based on the concept of self-determination. However, the failure of the liberal-democratic West to follow up on the Wilsonian promise after 1918 led to an eruption of anti-colonial nationalist movements in the colonial territories (Manela, 2007 cited in Renton, 2013). Uprisings and street protests against colonial rule in the Middle East suddenly occurred with unpredicted frequency. The impetus behind this explosion in the Middle East was the British Empire itself. This narrative suggests that the conflict between Jews and Arabs, rather than Israel and Palestine are largely a by-product of British colonial rule.

Renton further notes that although followed by the minority among the Jews, the Zionist movement was well established by the time WWI commenced. Modern Zionism originated in eastern and central Europe in the latter part of the nineteenth century, but it is in many ways a continuation of the ancient attachment of the Jews and the Jewish religion to the historical region of Palestine, where one of the hills of ancient Jerusalem was called Zion. By the time British imperial forces seized Jerusalem and southern Palestine from Turkey in December 1917, the British policy was clear that the country would not become a part of the post-war independent Arab area. Following the Balfour Declaration, the British Cabinet and the Foreign Office accepted that a future British administration in Palestine would have to support Zionism. This policy engendered the resolve of Zionists to achieve their aims by 1918, the first full year of British rule in Palestine. Across the Jewish diaspora, British-backed Zionism had come to be viewed widely as a movement that was on the verge of achieving its aims and had to be accommodated. Many Zionists believed that they were about to see the establishment of a Jewish state in Palestine; anything less would be a grave disappointment. It is here in this moment that we see the beginning of the conflict between Zionists and Palestinian nationalists for national sovereignty over Palestine.

Fields (1995) notes that during the early years of the Zionist movement in Israel (from 1915 to 1920) there was a philosophical disagreement over how the aims of Zionism could best be achieved among ardent proponents of Zionism. On one side, were relatively conservative individuals, such as David Ben-Gurion, who felt that political negotiation and settlement with the British and Arabs best served the interest of guaranteeing independence for Israel. At the other extreme were the ideological radicals, such as Vladimir Jabotinsky, who believed that the only way to secure a Jewish state was to use force and defend it militarily if necessary. After Turkey's defeat in 1917 during World War I, Britain gained control of Palestine. Eventually, in 1923, Britain was formally designated by the League of Nations as the legitimate administrator of Palestine. When Britain's position later began to deteriorate in Palestine, the relative power of the radical Zionist groups increased. This amplified militancy was also stimulated by Britain's retreat from pressing for a Zionist state, and the resurgence of Arab nationalism in the Middle East and North Africa region.

Ahdut Ha'avodah, an organization of early Zionists in Palestine, was established in 1920 to provide for the defense of Jewish settlements in Palestine against Arab attacks. This organization, along with other factions with similar views about the defense and establishment of the State of Israel evolved into a national defense movement under the leadership of the party. This organization became known as the Haganah (the Hebrew term for defense). In its infancy, the Haganah under Vladimir Jabotinsky's leadership was to be a militia defense force recognized and armed by the British Mandate Authorities (BMAs) (Fields, 1995, 3). However, as early as the 1920s, the British were skeptical of Haganah's motive and withheld the anticipated support, plunging the movement into a crisis of legitimacy. At the same time, the World Zionist Movement and other leading Jewish elements expressed similar skepticism, leading to deep differences with Haganah over its aims: "to strive for legal status from the British Mandate Authorities or pursue an immediate but clandestine self-defense movement" (Fields, 1995, 3). Throughout the 1920s, Haganah's existence elicited mixed reactions. It attracted praise or condemnation by both the BMAs and Jewish leaders depending on the political climate and issue. For example, the group was lauded after it prevented the massacre of Jews by Arabs in 1929 before the Mandate forces subdued the violence. Equally, the faction attracted bitter criticism for using violence against the BMAs.

In 1931, the Haganah split following internal conflicts. A new militant group, Hagana 'B,' was formed by the rebellious Avraham Tehomi as an antithesis to the antecedent movement. Meanwhile, the greater number of the leadership of the new outfit was ideologically inspired by the radical ideas of Jabotinsky, who exploited the break-away faction to further his long-term desire to build a self-defense capability against Arab provocation. As tensions among the BMAs, Arabs, and Jewish World society in Palestine intensified in the 1930s, Jabotinsky became more closely associated with Haganah 'B' because it approved of the idea of counter-terror operations against Arab terrorist acts (Fields, 1995, 4). In 1936, Haganah 'B' split again. This became the marker for the birth of Irgun. After the rupture, half retraced their footsteps to the original faction while the other half, mostly ideologically revisionists, regrouped under a new name, the Irgun, the National Military Organization, or Etzel (Fields, 1995, 4). Irgun aimed to provide the Jewish community with its defense, including through terrorism, against Arab violence. Militant self-defense was considered a fundamental duty in the aspiration and journey to form a Jewish state in Palestine. The Irgun, throughout its existence, was reflective of the politico-military ideology of its main leaders: Vladimir Jabotinsky, David Raziel, and Menachem Begin. Raziel and Begin believed that favorable political results could be achieved if supported by an armed force, terrorist or otherwise. Under their tutelage, the Irgun consistently employed armed force against the enemies of Zionism in support of political goals - the principal goal being to secure an independent Jewish Homeland (Fields, 1995, 5).

Several scholars have shown that there was pronounced Palestinian Arab opposition to Zionism before 1914, as well as deep Zionist concern about that opposition, and have argued that the clashes and tensions between Arabs and Zionists during this period established the key features of the conflict (Mandel, 1976 cited in Renton, 2013). Before 1914, despite the growth of Palestinian national sentiment and activity, an organized and explicitly Palestinian nationalist movement working for an independent state had not emerged (Renton, 2013). Palestinian Arab political opposition to Zionism, focused on Zionist land purchases and the fear that Zionist settlers aimed to establish a Jewish state, was widespread and increasing; but the large-scale, organized confrontation between Zionists and Palestinian Arabs had not appeared (Khalidi, 2008 cited in Renton, 2013). As early as 1918, and corresponding to the progress of Zionism and British policy on the same, Arabs established the first Palestinian nationalist organizations, which included the intellectual activist societies such as the Harvest of Studies, re-named the Literary Club and the Arab Club and the political elite body, the Muslim-Christian Association (al-Jam'iyya al-Islamiyya al-Masihiyya). These groups were committed to opposing political Zionism at all costs.

The contemporary history of Palestinian nationalism however began with the rise of the Palestine Liberation Organization (PLO) in the mid-1960s as a distinctive nationalistic movement (Arafat, 1982 cited in Gupta and Mundra, 2005). The early Palestinian struggle was subsumed within the broader Arab identity promoted by Gamal Abdel Nasser and the Ba'ath Party of Syria. The devastating war of 1967 and the success of a small band of fighters in inflicting heavy damage to a column of Israeli armed forces in the village of Karameh created an intense feeling of Palestinian pride separate from the wounded Arab identity (Singh, 2012). As a result of the ensuing political dynamics, several groups such as Fatah, the Syrian-sponsored Sa'iqa, the Popular Front for the Liberation of Palestine (PFLP), and its offshoot the Popular Front for Liberation of Palestine—General Command (PFLP–GC), all with diverse ideological orientation, merged under the umbrella of the PLO (cited in Gupta and Mundra, 2005; Singh, 2012). Among the various groups under the PLO, Fatah has been the largest, and mainly secular and considers itself the mainstream Palestinian organization and the legitimate voice on the Palestine question. While the PLO has been striving for a secular Palestinian state as it rose in popularity, the prospect of a peaceful settlement with the Jewish state brought about violent disagreements within the

Palestinian community. It pitted the largely secular and increasingly accommodating PLO against those holding a strong Islamic identity along with the ideology of not conceding any part of Palestinian soil to Israel. Hence, challenges to the PLO (in general) and Arafat (in particular) came primarily from two groups; Hamas and the Islamic Jihad. In November 1987, the PLO and the leadership of the intifada movement issued a fourteen-point declaration calling for a Palestinian state to coexist with Israel. A month later Hamas was officially founded.

Emerging during the first Palestinian Intifada, Hamas was established as the political and militant branch of the Palestinian Muslim Brotherhood to fight the Israeli occupation (Alsoos, 2021; Singh, 2012). The Muslim Brotherhood is an Islamist organization founded in Egypt and has wings, branches, and affiliations around the Muslim world. And the Brotherhood was particularly strong in Gaza, but when Egypt controlled Gaza, after the 1948 war, and until 1967, the Brotherhood was suppressed because the Egyptian government saw it as a political threat. The acronym *Hamas* means 'zeal' in Arabic, derives its roots from both religion (Islam) and *muqawama* (resistance) as evident in its official name Harakat al-Muqaawama al-'Islamiyya (the Islamic Resistance Movement) (Gupta and Mundray, 2005). Founding member, Abd al-Fattah Dukhan indicated that the name was coined on 10 December 1987, the integration of the term *muqawama* was inspired by the Islamic Resistance in the south of Lebanon which achieved success militarily against the Israeli occupation (Alsoos, 2021, 835). Gupta and Mundray (2005: 577) cogently write that:

> Although both Hamas and Islamic Jihad trace their origins to the Islamic Brotherhood movement in Egypt, there is a clear distinction in the order of priorities set forth by the two groups—particularly regarding the question of jihad. The Islamic Brotherhood, like many other fundamentalist Islamic movements, sees jihad as a general duty of all Muslims and proposed that first 'proper Islam' should be established throughout the Muslim world. Only after this primary goal is achieved, violent jihad should be directed against Israel. In contrast, the irredentist Hamas movement switched the two priorities. It maintained that first jihad should be directed at liberating all of Palestine, and then Muslims should direct their attention to the goal of restoring the "true faith" to the rest of the Islamic world. However, both groups absolutely reject any political arrangement that would result in the relinquishment of any part of Palestine to the non-believer.

Hamas was ideologically affiliated with the Brotherhood but strategically and tactically diverged in terms of sequencing of priorities. Resistance, to secure Palestinian statehood first, was weightier than the religious goals. Theocratisation of the state would only be realized once the occupying state is defeated and, *ipso facto*, supplanted by a Palestinian state led by a Hamas government.

By the way, the concept of *muqawama* as a militant framework was initially marginalized from Hamas' discursive formation. Rather, the term jihad was employed instead to explain Hamas' words and deeds (Alsoos, 2021, 836). It was not until the start of the Second Intifada in October 2000 that the framework of *muqawama* emerged and gradually came to constitute the master frame for the organization. The Palestinian-Israeli conflict was framed in the 1988 Charter as a religious cause between Muslims and Jews engaged until the day of judgment (Charter of the Islamic Resistance Movement (Hamas), 18 August 1988, cited in Alsoos, 2021). The *Introductory Memorandum* refutes this explanation and states that it is instead a conflict between 'Zionists' on the one side and 'Muslims and Arabs' on the other. Hamas's media spokesperson, Salah al-Bardawil, concurs that the Palestinian cause is a political problem in opposition to 'Zionism' (Salah al-Bardawil Hamas media spokesperson cited in Alsoos, 2021). Refuting religious agency and instead defining the key drivers of the conflict as colonialism, displacement, and dispossession aimed to redefine Hamas's worldview and counteract the negative impacts created by the generalized use of the term 'Jews' in the Charter. "The Introductory Memorandum is absolutist and inherently violent . . . Hamas considers Palestine wholly Muslim land, such that surrendering any of it would be sinful" (Simon and Stevenson 2003: 60). Both religious (theocratising the Palestinian state) and identity (Arab and Islam) redemption are intrinsically predicated on the complete annihilation of Zionism (Gupta and Mundray, 2005). And this radical goal requires not engagement, diplomacy, or compromise but armed violence. No wonder Hamas has never been equivocated on the goal as demonstrated in the remarks by Khaled Meshal, a Hamas political leader at the time, in December 2012 are instructive:

> Palestine is ours from the river to the sea and from the south to the north. There will be no concession on any inch of the land. We will never recognize the legitimacy of the Israeli occupation, and therefore there is no legitimacy for Israel, no matter how long it will take. We will free Jerusalem inch by inch, stone by stone. Israel has no right to be in Jerusalem (cited in Simon and Stevenson, 2003, 61).

CONCEPTUAL FRAMEWORK

This section heavily borrows from the works of Kydd and Walter who provide a framework for deciphering terrorism across groups and contexts. According to the authors, terrorist violence is a form of costly signaling. This provides a coherent framework upon which the strategies and tactics used by Irgun and Hamas can be comprehended and compared. Terrorists are too weak to impose their will directly by conventional force hence the resort to costly signaling. To this end, Lind, Schmitt, and Wilson (1989 cited in Berglund and Souleimanov, 2020) assert that terrorism is a form of asymmetric warfare or "fourth generation warfare because of the decentralized fashion and ability to adapt their strategies to make the most of their position as underdogs. Terrorists' legal status and weak capabilities impel them to communicate their power through costly signaling. According to Riley (2001 cited in Kydd and Walter, 2005), costly signals are actions so costly that bluffers and liars are unwilling to take them. By employing costly signaling, terrorists persuade audiences to do as they wish by altering the audience's beliefs through the terrorist's ability to impose costs and demonstrate commitment to their cause. Violence is meant to alter minds or influence the behavior of the target and the broader society afflicted by violence. "Because it is hard for weak actors to make credible threats *[through talking]*, terrorists are forced to display publicly just how far they are willing to go to obtain their desired results" (Kydd and Walter, 2006, 51). War itself, or the willingness to endure it, can serve as a forceful signal of resolve and provide believable information about power and capabilities (Riley, 2001 cited in Kydd and Walter, 2005). To obtain their political goals, terrorists need to provide credible information to the audiences whose behavior they hope to influence. Terrorists play to two key audiences: governments whose policies they wish to influence and the society on the terrorists' side whose support or obedience they seek to gain. Kydd and Walter aver that the targeted governments are central because they can grant concessions over the objectives that the terrorists are seeking. The terrorists' domestic audience is also important because they can provide resources to the terrorist group and must obey its edicts on social or political issues. Costly signaling in turn yields five strategies, rationally used in terrorist campaigns.

The five principal strategic logics of costly signaling in terrorism are attrition, intimidation, provocation, spoiling, and outbidding (Kydd and Walter, 2006). Kydd and Walter explain that in an attrition strategy, terrorists seek to persuade the enemy that the terrorists are strong enough to impose considerable costs if the enemy continues a particular policy. Terrorists using intimidation try to convince the population that the terrorists are strong enough to punish disobedience and that the government is too weak to stop them so that people behave as the terrorists wish. A provocation strategy is an attempt to induce the enemy to respond to terrorism with indiscriminate violence, which radicalizes the population and moves them to support the terrorists. Spoilers attack to persuade the enemy that moderates on the terrorists' side are weak and untrustworthy, thus undermining attempts to reach a peace settlement. Groups engaged in outbidding use violence to convince the public that the terrorists have greater resolve to fight the enemy than rival groups, and therefore are worthy of support. Based on this framework, the hypothesis of the chapter—Irgun and Hamas should be considered fraternal twins for they employed costly signals that were exuded in similar strategic logics—is presented and validated.

COMPARING IRGUN TO HAMAS' STRATEGIES AND TACTICS

There were three basic tenets of Irgun ideology as reflected in the teachings of Vladimir Jabotinsky: all Jews had a right to enter Palestine; only active retaliation would deter the Arabs; and only Jewish armed forces would ensure the Jewish State. It has been described as an Irish Republican Army (IRA) type guerrilla-terrorist organization (Fields, 1995, 6). The IRA sought the establishment of a republic, the end of British rule in Northern Ireland, and the reunification of Ireland. The IRA was created in 1919 as a successor to the Irish Volunteers, a militant nationalist organization founded in 1913 (Bowden, 1976). The IRA's strategy was to use armed force to undermine British rule in Ireland and thus assist in achieving the broader objective of an independent republic (Bloom and Horgan, 2008). The IRA used bombs and selective assassination of authorities to undermine the British interest in Northern Ireland. The violent action was part of the political culture of the IRA that was borrowed by the Irgun. By employing the gun and bomb of the IRA model, the Irgun sought to ensure that Jabotinsky's tenets were carried out. Menachem Begin's comments are especially instructive for characterizing Irgun as a terrorist entity:

> . . . the very existence of an underground, which oppression, hangings, tortures and deportations, fail to crush or to weaken must, in the end, undermine the prestige of a colonial regime that lives by the legend of its omnipotence. Every attack which it fails to prevent is a blow to its standing. . . . We never believed that our struggle would cause the total destruction of our people. We knew that Eretz Israel, in consequence of the revolt, resembled a glass house. The world was looking into it with ever-increasing interest and could see most of what was happening inside. . . . Arms were our weapons of attack; the transparency of the "glass" was our shield of defense. Served by these two instruments we continued to strike our blows at the structure of the Mandate's prestige (cited in Fields, 1995, 8).

This observation illustrates Irgun's determination to achieve its ultimate objective—the establishment of a State of Israel—using whatever means necessary. Begin's belief in creating tension, provocation, and destruction was the basis for the particular tactics used by Irgun throughout its existence. The tactics employed by the Irgun, exemplified by target selectivity, were mostly terrorist. Irgun activity encompassed more than the destruction of Arab and British installations, such as the British headquarters in Jerusalem at the King David Hotel (Fields, 1995, 7). The Irgun also sponsored a vociferous propaganda campaign against both British and Arabs in a weekly newspaper, published in Poland and distributed throughout Eastern Europe. These newspaper articles not only applauded Irgun's armed tactics but blatantly argued the case for an independent Jewish state in Palestine. All the same, the organization consisted of a group of cruel anti-Arab and anti-BMAs terrorists. Much of the Irgun effort was directed against the British to achieve an independent Jewish State. The rest of it was directed against the Arabs in retribution for attacks they had made earlier.

In terms of Hamas doctrine, it seeks the total demise of Zionism and Israel. Since its formation in the late 1980s, Hamas has been crystal clear about its opposition to Zionism and Israel. The group opposes any kind of negotiations or agreements that recognize the goals of Zionism or the state of Israel. Its leadership has unfailingly gushed incendiary remarks targeting the Jews, Zionism, and Israel. Over time, key leaders have been crystal clear that neither they nor Hamas will disarm nor give up militant action. The remarks made by one of the leaders of the organization validate this grounded position (quoted in London Filastin al-Muslimah, November 1996: 12–14):

> Hamas' jihad plan is the plan of a nation and not that of a movement. Neither Hamas nor the Palestinian people as a whole can end the jihad and the fighting against the occupation, as long as the occupation is still there and continues its arrogance and injustice on the ground against the people and their rights." Shaykh Jamal Mansur, Hamas leader in the West Bank (cited in Stein, 2014).

The remarks show that Hamas leaders believe that all of the lands on which the state of Israel was established belong to Arabs. Hamas does not equivocate in its outlook about its goals; all of its horizons require Israel's destruction. Stein (2014) further makes a fiery conclusion:

> Anyone who believes that Hamas' current fundamental beliefs are flexible enough to recognize Israel or that the organization will give up arms as a long-term political concession is simply naïve. As it has in the past Hamas may accept a tahdi'a or calming down of tensions, or even a temporary truce or hudna, negotiated by a third party, but for it to accept Israel as a reality is totally contrary to its ideological outlook. Removing/ending occupation for Hamas means Israel's destruction.

The radical doctrine of the non-state actor (Hamas), with its inevitably weak military power relative to the IDF, has forced the group to communicate its capabilities through costly signals. Thus Hamas, like Irgun, claim their relevance to the struggle for political independence in Palestinian territories based on terrorism. Their strategic choices thus make them fraternal twins in pursuing the same goal of statehood through the pursuit of strategies such as attrition, intimidation, and outbidding among other forms of signaling. Because of these strategies, Hamas has become the government of Gaza (the Palestinian proto-state—Singh, 2012) just like the Irgun became part of the coalition that formed the first government of Israel in 1948.

Attrition

The most important task for any terrorist group is to persuade the enemy that the group is strong and resolute enough to inflict serious costs so that the enemy yields to the terrorist's demands (Kydd and Walter, 2006). In an attrition campaign, the greater the costs a terrorist organization can inflict, the more credible its threat to inflict future costs, and the more likely the target is to grant concessions. Irgun used a war of attrition strategy against the BMAs. By targeting Britain with terrorist attacks, they eventually convinced the political leadership that maintaining control over these territories would not be worth the cost of British lives. The destruction of the King David Hotel in Jerusalem in July 1946 by Irgun, causing more than two hundred casualties (wounded or dead) was part of the equivocate display of power.

Hamas mostly adopted a strategy of violent street confrontations with the Israeli military during the first intifada in the late 1980s. And meanwhile, Hamas had been saying the true key is resistance, and resistance becomes the Palestinian way. As they begin to use more and more violence, Hamas' model, mostly suicide bombs, became more credible than Fatah's. Pape argues that suicide terrorism is employed by weak actors for whom peaceful tactics have failed and conventional military tactics are infeasible because of the imbalance of power. The strategy is to inflict costs on the enemy until it withdraws its occupying forces: the greater the costs inflicted, the more likely the enemy is to withdraw (Pape, 2003). On 29 August 2003, a Hamas operative detonated himself aboard a Jerusalem bus, killing twenty-one Israeli civilians and injuring over a hundred. Hamas immediately proclaimed that its attacks would continue (Simon and Stevenson, 2003, 59). Israel withdrew from Gaza in 2005, and it does so frankly because of constant Palestinian violence, especially violence by Hamas. Israel's precipitous withdrawal from southern Lebanon in May 2000 convinced Hamas that the Israeli leadership's resolve was weakening and encouraged Hamas leaders to initiate the second intifada in September 2000 (Kydd and Walter, 2006). Thus attacks by Hamas against Israel, particularly during the second intifada, were guided by attrition. In a letter written in the early 1990s to the leadership of Hamas, the organization's master bomb maker, Yahya Ayyash, said, "We paid a high price when we used only sling-shots and stones. We need to exert more pressure, make the cost of the occupation that much more expensive in human lives, that much more unbearable" (cited in Kydd and Walter, 2006, 60). A Hamas leader further declared in October 2005: "When we took up arms and launched [the second intifada], we succeeded in less than five years to force the Israelis to withdraw from the Gaza Strip. This fulfilled everyone's dream. I think we have to benefit from this experience by applying it accordingly to the West Bank and other occupied areas" (cited in Kydd and Walter, 2006, 63). Expressing similar sentiments, a Hamas spokesman quoted after the Intifada was unyielding: "When the intifada erupted, the power of Hamas was two percent, now it is 100 percent following 'the jihad capital' and the support that it derived among the Palestinian people's ranks" (cited in Stein, 2014), further adding that "As far as we in Hamas are concerned, we have never declared that we intend to stop our armed struggle against the occupation, negotiations or no negotiations" (Excerpts of interview with Ismail Haniyeh cited in Stein, 2014).

Intimidation

Intimidation is akin to the strategy of deterrence, preventing some undesired behavior utilizing threats and costly signals. It is most frequently used when terrorist organizations wish to overthrow a government in power or gain social control over a given population. It works by demonstrating that the terrorists have the power to punish whoever disobeys them and that the target is powerless to stop them (Kydd and Walter, 2006). An intimidation strategy can encompass a range of actions, from assassinations of individuals in positions of power to car bombings to the massacre of civilians. Irgun targeted BMAs with assassinations, including the public hanging of British soldiers. The Irgun emphasized that the two Britons—Clifford Martin and Mervin Paice—had been hanged after a guilty verdict was pronounced by the court-martial. Their charge sheets reflected five but identical offenses: illegal entry into Palestine; belonging to the occupying forces; spying on Jews; illegal carrying of arms; and plotting against the Jewish armed forces, the Irgun (Jewish Telegraphic Agency, 1947). In 1944, following BMAs policy to limit Jewish immigration, Irgun conducted a terrorist campaign against BMAs. The terror campaign culminated in the assassination of Lord Moyne, a British Minister Resident in the Middle East, in November (Paul et al., un, 5). On April 1, 1948, an Irgun unit destroyed the Arab village of Dir Yassen killing two hundred and fifty people. This act contributed heavily to the state of fear against Jewish attacks among the Palestinian Arabs. Although there is some debate about whether the unit involved in the attack was of Irgun origin, the fact remains that terrorist acts such as those perpetrated by Irgun are partly responsible for the present Palestinian refugee situation.

Concerning Hamas, the by-product of the Oslo Agreement was the strengthening of the PLO as the sole representative of the Palestinian people, a prospect that threatened its ideological rivals. In response, Hamas and Islamic Jihad stepped up their violent campaign against the Israeli government. In particular, they discovered the power of suicide attacks (Gupta and Mundray, 2005). The tactic of suicide bombing emerged as a strategic weapon of choice for the group. It would elicit little debate to state that suicide bombings—more than any other single form of political violence—have left their deepest imprint on global politics, particularly during the past decade (Gupta and Mundra, 2005, 573)—increased frequency and lethality of suicide attacks. Since 2000, most of the casualties of terrorism occurred against civilians within Israel (Frisch, 2009, 1051). Between 2000 and the end of 2005, 86 percent of Israeli fatalities were civilian and the overwhelming percentage of casualties (89 percent) was a result of suicide bombings that took place within the Green Line (Suicide Bombing, 2006 cited in Frisch, 2009, 1051).

Outbidding

Outbidding arises when two key conditions hold: two or more domestic parties are competing for leadership on their side, and the general population is uncertain about which of the groups best represent their interests (Bloom, 2005 cited in Kydd and Walter, 2006). The competition between Hamas and Fatah is a classic case where two groups vie for the support of the Palestinian citizens and where the average Palestinian is uncertain about which side he or she ought to back. Groups competing for power have the incentive to signal that they are zealots rather than sell-outs. Terrorist attacks can serve this function by signaling that a group has the will to continue the armed struggle despite its costs. The process is almost entirely concerned with the signal it sends to domestic audiences uncertain about their leadership and its commitment to a cause. As such, outbidding provides a potential explanation for terrorist attacks that continue even when they seem unable to produce any real results (Kydd and Walter, 2006).

The Irgun was competing for influence with two other terrorist organizations, namely Haganah and the Stern Gang. Zionists organizations in general differed in their political orientations and acceptable means of reaching their common goal—an independent Israel. Ben Gurion's Jewish Agency was a conservative group that believed in Arab-Israeli coexistence. The consistent terror campaign waged by the Irgun, its need for arms, and a defiant sense of independence from central authority led to the Altalena incident in June 1948. The Altalena, a ship used to transport men and arms, was sunk by the rival group Haganah on June 20, 1948, in Tel Aviv. In September 1948, the Irgun disbanded and joined with Haganah and Palmach forces forming Zahal—the Israeli National Defense Forces. Many authorities on the subject of terrorism and Israeli history have demonstrated that the activities of the Irgun served as a model for other subsequent terrorist movements with similar purposes (Fields, 1995, 19). Ironically, the chief adversary of Israel, the Palestine Liberation Organization, and now Hamas, could be included among those terrorist organizations that were heavily influenced by the Irgun model.

On Hamas' side, outbidding has been ingrained in its *modus operandi,* starting with the first Intifada. The first Intifada was a largely peaceful uprising that occurred on the West Bank in Gaza. The energy and activism associated with the Intifada made it impossible for the Brotherhood to let go of the opportunity despite being bound to a tradition of indirect role in politics. The risk was that if they stayed aloof during the uprising, they might lose to their rivals, especially Fatah. Hamas feared irrelevance and loss of support. So, they enter the fray, and they begin to use violence, but the identity they were pushing was different from Fatah's. Where Fatah pushed for a Palestinian identity, Hamas was for an identity that was both Palestinian and Islamic. Hamas became truly important during the 1990s. Early in the 1990s, Fatah morphed from a terrorist group to a negotiating partner of Israel, raising hopes for a peace deal. Hamas saw this development as ideologically unacceptable by the fact that it rabidly opposes peace with Israel. However, peace between Fatah and Israel would also mean that the former had a chance to consolidate its position and control of the Palestinian people. Hamas and Islamic Jihad resorted to suicide bombings to effectively disrupt peace talks. There were five suicide bombings in 1994 and these killed roughly 40, creating a dilemma for the Fatah and Israeli negotiations.

After the collapse of the peace negotiations in 1999, a second intifada in the 2000s occurred. During this turmoil, Hamas violence intensified with the rate of suicide bombings escalating. Israel's defense forces (IDF) responded by targeted assassinations and arrested, the Hamas gained credibility because Fatah had embraced negotiations, and negotiations failed. "Though it is in the interest of both Hamas and Fatah to forge unity as long as they both share the proximate goal of statehood, each party must buttress its popularity—for the perception of legitimacy will be required when the real test comes" (Simon and Stevenson, 2003, 61). For Hamas, violence bolsters its popular standing as the strongest defender of the Palestinian cause compared to the compromising Fatah or other secular organizations under the Palestine

Liberation Organisation (PLO). For instance, on 22 April 1997, a Hamas leader, Rantisi said:

> They [the Fatah-led Palestinian authority] openly say that their objective is to relinquish around 90 percent of the land of Palestine. Shall I give them a chance to achieve it? "Islam does not permit giving up one inch of Palestine and states that Palestine belongs to the Moslems, belongs to the Palestinian people, not to the Jews . . . Oslo boils down to relinquishing Palestine" (cited in Stein, 2014).

The remarks demonizing Fatah as sell-outs while self-praising Hamas as heroes render credence to de Mesquita's hypothesizes that nationalist movements are comprised of moderates and extremists, further positing that since the moderates are willing to negotiate, terrorist organizations become more militant following concessions to the enemy; the moderates leave the center stage of protest to cooperate with the authorities, while the resulting power vacuum is filled by the extremists (cited in Gupta and Mundra, 2005, 575). The model of Kydd and Walter also envisages the motive of spoiling or thwarting a potential peace deal between the enemy and the rivals of the terrorist group (Kydd and Walter, 2002). But in a more general sense, Hamas "has used the culturally and socially resonant norm of Palestinian heroic warfare to garner civilian support within the occupied territories" (Singh, 2012, 531).

Spoiling

The goal of a spoiling strategy is to ensure that peace overtures between moderate leaders on the terrorist's side and the target do not succeed (Stedman, 1997). Terrorists resort to a spoiling strategy when relations between two enemies are improving and a peace agreement threatens the terrorists' more far-reaching goals. Peace agreements alarm terrorists because they understand that moderate citizens are less likely to support ongoing violence once a compromise agreement between more moderate groups has been reached. Terrorist acts are particularly effective during peace negotiations because opposing parties are naturally distrustful of each other's motives and have limited sources of information about each other's intentions. The Israeli-Palestinian conflict, and in particular the Oslo peace process, has been plagued by spoilers. On the Palestinian side, Hamas's violent attacks coincided with the ratification and implementation of accords—occasions when increased mistrust could thwart progress toward peace. Hamas also stepped up its attacks before Israeli elections in 1996 and 2001, in which Labor was the incumbent party, in an effort to persuade Israeli voters to cast their votes for the less cooperative and less trusting hard-line Likud Party. Terrorism was especially effective after Arafat's electoral victory in 1996, when it became clear to the Israelis that Arafat was, at the time, a popular and powerful leader within the Palestinian community. This in turn suggested to the Israelis that Arafat was capable of cracking down aggressively on terrorist violence but was unwilling to do so, a sign that he could not be trusted to keep the peace (Kydd and Walter, 2006).

CONCLUSION

The Palestinian and Israeli struggles for self-determination and independence are colored with narratives that are more reflective of each other. In particular, both peoples believe they have been victims of historical injustices and claim the same territory which has been a salient feature in their counterclaims. Resistance movements in both nations have engaged in acts of terrorism in the pursuit of national self-determination and independence. Yet when one is exposed to the question of terrorism in the context of the protracted Palestinian struggle for independence, Hamas has been subjected to unfavorable stereotypes or projected as a profane movement compared to the Irgun's struggle for Jewish independence. It has been argued in this chapter that it is ahistorical to discount how the same strategy of terrorism was employed by the Jewish groups in the voyage towards the establishment of the state of Israel in 1948. Based on the conceptual framework of 'costly signaling,' similarities were ascertained between Irgun's strategies and tactics before 1948 and the Hamas' strategy and tactics in their search for the elusive Palestinian independence. Evidence presented shows that the Irgun and Hamas have employed similar terrorist strategies—attrition, intimidation, spoiling, and outbidding—validating the view that the two movements embraced the same strategy at different intervals. Indeed, comparing the two groups *modus operandi*, a compelling conclusion is that Hamas is continuing with the same rewarding terrorist strategies in a different epoch just as Irgun.

The implication of this conclusion is, while not suggesting that Hamas' resistance strategies are justified, it exposes that its designation as a terrorist group has been highly politicized. A frequently uninterrupted pattern is to treat terrorism through the lens of moral relativism, with an intense focus on Hamas. From a decolonial perspective, we need to be aware of the inherent tendency in Western political discourses and literature to use demeaning tropes that are never applied to its historical equal—the Irgun. Such narratives are endorsed through historical pedagogy and seem to suggest that those studying terrorism in the Middle East, in particular Israel and Palestine, need educational intervention through the case studies of Palestinian groups such as Hamas. While Hamas is globally elevated to a status of a vile organization and the most valuable lesson for terrorism against Israel, this might be happening at the expense of historical reference to Irgun as the role model for Hamas which is employing the strategies and tactics of terrorism. The dominant perspective thus provides intellectual direction and, *ipso facto,* structures the research agenda in terms of which terrorist groups to study and which ones not to study. This chapter has, however, cogently, demonstrated that the affinity between Irgun and Hamas is glaring in terms of the employment of costly signaling thus hardly circumscribing the construction of analogies in their respective quests for statehood.

REFERENCES

Alsoos, I (2021). From Jihad to Resistance: The Evolution of Hamas's Discourse in the Framework of Mobilization. *Middle Eastern Studies,* 57:5, 833–56.

Bloom, M and Horgan, J (2000). Missing the Mark: The IRA's Proxy Bomb Campaign. *Social Research,* 75:2, 579–614.

Bowden, T (1976). IRA (Irish Republican Army) and the Changing Tactics of Terrorism. *Political Quarterly,* 47:4, 425–37.

Christofer, B and Souleimanov, E. A (2020). What is (not) asymmetric conflict? From Conceptual Stretching to Conceptual Structuring. *Dynamics of Asymmetric Conflict*, 13:1, 87–98.

Fields, J. L (1995). Irgun Zvai Leumi: The Jewish Terrorist Element of the Arab-Israeli Conflict. https://apps.dtic.mil/sti/citations/ADA156178.

Frisch, H (2009). Strategic Change in Terrorist Movements: Lessons from Hamas. *Studies in Conflict & Terrorism,* 32:12, 1049–65.

Gupta, D. K and Mundra, K (2005). Suicide Bombing as a Strategic Weapon: An Empirical Investigation of Hamas and Islamic Jihad. *Terrorism and Political Violence,* 17:4, 573–98.

Jewish Telegraphic Agency (1947). Irgun Announces Hanging of Two British Soldiers; Warns of More Reprisals. https://www.jta.org/archive/irgun-announces-hanging-of-two-british-soldiers-warns-of-more-reprisals.

Kydd, A. H and Walter, B. F (2006). Strategies of Terrorism. *International Security,* 31:1, 49–80.

Kydd, A. H and Walter, B. F (2002). Sabotaging the Peace: The Politics of Extremist Violence. *International Organization,* 56: 2, 263–96.

Pape, P. A. 2003. The Strategic Logic of Suicide Terrorism. *American Political Science Review,* 97:3, 343–61.

Paul, C., Clarke, C. P., Grill. B and Dunigan, M (un). UK in Palestine, 1944–1947 Case Outcome: COIN Loss. https://www.jstor.org/stable/pdf/10.7249/j.ctt5hhsjk.9.pdf?refreqid=excelsior%3A833eb9c8dd9d63be0473e3a9029c66ef&ab_segments=&origin=.

Renton, J (2013). The Age of Nationality and the Origins of the Zionist-Palestinian Conflict. *The International History Review,* 35:3, 576–99.

Simon, S and Stevenson, J (2003). Confronting Hamas. *The National Interest,* 74:4, 59–68.

Singh, R (2012). The Discourse and Practice of 'Heroic Resistance' in the Israeli–Palestinian Conflict: The Case of Hamas. *Politics, Religion & Ideology,* 13:4, 529–45.

Stedman, S. J (1997). Spoiler Problems in Peace Processes. *International Security,* 22: 2, 5–53.

Stein, K (2014). Hamas Doctrine: Detest Israel—Hamas Principles for the Liberation of Palestine and Jihad against Zionism—In Their Own Words—Part III. https://israeled.org/hamas-doctrine-iii/.

II

Modern Palestine and the Struggle for Independence

5

The State of Palestine as a Sovereign Actor in the International Community

Implications for Its Legal Status

Konstantinos Magliveras and Gino Naldi

INTRODUCTION: HOW THE STATE OF PALESTINE CAME INTO EXISTENCE AND THE QUESTIONS OF ITS RECOGNITION

The seemingly intractable conflict over the international legal status of Palestine has a long history. Its origins would appear to lie in the Sykes-Picot Agreement of 1916, a secret treaty between Great Britain and France defining spheres of influence and control in the Ottoman Empire's area of the Middle East based on its partition should it be defeated in the First World War (*Exchange of Letters between France and Great Britain respecting the Recognition and Protection of an Arab State in Syria*, signed 9/16 May 1916, 221 CTS 323). The Balfour Declaration of 1917, which made known British support for the establishment of a "national home for the Jewish people" in Palestine, was to cause great difficulties (Quigley, 1990, pp. 8–11). However, following the conclusion of the First World War, Palestine was classified as a Mandate under British tutelage in accordance with article 22 of the *Covenant of the League of Nations*, opened for signature on 28 June 1919 (entered into force 10 January 1920) (Quigley, 1990, pp. 14–16). The Preamble of the Palestine Mandate, approved by the League of Nations Council in July 1922, put the Balfour Declaration, which had been adopted by other League members as well, into effect, "it being clearly understood that nothing should be done which might prejudice the civil and religious rights of existing non-Jewish communities in Palestine" (Palestine Mandate, signed 24 July 1922). The reference to a "civil right" could be understood as encompassing a right to self-determination, although it is doubtful whether the principle of self-determination amounted to a legally enforceable right at that time (Cassese, pp. 28–29). It is interesting to note that in its Advisory Opinion on *Legal Consequences of the Construction of a Wall in the Occupied Palestinian Territory* 2004 ICJ Rep. 136, 183, the International Court of Justice (ICJ) found that the references to the "legitimate rights" of the Palestinian people in the *Israel-Palestinian Interim Agreement on the West Bank and the Gaza Strip*, signed 28 September 1995, 36 ILM 551 (1997), included the right to self-determination.

In 1947, the United Nations (UN) adopted the Partition Plan for Palestine (UN General Assembly [UNGA] Resolution 181 (II), 29 November 1947), which proposed the creation of independent Palestinian and Jewish States upon the termination of the British Mandate of Palestine, envisaged to end no later than 1 August 1948 (Quigley, 1990, p. 37). However, Britain withdrew prematurely from Palestine on 15 May 1948, without ensuring an orderly transition of power (Colonial Office and Foreign Office, 1948), undermining the Partition Plan, which was never implemented as a result of opposition from Arab States which maintained that it was "unbalanced" (*Legal Consequences of the Construction of a Wall in the Occupied Palestinian Territory* 2004 ICJ Rep. 165) and the Palestinians themselves, who regarded it as incompatible with their right to self-determination (Quigley, 1989, p. 21). In 1988, the establishment of the State of Palestine (Palestine) was proclaimed by the Palestinian National Council, and acknowledged by UNGA Resolution 43/177, 15 December 1988, 27 ILM 1668 (1988). Some have considered this as an acceptance of Palestinian statehood (Quigley, 2011, pp. 751–53), but disputed by others (Benoliel & Perry, 2011, pp. 81–87; Crawford, 2006, pp. 440–41). In 1993, the Palestinian Liberation Organization (PLO) and Israel concluded the *Declaration of Principles on Interim Self-Government Arrangements*, signed on 13 September 1993, 32 ILM 1525 (1993) (Oslo Accords), which provides a framework for negotiation based on the implementation of the principle of "land for peace," the application of UN Security Council (UNSC) Resolutions 242 (1967) and 338 (1973) and the creation of a Palestinian Interim Self-Government Authority. The Oslo Accords and other later agreements, such as the *Israel-PLO Agreement on Preparatory Powers and Responsibilities* concluded on 29 August 2004 (34 ILM 455 [1995]), are transitional arrangements according to which, inter alia, the issue of borders, the future of Jerusalem, and the final status of the West Bank and Gaza, are to be determined in "permanent status" negotiations.

The Oslo Accords patently fails to acknowledge the existence of Palestinian statehood (Harris & Sivakumaran, p. 198), but the view has been expressed that it is not dependent on the peace process, it being merely "steps in the process of realization of Palestinian self-determination and statehood to which Palestine has been entitled to under international law from the Partition Resolution" (Orakhelashvili, 2019, p. 88). In 2003, the UNSC endorsed the Quartet Performance-based Roadmap to a Permanent Two-State Solution to the Israeli-Palestinian Conflict (UNSC Resolution 1515 (2003); UN Doc S/2003/529, Annex), which required the Quartet members (UN, USA, European Union, and Russian Federation, which, as the Soviet Union, had recognized Palestine in 1988), to promote the Palestinian State's international recognition, including possible UN membership, and ultimately envisaged an independent Palestine with agreed borders (UNSC Doc S/2003/529, 7 May 2003). These developments raise questions about the Palestinian strategy, which seems to have aimed at gaining universal international legitimacy for its claims to statehood. It does not appear that the PLO had suspended or abandoned its claims to statehood but that its policy was consistent with these agreements (Erakat, 2013, p. 27). Again, there are different views on this issue (Benoliel & Perry, 2011, pp. 84–85; Quigley, 2011, pp. 753–55). However, for a variety of reasons, the Oslo process has come to a standstill. Nevertheless, the Quartet remains ready to engage in a resumption of the peace process.

Presently, 139 countries have recognized Palestine but none of the G7 countries pending the results of direct, but stalled, negotiations between Palestine and Israel (Permanent Observer Mission of Palestine to the United Nations, 2021a; Sakran, 2020, p. 154). The UN Secretary-General (UNSG) has expressed his support for the Palestinian people's "legitimate right" to their independent State (UN Doc A/67/738, 8 March 2013, para. 8), while the UNGA is committed to the two-state solution in accordance with international law (UNGA Resolution 67/19, 29 November 2012; UNGA Resolution 74/11, 3 December 2019) and continues to reiterate the Palestinian people's right to self-determination and an independent State (UNGA Resolution 68/154, 18 December 2013, para. 1; UNGA Resolution 76/10, 1 December 2021, para. 12[b]). The EU's stance is similar to that of continued support for a negotiated two-state solution based on the pre-1967 borders leading to a viable, independent Palestinian State (European External Action Service, 2021; Fernández Sola, 2019, pp. 213–18). The United Kingdom also reflects this position adding that it will only recognize a Palestinian State at a time when the objective of peace is best served (Foreign & Commonwealth Office, 2018), thus connecting the question of statehood with the peace process.

Academic writers are divided as to whether Palestine qualifies as a State, with views ranging from full statehood to a state in *statu nascendi*, to quasi, functional, or limited statehood (Boyle, 2014; Quigley, 1989, pp. 25–33; Quigley, 2010, pp. 213–18; Crawford, 1990; Crawford, 2006, pp. 434–48; Worster, 2020; Sakran, 2019). Some question whether Palestine satisfies the criteria of statehood, especially that of control over territory (Malanczuk, 1997, p. 77). One jurist has expressed the view that Palestine indeed does, but that recognition is withheld because of wider political considerations (Lowe, 2007, p. 164), usually about not undermining the peace process. In its Advisory Opinion on *Legal Consequences of the Construction of a Wall in the Occupied Palestinian Territory*, 2004 ICJ Rep. 167, the ICJ declared that certain Palestinian territories constituted "occupied territories in which Israel had the status of occupying Power" and, as aforementioned, reaffirmed the right of the Palestinian people to self-determination. On the question of statehood, the ICJ appears to have suggested that Palestine was not yet at that time a state (*Legal Consequences of the Construction of a Wall in the Occupied Palestinian Territory* 2004 ICJ Rep. 162; Islam, 2019, pp. 10–11). In his Separate Opinion, Judge Elaraby was of the view that the "independence of the Palestinian Arab State has not yet materialized" (*Legal Consequences of the Construction of a Wall in the Occupied Palestinian Territory* 2004 ICJ Rep. 251, Separate Opinion of Judge Elaraby). However, the context in which this sentence was set suggests that he was referring to the fact that a sovereign Palestinian State's structures had yet to be built (Quigley, 2010b).

In light of the stalled Oslo process, Palestine has adopted a different strategy and since the 2010s it has intensified its efforts to join universal organizations, including UN specialized agencies, such as UNESCO (2011), UNIDO (2018), and UNCTAD (2018), the International Criminal Police Organization (INTERPOL) (2017) and the International Criminal Court (ICC) (2015), among others. Its application to join the UN (2011) still lingers undetermined in light of opposition in the UNSC, having been granted non-member observer State status in the UNGA the following year (UNGA Resolution 67/19) in accordance with UN practice (Crawford, 2006, pp. 179–82; Sands & Klein, 2009, p. 564). This is because, inter alia, the noun "State" in such instruments must denote the ordinary meaning of the word and signify "State for the purposes of international law" (Crawford, 2006, p. 179). But even before the 1988 proclamation, Palestine, as the PLO representing the people of Palestine (UNGA Resolution 3210 (XXIX), 14 October 1974), had been recognized as having limited international personality (*Arafat and Salah*, Italian Court of Cassation, Judgment of 28 June 1985, English translation in [1986–1987] *Italian Yearbook of International Law* 7, p. 295), had been admitted to regional organizations, e.g., the League of Arab States (LAS) (1976) and the Organization of Islamic Cooperation (OIC) (1969), where no opposition was to be expected. As is later explained, it has also acceded to many multilateral agreements, including all UN core human rights treaties.

While Palestine considers that its participation in IOs and international treaties are not connected to the peace process, Israel has consistently argued that Palestine's seeking membership in IOs is part and parcel with it. Thus, when, as will later be explained, Palestine sought to become a member of UNCTAD in 2018, Israel objected because it considered that, by unilaterally seeking membership in UN bodies, Palestine was attempting to evade bilateral negotiations in violation of the framework of the agreed negotiations. Moreover, Israel claimed that Palestinian efforts to gain membership in UN bodies are neither reflection nor evidence of its legal status under international law nor do they constitute recognition of any kind (United Nations Conference on Trade and Development, 2018a).

Notwithstanding these long-held views, the prevailing political and economic realities have arguably led to an unprecedented development: the participation of both Israel and Palestine as founding Members in the same regional intergovernmental organization, the East Mediterranean Gas Forum (EMGF), the *Statute* of which was signed on 22 September 2020 (entered into force on 9 March 2021). Their simultaneous original membership in EMGF presumably shows that Israel does recognize and accepts that Palestine enjoys a certain measure of statehood. Naturally, membership in the same IO does not entail the automatic recognition of a State of Palestine by the State of Israel. However, their parallel presence in the negotiations of the *EMGF Statute*, namely an IO's founding instrument, leads to the conclusion that the State of Israel accepts Palestine's ability to act in the international community as a de facto state, i.e., not as a mere political entity.

After offering a detailed overview of Palestine's record in seeking membership in international organizations and participating in multilateral treaties, this chapter examines certain proceedings brought by Palestine before transnational judicial and quasi-judicial organs having potentially significant implications for its statehood. The following actions will be examined (they were made possible on account of Palestine's accession to international treaties): (a) the inter-State communication to the Commission on Elimination of Racial Discrimination (CERD) against Israel submitted in 2018; CERD upheld Palestine's locus standi; (b) proceedings against the United States before the ICJ arising from US President Trump's recognition of Jerusalem as Israel's capital and the relocation of the US Embassy from Tel Aviv to Jerusalem lodged in 2018; the issue of the ICJ's jurisdiction currently pending; and (c) the referral in 2018 of the *Situation in the State of Palestine* to the Prosecutor of the International Criminal Court (ICC) pursuant to articles 13(a) and 14 of the *Statute of the International Criminal Court*, opened for signature 17 July 1998, 2187 UNTS 3 (entered into force 1 July 2002) (Rome Statute), currently pending, which followed its lodging in 2015 of a declaration under article 12(3) Rome Statute accepting the ICC's jurisdiction over alleged crimes committed "in the occupied Palestinian territory, including East Jerusalem, since June 13, 2014," and its accession to the Rome Statute also in 2015. Despite these developments, Palestine's legal status as a sovereign actor is still undecided in the international community. However, this chapter argues that these events may support Palestine's claims to statehood and, accordingly, its ultimate goal to be universally acknowledged as an independent, sovereign State.

PALESTINE'S SUCCESSES AND FAILURES IN BEING ADMITTED TO INTERNATIONAL ORGANIZATIONS AND UN-SPECIALIZED AGENCIES

As has been previously mentioned, Palestine, represented by the PLO, was admitted to the LAS in September 1976. LAS recognized the PLO as the Palestinian people's legitimate representative in 1974 (League of Arab States, 1974). Following its Declaration of Independence in 1988, the State of Palestine succeeded to this seat. According to article 1 of the *LAS Charter,* which opened for signature on 22 March 1945, 70 UNTS 237 (entered into force on 11 May 1945) membership is based on being an independent Arab State. However, the decisive factor appears to have been that Palestine had been participating in all LAS activities (League of Arab States Council, 1976). Taking advantage of its LAS membership, Palestine has participated in Conferences organized by UN Specialized Agencies in which it is not a member and partaken in deliberations under UN auspices as if it were a UN Member State. Thus, when, in 2018, the UNGA was deliberating organizing a conference for establishing a Middle East zone free of nuclear weapons and other weapons of mass destruction, Egypt submitted the revised draft text of the Decision to commence the conference (UN Doc A/C.1/73/L.22/Rev.1, 17 October 2018). As the draft Decision was submitted on behalf of the entire LAS membership, it was considered to have been presented by Palestine as well. Consequently, when the UNGA approved the conference's first session (UNGA Decision 73/546, 22 December 2018), which took place in November 2019, all LAS members were invited to attend. Effectively, this allowed Palestine to participate as if it had the status of UN membership (Magliveras, 2021). Palestine also participated in the conference's second session held in November/December 2021 (UN Doc A/CONF.236/2021/4, 3 December 2021).

Palestine is an original member of the OIC, founded in 1969, pursuant to article VIII of the original *OIC Charter*, opened for signature on 4 March 1972, 914 UNTS 111 (entered into force 28 February 1973). It is also a member of specialized institutions attached to the OIC, e.g., the

Islamic Development Bank and the Islamic World Educational, Scientific, and Cultural Organization. However, these events have been rationalized as politically expedient based on frustrated self-determination and therefore not to be relied upon as substantiation of Palestine's statehood, at least beyond the limits of the Arab and Islamic worlds (Sands & Klein, 2009, pp. 538–39).

The prize for Palestine is admission to the UN. This is because it is universally recognized as "usually the shortest and quickest route to recognition of statehood" (Aust, 2010, p. 18) and because, for practical purposes, the UN has become "the collective arbiter of statehood through the process of admission" (Dugard, 1987, p. 126). Importantly, UN practice "has attributed to the term 'State' in Article 4(1) [of the UN Charter] the meaning it has under general international law" (Crawford, 2006, p. 179). Palestine's application (UN Doc A/66/371-S/2011/592, 23 September 2011) has not been successful as it became apparent that it could not garner the necessary support of the required number of UNSC members, nine. Even if had, it has been argued that the United States would have cast its veto to defeat any resolution recommending Palestinian membership (Imseis, 2021, p. 866).

However, no formal vote on Palestine's application has so far been taken and it could therefore be reactivated at any time. When its application was referred to the UNSC Committee on the Admission of New Members, the question of whether Palestine met the criteria for admission to membership, as set out in article 4 of the UN Charter, was discussed at length (UN Doc S/2011/705, 11 November 2011). Doubts were raised as to whether it was a "peace-loving State" since Hamas, a powerful militant group, was committed to armed struggle and rejected peace with Israel. It was observed to the contrary that Palestine and its government, the Palestinian Authority, was committed to the peace process. It is noteworthy that in 2015 Palestine acceded to the *Hague Convention for the Pacific Settlement of International Disputes*, opened for signature on 18 October 1907 (entered into force 27 November 1909), and thus became a member of the Permanent Court of Arbitration (Hamamoto, 2019, pp. 137–38). While reservations were expressed as to whether Palestine was able to accept and perform the UN Charter's obligations, its application did contain a solemn undertaking to meet all commitments. As to the criteria of statehood, it was questioned whether Palestine fulfilled the requirements of territory and effective government since Hamas controlled the Gaza Strip. As to the criterion that a State has the capacity to enter into relations with other States, it was argued that, under the Oslo Accords, the Palestinian Authority had limited capacity to conduct foreign relations. But it was pointed out that Palestine had been recognized as a State by many States and had joined several IOs and international fora, such as the Group of 77 and the Non-Aligned Movement. While the Committee concluded that it was unable unanimously to recommend Palestinian membership, some members' positions have been subjected to reasoned criticism for "unduly narrow application" of the statehood criteria and introducing conditions extraneous to Article 4(1) of the UN Charter (Imseis, 2021, pp. 866–77).

The indecisiveness of the UNSC discussions on the underlying issue of statehood has arguably other ramifications as well, including whether Palestine could benefit from article 35(2) of the UN Charter. It stipulates that States, not UN Member States may bring to UNSC or UNGA attention any dispute to which it is a party, provided they have already accepted the UN Charter obligations on the pacific settlement of disputes. Two observations should be made. First, this mode of participation in UNSC deliberations is separate from the one envisaged in article 32 of the UN Charter, whereby non-UN Member States, which are parties to disputes considered by the UNSC, shall be invited to participate in the relevant discussions, but without the right to vote. Second, was Palestine to bring a dispute to the UNGA's attention under article 35(2), this organ may treat the statehood question quite differently from the way the UNSC would have addressed it.

Despite the inconclusive outcome of UNSC deliberations, in November 2012 Palestine, as has already been mentioned, succeeded in the UNGA granting it non-member observer State status. That the relevant decision (UNGA Resolution 67/19) was approved by 138 Members with only nine against suggests that more than two-thirds of the UN membership might support a Palestinian application, but this does not necessarily follow: some writers have argued that the positive vote did not imply recognition (Hamamoto, 2019, pp. 130–31), while others have interpreted Resolution 67/19 as acceptance of Palestinian statehood by the international community (Imseis, 2021, pp. 22–23; Orakhelashvili, 2019, p. 88; Quigley, 2013). Thus, while it was viewed as an exercise in collective recognition (Akande, 2012), it was also contended that it did not "alter or clarify Palestine's legal status . . . despite the term state being on the label, the status of a non-member state does not carry an implicit confirmation of statehood analogous to UN membership" (Vidmar 2013, p. 27). Despite this dichotomy of opinion, the significance of this status was that Palestine could "participate fully and on an equal basis with other States in conferences that are open to members of specialized agencies or that are open to all States" (UN Doc A/67/738, para. 7).

Before being granted non-member observer State status, Palestine's applications for membership in UN specialized agencies were treated in opposing ways, as the following two cases reveal. The first concerns its unsuccessful bid for full membership of the World Health Organization (WHO) in 1989. According to article 3 of the *Constitution of WHO*, opened for signature on 22 July 1946, 14 UNTS 185 (entered into force 7 April 1948) membership is open to "all States." The official reason given for not proceeding with Palestine's application was that the "legal and other issues related to the application of Palestine for membership . . . required further detailed study" (World Health Organization, Resolution WHA 42.1, 12 May 1989). Arguably, that the United States threatened to withhold its funding where Palestine admitted to membership must have played a role (Kirgis, 1990, p. 218). It has been suggested that for the same reason, Palestine finally decided not to submit a fresh application in 2018 (Zaracostas, 2018, p. 2199).

The second case concerns its application to join UNESCO. On 31 October 2011, UNESCO's General Conference voted to admit Palestine as a Member State (UNESCO 2012, p. 616). According to article II (2) of the *Constitution of the United Nations Educational, Scientific and Cultural Organization* opened for signature on 16 November 1945, 4 UNTS 275 (entered into force 4 November 1946), "States not Members of the United Nations Organization may be admitted to membership of [UNESCO], upon recommendation of the Executive Board, by a two-thirds majority vote of the General Conference." In the absence of any definition of "state" in UNESCO's *Constitution*, its competent organs were of the view that Palestine met the required criteria and constituted a "state" for its purposes. However, it seems that many States supporting Palestine's admission were careful to explain that it was limited and did not have wider implications for its statehood (UNESCO, 2015, pp. 311 et seq.; Hamamoto, 2019, pp. 136–37).

Palestine's admission to UNESCO was significant in one particular respect; it enabled it to apply for membership in other specialized agencies. In 2018, it was admitted to UNIDO. The relevant provision in the *Constitution of the United Nations Industrial Development Organization*, opened for signature 8 April 1979, 1401 UNTS 3 (entered into force 21 June 1985) art 3(a), provides that membership is open to any State which is a member of the UN or another Specialized Agency. Under Article 24(2), all that was required was for Palestine to accede to UNIDO's *Constitution*. These provisions are examples of the so-called Vienna formula, the entry-into-force or accession clauses in accordance with article 83 of the *Vienna Convention on the Law of Treaties*, opened for signature 23 May 1969, 1155 UNTS 331 (entered into force 27 January 1980), which allows applicant States, not UN members but members of another Specialized Agency, to become a party to a treaty, thereby sidestepping the veto of a UNSC permanent member (United Nations, 1999, paras. 79–80). As a UNESCO member, Palestine satisfied the necessary conditions.

However, the use of the "Vienna formula" may not always lead to entering UN specialized agencies. Thus, in 2019, Palestine was unsuccessful in joining the Universal Postal Union (UPU) (Universal Postal Union, 2019). According to the *UPU Constitution*, the *Constitution of the Universal Postal Union* opened for signature on 10 July 1964, 611 UNTS 62 (entered into force 1 January 1966) art 11(2), (4)), any *sovereign country* (emphasis added), which is not already a UN member, may be admitted with the support of at least two-thirds of the membership. But Palestine failed to receive the requisite support; out of 192 Members, only eighty-six returned valid ballots and, of them, fifty-six voted in favor. One can only speculate why its application was unsuccessful; because voting was by postal ballot and many States failed to reply at all or reply on time and/or because certain States could not overcome their unease at the wider implications of requiring applicants (in case, Palestine) to be a "sovereign country," which is tantamount to unfettered statehood.

Still, the previous year (June 2018), Palestine had successfully joined UNCTAD, which is not an UN-specialized agency, but an intergovernmental body initially established as a UNGA organ (United Nations Conference on Trade and Development, UNGA Resolution 1995 (XIX), 30 December 1964, Section I). UNCTAD's membership clause is based on the "Vienna formula," in that members of specialized agencies are eligible (UNGA Resolution 1995 (XIX), Section II (1)) (United Nations Conference on Trade and Development, 2018).

But Palestine has been successful in its bids to join IOs outside the UN system. After two unsuccessful attempts, in September 2017 it was finally admitted to the International Criminal Police Organization-INTERPOL (Resolution No. 13, GA-2017–86-RES-13, 86th INTERPOL General Assembly, 2017). Palestine first applied in 1999 but the Secretary-General turned it down as it was not considered a sovereign State recognized by the UN. In 2010, another bid was rejected on similar grounds (INTERPOL, n.d., pp. 12–13). In 2017, in a secret General Assembly ballot, Palestine just met the two-thirds majority required under article 4 of the *INTERPOL Constitution*, the *Constitution of the International Criminal Police Organization* (entered into force on 13 June 1956). According to this provision, "[A]ny country" may apply to join but no further explanation of this somewhat unhelpful term is provided. Even though INTERPOL had interpreted it to mean "sovereign State, recognized as such by the international community as a whole" (INTERPOL, n.d., pp. 5–15), its admissions practice had not been wholly consistent. Thus, in 2017, General Assembly Resolution GA2017–86-RES-01, titled "The process of membership of INTERPOL," sought to define article 4 and clarify the conditions for membership, a resolution that did not apply to the case of Palestine. That the term "country" in said provision was to be interpreted as "state" was endorsed. It was further agreed that applicant countries should testify that they meet the statehood criteria and indicate whether they are UN members or UN Observer States, or members of other IOs.

Regarding the Inter-Parliamentary Union (IPU), on 15 October 2008, its 119th Assembly admitted the Parliament of Palestine as a full-fledged member (IPU, 2018). According to article 1 of the *Statutes*, *Statutes of the*

Inter-Parliamentary Union last amended in October 2019, the IPU is the international organization of the Parliaments of sovereign States. Pursuant to article 3(2), membership is open to any Parliament constituted in conformity with the basic law of a territorial entity, whose aspirations and entitlement to statehood have been recognized by the UN and enjoys the status of UN Permanent Observer with substantial additional rights and privileges. Palestine had achieved the latter when, on 7 July 1998, under UNGA Resolution 52/250, in its capacity as Observer, it was conferred additional rights and privileges, including the right to participate in the UNGA general debate and to exercise the right of reply.

Finally, the case of the World Trade Organization (WTO) should be noted. Palestine first sought observer status, which would then have opened the way for a full membership application. However, this strategy proved unsuccessful. Specifically, Palestine requested observer status in October 2009 (WTO 2009), which failed. It then reapplied six months later (WTO 2010a), but the request was not included in the agenda of the General Council meeting in May 2010 (WTO 2010b) and, consequently, was never deliberated. While Palestine appears not to have taken any action since then, it is instructive to note that, pursuant to article XII (1) of the *Marrakesh Agreement Establishing the World Trade Organization*, signed 15 April 1994, 1867 UNTS 3 (entered into force 1 January 1995), it is not only States but also separate customs territories possessing full autonomy in the conduct of their external commercial relations, which may accede to the Marrakesh Agreement. Even though Palestine has already claimed that it constitutes a separate customs territory (WTO 2009), apparently it has not pursued this avenue to apply for membership.

There are different schools of thought as to the implications of these events for Palestinian statehood. A strict positivist approach maintains that statehood is not inherent in admission to IOs and that membership does not equate to formal statehood under international law. It is asserted that membership in IOs, as well as participation in international treaties, cannot lead to "implicit" state creation (Vidmar, 2013). Palestine is accepted as a State for limited or procedural purposes and restricted to the specific nature of the relevant IOs without further implications for its statehood (Shany, 2010, pp. 334–35; Sakran, 2020, pp. 44–76; Worster, 2020, p. 53). But giving different interpretations of 'statehood' is not free of difficulties (Hamamoto, 2019, p. 140). While the assertion that many IOs treat quasi-States as if they were a State on a "case-by-case, functional and relative basis" (Worster, 2020, pp. 40, 71–75) appears correct from a strictly legal point of view, actual state practice may well deviate. The contrary view is that admission to IO membership may constitute evidence of statehood. The view has been expressed with reference to the UN that "admission raises a very strong presumption that the new Member is a State" (Aust, 2010, p. 187), that membership may constitute *prima facie* evidence of statehood (Brownlie, 2008, p. 94), or that it "establishes a strong presumption that an entity is a state" (Klabbers, 2009, p. 94).

While it has further been suggested that admission ought to constitute "sufficient proof of the existence of the requirements of statehood" (Lauterpacht, 1948, p. 402), the status of certain States admitted to the UN was arguably uncertain (Imseis, 2021, pp. 861–63; Klabbers, 2009, p. 94; Worster, 2020, pp. 75–77). In such instances of doubt surrounding statehood, admission to an IO such as the UN, in addition to the applicability of the right to self-determination, could compensate for the lack of meeting fully the statehood criteria. Such an event, while not conclusive of statehood, is no doubt of considerable evidentiary value. Moreover, given that invariably the IOs' constitutive instruments do not define a "state" for the purposes of admission, the IO's organ competent to determine membership questions must decide whether the entity seeking admission meets the criteria (Osieke, 1980, p. 220). Thus, in its Advisory Opinion on *Conditions of Admission of a State to Membership in the United Nations* 1948 ICJ Rep. 57, 62–63, the ICJ stated that the conditions for UN admission are subject to the judgment of the Organization and, in the last analysis, that of its members, which must be exercised in good faith. But it would be naïve in the extreme to suppose that political considerations play but a limited part in the admissions process notwithstanding that strictly speaking they should be impermissible (Imseis, 2021, p. 867). In other instances, where the membership criteria may not be so prescriptive, political considerations may be considered, since existing Member States are the sole arbiters of who is going to join their IO. Ultimately, Palestine's admission to several IOs supports its claim that it qualifies as a State under both the constitutive and declaratory doctrines of recognition (Hamamoto, 2019, pp. 140–44).

PALESTINE'S ACCESSION TO INTERNATIONAL TREATIES, ESPECIALLY UN-HUMAN RIGHTS CONVENTIONS AND CONVENTIONS ON DISARMAMENT

As mentioned above, Palestine's attainment of UNGA observer status and membership in UNESCO facilitated its participation in several international instruments. In April 2014, it acceded to most of the core human rights treaties and several humanitarian law treaties, amongst others (Permanent Observer Mission of Palestine to the United Nations, 2021b), including the *Hague Convention (IV) on War on Land*, opened for signature 18 October 1907 (entered into force 26 January 1910); the *Geneva Protocol on Asphyxiating or Poisonous Gases, and of Bacteriological Methods*, opened for signature 17 June 1925, the *Convention on the Prevention and Punishment of Genocide*, opened for signature 9 December 1948, 78 UNTS 277 (entered into force 12 January 1951), and the *Convention on the Non-Applicability of Statutory Limitations to War Crimes and Crimes Against Humanity*, opened for signature 16 December 1968, 754 UNTS 73 (entered into force 11 November 1970). But in 1989, its request to accede to the *Geneva Conventions* of 12 August 1949 failed. The depositary, Switzerland, did not take a position on the controversy over Palestinian statehood and left it to the States Parties to make their findings (Swiss Federal Department of Foreign Affairs, 2007, para. 3.1; Crawford, 2006, p. 440). However, in 2014 Palestine was successful in acceding to the Geneva Conventions and *Additional Protocols I*, opened for signature 8 June 1977, 1125 UNTS 3 (entered into force 7 December 1978), *II*, opened for signature 8 June 1977, 1125 UNTS 609 (entered into force 7 December 1978), and *III*, opened for signature 8 December 2005, 45 ILM (2006) 558 (entered into force 14 January 2007) (SWI swissinfo.ch, 2014).

Since the mid-2010s, Palestine has also participated in most international treaties prohibiting the production, stockpiling, transfer, and use of weapons of mass destruction but also arms either through accession or as an original party. In particular: (a) on 2 January 2015, it acceded to the *Convention on Cluster Munitions*, opened for signature 3 December 2008, 2688 UNTS 39 (entered into force 1 August 2010); (b) on 5 January 2015, it acceded to the *Convention on Prohibitions or Restrictions on the Use of Certain Conventional Weapons Which May Be Deemed to Be Excessively Injurious or to Have Indiscriminate Effects*, opened for signature 10 April 1981, 1342 UNTS 137 (entered into force 2 December 1983); (c) on 10 February 2015, it acceded to the *Treaty on the Non-Proliferation of Nuclear Weapons* (NPT), opened for signature 1 July 1968, 729 UNTS 161 (entered into force 5 March 1970); (d) on 29 December 2017, it acceded to the *Arms Trade Treaty*, opened for signature 3 June 2013, 3013 UNTS 269 (entered into force 24 December 2014); (e) on 29 December 2017, it acceded to the *Convention on the Prohibition of the Use, Stockpiling, Production and Transfer of Anti-Personnel Mines and on their Destruction*, opened for signature 18 September 1997, 2056 UNTS 211 (entered into force 1 March 1999); (f) on 22 March 2018, it ratified the *Treaty on the Prohibition of Nuclear Weapons* and became an original state party, opened for signature 20 September 2017, 57 ILM 347 (2018), (entered into force 22 January 2021); and (g) on 17 May 2018, it acceded to the *Convention on the Prohibition of the Development, Production, Stockpiling and Use of Chemical Weapons and on Their Destruction*, opened for signature 3 September 1992, 1975 UNTS 45 (entered into force 29 April 1997) (Organisation for the Prohibition of Chemical Weapons, 2018).

The latter treaty action is of particular interest for two reasons. First, under article XX of the *Convention*, it is open to any 'State,' which can be alluded by Palestine as further evidence of practice in the international community accepting it as a 'State.' Second, because ipso facto Palestine became a member of the implementing body, the Organization for the Prohibition of Chemical Weapons (OPCW) established under article VIII thereof. Presently, the only UN member not participating in OPCW is Israel, which signed the Convention on 13 January 1993.

Some of these treaties rely on the "Vienna formula" whereas others employ the "all States formula," ie, treaties adopted by the UNGA that are "open to participation by 'all States' without further specifications" (United Nations, 1999, paras. 81–83). According to one writer, Palestine's extensive treaty practice proves its capacity to enter into relations with other States (Quigley, 2010, p. 213). However, this is because this ability is not restricted to States only but exists for non-State entities too (Crawford, 2006, p. 444). Arguably, the mere act of signing a multilateral treaty, especially if the State in question had not participated in the deliberations, is not, at face value, evidence of transacting with other States. On the contrary, entering into bilateral agreements is because they expressly show the wish to transact with a specific State and to regulate particular issues between them. On the other hand, if a State, like Palestine, which has not received universal recognition, routinely signs/accedes to multilateral treaties and there is no opposition, or only very limited, from the State parties, clearly this would suggest that they recognize it as having the same rights and obligations as they do. In other words, the State parties had the opportunity to object; that they did not, notwithstanding the reasons why cannot but reveal a measure of their acquiescence. Consequently, silence by State parties, if observed over longer periods, may lead to legitimate expectations for the State in question: according to the law of treaties, State parties to multilateral treaties may exclude treaty relations with an entity they do not recognize (*State of Palestine v Israel*, CERD/C/100/5, 12 December 2019, paras. 3.13–3.16). As is explained later, the United States took this action in relation to Palestine's accession to the *Vienna Convention on Diplomatic Relations*, opened for signature 18 April 1961, 500 UNTS 95 (entered into force 24 April 1964) and to the *Optional Protocol of the Vienna Convention on Diplomatic Relations, concerning the Compulsory Settlement of Disputes*, opened for signature 18 April 1961, 500 UNTS 241 (entered into force 24 April 1964), respectively, in 2014 and 2018. However, such a rule does not apply to human rights treaties since they have a special status (*State of Palestine v Israel*, CERD/C/100/5, 12 December 2019, paras. 3.20–3.37).

THE STATE OF PALESTINE RESORTS TO INTERNATIONAL JUDICIAL AND QUASI-JUDICIAL ORGANS AGAINST OTHER STATES TO PROTECT ITS INTERESTS

A. Inter-State communication against Israel before the Committee on the Elimination of Racial Discrimination

Regarding the core human rights treaties to which Palestine is a party, of special significance is the *International Convention on the Elimination of All Forms of Racial Discrimination*, opened for signature on 21 December 1965, 660 UNTS 195 (entered into force 4 January 1969) (ICERD). Palestine acceded on 2 April 2014 and ICERD entered into force for it on 2 May 2014 (UN Depositary Notification, UN Doc C.N.179.2014. TREATIES -IV.2). Israel responded by communicating to the UNSG, the depositary of ICERD, that Palestine, inter alia, did not satisfy the criteria for sovereign statehood under international law, that it lacked the legal capacity to become an ICERD party and, consequently, did not consider Palestine a party and its request for accession had no legal validity (Israeli reservation Communication, 16 May 2014, UN Depositary Notification, C.N.293.2014. TREATIES- IV.2). In April 2018, Palestine submitted an inter-State communication to the Committee on the Elimination of Racial Discrimination (CERD) against Israel, alleging multiple violations of ICERD regarding Palestinian nationals living in the occupied Palestinian territory and in East Jerusalem (Communication submitted to the Committee on the Elimination of Racial Discrimination, 2018; Eiken, 2020; Tamada, 2021, pp. 14–21). Palestine asserted that CERD had jurisdiction to entertain the complaint because, inter alia, as a member of UNESCO it had become a legitimate contracting party to ICERD. Furthermore, UN human rights treaty bodies had requested that it submit the mandatory periodic reports, thereby proving that they considered it a proper 'contracting' party to those treaties (*State of Palestine v Israel*, CERD/C/100/3, 12 December 2019, paras. 2.3, 2.4.). Notwithstanding Israel's claims that CERD lacked jurisdiction on the grounds specified above in the communication to the UNSG, CERD upheld Palestine's standing to bring the case finding, inter alia, that Palestine was a valid State party (*State of Palestine v Israel*, CERD/C/100/5, 12 December 2019). It reached this conclusion based on two key points. First, Palestine had been accorded non-member observer State status in the UN pursuant to the aforementioned Resolution 67/19.

Accordingly, it has been considered a "State" for the purpose of participation in the multilateral treaties for which the UNSG acts as a depository. Secondly, agreeing with Palestine's submission, the accession requirements of articles 17 and 18 ICERD refer to a "State member of any of [the UN] specialized agencies"; as a member of UNESCO since 2011, Palestine satisfied the necessary conditions. The UNSG, in the capacity of ICERD depositary, saw no reason to challenge Palestine's instrument of accession. Thus, Palestine was recognized as a State under the "Vienna formula." CERD observed further that Palestine had submitted a periodic report in accordance with article 9 ICERD (*Palestine v Israel*, para. 3.9). The UN Office of Legal Affairs had reached similar conclusions (Memorandum of the Office of Legal Affairs, 23 July 2019, paras. 17–18). In light of Palestine fulfilling the formalities of accession, it is difficult to see how CERD could have come to a different conclusion: as far as it was concerned, Palestine was unquestionably a State party (Eiken, 2020).

B. Proceedings against the United States before the International Court of Justice

In September 2018, Palestine initiated proceedings against the USA before the ICJ regarding a dispute concerning alleged violations of the *Vienna Convention on Diplomatic Relations*, to which it had acceded on 2 April 2014 (*Relocation of the United States Embassy to Jerusalem (Palestine v United States of America)*, Application Instituting Proceedings, 28 September 2018; Galbraith, 2019b). Palestine alleges that relocating the US Embassy in Israel to Jerusalem, which was effected following the US president's recognition of Jerusalem and not Tel Aviv as Israel's capital (Galbraith, 2018), constituted a violation of the *Vienna Convention*. As a basis for the ICJ's jurisdiction, Palestine relied on Article I of the *Optional Protocol to the Vienna Convention on Diplomatic Relations* acceded in April 2018, and on article 35(2) of the ICJ Statute under which it has recognized the ICJ's competence. The United States has treated Palestine's actions in relation to these two instruments as "purported accession." On 13 May 2014 and 1 May 2018, it submitted communications to the UNSG, the depositary of both treaties, declaring that it does not consider itself to be in a "treaty relationship" with Palestine under, respectively, the *Vienna Convention* and the *Optional Protocol*.

The immediate US reaction to these proceedings was to withdraw from the *Optional Protocol* (Galbraith, 2019a), and the UNSG received a communication to this effect on 12 October 2018. This decision has not been reversed by the Biden Administration at the time of writing. However, this move is unlikely to deprive the ICJ of jurisdiction since its jurisdiction is usually assessed on the date the act instituting proceedings was filed (*Application of the Convention on the Prevention and Punishment of the Crime of Genocide [Croatia v Serbia], Preliminary Objections*, 2008 ICJ Rep. 412, para.79).

Moreover, the United States informed the ICJ by letter that it would not participate in the meeting with the ICJ President and Palestine, which had been scheduled for 5 November 2018 to ascertain the parties' views regarding questions of procedure, that it was manifest that the ICJ had no jurisdiction in the case and asked that it be removed from the list of pending cases. However, Palestine was present at the meeting and expressed the wish that the ICJ decide in favor of its claim. Notwithstanding the US refusal to partake in the meeting, the ICJ regarded that its letter questioned both its jurisdiction and the application's admissibility and ordered both litigant parties to present their written observations (Memorial and Counter-Memorial) by 15 May 2019 and 15 November 2019, respectively. (*Relocation of the United States Embassy to Jerusalem, Order of 15 November 2018 [Palestine v United States of America]*, 2018 ICJ Rep. 708). As neither litigant party has complied with the order or requested a time extension, Palestine's request that the ICJ decide in its favor, which can only happen if the ICJ delves into merits, a procedural right envisaged in article 53 ICJ Statute when the other litigant party does not appear before the ICJ, is meaningless. The ICJ has made it clear that it will not discuss merits unless it has first convinced itself that it has jurisdiction.

While one cannot speculate why Palestine did not submit the Memorial, suffice to mention the following on its *locus standi*. According to article 34(1) ICJ Statute, "[O]nly states may be parties in cases before the Court." States, not UN Members may become a party to the ICJ Statute under article 93(2) UN Charter, but this route is problematic for Palestine because of the UNSC's role. However, Palestine has been able to rely on an alternative option, article 35(2) ICJ Statute, whereby the ICJ is also open to other States not parties to its Statute. In particular, the relevant conditions shall, subject to the special provisions contained in treaties in force, be laid down by the UNSC, which must ensure that they are not placed in a position of inequality before the ICJ. Said conditions were set out in UNSC Resolution 9 (1946): a State not a party to the Statute shall have access to the ICJ if it has previously deposited a declaration, inter alia, accepting its jurisdiction. On 4 July 2018, Palestine deposited such a declaration (International Court of Justice, n.d.).

C. Proceedings against Israel before the International Criminal Court

As mentioned above, on 1 January 2015, Palestine, invoking Article 12(3) of the Rome Statute, filed a declaration accepting the ICC's jurisdiction over alleged crimes perpetrated in the occupied Palestinian territory since June 2014, while the following day it acceded to the Rome Statute (it came into force for Palestine on 1 April 2015 (C.N.13.2015.TREATIES-XVIII.10 [Depositary Notification] 6 January 2015). A fortnight later, the ICC Prosecutor announced the opening of a preliminary examination into the *Situation in the State of Palestine* to determine whether the criteria for commencing an investigation were met. While the preliminary examination was ongoing, in May 2018, Palestine pressed ahead: by citing this time articles 13(a) and 14 of the Rome Statute (they allow a State party to refer to the Prosecutor a situation by claiming that crimes within ICC jurisdiction have been committed and to request the Prosecutor to investigate it and determine if specific persons should be charged), it referred the *Situation in the State of Palestine* since June 2014 with no end date (Palestine, 2018). The referral's legal consequence was that the Prosecutor was no longer required to seek the authorization of the competent Pre-Trial Chamber to open an investigation if the Prosecutor was satisfied that all relevant criteria were met (cf articles 15(3) and 53(1) Rome Statute). In December 2019, the Prosecutor announced that the preliminary examination had found that they were fulfilled but hesitated to start the investigation before the territorial scope of the ICC's criminal jurisdiction in this *Situation* had been fully clarified. Presumably, the Prosecutor wanted to pre-empt any future challenges to jurisdiction or the case's admissibility (cf article 19 Rome Statute). Thus, in January 2020, a request to that effect was made to the three-member Pre-Trial Chamber I ([ICC Prosecutor, 2020], which delivered a majority Decision in February 2021 finding that territorial jurisdiction extended to the territories occupied by the State of Israel since 1967, namely Gaza and the West Bank, including East Jerusalem (ICC Pre-Trial Chamber I, 2021).

Pre-Trial Chamber I made it very clear that it was neither determining the question of Palestine's statehood under international law nor adjudicating a border dispute (or indeed the question of the borders) between Israel and Palestine; these were matters to be resolved in bilateral discussions and the context of a negotiated agreement. Without underestimating the significance of having confirmed that Palestine is a valid State party to the Rome Statute, arguably, the importance of the Decision lies elsewhere, namely in that Palestine was successful in ending the impunity over crimes allegedly committed in the occupied Palestinian territory since June 2014 or those that may be perpetrated in the future. Thus, even if the UNSC is unable, for whatever reason, to deal with such alleged crimes, the ICC Prosecutor has to authority to investigate them and bring charges against those allegedly responsible without being constrained by the unresolved issue of Palestinian statehood.

CONCLUSION

The main argument of this chapter is that, even though Palestine has been recognized as an independent State by the majority of States, its statehood has not been accepted by the politically influential States as represented in the G7. As a result, for several years now, it has tried to strengthen its position by systematically following a diplomatic strategy of active involvement in the international arena. This strategy has three main strands: (a) partaking in a large number of treaties either through accession or by becoming an original party, (b) membership of IOs, primarily of the UN family, and (c) recourse to international courts and quasi-judicial bodies in support of its rights and to challenge the legality of acts by third States. Thus, it is manifestly aimed at enabling Palestine to behave like a "normal" (sovereign) State and overcome the problems and limitations resulting from its continued non-recognition by powerful States. On the whole, it has been successful and has paid off. Palestine is treated as a State for the purposes of several IOs and multilateral institutions. It has allowed Palestine to have a significant voice in global affairs compared to the limitations imposed by non-recognition and, in a large measure, to be treated as a (quasi) sovereign State. Nevertheless, this strategy has its critics who contend that while "Palestine, in many respects, has the capacity to act like a state international; yet, such a capacity does not create Palestinian statehood" (Vidmar, 2013, p. 41). Whereas few would deny that Palestine has international personality and the capacity to act in the global society, the crucial question remains its extent. It would seem, therefore, that the jury is still undecided on the issue of Palestinian statehood.

REFERENCES

Akande, D. (December 3, 2012). Palestine as a UN Observer State: Does this Make Palestine a State? *EJIL: Talk!* https://www.ejiltalk.org/palestine-as-a-un-observer-state-does-this-make-palestine-a-state/.

Application of the Convention on the Prevention and Punishment of the Crime of Genocide (Croatia v Serbia), Preliminary Objections, 2008 ICJ Rep. 412.

Arafat and Salah, Italian Court of Cassation, Judgment of 28 June 1985. English translation in (1986–1987) *Italian Yearbook of International Law*, *7*, 295–98.

Arms Trade Treaty, opened for signature on 3 June 2013, 3013 UNTS 269 (entered into force 24 December 2014).

Aust, A. (2010). *Handbook of International Law* (2nd ed.). Cambridge University Press.

Benoliel, D. & Perry, R. (2011). Israel, Palestine and the ICC. *Michigan Journal of International Law*, *32(1)*, 73–128.

Boyle, F. (1990). The Creation of the State of Palestine. *European Journal of International Law, 1*, 301–06.

Brownlie, I. (2008). *Principles of Public International Law* (7th ed.). Oxford University Press.

Cassese, A. (1995). *Self-Determination of Peoples: A Legal Reappraisal*. Cambridge University Press.

Cerone, J. (2012). Introductory Note to the Admission of Palestine to UNESCO and Related Documents. *International Legal Materials, 51(3)*, 606–09.

Colonial Office and Foreign Office, *Palestine: Termination of the Mandate*. 15 May 1948. https://ismi.emory.edu/resources/primary-source-docs/1948%20-%20PALESTINE-HMG%20termination%20of%20Mandate%201948.pdf.

Communication submitted to the Committee on the Elimination of Racial Discrimination by the State of Palestine pursuant to article 11 of the International Convention on the Elimination of All Forms of Racial Discrimination. (April 23, 2018). ICERD-ISC-2018/3.

Conditions of Admission of a State to Membership in the United Nations 1948 ICJ Rep. 57.

Convention on Cluster Munitions, opened for signature on 3 December 2008, 2688 UNTS 39 (entered into force 1 August 2010).

Convention on the Non-Applicability of Statutory Limitations to War Crimes and Crimes Against Humanity, opened for signature 16 December 1968, 754 UNTS 73 (entered into force 11 November 1970).

Convention on the Prohibition of the Development, Production, Stockpiling and Use of Chemical Weapons and on Their Destruction, opened for signature on 3 September 1992, 1975 UNTS 45 (entered into force 29 April 1997).

Convention on the Prohibition of the Use, Stockpiling, Production and Transfer of Anti-Personnel Mines and on their Destruction, opened for signature 18 September 1997, 2056 UNTS 211 (entered into force 1 March 1999).

Convention on Prohibitions or Restrictions on the Use of Certain Conventional Weapons Which May Be Deemed to Be Excessively Injurious or to Have Indiscriminate Effects, opened for signature 10 April 1981, 1342 UNTS 137 (entered into force 2 December 1983).

Convention on the Prevention and Punishment of Genocide, opened for signature on 9 December 1948, 78 UNTS 277 (entered into force 12 January 1951).

Crawford, J. (1990). The Creation of the State of Palestine: Too Much Too Soon? *European Journal of International Law, 1*, 307–13.

Crawford, J. (2006). *The Creation of States in International Law* (2nd ed.). Oxford University Press.

Dugard, J. (1987). *Recognition and the United Nations*. Cambridge University Press.

East Mediterranean Gas Forum, *Statute*, opened for signature on 22 September 2020 (entered into force on 9 March 2021).

Erakat, S. Palestinian Liberation Organization Legal Brief in Support of Legal Recognition of the State of Palestine. In M. Qafisheh (Ed.), *Palestine Membership in the United Nations: Legal and Practical Implications* (pp. 14–29). Cambridge Scholars Publishing.

European External Action Service. (2021). *Middle East Peace process*. https://eeas.europa.eu/headquarters/headquarters-homepage_en/337/Middle%20East%20Peace%20process.

Exchange of Letters between France and Great Britain respecting the Recognition and Protection of an Arab State in Syria, signed 9/16 May 1916, 221 CTS 323.

Fernández Sola, N. Collective Recognition? The Case of the European Union. In W. Czapliński & A. Kleczkowska (Eds.), *Unrecognised Subjects in International Law* (pp. 195–225). Scholar Publishing House.

Foreign & Commonwealth Office, Statement by Ambassador Jonathan Allen, Chargé d'Affaires, at the Security Council Briefing on the Middle East, 20 February 2018. https://www.gov.uk/government/speeches/reaffirming-uk-commitment-to-a-two-state-solution-which-ends-the-israeli-palestinian-conflict.

Galbraith, J. (2018). Contemporary Practice of the United States. *American Journal of International Law, 112(2)*, 306–10.

Galbraith, J. (2019a). Contemporary Practice of the United States. *American Journal of International Law, 113(1)*, 132–41.

Galbraith, J. (2019b). Contemporary Practice of the United States. *American Journal of International Law, 113(1)*, 143–49.

Geneva Conventions of 12 August 1949. https://www.icrc.org/en/doc/assets/files/publications/icrc-002-0173.pdf.

The Hague Convention for the Pacific Settlement of International Disputes, opened for signature on 18 October 1907 (entered into force on 27 November 1909). https://docs.pca-cpa.org/2016/01/1907-Convention-for-the-Pacific-Settlement-of-International-Disputes.pdf.

Hague Convention (IV) Respecting the Laws and Customs of War on Land, opened for signature on 18 October 1907, (entered into force 26 January 1910). https://www.refworld.org/publisher,HAGUE,3ddca4e14,0.html.

Hamamoto, S. (2019). Status of Unrecognised Subjects: Recent Practice of "Collective Recognition": Admission to or Granting a Status in an International Organisation. In W. Czapliński & A. Kleczkowska (Eds.), *Unrecognised Subjects in International Law* (pp. 125–46). Scholar Publishing House.

Harris, D. & Sivakumaran, S. (2020). *Cases and Materials on International Law* (9th ed.). Sweet & Maxwell.

ICC Pre-Trial Chamber I. (2021, February 5). *Decision on the 'Prosecution request pursuant to Article 19(3) for a ruling on the Court's territorial jurisdiction in Palestine.'* ICC-01/18–143. https://www.icc-cpi.int/CourtRecords/CR2021_01165.PDF.

ICC Prosecutor. (2020, January 22). *Prosecution request pursuant to Article 19(3) for a ruling on the Court's territorial jurisdiction in Palestine*. ICC-01/18–12. https://www.legal-tools.org/doc/clur6w/.

Imseis, A. (2021). On membership of the United Nations and the State of Palestine: A critical account. *Leiden Journal of International Law*, *34(3)*, 1–24.

International Court of Justice. (n.d.). *States not parties to the Statute to which the Court may be open*. https://www.icj-cij.org/en/states-not-parties.

Inter-Parliamentary Union. (2018). 119th Assembly of the Inter-Parliamentary Union and Related Meetings, CL/183/3(a)-R.2 Item 3, 14 October 2008. Recommendation of the Executive Committee on the Subject of the Membership of the Parliament of Palestine in the Inter-Parliamentary Union.
https://unispal.un.org/UNISPAL.NSF/0/48DC47CD7B25AFBC852574E400561E85.

International Criminal Court, *Statute*, opened for signature 17 July 1998, 2187 UNTS 3 (entered into force 1 July 2002).

International Criminal Police Organization, *Constitution*, (entered into force 13 June 1956).

INTERPOL. (n.d.). *INTERPOL Membership—Historical Perspective*. https://www.interpol.int/Who-we-are/Legal-framework/Membership-of-INTERPOL.

Islam, M. (2019). The Case of Palestine Against the USA at the ICJ: A Non-Starter or Precedent-Setter? *Georgia Journal of International and Comparative Law, 48(1)*, 1–27.

Israel-Palestine Liberation Organization: Interim Agreement on the West Bank and the Gaza Strip, signed 28 September 1995. (1997). *International Legal Materials, 36(3)*, 551–649.

Israel-Palestine Liberation Organization: Agreement on Preparatory Powers and Responsibilities, signed 29 August 1994. (1995). *International Legal Materials, 34(2)*, 455–81.

Israel-Palestine Liberation Organization: Declaration of Principles on Interim Self-Government Arrangements, signed 13 September 1993. (1993). *International Legal Materials, 32(6)*, 1525–44.

Kirgis, F. L. (1990). Admission of "Palestine" as a Member of a Specialized Agency and Withholding the Payment of Assessments in Response. *American Journal of International Law, 84(1)*, 218–30.

Klabbers, J. (2009). *An Introduction to International Institutional Law* (2nd ed.). Cambridge University Press.

Lauterpacht, H. (1948). *Recognition in International Law*. Cambridge University Press.

League of Arab States, *Charter*, opened for signature on 22 March 1945, 70 UNTS 237 (entered into force 11 May 1945).

League of Nations, *Covenant*, opened for signature 28 June 1919 (entered into force 10 January 1920). https://www.un.org/unispal/document/auto-insert-199451/.

Legal Consequences of the Construction of a Wall in the Occupied Palestinian Territory 2004 ICJ Rep. 136.

Lowe, V. (2007). *International Law*. Oxford University Press.

Magliveras, K. (2021). The Conference on the Establishment of a Middle East Zone Free of Nuclear Weapons and Other Weapons of Mass Destruction: Too Little, Too Late? In J. Black-Branch & D. Fleck (Eds.), *Nuclear Non-Proliferation in International Law*, Vol. VI (pp. 113–33). T.M.C. Asser / Springer.

Malanczuk, P. (1997). *Akehurst's Modern Introduction to International Law* (7th rev. ed.). Routledge.

Marrakesh Agreement Establishing the World Trade Organization, signed 15 April 1994, 1867 UNTS 3 (entered into force 1 January 1995).

Naldi, G. & Magliveras, K. (2023). *The East Mediterranean Gas Forum: A Regional Institution Struggling in the Mire of Energy Insecurities*. International Organizations Law Review, 20 (forthcoming).

Optional Protocol of the Vienna Convention on Diplomatic Relations, concerning the Compulsory Settlement of Disputes, opened for signature 18 April 1961, 500 UNTS 241 (entered into force 24 April 1964).

Orakhelashvili, A. (2019). *Akehurst's Modern Introduction to International Law* (8th ed.). Routledge.

Organization for the Prohibition of Chemical Weapons. (2018, June 21). *State of Palestine Joins the Organisation for the Prohibition of Chemical Weapons* [Press Release]. https://www.opcw.org/media-centre/news/2018/06/state-palestine-joins-organisation-prohibition-chemical-weapons.

Organization of Islamic Cooperation, *Charter*, opened for signature 4 March 1972, 914 UNTS 111 (entered into force 28 February 1973).

Osieke, E. (1980). Admission to Membership in International Organizations: The Case of Namibia. *British Yearbook of International Law, 51*, 189–229.

Palestine. (2015, May 15). *The State of Palestine - Referral by the State of Palestine Pursuant to Articles 13(a) and 14 of the Rome Statute*. PAL-180515-Ref. https://www.legal-tools.org/doc/69852a/.

Permanent Observer Mission of Palestine to the United Nations. (2021). *Diplomatic Relations*. http://palestineun.org/about-palestine/diplomatic-relations/.

Permanent Observer Mission of Palestine to the United Nations. (2021). *International Instruments*. http://palestineun.org/category/treaties-conventions/.

Protocol Additional to the Geneva Conventions of 12 August 1949, and Relating to the Protection of Victims of International Armed Conflicts (Protocol I), opened for signature 8 June 1977, 1125 UNTS 3 (entered into force 7 December 1978).

Protocol Additional to the Geneva Conventions of 12 August 1949, and Relating to the Protection of Victims of Non-International Armed Conflicts (Protocol II), opened for signature 8 June 1977, 1125 UNTS 609 (entered into force 7 December 1978).

Protocol Additional to the Geneva Conventions of 12 August 1949, and Relating to the Adoption of an Additional Distinctive Emblem (Protocol III), opened for signature 8 December 2005, 45 ILM (2006) 558 (entered into force 14 January 2007).

Protocol for the Prohibition of the Use in War of Asphyxiating, Poisonous or Other Gases, and of Bacteriological Methods of Warfare, opened for signature 17 June 1925. https://unoda-web.s3-accelerate.amazonaws.com/wp-content/uploads/assets/WMD/Bio/pdf/Status_Protocol.pdf.

Quigley, J. (1989). Palestine's Declaration of Independence: Self-Determination and the Right of the Palestinians to Statehood. *Boston University International Law Journal, 7(1)*, 1–33.

Quigley, J. (1990). *Palestine and Israel: A Challenge to Justice*. Duke University Press.

Quigley, J. (2009). The Palestine Declaration to the International Criminal Court: The Statehood Issue. *Rutgers Law Record, 35(1)*. http://lawrecord.com/files/35_Rutgers_L_Rec_1.pdf.

Quigley, J. (2010). *The Statehood of Palestine: International Law in the Middle East Conflict*. Cambridge University Press.

Quigley, J. (2011). Palestine is a State: A Horse with Black and White Stripes is a Zebra. *Michigan Journal of International Law, 32(4)*, 749–64.

Quigley, J. (2013). Palestine Statehood and International Law. *Global Policy Essay.* https://www.globalpolicyjournal.com/sites/default/files/pdf/Quigley%20-%20Palestine%20statehood%20and%20international%20law%2001.13_0.pdf.

Relocation of the United States Embassy to Jerusalem, Order of 15 November 2018 (Palestine v United States of America), 2018 ICJ Rep. 708.

Sakran, S. (2020). *The Legal Consequences of Limited Statehood: Palestine in Multilateral Frameworks*. Routledge.

Sands, P., & Klein, P. (2009). *Bowett's Law of International Institutions* (6th ed.) Sweet & Maxwell.

Shany, Y. (2010). In Defence of Functional Interpretation of Article 12(3) of the Rome Statute. A Response to Yaël Ronen. *Journal of International Criminal Justice, 8(2)*, 329–43.

State of Palestine v Israel, CERD/C/100/3, 12 December 2019.

State of Palestine v Israel, CERD/C/100/5, 12 December 2019.

SWI swissinfo.ch (April 11, 2014). *Palestinians join Geneva Conventions*. https://www.swissinfo.ch/eng/rules-of-war_palestinians-join-geneva-conventions/38371102#:~:text=Palestinians%20join%20Geneva%20Conventions%20The%20original%20document%20of,in%20the%20Field%2C%20signed%20in%201864%2C%20is%20displayed.

Swiss Federal Department of Foreign Affairs, Directorate of International Law, Treaty Section. (2007). *Le rôle de la Suisse en tant que dépositaire des Conventions de Genève*. https://www.eda.admin.ch/dam/eda/fr/documents/aussenpolitik/voelkerrecht/role-de-la-suisse-d%C3%A9positaire-des-conventions-de-geneve_FR.pdf.

Tamada, D. (2021). Inter-State Communication under ICERD: From ad hoc Conciliation to Collective Enforcement? *Journal of International Dispute Settlement, 12(3)*, 405–26.

Treaty on the Non-Proliferation of Nuclear Weapons, opened for signature 1 July 1968, 729 UNTS 161 (entered into force 5 March 1970).

Treaty on the Prohibition of Nuclear Weapons, opened for signature 20 September 2017, 57 ILM 347 (2018), (entered into force 22 January 2021).

UNESCO. (2012). UNESCO Resolution to Admit Palestine. *International Legal Materials, 51(3)*, 610–22.

United Nations. (1999). *Summary of Practice of the Secretary-General as Depositary of Multilateral Treaties*. United Nations.

United Nations Conference on Trade and Development. (2018a, June 6). *Israel objects to Palestinian membership—Statement*. https://embassies.gov.il/UnGeneva/priorities-statements/ScienceTechnologyDevelopment/Pages/20180606-Israel-objects-to-Palestinian-membership-request-in-UNCTAD.aspx.

United Nations Conference on Trade and Development. (2018b). *Annual Report 2018*. https://unctad.org/system/files/official-document/dom2019_en.pdf.

United Nations Educational, Scientific and Cultural Organization, *Constitution of*, opened for signature 16 November 1945, 4 UNTS 275 (entered into force 4 November 1946).

United Nations Educational, Scientific and Cultural Organization, Records of the General Conference 36th session, Vol. 2 Proceedings, 2015. https://unesdoc.unesco.org/ark:/48223/pf0000235201.

United Nations General Assembly, Report of the Secretary-General. (2013). *The Status of Palestine in the United Nations*. UN Doc A/67/738.

United Nations High Commissioner for Human Rights. (2014, May 2). *Press briefing notes on Palestine* [Press Release]. https://unispal.un.org/UNISPAL.NSF/0/262AC5B8C25B364585257CCF006C010D.

United Nations Industrial Development Organization, *Constitution of*, opened for signature 8 April 1979, 1401 UNTS 3 (entered into force 21 June 1985).

Universal Postal Union, Constitution, opened for signature 10 July 1964, 611 UNTS 62 (entered into force 1 January 1966).

Universal Postal Union. (2019, September 18). The State of Palestine has not been admitted to the Universal Postal Union (UPU) after a postal ballot of the organization's member countries [Press Release]. https://www.upu.int/en/News/2019/9/UPU-issues-statement-on-membership-application-from-State-of-Palestine.

Vienna Convention on Diplomatic Relations, opened for signature 18 April 1961, 500 UNTS 95 (entered into force 24 April 1964).

Vienna Convention on the Law of Treaties, opened for signature 23 May 1969, 1155 UNTS 331 (entered into force 27 January 1980).

World Health Organization, *Constitution*, opened for signature 22 July 1946, 14 UNTS 185 (entered into force 7 April 1948).

World Trade Organization. 2009. Palestine—Request for Observer Status, Communication from Palestine Addendum. WT/L/770/Add.1, 23 October 2009.

World Trade Organization. 2010a. Palestine—Request for Observer Status, Communication from Palestine. WT/L/792, 13 April 2010.

World Trade Organization. 2010b. General Council: Meeting of 4–5 May 2010, Proposed Agenda.

https://www.wto.org/english/thewto_e/gcounc_e/meet_may10_e.htm

Worster, W. (2020). Functional Statehood in Contemporary International Law. *Brooklyn Journal of International Law, 46(1)*, 39–98.

Zaracostas, J. (2018). Palestine not to seek full membership of WHO. *The Lancet, 391*, 2199.

6

The State of Palestine

Between Abstraction and Reality

Federica Stagni

INTRODUCTION

The Palestinian question has been addressed from a number of different perspectives: international relations theory, human rights law, ethnonationalism studies, area studies, social movements theory, democratization theory, and oriental and Islamic studies. The most convincing approach seems to highlight settler colonialism. Several authors have explored the different theoretical applications of this framework. Consequently, the current challenge is to evaluate its practical and potential applications (Veracini, 2016). A decolonial theory as a response to settler-colonialism argues, for example, for the decolonization of the land historically known as Palestine, "*from the (Jordan) river to the (Mediterranean) sea.*" However, as I will outline throughout the chapter, the practical feasibility of such an action is often put into question. Due to international support, Israel has become an economically developed and powerful state that would never give up its territory. How come this historical unfolding of the Israeli nation-state has made the prospect of an independent Palestinian state virtually impossible? How can the settler colonial framework explain this impasse as well as the more general tenets of Israel's relentless occupation of Palestine?

In recent years, the idea of one democratic state all over historic Palestine as the best solution to the conflict has re-emerged. The Palestinian liberation movement, before the catastrophe of 1948 (the Nakba), and its succeeding formal organization, the Palestinian Liberation Organization (PLO), had adopted the idea of the creation of a single bi-national democratic state. The PLO abandoned this project in the late eighties to start diplomatic negotiations leading to the Oslo Accords of 1993. Their leadership hoped that this agreement would enable the building of an independent Palestinian state on the territories that Israel occupied in 1967. At the same time, Israel strengthened its colonial control, splintering the West Bank, East Jerusalem, and Gaza into isolated cantons, fractured by settlements, checkpoints, military bases, and fences. As a result, the two-state solution is too compromised if not already dead. On this basis, I will use this chapter to argue for the establishment of one democratic state, rather than an independent Palestinian state next to the Israeli one (Hilal, 2007).

I analyze social movement campaigning with a focus on the cooperation between different activist organizations. Despite these organizations belonging to either of the two different national groups, I witnessed how they join forces to implement concrete acts of prefigurative politics, making the one-state solution into a real option to overcome the current political stalemate. While there is only a minority of activists working towards this solution, their open embracement of an anti-colonial discourse and a decolonial address the settler-colonial roots of the conflict. The chapter starts with a historical introduction to the Palestinian context, reviewing applications of the settler-colonial framework in the context of Palestine. I follow up with a critique of the dichotomy created by such an approach, looking at the impacts of illustrating the colonized and the colonizers as seemingly inevitable competing entities. I then present the results of a campaign, the #savesusyia campaign, carried out by both Israeli and Palestinian activist organizations. This effort is relevant because it shows a successful decolonial collaboration that was able to save the village of Susiya in area C (which is still standing at the moment of writing). The final part of the chapter highlights how future arrangements for Palestine need to address the settler-colonial responsibility that Israel holds toward Palestinians. This recognition is necessary to make the creation of one state in which Israeli and Palestinians have equal rights a concrete option.

A THEORY OF RELATIONAL VARIANCE

The imperative of altering territorial boundaries and imposing new demographic and socio-political facts on the ground has broken up geographies and identities across history: from Turtle Island to Aotearoa, from South Africa to Sapmi, from Palestine to Australia, in Mexico, Algeria, Cyprus, Kenya or Western Sahara. Literature on these issues has repeatedly revealed, there is no unique trajectory for approaching the settler-colonial phenomena. Moreover, there is no all-encompassing definition to account for all the different variations and occurring complexities. Nevertheless, a common starting point is to understand settler colonialism not as a single event but as a process. A primary tactic of colonization is, in one way or another, to eliminate the native population and construct and impose a different society. Studying the Israeli settler-colonial reality requires the introduction of differentiated perspectives from which to analyze the present context. A debate regarding the structure and the aftermaths of Zionist settler colonialism is therefore paramount. To identify the inseparable connection between ethnic, social class, national, race, and gender narratives, we must understand the various actors' entanglement in the development of this particular settler society (Daniele, 2020).

Since the nineteens, there has been renewed attention both in academia and political circles to use the settler-colonial framework[1] in the study of Israel's ongoing occupation of Palestine. While the Oslo Accords are continuously deemed dead, their impact on Palestinian life is highly tangible. Understanding Israel as a settler-colonial state opposes both the fragmentation of the imaginary and the imposed separation of Palestinian society on the ground. This framework allows us to move beyond the discourse surrounding the Oslo accords, for example, their emphasis on conflict resolution, peacebuilding, and dialogue between two supposedly equal sides. At the same time, "settler-colonial studies" have grown and been consolidated, manifested in increasing numbers of new journals, publications, blogs, books, and conferences on the issue. While settler colonialism is not a new analytical tool, its crystallization as a relevant academic framework in Western academia has emerged relatively recently. Discussions of Zionism as a settler colonial endeavor continue to ignore the rich historical scholarship on the colonization of the Palestinian land (Pappe, 2017). As Ilan Pappé has retraced, early Zionists from the late nineteenth century onwards explicitly referred to Palestine as a settler-colonial destination, amongst alternative potential countries for accommodating the Jewish diaspora such as Uganda and Madagascar, South America and Azerbaijan (Pappe, 2017, p. 22). Settler-colonial frameworks can historicize the colonization of Palestine as a process that began long before the creation of the State of Israel. Such accounts build upon the earlier scholarship of, for example, Fayez A. Sayegh (1965), Maxime Rodinson (1973), Gershon Shafir (2016), Nira Yuval- Davis (1997), and Daiva Stasiulis (1995), Nahla Abdo (1993), and the body of Palestinian anticolonial writings that have not necessarily used the settler-colonial analytic, but have created the foundation for contemporary research on land appropriation Naseer Aruri (1989), Raja Shehadeh (1988), Walid Khalidi (1992) George Bisharat (1994); border controls and surveillance Yusif A. Sayigh (1997), Zureik (2001), Lisa Hajjar (2005); political economy, Nadera Shalhoub-Kerkovian and Rachel Busbridge (2014), Mandy Turner and Omar Shweiki (2014); and displacement, Farsakh (2011), Rosemary Sayigh (2007) and George Bisharat (1994).

Settler colonialism is a type of colonization that attempts to replace the native population of the colonized land with a new society of settlers. Similar to other forms of colonization, these processes are based on exogenous domination. Typically, colonizing authorities claim ethnic legitimacy (Wolfe, 2006; Stoler, 2013), or their racist and supremacist behavior towards the original inhabitants. Rodinson found how this multi-layered system of oppression is a key characteristic of Israeli domination of Palestinians. In his seminal publication "Israel a Colonial-Settler Society," he writes: "*the State of Israel on Palestinian soil is the culmination of a process that fits perfectly into the great European-American movement of expansion in the nineteenth and twentieth centuries whose aim was to settle new inhabitants among other peoples*" (Rodinson, 1973, p. 91). Despite potential controversy within parts of the settler society, colonization has clear repercussions on many aspects of Palestinian and Israeli social life, such as redistributive and socio-economic inequalities, educational possibilities, freedom of movement, and the possibility of the two groups working together (Chomsky & Pappé, 2015; Taghdisi-Rad, 2014). Although colonialism is often seen as a concluded "historical period," its power relations and the system of meanings are still imposed on the majority of people in the world today (Stoler, 2013).

Another element that can help us see the importance of classifying Israel as a settler-colonial state is its geographical organization of land and the fragmentation of the Palestinian territories (Veracini, 2016, p. 1). Today, Jewish settlements and infrastructures back the colonization in both Israel and the Occupied Palestinian Territories (OPTs) impacted roughly 85 percent of what was Palestinian land before the construction of the Israeli state (Fields, 2018, p. 18). Additionally, Israel's settler-colonial effort has determined the fragmented characteristic of the different territorial entities that make up Palestine as it is today. This context cannot be reduced to an occupation of the past when it is still ongoing (Veracini, 2016). In particular, since the US "Deal of the Century" dealt a so-called *carte blanche* or a free pass to the Israeli annexation of the West Bank, expansion efforts show no sign of stopping (Falk & Tilley, 2017).

This settler-colonialism has detrimental implications on the possibility of Israelis and Palestinians working together because of a shared future. Relations between the two peoples are one of colonized and colonizers or settlers and natives, conditioned by the undeniable racist origins of colonialism (Hilal, 2007, p. 3). As some Israeli scholars (Kedar, 2003; Pappe, 2017) have stressed, the state of Israel is a Jewish state that conceptualizes Judaism as a nation - not a religion nor an aspect of culture (Yiftachel, 1999). his understanding of Judaism, historically conceptualized by Theodor Herzl, has two main implications. First, those who are citizens of the country without being Jewish do not belong to the Israeli nation. They are *de facto* second-class citizens. Second, such a conceptualization mainly came from Western European *Ashkenazi Jews*. Meaning, the Jewish national identity itself is subjected to several segmentations. Middle Eastern Jews, called *Mizrahi*, are also discriminated against by the majority *of Ashkenazi Jews.* These aspects show how the contextual type of control and colonization is a racial one (Dahan-Kalev, 2001). Another example of this racial paradox is emphasized by Giulia Daniele (2020), looking at tensions between the role of Israel's Mizrahi majority as a Zionist settler-colonial endeavor and their marginalization from the mainstream Zionist discourse. Understanding Israeli colonization through the different intersections of oppression shows the historical and present role of racism.

A settler-colonial framework further allows for the articulation of more complex discussions concerning the making and unmaking of settler-indigenous relations in Palestine-Israel, as well as the possibility of a coexistence via decolonization (Todorova, 2019, p. 2). Teodora Todorova defines the cooperation between settler-indigenous groups as "decolonial solidarity" as a "*process which begins with an acknowledgment of solidarity protest as located in contested indigenous sovereign space where solidarity between the settler and indigenous is premised on working for, towards a vision of struggle with the colonial power*" (Todorova, 2019, p. 3). Giulia Daniele (2020) and Teodora Todorova (2019) successfully challenge the dichotomy colonized/colonizer, occupied/occupier showing the existence of other "*forms of oppression, power asymmetry and discrimination that have been generated by Zionist settler colonialism concerning other marginalized actors since the very beginning of the establishment of the Jewish state*" (Daniele, 2020 p. 465).

This contribution adds another wedge in the opening created by Giulia Daniele and Teodora Todorova that I define as "relational variance." This concept includes types of relations that diverge from the norm surrounding the predominant debate on the situation in Palestine. I thereby establish relational agency which challenges power structures and mitigates inter-personal asymmetries. This relational agency is shaped by defection from the norm. In the context of this chapter, decolonial efforts of defection from the norm are represented by Israeli activists and international Jewish organizations that mobilize alongside Palestinian ones. Relational variance does not challenge the settler-colonial framework's explanatory capacity. Instead, I propose this concept as a way to stress how pre-defined contexts, where most of the relationships respond to the settler-indigenous ways of interaction, can result in unexpected cooperation.

My research adds to the field of Relational Sociology as outlined by Mustafa Emirbayer's 1997 "*Manifesto for a Relational Sociology*." He finds that, in this research field, central elements of social life are assumed to be constituted by interactions, relations, and exchanges. However, these elements do not merely entail the interaction across "spaces" or "contexts" but are rather concerned with how relations are performed (Jasper, 2015). These performative relations have varying impacts on social structures. Most of the time, interpersonal relationships reproduce systemic violence and inequalities. As this chapter shows, there are instances of diversion from these normative relationships with significant impacts on social change and structural oppression. I depart from the epistemological cornerstone of relational sociology, assigning a central role to interpersonal interactions as well as to the agency of social actors. As a result, the concept of "relational variance" merges two epistemological standpoints. One is the insight derived from a relational approach to the social realm, and the second comes from the settler-colonial framework. Although the type of relations characterized in a settler-colonial society is concerned with settler and indigenous people, there is a residual possibility that some relations "depart from the mean." In their practice, the actors become positive deviants, enabling and unfolding relational variance. Indigenous-settler relations have major implications in terms of power asymmetries. As these relations unfurl, the existence of relational variance provides critical new reflections on how to address asymmetries across settler-colonial realities more broadly. As the empirical case in this chapter shows, it is precisely in the multidimensional space of relational variance that structural and imaginary changes can escape the seemingly inevitable chokehold of the status quo.

A CASE OF "RELATIONAL VARIANCE": THE SAVE SUSIYA CAMPAIGN

When I first visited Palestine, I went as an activist. For the next stay, I came as a researcher. From the very moment, I crossed the imaginary green-line,[2] it was self-evident that the Oslo Accords had already exhausted their potential for change. Contacts between Palestinians and Israelis are constant and, in certain areas, even frequent. However, the racial and economic interests maintaining business as usual prevent a serious reflection on the prospect of a one-democratic state with the end of the occupation. The current situation is destined to change for two reasons: 1) the management of the Occupied Palestinian Territories represents a real limit to Israel's claims to democracy and undermines its credibility as a democratic state; 2) the international civil society is growing weary, witnessing a continuous violation of Palestinian human rights. The Boycott, Divestment, Sanctions (BDS) movement and certain sectors of the Israeli-Palestinian civil society have shown that is time to take into account a real plan of decolonization.

Based on these initiatives, this chapter explores the #savesusiya social movement campaign that saw the cooperation of Palestinian and Israeli activists through a decolonial coalition. The campaign resulted in the saving of a village in the South Hebron Hills: Susiya. The Palestinian village of Khirbet Susiya has existed for over a century, appearing on maps as early as 1917, decades before Israel began its West Bank occupation policy[3]. In 1982, the Israeli government gave its approval to start the construction of the settlement Susia (the name is spelled differently from the Palestinian village, but they pronounce the same). One year later, the construction work for the settlement starts. However, settlements have always been illegal under international law. As a result, the Israeli government had to construct a "legitimate" excuse to appropriate Palestinian land. An Israeli organization fighting the use of cultural heritage classifications to dispossess disenfranchised communities, *Emek Shaveh,* reported the Susia settlement was established after the discovery of a synagogue and the antiquities site. More than two hundred people were living in the area until in 1986, the entire community was expelled from the site, and forced to move into encampments and caves outside the vicinity of the ruins. Signs have been placed by the Israeli Civil Administration around the site, which today is presented as an ancient Jewish settlement, and an entrance fee has to be paid. The indigenous Palestinians who lived there were not given any information about the excavations or any type of compensation.

Once expelled from their village, the Palestinians moved to caves or tents on their privately owned farmland, in Rujum al-Hamri, near the Susia settlement and the original village site. In 2001, during the second intifada and a short time after Palestinians killed an Israeli from the neighboring Susia settlement, the Israeli military expelled former inhabitants even from this area. The military had no official mandate for this action nor did they provide the residents with an explanation for this second expulsion. While Israel claims the structures in Khirbet Susiya are illegal because they were built without building permits, it is also known (Margalit, 2006; Margalit, 2018) that Israel's civil administration has a policy of refusing to issue building permits to Palestinians in Area C. Although the Israeli court accepted the villagers' ownership of the land, it ruled that they did not have construction permission. All attempts to obtain building permits, appeals, and requests for amnesty were rejected. Today the village of Susiya has one hundred structures that serve about 340 residents.[2]

While mobilizations for the campaign started already in 2012, the media only picked up after the introduction of the campaign's #savesusiya in May 2015. This increased attention happened at the same time as the Israeli

Civil Administration issued the demolition orders for most of the village's structures, peaking in July 2015. Thanks to a tremendous outpouring of international support, and joint actions of many different groups and organizations, including significant international media coverage, Susiya was not demolished, and the demolition order was frozen. This result is a success for the activists for many reasons. An analytical perspective could consider success in various ways, for example, concerning outcomes, the cycle of protests, campaign phases, relational approach, coalition building, or political opportunity structure (POS). I focus on the relational mechanisms of mobilization, particularly how they influence genuine cooperation and processes of coalition-building between the indigenous Palestinian population, and Israeli and International Jews.

Most of the activists were together in another Palestinian village nearby, At-Tuwani, when they received the news that the Israeli government had decided to demolish the whole village. In response, they started a meeting to decide how to proceed after the failure of their "master plan" and the legal action. One of the present activists described their feeling in an interview: "*During the meeting, I was very pessimistic because this is my nature. I'm a pessimist. I said, you know, we were working there for 15 years. But the situation seems so drastic at that time, that I didn't believe that we could help much. What I said in that meeting, was: 'We will try. We will do our best but don't have high expectations. You know, it's like, we saw that in a few weeks, the Civil Administration will demolish Susiya and that was very much the atmosphere for me, very gloomy atmosphere* (IS9)."

Activists deployed all their resources and contacts to launch a broad outreach campaign to gather activists from both sides. Surprisingly, some Susiya residents, through the help of the international organization Rebuilding Alliances, were able to go to the US Congress and present their cases.[4] On this occasion, Senator Dianne Feinstein, from the Democratic Party and of Jewish origin, made a public statement to declare her support of the activists' claims and the Palestinian right to their land.[5] This was something most activists had never thought would have happened. After these statements, demolitions were suspended. A Palestinian activist from the South Hebron Hills Popular Committee said: "*We are talking about the early stages of the campaign. So you needed a kind of very strong agency in this case who can raise your voice. But from the voices of the people, I think the Israeli activists and the human rights organizations, in addition to some Palestinian organizations, played this agency role by spreading the message of the people. In return, everyone brought more solidarity to the people, to the South Hebron Hill, so, Susiya has this voice, and later on, they started to build their capacities*" (p.2).

For a while, the first large demonstrations, reaching the US Congress, and the wide variety of international actions and declarations from diplomats and government representatives halted the destruction of the village. However, demolition orders were issued again in 2016 and a new cycle of protests took place. The situation remained unsettled until November 2017, when the Israeli government pledged to demolish the village in fifteen days. Another US response to this threat managed to stop the demolition yet again. Senators Dianne Feinstein and Bernard Sanders, who is also of Jewish origin, together with eight of their Democratic colleagues, joined a call on Israeli Prime Minister Benjamin Netanyahu to stop the demolition of the Palestinian village of Susiya and the Bedouin community of Khan al-Ahmar in the West Bank.[6]

The same events unfolded again in 2018 when Democratic Representative Jan Schakowsky, issued a statement following the Israeli High Court of Justice's approval of the planned demolition of the West Bank Palestinian village of Susiya:

> 76 members of the House of Representatives, led by myself and Congressman John Yarmuth, sent a letter to Prime Minister Netanyahu urging him not to demolish Palestinian villages like Khan al-Ahmar and Susya. In the letter, we stated that 'the destruction and displacement of such communities would run counter to the shared US and Israeli values, while further undermining long-term Israeli security, Palestinian dignity, and the prospects for peacefully achieving two states for two people.' This remains true—these demolitions must be halted.

They directly addressed Israeli Prime Minister Benjamin Netanyahu who had no alternative but to accept the US decision and influence. After 2018, there were other actions of solidarity. Even though the demolition orders are still valid and could be enforced at any moment, the village still stands. The strong network of solidarity built through time around the village is in abeyance waiting to be re-activated in case of need. The story told so far is what emerges from newspapers and press releases. But there is another story of continuous struggle and tactics. A story of coexistence between activists who come from a conflict-ridden area in which identities determine most of their life choices. Activists, who against all odds decided to engage with different ways of working together.

The #savesusiya campaign is not only an example of a social movement's success. It is emblematic of a type of mobilization that is getting increasingly common in the South Hebron Hills area: Israeli and international Jews who ally in solidarity with Palestinian activists (Shamir & Rouger, 2021). The Oslo Accords imposed the control of area C under the total administrative and military rule of Israel, but apart from that, four other aspects characterize this area:

1. The Jewish religious settler ideology considers this area "Judea," an integral part of the promised land and Eretz Yisrael. This view makes the area a particularly attractive destination for settlers. Despite the fact that settlements are illegal, Israel's state-sanctioned settlements are growing in number and dimension. Moreover, these settlements exploit Palestinian natural resources without paying taxes to the Palestinian Authority (PA).
2. Area C was and is the backdrop to the relentless construction of the separation wall, declared illegal by the International Court of Justice.[7] This blatant violation of human rights and the symbolic dimension of the wall moved the imagination of many Israeli citizens, many of whom joined demonstrations against the construction of such a separation barrier. Some campaigns, for example, the one in Bilin, succeeded in halting the construction of the wall and favored contacts between the two communities.
3. Area C is under Israeli administrative and military rule, which places the area under *de facto* Israeli control and responsibility.
4. The South Hebron Hills area is closer to the Israeli border, making Israeli activists' access easier and swifter in case of emergency from both the Jerusalem area and the South of Israel (Ber Sheva area). All these elements made the Hills southern of Yatta the scene of several long-standing joint campaigns of Palestinians and Israelis and international Jewish activists. These coalitions were built on a block of concrete, even though not always explicit, decolonial efforts, and the idea of a shared future and coexistence. The nurturing of this solidarity was possible thanks to constant relational caring by the activists.

Social Movement scholars have for a long time considered the impact of relations, and relational mechanisms concerning different elements of social movement's creation, endurance, and disengagement. McAdam, Tilly, and Tarrow's studies of contentious politics conceptualize these dynamics as a "*delimited class of changes that alter relations among specified sets of elements in identical or closely similar ways over a variety of situations*" (McAdam, Tarrow, & Tilly, 2001, p. 24). At the relational level, the most commonly highlighted aspect is *brokerage* via the production of new connections between previously unconnected actors; *diffusion* is defined as the spread of forms of contention, an issue, or a way of framing it from one site to another; *coordinated action* presented as an occurrence when two or more actors engage in mutual signaling and the parallel making of claims on the same object (McAdam, Tarrow, & Tilly, 2001).

So far most of the literature falls short of theorizing both relational variance and the dynamics of contextual characteristics related to conflict, mistrust, and racism. Consequently, I focus on the strategies practiced by activists which are usually left out of the literature. My ambition with this case study is to reduce the underlying asymmetries of power between the represented groups, and that this approach may be replicated in a wider movement toward the creation of one democratic Palestinian state.

RELATIONAL MECHANISMS TO MANAGE POWER ASYMMETRY

The main obstacle to cooperation through relational variance, underlined by most of the activists I interviewed, concerned the power asymmetries between Israelis and international Jews, and Palestinians. In the next section, I will consider three of the strategies put into place by activists to manage such a power differential, emerging from settler colonial domination. In addition, I will report some of the activists' reflections on the future of Israel and Palestine that might be considered for a wider mobilization toward the imagery of one democratic state.

Recognizing Asymmetry

For a long time Israeli-Palestinian joint activities have been studied from a peace-building/-making standpoint (Bar-On, 1996; Gawerc M. I., 2012; Hallward, 2011; Svirsky G. , 2004; Svirsky M. , 2017; Bar-Siman-Tov, 2004; Emmett, 2003). Such an approach widely underestimates, and sometimes even reinforces, the large power asymmetry existing between the two groups. This paradigm was largely bolstered by the so-called people-to-people initiatives[8] (Maoz, 2004; Naser-Najjab, 2019; Tamari, 2005; Pundak, 2006; Shira & Avivit, 2006; Golan & Zahira, 2006). As I previously described, the premises of these peace-building attempts had a strong bias, relying heavily on an *equalization* aimed at "*treating the rival as an equal partner contrary, to previous belief in the superiority of 'our side*'" (Herzog & Hai, 2005, p. 8). Although the intentions behind this assumption were probably honorable and legitimate, this perspective disregarded the colonial nature of the conflict, similar to many other perspectives. Consequently, Palestinian dispossession was watered-down.

The type of organizations and applied methodologies were multiple, including equal representation of both sides in the organizational hierarchy, long-term projects, large conferences, intimate meetings, seminars, one-day events, training sessions, round-table dialogues, and field activities. An underlying idea of these attempts was that equal representation and constant interactions between the two groups, by including directors and moderators from each nationality, would have ensured equality and symmetry between Israeli-Jews and Palestinians (Maoz, 2004, p. 569). However, performing a sort of "formal equality" to eliminate the disproportionate power asymmetries existing between the two groups is profoundly misleading. Indeed, most of these people-to-people initiatives failed after the second intifada and the construction of the Separation Wall.[9] Mindful of potential limits and animated by decolonial awareness, activists involved in the #savesusiya campaign started their joint activism from the recognition of these structural asymmetries.

People on both sides described this cooperation in a very similar way, stressing the importance to recognize such asymmetric relations: *"A praxis that's based on connection. And it's not a connection like everybody's friends, and we hold hands and sing. It's a connection that's built on mutual recognition of asymmetry and mutual appreciation of what that asymmetry can also allow, what it enables (IS4)."* Israelis are free to move wherever they wish to. Palestinians are denied the right to mobility. Israelis provide humanitarian aid while Palestinians are most of the time the "recipients" of such aid. Israelis—whether they like it or not—are part of the occupying nation, while Palestinians are the occupied nation. Israelis have easy, direct contact with the rest of the world, while Palestinians constantly need to prove to the West that they are not "terrorists." Because of such asymmetries, which increased over the recent years, it is difficult to maintain the essence of reciprocal relations: *"There are two dangers here. One is of becoming professional philanthropists; the other is of embracing the illusion that we can be saviors. From our work, we continuously learn how to walk the fine line of mutuality even when the external reality is so asymmetric" (IS2).*

Every activist faces this asymmetry dilemma at a certain point, and internationals too. Palestinians do not usually like to talk about such an asymmetry. In most of the interviews, they tried to move the discourse on why working with Israeli activists is not considered "*normalization*"[8]. This was made very clear by a Palestinian activist who participated in the research: "*Sometimes there are other groups and they say we are 'normalizing' but this is something not right because we didn't, for example normalizing is to come to sell settlers more land, but we all resist the settlers, they [Israeli activists] come to join the resistance. I want to make it clear that this is like that, and usually, these people say: 'This is normalizing,' but this is not*" (p. 3).

One of the Israeli activists highlights their understanding of these asymmetries:

> *"Of course, you meet the asymmetry and people are telling you: 'you are lucky, you don't have to face all those hardships that we are facing in our everyday life.' But in reality, on the other side, when we are under the threat of rockets from Gaza, our friends in Southern Hebron and Susiya and elsewhere, tell us to come, come and stay with us. Here is safer than in your kibbutz [. . .] [Asymmetry] It's the rule of the game, and then you have to work within it. So the basic is another aspect. The question is whether we are the Israelis, or we are individuals in front of you. Especially during operations, like there is a war in Gaza between Hamas and Israel. Especially during those operations that happen from time to time, and there is a real danger and raise in tensions between the Palestinian and Israelis. We come to meet those people, our friends in Southern Hebron and we are the only Israelis that they encounter, just on a personal level"* (IS 9).

Western approaches to encounter and collaboration have long been criticized for reinforcing colonial legacies. Most of these initiatives have their foundations in liberal multiculturalism that focuses on individual cultural differences instead of structural group differences. In this way, it blanks over the specific histories that determine existing inequalities (Beausoleil, 2020, p. 7). Most of the activists, from both sides, have underlined the importance of trying to manage asymmetries of power between the two groups. This is essential for any social movement that finds itself dealing with discriminated minorities. Gender, racial and economic divides create asymmetries of power. This is why the more strategies are identified to deal with such asymmetries the more likely cooperation across divides will be.

1. Leave for Palestinians (the Historically Discriminated Group) the Actions Initiative

Many Israeli activists have underlined the need to listen to and follow the Palestinian leadership when organizing and structuring collective actions. They have described this approach as the need of accepting the role of the "*junior partner*": "*we understood that even though we're partners, we are the junior partners. In other words, it's a Palestinian-led struggle*" (IS8). In other words, the recognition of these asymmetries is about accepting to do something that you, as an Israeli or international Jew, would not have thought about but is meaningful to the movement.

A 2016 action exemplifies this approach in practice when a mixed group of activists visited the ancient synagogue from where some of the families were evicted in the '80s, paying the entrance ticket and remembering the living

Nakba.[10] *"We said we want to go home. We want the whole village to walk across the highway and to go to our original village of Susiya where we were, where many of us were born in the caves, many of us lived and died in these caves and on the agricultural land that's now been turned into a settlement/ archaeological site. Before that action, I think maybe three or four people from the community had ever gone back since they were forced off that land when the Israeli government expelled them and turned it into an archaeological site. I was born here. I want to see where I was born, even though it's literally across the road. This would be the most meaningful thing for the grandparents and the children to go back and visit. We won't stay. We can't stay at that time. We can't stay. Maybe in the future, we will do something where they can reclaim it. And we help them go back and they stay there until they're forced out. But at that point, we want to go back. I want the kids of Susiya to get to see where their parents were born, where their grandparents grew up" (P4).* Palestinian activists and Susiya inhabitants together with Israelis and international Jews visit the historical site from which Palestinians were expelled in the '80s. According to the interviewees, Israelis were ready for a more confrontational type of collective action, but Palestinians decided to pay a ticket to visit the site of their personal Nakba. This moment was mentioned by many interviewees as an unexpected but very powerful moment. An Israeli activist who took part in this action said: *"What we do is like we call in question everything that we're doing with the Palestinian communities that are there. So, like all of our processes start with what our Palestinian partners want and need from us. What do they want? How many people do they want in their communities? What do they want these people to be doing in their communities, when we have done press releases and these kinds of things, all of the languages get to run through the coalition and the coalition media people to make sure that everyone feels like their language and ideas are reflected. Sometimes, the process of planning a single action takes like eight months because of how, you know, genuinely collaborative and Palestinian-led, right? The lingua franca, the working language is often English. So we have both Arabic and Hebrew speakers on sort of all sides, but sometimes like you'll be in one of these big coalition meetings and something will happen. And then all of a sudden, the Palestinians start talking in Arabic, not talking to us, talking among themselves. They're like: 'We've got a thing to figure out.' And it is fine, we say 'cool.' We don't have to be inside every conversation or every decision-making analysis. We also try to make sure that when we're talking to journalists [. . .], especially the Israeli media, wants to make the story of some of these Palestinian villages a story about Jews doing resistance. I hate that. That is not the fucking story here. We also do massive debriefs. So after every action, after every campaign, we sit down with each one of our Palestinian partners and assess what went well, what went badly, and how do we change? These are processes of accountability that are really important. I feel like co-visioning and accountability and trying to control for asymmetrical power forces. They don't eliminate them they're still in the world. But I think the thing I'm really proud of is really trying to tackle those hand in hand: these are the conditions of our work, and we have an obligation to respond to them and to try to find ways of counteracting structural power imbalance, even if we can't eliminate it" (IS3*). Israeli activists offer themselves as human shields, defenders, advocators for human rights in Israel. But, once they do join activities and participate in collective actions, the question of how to carry them out and with what strategies, is decided by Palestinians.

2. Sharing (Meaningful) Life Experiences

Sleepover actions were a common tool to prevent unexpected demolitions overnight. The presence of Israeli activists, in particular, is a strong deterrent to the Israeli Defence Forces' (IDF) violations of human rights. These actions did not start during the 2015 campaign as reported by the media. They started with the very beginning of the cooperation surrounding the #savesusiya campaign. The additional advantage of sharing day-by-day activism is certainly the creation of strong links and relations of trust with the Palestinian activists living in the village, or those Palestinians who came to support the struggle. The "sleepover tool" was mentioned by all the activists who took part in the campaign as one of the most useful tactics and potentials for movement building. *"But I think that some 90 people slept in Susiya and I had never been part of something like that [. . .] there was something truly different and transformative about sleeping over" (IS4). "Well, we were sleeping there during the campaign, sleeping in Susiya, this also encouraged people to stay and to maintain in the campaign"* (p. 2).

This strategy also mitigated one of the strongest manifestations of asymmetry: the rich ones, the powerful ones, the Whites, and the "humanitarians" always have a place where to "come back" away from what could be called "subalterns' misery" after joining an action. This is equally the case for the whole humanitarian and development aid complex that, most of the time, dictates the relationship between the Global South and the Global North (Gawerc M., 2019, p. 61). All interviewed activists considered these sleepovers, which lasted for several days, in combination with a tangible "not-to-leave-and-go-back-to-your-privilege" as a crucial moment. On the one hand, it was a way to manage the enduring asymmetry that makes cooperation so hard. On the other hand, it proposes a concrete image of "sharing the land" and sharing a future.

This act of staying was very much felt also by Palestinian activists who stated: "*Susiya was an example of Israeli-Palestinian cooperation? Yes. Because they stayed those nights. They didn't leave*" (p. 2).

What should be stressed for these types of collective action repertoires, is that they all pay a lot of attention to the relational level of activism together with the need to address structural types of oppression. These strategies are concrete tools to allow relational variance to emerge and flourish.

WHAT IS NEXT FOR PALESTINE?

The main potential of a single-state democracy is to shift the territorial grounding of the current confrontation, dismantle normative ethnicity, and challenge issues commonly linked to the present demographic distribution. This approach simultaneously puts into question the legitimacy of predominating politics and power asymmetries. This single state could take many different forms, but it must guarantee the end of occupation and the Gaza blockade. When asking activists about their reflections on the future of Palestine, only one out of twenty interviewees that took part in the #savesusiya campaign advocated for the two-state solution. All the other activists were convinced that, given the previously described situation of the conflict, the existence of an independent Palestinian state as envisioned by a two-state-solution is unfeasible: "*I see that with all the settlements expansion and what is happening in the West Bank, there's no more space for the two-State solution. I think something else should be developed to end this conflict and improve the future of Palestinians*" (p. 8).

"*I think the two-state solution has two main problems. One is that it's an injustice for the Palestinians. Because there are many Palestinians that are refugees and are refugees from '48. And it's an injustice to them. And the other thing is that the situation on the ground is that there are settlers all over the West Bank. So I don't think it's happening. It's out of reality. I don't know. I don't think it will happen. And I don't see the atmosphere. The political atmosphere in Israel would not allow that. I don't see it would be a solution*" (IS 7).

Both Palestinian and Israeli activists working together are aware of the practical impossibility of creating an independent Palestinian state in co-existence with an Israeli state in Palestine. However, this is not only impracticable but also unfair. Palestinians were living in that land since time immemorial. They deserve reparations and the possibility to return to their land as a state by the UN Resolution 194 of 1948. Palestinians that I interviewed understand that this does not mean "liberating" the land from non-Palestinians. Instead, the ongoing crimes of the Zionist project under the state of Israel are an unfinished colonial enterprise that necessitates the ongoing violation of human rights. For centuries Jewish people in Europe have been victims of anti-Semitism, persecution, and horrific violence surmounting genocide. Amidst all this hopelessness, the #savesusiya provided a glimpse towards a future in which the land of Palestine is a shared homeland for Jews and Palestinians. Coming together across differences, this future would be a glorious victory for the persistence of love over hate, and self-determination over oppression. To come closer to this prospect, Israel needs to immediately set a stop to their ethnocracy (Yiftachel, 1999). This means also a stop to re-affirmations via legal instruments, like the 2018 Nation-State Law which outlines the right of self-determination to "the Jewish people," excluding indigenous Palestinians. This law—which has distinct colonial characteristics—guarantees the ethnic-religious character of Israel as exclusively Jewish and entrenches the privileges enjoyed by Jewish citizens. Simultaneously, the law is anchored in discrimination against Palestinian citizens, legitimizing exclusion, racism, and systemic inequality. These issues must be addressed comprehensively to direct energies towards the construction of one democratic state: "*Now this is not life for Palestinians here in South Hebron Hills. We cannot move, we have no money, I think there should be one state, with equal rights, everyone with equal rights: Palestinians and Jews*" (p. 2).

CONCLUSION

Palestinians face a critical moment in their confrontation with Israeli settler-colonialism. They cannot accept a Bantustan-like state—encircled by walls and electronic fences—on approximately 12 percent of their historical land, nor can they accept a denial of the right to return, or not having Jerusalem as capital (Hilal, 2007, p. 17). A client and dependent Palestinian state will never be able to provide Palestinians with the necessary freedom, justice, and emancipation, as sought by any people (Hilal, 2007, p. 19). Currently, the most discussed solutions are a one-state or a bi-national state. The bi-national state model provides a sharing of power between Jewish and Palestinians that could take various negotiable forms, but with an emphasis on collective rights. The other model is a secular democratic state with no distinction between citizens according to religion, ethnicity, or national origin, emphasizing individual rights. The main reason for the incompatibility of a one-state solution resides in the Zionist colonial ideology and its insistence on a Jewish state conceptualizing Judaism as a nation, not a religion or an aspect of culture (Hilal, 2007, p. 21).

However, as I showed in the above-outlined empirical case, the very presence of Jewish Israelis resisting colonial land expropriation side-by-side with

Palestinians represents settler-indigenous cooperation that challenges exclusionary ethnonational mobilization. Additionally, it directly questions the representation of Palestinians as an existential threat to Israel and proposes a decolonial alternative to the settler-colonial state. Shared experiences of colonial violence during protest actions, such as the ones to avoid house demolition in the South Hebron Hills, created previously unthinkable decolonial coalitions and revealed relational variance between Israelis and Palestinians. The "*decolonial outcome*," even though not indefinitely reflected in a concrete success or failure of these alliances, is arguably a symptom of a wider movement that advocates the creation of one democratic state.

In this view, we can see the critical importance of achieving justice and permanent peace lies within the dismantling of the settler-colonial regime in historic Palestine, establishing a new political system based on full civil equality, and the full implementation of the Palestinian refugees' Rights of Return. Many activists and groups, Palestinians, Israelis, and internationals, have recently started to evaluate this option both theoretically and practically. This chapter has looked at how the resisting Israeli and Palestinian civil society has developed strategies to reach this aim. Indeed, this political project makes sense only as far as both populations and communities support such an effort. It will be a long and hard project but something has started changing. The type of prefigurative resistance actors in the South Hebron Hills are performing is the right step in this direction. To conclude, we should be adamant in joining their arguments for the establishment of one democratic state, from the River to the Sea.

REFERENCES

Abdo, N. (1993). Middle east politics through feminist lenses: Negotiating the terms of solidarity. Alternatives, 8.1; 29–38.

Alimi, E., Bosi, L., & Demetriou, C. (2015). The dynamics of radicalization: a relational and comparative perspective. Oxford University Press.

Aruri, N. (1989). The recolonization of the Arab world. Arab Studies Quarterly, 273–86.

Atshan, S. (2020). Queer Palestine and the Empire of Critique. Stanford University Press.

B'Tselem. (2010). Hook and By Crook: Israel's Settlement Policy in the West Bank, Summary.

Bar-On, M. (1996). In pursuit of peace A history of the Israeli peace movement. US Institute of Peace Press.

Bar-Siman-Tov, Y. (2004). From Conflict Resolution to Reconciliation. New York: Oxford University Press.

Beausoleil, E. (2020). "Gather your people": Learning to listen intergenerationally in settler-indigenous politics. *Political Theory*, 48(6), 665–91.

Bensky, T. (2007). Breaching events and the emotional reactions: Women in Black in Israel. In H. Flam, & D. King, Emotions and social movements (pp. 67–88). Routledge.

Bisharat, G. E. (1994). Displacement and social identity: Palestinian refugees in the West Bank. Center for Migration Studies special issues, 11(4), 163–88.

Bohrer, A. (2019). Marxism and intersectionality: Race, gender, class and sexuality under contemporary capitalism. Bielefeld: transcript Verlag.

Bourdieu, P. (2000). Propos sur le champ politique. Lyon: Presses Universitaires Lyon.

Chomsky, N., & Pappé, I. (2015). On Palestine. Haymarket Books.

Crenshaw, K. (1989). Kimberle Crenshaw. In The University of Chicago Legal Forum (pp. 139–67). Chicago: Chicago University Press.

Dahan-Kalev, H. (2001). Tensions in Israeli feminism: The Mizrahi Ashkenazi rift. Women's Studies International Forum, Vol. 24, No. 6, pp. 669–84.

Daniele, G. (2020). Mizrahi Jews and the Zionist settler colonial context: between. Settler Colonial Studies, 461–80.

Darweish, M., & Andrew, R. (2015). Popular Protest in Palestine. London: Pluto Press.

Degani, A. (2016). From Republic to Empire. Israel and the Palestinians after 1948. In V. Lorenzo, & C. Edward, The Routledge Handbook of the History of Settler Colonialism (pp. 353–65). Taylor & Francis.

della Porta, D. (2014). Mobilizing for democracy: comparing 1989 and 2011. OUP Oxford.

Dépelteau, F. (2018). Relational Thinking in Sociology: Relevance, Concurrence, and Dissonance. In F. Dépelteau, he Palgrave handbook of relational sociology (pp. 3–34). London: Palgrave Macmillan.

Emirbayer, M. (1997). Manifesto for a relational sociology. American journal of sociology, 103(2), 281–317.

Emmett, A. (2003). Our sisters' promised land: women, politics, and Israeli-Palestinian coexistence. The University of Michigan Press.

Falk, R., & Tilley, V. (2017). Israeli Practices towards the Palestinian People and the Question of Apartheid. Beirut: United Nations.

Farsakh, L. (2011). The one-state solution and the Israeli-Palestinian conflict: Palestinian challenges and prospects. The Middle East Journal, 65(1), 55–71.

Fields, G. (2018). Enclosure. Palestinian Landscape in a Historical Mirror. University of Californian Press.

Gawerc, M. (2019). Endeavoring to Change History: Palestinian-led Transnational Coalitions in the Occupied West Bank. Bringing Down Divides: Research in Social Movements, Conflicts and Change, 43, 39–61.

Gawerc, M. I. (2012). Prefiguring Peace: Israeli-Palestinian peacebuilding partnerships. Lanham: Lexington Books.

Golan, G., & Zahira, K. (2006). Women's People-to-People Activities: Do We Do It Better? Palestine - Israel Journal of Politics, Economics, and Culture, 58–63.

Hajjar, L. (2005). Courting Conflict: The Israeli military court system in the West Bank and Gaza. The University of California Press.

Hallward, M. C. (2011). Struggling for a Just Peace Israeli and Palestinian Activism in the Second Intifada. Gainesville: University Press of Florida.

Herzog, S., & Hai, A. (2005). What do people mean when they say'people-to-people'? Origins, definitions, goals, and methods. Palestine-Israel journal of politics, economics, and culture 12.4/1, 8–15.

Hilal, J. (2007). Palestine: the lats colonial issue. In J. Hilal, Where Now For Palestine? The Demise of the Two-State Solution (pp. 1–29). London: Zed Books.

Hooks, B. (2015). Feminist Theory from the margin to center. New York: Routledge.

Jasper, J. M. (2015). Introduction Playing the Game. In J. Jasper, & J. Duyvendak, Players and Arenas The Interactive Dynamics of Protest (pp. 9–34). Croydon: Amsterdam University Press.

Kedar, A. (2003). On the legal geography of ethnocratic settler states: Notes towards a research agenda. Current Legal Issues, 5, 401–41.

Khalidi, W., Elmusa, S., & Ali, M. (1992). All that remains: The Palestinian villages occupied and depopulated by Israel in 1948. Institution for Palestine Studies.

Maoz, I. (2004). Peace Building in Violent Conflict: Israeli-Palestinian Post-Oslo People-to-People Activities. International Journal of Politics, Culture and Society, 563–73 Vol. 17, No. 3.

Margalit, M. (2006). Discrimination in the Heart of the Holy City. Jerusalem: International Peace and Cooperation Center.

Margalit, M. (2018). Gerusalemme la Città Impossibile. Chiavi per Comprendere l'Occupazione Israeliana. Milano: Edizioni Terra Santa.

McAdam, D., Tarrow, S., & Tilly, C. (2001). Dynamics of Contentious. Cambridge: Cambridge University Press.

Messerschmid, C. (2014). Hydro-Apartheid and Water Access in Israel-Palestine: Challenging the Myths of Cooperation and Scarcity. In M. Turner, & O. Shweiki, Decolonizing Palestinian Political Economy (pp. 53–76). London: Palgrave Macmillan.

Mitchell, T. (2000). Native vs. Settler: Ethnic Conflict in Israel/Palestine, Northern Ireland, and South Africa. Westport: Greenwood Publishing Group.

Naser-Najjab, N. (2019). The Oslo People-to-People Program and the Limits of Hegemony. Middle East Critique, 425–43.

Pappe, I. (2017). Ten myths about Israel. Verso Books.

Pundak, R. (2006). Looking Back: An Evaluation of People-to-People. Palestine - Israel Journal of Politics, Economics, and Culture, 34–38.

Rodinson, M. (1973). Israel A Colonial-Settler State? New York: Monad Press.

Runciman, W. G. (1966). Relative deprivation & social justice: Study attitudes social inequality in 20th century England.

Salaita, S. (2016). Inter/nationalism: Decolonizing Native America and Palestine. Universtiy of Minnesota Press.

Sayegh, F. A. (1965). Zionist colonialism in Palestine. Beirut, Lebanon: Research Center, Palestine Liberation Organization.

Sayigh, R. (2007). Women's Nakba Stories: Between Being and Knowing. In A. Sa'di, & L. Abu-Lughod, Nakba: Palestine, 1948, and the Claims of Memory (pp. 135–61). New York: Columbia University Press.

Sayigh, Y. (1997). Armed struggle and the search for state: The Palestinian national movement, 1949–1993. Clarendon Press.

Shafir, G. (2016). Theorizing Zionist Settler Colonialism in Palestine. In L. Veracini, & E. Cavanagh, The Routledge Handbook of the History of Settler Colonialism (pp. 339–52). Taylor & Francis.

Shalhoub-Kerkovian, N., & Busbridge, R. (2014). En)gendering De-development in East Jerusalem: Thinking Through the "Everyday." In M. Turner, & O. Shweiki, Decolonizing Palestinian Politica Economy (pp. 77–96). Palgrave Macmillan.

Shamir, J., & Rouger, N. (2021, February 23). A Youth-led Palestinian Protest Movement Is Rocking the Hills South of Jerusalem. Haaretz.

Shehadeh, R. (1988). Occupier's Law and the Uprising. Journal of Palestine Studies 17.3, 24–37.

Shira, H., & Avivit, H. (2006). What Do People Mean When They Say 'People-to-People'? Origins, Definitions, Goals and Methods. Palestine—Israel Journal of Politics, Economics, and Culture, 8–15.

Stoler, A. L. (2013). Imperial Debris: on ruins and ruination. Duke University Press.

Summary, B. (1982, April 29). New Settlements in the West Bank. BBC Summary of World Broadcasts.

Svirsky, G. (2004). Local coalitions, global partners: The women's peace movement in Israel and beyond. Signs: Journal of Women in Culture and Society, 29(2), 543–50.

Svirsky, M. (2017). Arab–Jewish Activism in Israel–Palestine. Abingdon: Routledge.

Taghdisi-Rad, S. (2014). The Economic Strategies of Occupation: Confining Development and Buying-off Peace. In M. Turner, & O. Shweiki, Decolonizing Palestinian Political Economy: De-development and Beyond (pp. 13–31). London: Palgrave Macmillan.

Tamari, S. (2005). Kissing Cousins: A Cautionary Note on People-to-People Projects. Israel Journal of Politics, Economics, and Culture, 16–19.

Tarrow, S. (2011). Power in movement: Social movements and contentious politics. Cambridge: Cambridge University Press.

Tarrow, S. (2015). Contentious Politics. In D. Della Porta, & M. Diani, The Oxford Handbook of Social Movement Studies (pp. 86–107). Oxford: Oxford University Press.

Tarrow, S., & Tilly, C. (2007). Contentious politics and social movements. In C. Boix, & S. C. Susan, The Oxford handbook of comparative politics. Oxford: Oxford Handbooks of Political.

Todorova, T. (2019). Vulnerability as a politics of decolonial solidarity: the case of the Anarchists Against the Wall. Global Studies in Culture and Power, 1–18.

Turner, M., & Shweiki, O. (2014). Introduction: Decolonizing the Study of the Political Economy of the Palestinian People. In M. Turner, & O. Shweiki, Decolonizing Palestinian Political Economy: De-development and Beyond (pp. 1–12). London: Palgrave Macmillan.

Veracini, L. (2016). Settler Colonialism as a Distinct mode of domination. In L. Veracini, & E. Cavanagh, The Routledge Handbook of the History of Settler Colonialism (pp. 1–8). Taylor & Francis.

Wolfe, P. (2006). Settler Colonialism and the Elimination of the Native. Journal of genocide research, 8(4), 387–409.

Yiftachel, O. (1999). "Ethnocracy": The Politics of Judaizing Israel/Palestine. Constellations, 364–90.

Yuval-Davis, N. (1997). Gender and Nation. London: Sage.

Zureik, E. (2001). Constructing Palestine through surveillance practices. British Journal of Middle Eastern Studies, 28(2), 205–27.

NOTES

1. For an in-depth analysis of different contexts of settler colonialism, see: Ran Greenstein, Genealogie of Conflict: Class, Identity, and State in Palestine/Israel and South Africa (Hanover SETTLER COLONIAL STUDIES 1 Wesleyan University Press, 1995); Scott L. Morgensen, 'The Biopolitics of Settler Colonialism Right Here, Right Now,' *Settler Colonial Studies* 1, no. 1 (2011): 52–76; Lorenzo Veracini, *Israel and Settler Society* (London: Pluto Press, 2006); Lorenzo Veracini, *Settler Colonialism: A Theoretica Overview* (Basingstoke: Palgrave Macmillan, 2010); Patrick Wolfe, *Settler Colonialism and the Transformation of Anthropology* (London: Cassell, 1999); Patrick Wolfe, *Traces of History: Elementary Structures of Race* (London and New York: Verso, 2016).

2. The Green Line, also known as the 1949 Armistice Agreement is the dividing line established in the 1949 Arab-Israeli Armistice Agreements. It is not a legislative border but it is a de facto demarcation line between Israel from the rest of the POT.

3. The presence of the village was mentioned by the geographer David Grossman in his book *Expansion and Desertion: The Arab Village and Its Offshoots in Ottoman Palestine* [in Hebrew].

4. https://www.timesofisrael.com/palestinians-bring-plight-of-threatened-village-to-us/ and https://www.haaretz.com/senator-feinstein-urges-netanyahu-not-to-demolish-palestinian-village-1.5380462.

5.Here the senator's tweet with a picture together with Nasser Nawaja'a: https://twitter.com/senfeinstein/status/927942821096624128 and an archival document in which she is with the children of Susiya in her office http://hosted-p0.vresp.com/327262/38be994ecf/ARCHIVE#.VgRMLCshcuc.twitter.

6. https://www.feinstein.senate.gov/public/index.cfm/2017/11/senators-to-netanyahu-stop-israeli-demolition-of-west-bank-villages.

7. https://www.icj-cij.org/en/case/131.

8. Each year since the signing of the Oslo peace agreements in 1993, there have been numerous programs of Israeli-Palestinian activities aimed at peace building (see Adwan & Bar-On, 2000; Chaitin, Obeidi, Adwan & Bar-On, 2002, Albeck, Adwan & Bar-On). These meetings ranged from onetime single events to long-term and continuous series of meetings, and from youth encounters to dialogues among

schoolteachers, university students, university professors, and other professionals (Bar-On, 1996). The idea behind these meetings was to foster dialogue and in order to cease the conflict (Maoz, 2004). For those interested in having a deeper understanding of these initiatives, I would suggest a very brief article by Herzog and Hai titled "*What do people mean when they say 'people-to-people'? Origins, definitions, goals and methods*" (2005).

9. The Israeli West Bank barrier (also known as the Israeli West Bank wall or Israeli West Bank fence) is a separation barrier in the West Bank. Israel describes the wall as a necessary security barrier against terrorism; Palestinians call it a racial segregation or apartheid wall. At a total length of 708 kilometres (440 mi) upon completion, the route traced by the barrier is more than double the length of the Green Line, with 15 percent of the barrier's length running along the Green Line or inside Israel, while the remaining 85 percent is inside the West Bank going up to 18 kilometres (11 mi) from the West Bank border, isolating about 9 percent of the land and twenty-five thousand Palestinians from the rest of West Bank.

10. Literally, the Palestinian catastrophe of 1948, known mainly in the Arab world, and among Palestinians in particular, as nakba (Arabic: النكبة, al-Nakba, literally "disaster," "catastrophe," or "cataclysm"), is the exodus of the Palestinian Arab population during the civil war of 1947–1948, at the end of the British Mandate, and during the Arab-Israeli war of 1948, after the founding of the State of Israel. Nakba is the name assigned to this event by historiography, not only in Arabic. During this conflict, more than seven hundred thousand Palestinians were expelled from towns and villages, and were subsequently denied any right to return to their lands, both during and after the conflict.

7

Toward a Global Agenda

Resolving the Israeli–Palestinian Conflict

Idowu Johnson

INTRODUCTION

The Israeli–Palestinian conflict, which has pitted two peoples (Jews and Palestinian Arabs) against one another, is one of the longest and most violent conflicts in modern history. The ramifications of its daily events go well beyond the clashing parties and attract the attention of millions of people in many parts of the world. The conflict is categorized as a complex conflict that is resistant to peaceful solutions (Dowty, 2008). Some of the several factors that constitute the complexity of the conflict include but are not limited to religious differences between the warring factions, strong historical antecedents, as well as a concrete sense of entitlement by the two belligerents to statehood (Bickerton & Carla, 2010).

Over the last seventy years, the Middle East has been characterized by widespread violence and war as disputes over territory and religious freedom have heightened tensions between the Israelis and Palestinians. While the Israelis on one hand are armed by the Jewish narrative of the quest for national restoration and scriptural convictions of being the sole and direct owner of the area presently occupied by the Palestinians, the Palestinians are motivated by the claim that the land in all sense of righteousness belongs to them; and the eventual Israeli invasion of the land is in the true sense of the word a violation. The evolution of these two extreme claims and counter-claims can be traced first to the exigent need of the Jews to find a place for themselves that they can call home after the horrendous experience of the Holocaust (Morris 2009, p. 42).

The quest of the Israelis to re-establish their statehood was borne out of not only the need to escape from any further embarrassment as experienced in the Holocaust, but a desire to establish a strong defense against any attack on their nationhood as well as reclaim lost territory. This invasion from the Palestinian narrative cannot be regarded as an act of aggression. This laid the foundation for the implosion that was to follow in 1948, which later earned the name Arab-Israeli war. The conflict since then has been on the rise and has encouraged several dynamics in the struggle over territorial ownership of the land that both parties lay claim to. This conflict has already taken a global outlook, judging from the interference and the interest of several powerful states of the world which directly or indirectly shapes the perception and reaction of their allies towards the conflict.

With no absolute solution to resolving the conflict and the—United States' recognition (under the Trump administration) of the city of Jerusalem as the capital of Israel, peace is far from the conflict. However, the conflict raises global concern as many states are now at war against violent ideological fundamentalist groups. This poses a serious threat to international peace and security. It is against this background that this paper examines a global peaceful settlement framework that can resolve the conflict. This paper utilizes descriptive and qualitative methods by relying on secondary materials (books, journals, government publications, magazines, and internet materials) to analyze the trend in Israeli–Palestinian conflict.

This chapter begins with an introduction. After this, it explores the discourse on the historical exploration of the conflict between Israel and Palestine, it proceeds to the recent development of the conflict. The next section examines the global outlook and parties to the conflict. This was followed by an analysis of the consequences of the conflicts, as well as peacebuilding efforts in resolving the conflict. The last section of the paper explores suggestions for a global settlement framework for resolving conflict. The final section of the paper is the conclusion.

HISTORICAL EXPLORATION OF THE ISRAELI–PALESTINIAN CONFLICT

Israel is a land that could be described as the survivor of ancient conspiracy and external conquest. Historians and anthropologists said Israel had existed as far back as 900 BCE. The state of Israel shares its northern border with Lebanon, its northeastern border with Syria, its eastern border with Jordan, as well as the Palestinian territories of the West Bank and Gaza strip respectively to the east and west; and finally, it shares with Egypt its southwest border. On the other hand, the state of Palestine, best pronounced as *Dawlat Filastin* in Arabic, currently refers to the geographical area known as the Levant. The state of Palestine is currently bordered to the west by the Mediterranean Sea, and it is bordered to the south by Egypt and to the north and east by Israel (CIA, 2017).

The conflict between Israel and Palestine dates back to the biblical era. The Israelis claimed Palestine based on God's promise to the Jewish and the fact that it was historically the land of the Jewish Kingdom of Israel until its devastation by the Roman Empire (Chao, 2011). It is important to note that today referred to as Israel and the Palestinian territories in this part of the world were originally just called Palestine, named after twelfth-century Greeks who lived near modern Tel Aviv and Gaza (Ismail, 2020). The Palestinians involved their continued existence in the area as a ground not to give the land and had been unwilling to provide their land as a remedy for European injustice.

The birth of major nationalist movements in the nineteenth and early twentieth centuries among the Jews and the Arabs in attaining sovereignty in the Middle East for their people aggravated the conflict. The movements are classified as Zionism and Arab nationalism. These two historic movements of Arab nationalism and Zionism had been building up significantly since the nineteenth century with the aims of achieving emancipation and self-determination, both revolving around the concept of identity, nationhood, history, religion, and culture (Schelze 1999, p. 1). Zionism promoted the belief that Jews were entitled to Palestine and fuelled their zeal in pursuing their fight and struggle to have self-determination. Arab nationalism, on the other hand, was born out of the shared language, religion (Islam), and history of the Middle East region, and therefore Arab nationalists aspired to political cooperation through the Arab League (Bell 2001, p. 176). The Arabs often perceived western rulers to be pro-Israel. The collision between those two forces in the southern Levant eventually escalated into the Israeli–Palestinian conflict in 1947 and expanded into the wider Arab-Israeli conflict later (Ortiz 2015, p. 3).

Specifically, British policy during World War I helped create the conditions for conflict between Jews and Arabs in Palestine and most of the Middle East. During the war, Great Britain pursued a policy of urging open revolt by the Arabs against the Ottomans (allied with Germany and Austria) who ruled most of the Middle East, in return for British support of Arab independence. At the same time, to gain greater Jewish support for the Allied war effort as well as leverage American Jewish pressure to get the United States to enter the war, Britain issued the Balfour Declaration, which was a pledge to support a national homeland for Jews in Palestine. At the end of the war, the newly formed League of Nations determined that the peoples of the former lands of the Ottoman Empire were not ready yet for independence so the league gave Britain and France mandates to govern these territories until independence was possible. With the British mandate over Palestine about to expire, a decision on what to do with the land had to be made. Unable to develop a plan that would appease both the Jewish and Arab people, the British handed over the mandate to the United Nations, who ultimately decided to partition the land and affirm the creation of the state of Israel in 1948 (Wistrich 1997, p. 13). The Israeli state was declared unilaterally on May 14, 1948, in Tel Aviv. Chaim Weizmann was declared the first president and Ben-Gurion, the first prime minister.

The declaration of an Israeli state by the UN infuriated the neighboring countries, thereby declaring war against the new state of Israel and invading it. Syria, Saudi Arabia, Iraq, Lebanon, and Egypt (Arab League) declared war (Bickerton & Carta 2010, p. 36). Even though the Arabs together outnumbered the Jews, the Israeli army was smaller, and Israel was more organized and prepared and had the support of the United States. The Palestinian Arabs refused to give up their land and believed the UN process to be favorable to only the Jewish people. After nearly a year of combat and thousands of lives lost, separate armistice agreements between Israel and each of the Arab states eventually ended the war. The Jewish people came out victorious, gaining the land granted to them by the UN as well as additional land won through the conflict (Rodriguez 2020, p. 15).

For several decades, the Israeli and Arab communities continue to engage in violent conflict. In 1967, the ongoing tension between Israel and its Arab neighbors broke out into a full-scale war. The Six-Day War of 1967 was an attempt by Arab forces to regain control of the land as relations between the Arab states and Israel had not been fully normalized (Nasrallab 2013, p. 56). As a result of swift and stunning military victories, Israel occupied the Sinai Peninsula (Egyptian), the Golan Heights (Syrian), Gaza, the West Bank, and East Jerusalem. Each of these territories came under military occupation. The occupation led to over two hundred thousand Palestinians fleeing to Jordan (USIP, nd). War broke out once again in 1973, when Egypt and Syria surprised Israel with a daring military attack. Ultimately, the Arab armies were pushed back, but it became clear to Israel that occupying land and military superiority did not ensure security from attack. As Israeli nationalism and pride were going strong, so were Arab resentment and hostility. Palestinians who now lived under Israeli rule were dealing with retaliatory repression and discrimination. Tired of their treatment under Israeli rule, in 1987 the first Intifada broke out (Nasrallah 2013, p. 56). It was characterized by mass protests and often violent riots, and it was a sign that relations between the two groups were still contentious.

In the early 1990s, international efforts to settle the conflict had begun, in the light of the success of the Egyptian–Israeli peace treaty of 1982 and due to the ongoing conflict with no end in sight. Eventually, the Israeli–Palestinian peace process led to the Oslo Accords of 1993 (Bickerton & Carla 2010, p. 101). The Oslo Accord allowed the Palestinian Liberation Organization to relocate from Tunisia and take ground in the West Bank and Gaza strip; thereby establishing the Palestinian National Authority. The peace process also faced great opposition among radical Islamic elements of Palestinian society, such as Hamas, who immediately initiated a campaign of attacks targeting Israelis. From Israel, the peace process was also heavily criticized resulting in the assassination of Israeli Prime Minister Yitzhak Rabin. Rabin was assassinated by an Israeli fanatic who disagreed with the peace accords. This struck a serious blow to the peace process, resulting in the withdrawal of the newly elected government of Israel in 1996 (Ortiz 2015, p. 7).

The second Intifada occurred again in the year 2000 as a result of the failed Oslo peace process. The Israeli army once again faced off against unarmed civilians enraged by the occupation of their land and second-class treatment. Many on both sides saw this second breakout as the official abandonment of a peaceful resolution. With every attempt by the Palestinians to seek retribution, Israeli forces increased the security and hostility toward those living in their declared state (Rodriguez 2020, p. 17). This was marked by violence, which lasted until 2005, causing 130 fatalities and Israel disengaging from Gaza. In the same year, 2005, Israel removed every soldier and every Jewish settler from Gaza. Israel and its Supreme Court formally declared an end to the occupation, affirming that it had no effective control of what happened in Gaza (Josh, 2009). In 2006, Hamas took power by winning a plurality of 44 percent in a Palestinian parliamentary election. Israel demanded that Hamas agreed to accept previous agreements between Israel and Palestine, forswear violence and most importantly recognize the right of Israel to exist. This led to renewed violence, with Hamas taking full control of Gaza and Israel imposing a naval blockade on the Gaza strip, and a ground blockade of the Egyptian border with cooperation from Egypt (Ortiz 2015, p. 7). In addition, tensions between Israel and Hamas, who gained financial and political support from Iran, escalated until late 2008, when Israel launched several strong military operations. By February 2009, a cease-fire was signed with international mediation between the parties, though small and sporadic eruptions of violence continued.

RECENT DEVELOPMENTS

The current state of Israel and the Palestinian territories is very devastating. Sustained clashes between Israelis and Palestinians have persisted, with the most significant surge of violence taking place between October 2015 and mid-2016 and then again in July–August 2017 (Israeli Ministry of Foreign Affairs, 2017). Israel has constantly blamed Hamas for orchestrating the event even though its allegation was firmly denied by the Palestinian Islamist militant group. Protests and demonstrations became the hallmark of the region. In addition to protests and demonstrations, most of the violence from the Palestinian side consisted of stabbings and vehicular attacks against Israeli passersby and security forces. It has been observed that between January 2015 and December 2017, Palestinians killed sixty-two Israeli citizens and soldiers in the West Bank and Israel, and injured 427 Israeli civilians and security officers in the West Bank and Israel. During that same period, Israeli security forces killed 269 Palestinians and injured 22,688 Palestinians in the West Bank and Israel, including bystanders, protesters, and suspected assailants (The War Report 2017, p. 2).

On December 6, 2017, President Donald Trump's recognition of Jerusalem as the capital of Israel provoked the global condemnation of that policy statement. The long-term impact of that decision and any legal and diplomatic consequences are not yet clear. But its most immediate impact is well known. To be sure, Palestinian president Abbas responded to President Trump's announcement by stating that Palestine no longer recognized the United States as a mediator in the peace negotiations. Hamas quickly responded with rocket attacks against Israeli towns close to the Gaza border, following a declaration of a "day of rage" by Palestinian factions in protest of President Trump's announcement. The Israeli military responded by launching airstrikes on Gaza and killing at least two Palestinians (The War Report, 2017). To this end, the international community condemned President Trump's pronouncement. The UN General Assembly in particular passed a resolution by an overwhelming majority declaring that the status of Jerusalem can only be resolved through negotiations in line with relevant UN resolutions. Thus, Trump's totalitarian tendencies, along with his unyielding support for Israel regardless of their actions, have disqualified the United States from continuing to play a role in peace negotiations. Of course, there was no viable solution to the conflict up till the time Trump handed over power to Joe Biden (the current US president in 2023).

GLOBAL OUTLOOK AND PARTIES TO THE CONFLICT

The Palestinian–Israeli conflict has already taken a global outlook, judging from the interference and the interest of several powerful states of the world that directly or indirectly shapes the perception and reactions of their allies toward the conflict. The position of many of these states and groups is also not devoid of both national and religious interests. The parties to the conflict are numerous. Both Israel and Palestine are the principal parties to the conflict. However, the position of the powerful western states in the conflict cannot be underestimated. Fatah in the West Bank and Hamas (the two key political factions in Palestine) are also parties to the conflict. For clarity, the position of Britain, the United States, Hamas, and Fatah are examined below:

1. Great Britain

The genesis of international support for Zionism and the Jews‘ national liberation movement can be traced back to Great Britain's Balfour Declaration of November 2, 1917. Thus the British government declared its commitment to the establishment of a "Jewish National Home", in Palestine, which constitutes the root cause of the Palestinian Question. Britain's commitment had proved to be a continuous history of protest, disturbances, and rebellion, as the Palestinian Arabs made clear their fears and objectives for its implementation and their demand for national self-determination (Fildis & Nisanci 2019, p. 17). With the Balfour declaration in 1917, and ending with the recognition of the state of Israel in 1948, virtually all the steps undertaken by Britain were contrary to the international legal order it had helped create. Palestinian Arabs suffered the consequences of British actions, which culminated in the creation of a new state (Terry, 2017).

Quite obviously, the Balfour declaration made the goal of establishing a national home for the Jewish people in Palestine an article of international law. The increasing levels of Jewish immigration to Palestine triggered violent Arab riots from 1920–1921. But the influx of Jewish immigrants gradually emboldened Zionist leaders, who began organizing their militia, the Haganah, to protect their interests and lay the foundations for a sovereign state. The conflict between Jews and indigenous Arabs erupted again in the Arab riots of 1936–1939 over rising Jewish immigration and this time the British helped smother the more widespread Arab resistance and then actively disarmed the indigenous population (Abrams 2008, p. 11). The Palestinian notables felt that the brutal suppression of the 1936 revolt exposed Britain's real agenda. Even without this brutality, the nationalist notables felt betrayed by Britain, which had constantly violated its promises to the Palestinians since 1916. Great Britain's competing promises to Arab leaders and Zionists for sovereignty over Palestine laid the earliest foundation for today's Israeli–Palestinian conflict.

2. The United States of America

While it is very glaring that British support for Zionism was most responsible for the early victories of Zionism over Arab rights in Palestine, the United States can be regarded as the primary sponsor of Zionism and Israel during the Cold War. The fact that the United States was the first nation to recognize Israel was a testament to the Pro-Zionist character of U.S. foreign policy.

The United States has proven over the years to be an unrepentant ally of Israel and this put them in a rather strategic position in the conflict. The United States supports the State of Israel with significant amounts of financial assistance as well as diplomatic aid. The love cost between the United States and Israel can be traced to the days of the Cold War when the United States at all costs wanted to displace the Soviet Union from its global strategic position. The United States enhanced its relationship with Israel and used Israel to eliminate the growing influence of the Soviet Union in the Middle East. Taken as a whole, the U.S.–Israeli special relationship has contributed both to the creation and the perpetuation of the Israeli–Palestinian conflict. The U.S. foreign policy has consistently endorsed Zionism and contributed substantively to the ongoing denial of the Palestinian Arab right to self-determination. The fulfillment of the Zionist vision for a Jewish state in Palestine has entailed significant, long-standing costs for Palestinians. On the other hand, Israel has become one of the most prosperous and powerful nations in the world. Actions by successive U.S. administrations have enabled Israel to grow in military and economic strength. That strength has allowed Israel to justifiably defend itself against invasion and terrorism but has also allowed Israel to conduct offensive wars and expand its territorial control through both annexation and military occupation with little or no U.S. resistance (Abrams 2008, p. 44).

In recent times, the U.S. interest in the state of Israel has not waned and this can be seen in President Trump's decision on December 6, 2017, to recognize Jerusalem as the capital of Israel. Under the Trump administration, U.S. policy shifted in a direction that more explicitly favored Israel over the Palestinians. Actions of note included suspending U.S funding for the Palestinians, recognizing Jerusalem as Israel‘s capital and opening an embassy there, and adopting measures to treat Israel; settlements in the West Bank more like areas in Israel proper (Congressional Research Service, 2021). Although the Biden administration officials have stated their intention to improve U.S.–Palestinian ties, and probably plan to resume humanitarian, security, and economic development aid for Palestinians, the status of Jerusalem as the capital city of Israel is yet to be resolved.</indent.

3. Hamas

Hamas is one of the parties to the conflict between the Israelis and the Palestinians. Hamas (an Arabic acronym for "Islamic Resistant Movement") is the U.S.-designated terrorist organization and Fatah's main rival for leadership of the Palestinian national movement. The group grew out of the Muslim Brotherhood, a religious and political organization founded in Egypt in 1928 with affiliates and sympathizers throughout the Arab world (Congressional Research Service, 2021). Hamas ideology combines Palestinian nationalism with Islamic fundamentalism. Hamas' emergence as a major political and military group can be traced to the first Palestinian *intifada* (or uprising) that began in the Gaza strip in 1987 in resistance to what Hamas terms the Israeli occupation of Palestinian-populated lands.

As a violent Islamic extremist group, it has conspicuously established its goals as taking over the land presently occupied by Israel. The group presented an alternative to Yasser Arafat and his secular Fatah movement by using violence against Israeli civilians and military targets just as Arafat began negotiations with Israel. Hamas took a leading role in attacks against Israelis; including bombing target civilians during the second intifada, between 2000 and 2005. Shortly after Arafat died in 2004, the group decided to directly involve itself in politics. In 2006, a year after the election of Fatah's Mahmoud Abbas as Palestinian Authority President, and just a few months after Israel's military withdrawal from the Gaza strip, Hamas defeated Fatah in Palestinian legislative council elections (Congressional Research Service 2021, p. 29). The conflict of interests that ensued between Hamas and other protestant groups in the country, such as the Palestinian Legislative Council and the Palestinian Liberation Organization, threw a big challenge at Hamas and eventually escalated into violent conflicts between the PLO and Hamas. It is very important to note that Hamas receives support from many sources, including some states. Along with some other non-PLO factions, Hamas has historically received much of its political and material support (including funding, weapons, and training) from Iran. Hamas became distant from Iran when it broke with Syria's government in the early years of the country's civil war. However, the Hamas–Iran relationship reportedly revived financially around 2017 (Eldar 2017). Indeed, the extremely violent activities of Hamas have earned it a reputation as a terrorist organization in the United States of America, the European Union as well as the United Kingdom.

4. Fatah

The Palestinian Liberation Organization (PLO) is recognized by the United Nations (including Israel since 1993) as the sole legitimate representative of the Palestinian people, wherever they may reside. Founded in 1964, and since 1969, has been dominated by the secular nationalist Fatah movement. Fatah, the secular nationalist movement formerly led by Yasser Arafat has been the largest and most prominent faction in the PLO for decades. Since the establishment of the PA and limited self-rule in the West Bank and Gaza in 1994, Fatah has dominated the PA, except during the period of partial Hamas rule in 2006–2007. Fatah's 1960 charter continues to include clauses calling for the destruction of the Zionist state and its economic, political, military, and cultural support. Both PLO and PA are largely under the control of Fatah, which has dominated the political landscape of the Palestinians for years. The involvement of these groups operating in Gaza and the West Bank has prolonged the conflict with grave humanitarian catastrophe and huge material destruction.

CONSEQUENCES OF ISRAELI–PALESTINIAN CONFLICT

The protracted Israeli–Palestinian conflict has resulted in several consequences. One main obvious consequence was the destruction and loss of life. Not only was there the loss of life from soldiers on both sides, but also innocents were murdered. Also, the conflict led to a growing number of Palestinian refugees. Regardless of the exact number, the truth remains that there was a significant number of Palestinians who were left homeless as a result of the prolonged conflict. It is the solution to this problem that caused further disputes between Arabs and Jews. The Jewish argument was that Palestinians should be integrated into the Arab states, whereas the Arabs argued that refugees should be able to return to their rightful homes (Schulze 1999, p. 16).

Similarly, the conflict led to territory changes. For Israel this was arguably positive, having increased its territory by 21 percent in comparison to the partition resolution boundaries. However, this partition remains controversial among Palestinians, because they have undergone extraordinary change since 1948 in which the Palestinians have been transformed into a "mobile people" (Freedman 1979, p. 218).

More importantly, the protracted conflict between Israel and Palestine has since put the world in extreme danger as the conflict has transformed into international terrorism against the initial struggle over territorial claims. Although terrorism had been existing before the six-day War of 1967, it, however, became rooted in the Israeli–Palestinian conflict. Beyond the major actors in the conflict, the war between Israel and Palestine has attracted hundreds of thousands of volunteers who are Islamic radicals on a Jihad mission globally to fight for the Islamic State of Palestine. This newly inspired terrorism did not only face the state of Israel as the major culprit but also seek its major allies as the United States and European Countries as its major target. The precariousness of the forms of terror and the target of terror was experienced when the world's avowed most powerful country, taken by rude shock was attacked by an Islamic fundamentalist and extremist group, popularly known as Al-Qaed on September 11, 2001. The 9/11 attack has since been followed by several massive onslaughts on the citizens of the United States, the United Kingdom, and France among others (Israel Ministry of Foreign Affairs, 2017). These myriads of attacks have not only shaped global security but desperate security measures are being put in place by most countries of the world to immune them against possible terrorist attacks. Therefore, the conflict between Israel and Palestine is not far from the cause of terrorism that the international community currently contend with.

PEACEBUILDING EFFORTS IN RESOLVING THE ISRAELI–PALESTINIAN CONFLICT

The Israeli–Palestinian conflict is a great concern to the international community. Many countries, especially the United States, have attempted to resolve the conflict and bring peace to the region. In September 1978, during a conference at Camp David organized by American president Jimmy Carter, Israel prime minister Menachem Begin, and Egyptian president Anwar Sadat signed a peace agreement between the two countries, which led to an Israeli withdrawal from Sinai (Carter, 2009). Even though Israel and Egypt had begun negotiations, conflicts within Israel were escalating.

However, some strategic and micro-political considerations are traceable, in particular, to the end of the Cold War and the aftermath of the Gulf War; which eventually brought the two sides to the negotiating table at the Madrid Conference in 1991 and the subsequent talks in Washington, D.C (Kelman, 1997). A series of talks between the Israeli government, individual Arab states, and the PLO was initiated. These talks, however, never developed momentum. However, some Israeli and Palestinian leaders sought a less public and politically charged environment and entered into secret discussions in Norway. The result was the signing of the Oslo Accords by Israeli leader Yitzhak Rabin and PLO leader Yasser Arafat in 1993. According to the Oslo Agreement, Israel would withdraw forces from Gaza and the West Bank town of Jericho and grant greater autonomy to the Palestinians. Eventually, Palestinians would be able to elect a self-Government Authority in these areas. In return, the PLO agreed to recognize the state of Israel, a step that Israelis felt was vital to their security.

In 1994, a Palestinian Authority was established under Arafat, and Jordan joined Egypt in recognizing the state of Israel. Critics of the Oslo Accords charged that the agreement did not address many of the serious issues that still divided the two peoples. Unfortunately, these issues were never resolved, and both sides failed to honor parts of the agreement. Israel increased its settlements in Palestinian lands, and Palestinians responded by increasing attacks on settlers. Extremism on both sides led to a further escalation of the conflict.

There are many peace initiatives put in place after the Oslo Accords, although none has maintained momentum. For instance, the Geneva Accord (2003), sponsored by the Geneva initiative was a Track II (unofficial) initiative drafted by high-level Israelis and Palestinians with experience in government. Like Oslo Accords, the Geneva Initiative aimed at two-state solutions. Unlike Oslo, the Geneva Initiative sought to address the permanent status issues like borders, Jerusalem, refugees, and settlements that had evaded Oslo negotiators (Hallward 2011, p. 192).

In June 2002, the European Union published the Seville Declaration, which insisted that negotiation is the only means to resolve the conflict. According to the EU:

> The objective is an end to the (Israeli military) occupation and the early establishment of a democratic, viable, peaceful and sovereign state of Palestine based on the 1967 borders, if necessary with minor adjustments agreed upon by the parties. The result should be two states living side by side within secure and recognized borders enjoying normal relations with their neighbors (Council of the European Union 2002).

The EU being a member of the Quartet on the Middle East, continue to stand firm, along with the United States, Russia, and the UN, in support of a two-state solution to the Israeli–Palestinian conflict. Unfortunately, EU efforts to promote democratic reform of the PA have fallen apart since the election of the Hamas–led government in January 2006. In a sign of diplomatic convergence, both the United States and the EU have labeled Hamas a terrorist organization and frozen direct budget support for the PA through economic sanctions. Instead of funding the PA, a temporary international channel has been created to provide direct humanitarian assistance to the Palestinian people. In addition, the provisional Fatah government in the West Bank receives some direct funds. However, the Quartet continues to call for a new Palestinian government capable of meeting and implementing the three principles of non-violence, recognition of Israel's right to exist, and acceptance of existing agreements and obligations (Abrams 2008, p. 63).

In recent decades, the United States has been a key facilitator of efforts to resolve the Israeli–Palestinian conflict. The basic U.S. formula for resolving the Israeli–Palestinian conflict has been well established as a two-state solution since the Clinton administration. The last peace proposal dates back to 2010, following the election of U.S. president Barack Obama. In November 2009, President Obama persuaded Prime Minister Netanyahu to agree to a ten-month partial freeze on settlement construction in the West Bank. President Abbas said this plan did not cover East Jerusalem and wanted a guarantee of a Palestinian state based on 1967 lines. Unfortunately, U.S. negotiators subsequently failed to persuade Prime Minister Netanyahu's coalition government to renew the moratorium, or to convince President Abbas to resume negotiations without an end to all settlement activities on occupied territory (Corlaten 2018, p. 8). However, the election of Donald J. Trump has dramatically shifted U.S. policy toward the conflict, which has ultimately made the situation worse. Trump's aggressive support of Israel has stifled peace negotiations and has made the prospect of a peaceful resolution impossible (Rodriguez, 2020). However, the new president of the United States (Joe Biden) has promised to "reverse the Trump administration's destructive cutoff of diplomatic ties with the Palestinian Authority and cancellation of assistance programs that support Israeli–Palestinian security cooperation, economic development, and humanitarian aid for the Palestinian people in the West Bank and Gaza" (Rodriguez 2020, p. 31). Developments, since Joe Biden assumed office in 2021, have not changed the pattern of the Israeli–Palestinian conflict. Gaza became a focal point of the Israeli–Palestinian conflict, leading to Israeli attacks on the area, and Palestinian attacks on Israeli citizens. Thus, the Israeli-Palestinian conflict seems increasingly intractable.

GLOBAL SETTLEMENT FRAMEWORK IN RESOLVING THE CONFLICT

The intense animosity between Israel and Palestine requires a global settlement framework that will bring a lasting solution to the protracted conflict. The international community must support all UN agendas in resolving the Israeli–Palestinian conflict. In the first instance, a comprehensive peace, consistent with the United Nations Charter that will fulfill U.N. Security Council resolutions 242 and 338 is very crucial in resolving the Israeli–Palestinian conflict. Thus, the two-state solution is consistent with UNSC resolutions 242 and 338 as well as the roadmap for peace designed by the Quartet on the Middle East. This framework is of the view that the state of Israel and Palestine will live side by side in peace and security. To the extent that Israel will recognize Palestine as the national home of the Palestinian people and all its citizens, and Palestine will recognize Israel as the national home of the Jewish people and all its citizens. However, the Quartet could ease the burden on Israel by helping to finance such compensation. On the other hand, final status negotiations, which need to include Palestinian leaders from Hamas, Fatah, and possibly other factions, would have to resolve the remaining disputes regarding official borders, the dismantling of Israeli settlements, access to water resources, security arrangements, and sovereignty over Jerusalem (Abrams 2008, p. 97). The parties will agree to the full and orderly implementation of the terms of the agreement, per agreed means, methods, sequencing, timelines, and provision.

In finding a lasting solution to Israeli–Palestinian conflict the international community must realize that the issue at stake is not based only on claims over territory. While territorial claims remain true in academic and policy terms, there is a problem with approaching this issue on territorial considerations alone. Thus, religion as an issue in Israeli–Palestinian conflict is very crucial. Religion plays a key role both in the development of war rationale and in the structural makeup of Israeli and Palestinian's social and political infrastructure. At the core of this conflict, legal claims over territory are tightly intertwined with religious history. In this regard, any peace plan that tries to bridge these territorial claims, with a two-state solution, must take into account the religious component. To adopt a secularized, western conception of a peaceful solution would risk overlooking the important connections that exist between religion and both parties' claims over territory (Suazo 2021, p. 4). In addition, Jerusalem has to be declared an international city accessible to Jews, Christians, and Muslims because of the significance of the city to three monotheistic religions. This is why Joe Biden of the United States must reverse Donald Trump's decision of declaring Jerusalem as the capital city of Israel.

In line with the priority given to the status of refugees by the UN, and given the suffering experienced by Palestinian refugees, such refugees will have the right to return to the State of Palestine. This must be consistent with the absorptive capacity and laws of the state. Those refugees who choose not to exercise their right to return to the State of Palestine or who are prevented from returning by the state of Palestine will be assisted in resettling in their countries of current residence or in other countries willing to receive them while respecting the sovereign rights of those states. The state of Israel will offer a program of family reunification, including citizenship, for a limited number of refugees. An international fund must be established to help defray compensation and resettlement of Palestinian refugees and Jewish refugees from Arab countries.

Furthermore, there is a need for a global security strategic framework between the two parties. This agreement will base Israeli–Palestinian security relations on mutual trust and the advancement of joint interests and cooperation. The agreement will stipulate that each state will refrain from the threat or use of force or weapons (conventional and non-conventional) against each other, or from other actions or activities that adversely affect the security of the citizens, residents, and territorial integrity or political independence of the other. In the same vein, the security of Israeli borders must be guaranteed by the big powers in the Security Council of the United Nations or through a joint defense pact with the North Atlantic Treaty Organization (NATO) and if that is going to be cumbersome the United States should openly guarantee the security of Israel. Whatever the geography of the Palestinian state turns out to be, it must be free and seen to be free from Israel and incredibly from the kind of current Egyptian blockade. Palestine must also recognize Israel without any qualification (Osuntokun 2021, p. 21). However, the two states must refrain from organizing, instigating, inciting, assisting, or participating in any acts of threats or aggression against each other. Also, members of the Quartet must be prepared to deal with extremists on both sides who will reject any compromise agreement. Therefore, ending this conflict should be a major national security priority for the United States and other Western countries.

More importantly, peace in the Middle East would have to be accompanied by generous financial assistance from the European Union whose members were vicariously responsible for the Israeli–Palestinian problem. The countries in the Middle East swimming in an ocean of oil must be pressured to make huge donations towards the development of the new Palestinian State rather than funding the development of rockets in Gaza. The important thing is that the Palestinians must be made so comfortable that extremist parties like Hamas and Islamic Jihad committed to the destruction of Israel would not be as attractive to frustrated and bedraggled people as they are currently attracted to them (Osuntokun 2021, p. 21). In addition, the United States and the European Union should provide extensive diplomatic and financial support to the fledgling Palestinian state to ensure its survival, institutional development, and economic progress. Now, the U.S. foreign policy of virtually unconditional support for Israel must come to an end. A more balanced foreign policy approach is required, one which respects equally the political and human rights of Israelis and Palestinians and makes U.S. support contingent on Israel‘s compliance with U.S. policy preferences (Abrams 2008, p. 105).

Lastly, the prospect for regional harmony and stability in the Middle East; especially in resolving the protracted Israeli–Palestinian conflict depends largely on the leadership role of the United States. The United States should play a leadership role in strongly espousing proposals that include the essential components of pertinent United Nations resolutions, the Roadmap of the International Quartet, the Oslo Agreement, the peace offer of the Arab nations endorsed by other Muslim states, the Camp David Accords, and the Geneva Accord (Carter 2009, p. 179). Even more pertinent is the fact that the United States and Israel should have stable and friendly diplomatic and trade relations with the antagonistic factions in Palestine and with Lebanon, Syria, and all other Arab nations. To achieve this global settlement framework, positive leadership from the international community, the Israelis, and the Palestinians are crucial. In the same vein, the international community should establish an international mechanism to monitor and implement the underlying framework.

CONCLUSION

The Israeli–Palestinian conflict that began in the mid-twentieth century can be regarded as the most lengthened conflict in human history. The complexities of the conflict have resulted in serious acrimonious, hateful, and belligerent aspirations among the two sides. Some of the several factors that constitute the complexity of the conflict include but are not limited to religious differences, strong historical antecedents as well as concrete entitlements by the two belligerents to statehood. This seemingly unending conflict which has defiled solutions seems to attract different interests from different quarters ranging from states' interests to religious interests majorly between the Muslim and Christian divide. The numerous strategies aimed at promoting peace in the area have yielded little or no success as the belligerents currently hold on to several positions which are not limited to bilateral recognition of sovereignty and statehood, the definition of borders, pattern and design of security agreement, right to water, ownership of Jerusalem and freedom of movement, mostly for the Palestinians. The perspective of this paper is that ending the Israeli–Palestinian conflict requires the cooperation of the international community. With cooperation between Israel and Palestine and the commitment of the United States, European Union, and Arabs states, the framework suggested in this paper will bring lasting peace to the Middle East. An International Peace Conference should be held where all stakeholders, academics, policymakers, and peace practitioners will suggest various measures to end the prolonged Israeli–Palestinian conflict. In addition, the global peaceful settlement framework should be signed by all member states of the United Nations Organization. A well-established international mechanism to monitor and facilitate the implementation of the proposed framework should be a priority of the international community. In conclusion, the Arabs and the

Israelis will have to bury their old hatchet and work toward the achievement of bringing a lasting solution to the Middle East crisis.

REFERENCES

Abrams, W.A. (2008). Israel and the Palestinians in U.S. foreign policy: Past, present, future. Unpublished Masters of Arts Thesis. The University of Georgia.

Bell, P.M.H. (2001). *The world since 1945: An international history*. London: Bloomsbury Publishing Plc.

Bickerton, I.I. & Carla, L.K. (2010). *A history of the Arab-Israeli conflict*. Boston: Prentice Hall.

Carter, J. (2009). *We can have peace in the holy land: A plan that will work*. New York: Simon & Schuster.

Central Intelligence Agency (2017).

Chao, K. (2011). *Isratin: The one-state solution to the Israeli–Palestinian* conflict.

Congressional Research Service (2021). *Israel: New prime minister and U.S. relations in brief. https://crsreports.congress.gov.*

Corlaten. T. (2018). The Israeli–Palestinian peace process: The role of the Council of Europe. Doc. 14484 Report. Parliamentary Assembly.

Council of the European Union (2002). "Presidency conclusion." Online at: http://www.consilium.europa.eu/ueDocs/cms.

Dowty, A. (2008). *Israel/Palestine*. Cambridge: Polity Press.

Elder, S. (2017). Hamas turns to Iran. *Al-Monitor*, July 6.

Fildis, A.T. & Nisanci, E. (2019). "British colonial policy divide and rule": Fanning Arab rivalry in Palestine. *UMRAN International Journal of Islamic and Civilization Studies*, 6(1), 15–30.

Freedman, R.O. (ed) (1979). *World politics and the Arab-Israeli conflict*. Oxford: Pergamon Press Inc.

Hallward, M. (2011). Pursuing "peace in Israeli/Palestine. *Journal of Third World Studies*, 28 (1), 185–202.

Ismail, R. & Fraser, P.M. (2020). "Palestine." *Britannia*, Encyclopedia Britannica.

Israel Ministry of Foreign Affairs (2017).

Kelman, H.C. (1999). The interdependence of Israeli and Palestinian national identities: The role of the other in existential conflict. *Journal of Social Issues*, 55(3), 581–600.

Levs, J. (2009). "Is Gaza occupied territory?" CNN.

Morris, B. (2009). *One state, two states: Resolving the Israeli–Palestinian conflict*. Yale: Yale University Press.

Nasrallah, N. (2013). The first and second Palestinian intifadas. In D. Newman & J. Peters (eds.) *Routledge handbook on the Israeli–Palestinian conflict*. London: Routledge.

Ortiz, A.M. (2015). The Israeli–Palestinian conflict: An analysis of Palestine's bid for statehood. *CEI International Affairs*, 7 (11), 1–31.

Osuntokun, J. (2021). Israeli–Palestinian conflict. *The Nation Newspaper*. Lagos: Nigeria.
Rodriguez, M. (2020). *The Israeli–Palestinian conflict in the Trump era: A human rights perspective*. Trinity College Digital Repository.
Schulze, K.E. (1999). *The Arab-Israeli conflict*. Harlow: Pearson Education Ltd.
Suazo, A.E. (2015). Explore related peacebuilding organizations *Peace Insight*. Retrieved online 7 September 2021.
Terry, P.C.R. (2017). Britain in Palestine (1917–1948): Occupation, the Palestine mandate, and international law. *University of Bologna Law Review*, 2(2), 187–251.
The War Report (2017). *The armed conflict in Israel–Palestine.* Geneva Academy.
United States Institute of Peace. "Simulation on the Israeli–Palestinian conflict." www.uisp.org.
Wistrich, R.S. (1997). Israel and the holocaust trauma. *Jewish History*, 11(2), 13–20.

III

Taiwan's Nationalism and Sovereignty

8

Kurdayeti and Taiwan Rentong

Identity and Nation Building in Under-Recognized States

Dean Karalekas

INTRODUCTION

The question of why some countries hold together over time while others break apart, often along ethnic and religious rifts, has long consumed scholars and policymakers. Identifying the factors that led to the success of a particular nation-building project—especially if those factors are replicated under otherwise very different circumstances elsewhere in the world—would be an invaluable tool in fostering peace and stability in an all-too-unstable international environment.

The phrase "nation-building" is often used synonymously with other terms, such as "state building," "democratization," and "modernization." Though these concepts are indeed intimately related, there are important distinctions between them (Stephenson 2005). US policymakers, for example, use the term "nation building" to refer to efforts to achieve democratization in a polity overseas, often through the use of the armed forces, and usually in the aftermath of war (Dobbins 2003). However, this perspective conflates the term "nation" with "state," and would be more accurately described as "state building." A state, as famously defined by Max Weber (1946), is "a human community that (successfully) claims the monopoly of the legitimate use of physical force within a given territory." What then is a nation, if not a state?

Stephenson (2005) cites a longstanding definition of a nation as a group or race of people with shared history, traditions, and culture, and often with a common religion and language. The United Kingdom, a state, can be seen as comprising four nations: the English, Irish, Scottish, and Welsh. The project of nation-building, therefore, is not the incorporation of a polity into a distinct nation-state, but rather the social construction of the aforementioned history, traditions, and culture to create a common identity and hence loyalty to a set of political ideas and institutions designed to reflect the culture's values.

It is these components, and how they impact the question of identity, that this chapter will examine in this case study of two historically recent examples of nation-building: the Republic of China (ROC) on Taiwan and the Kurdistan Region of Iraq (Rokkan 1971; Stephenson 2005).

Geopolitically, there might at first glance seem to be little similarity between Taiwan and Kurdistan. Taiwan is an island whose main security threat is invasion by an expansionist communist superpower, whereas Iraqi Kurdistan is a landlocked area threatened by Islamic insurgents and regional powers of roughly equal military balance. They are situated on different continents, have different languages and cultural influences, and have a minimum of contact between them. On closer inspection, however, the two do share certain remarkable similarities: They both represent nationhood projects predicated on an ethnic identity that is distinct from the one in which they risk being subsumed; they both employ the concept of "imagined community" to establish unity among their members; and they both, unlike the powers that surround them in their respective regions, demonstrate a propensity to cherish Western values such as democracy and political freedom. To what degree these similarities are linked is a topic worthy of study.

ETHNIC IDENTITY

In both countries under discussion, participation in politics is largely influenced by ethnic identity. In East Asia, as in the Levant, nations are roughly divided according to ethnicity, tribe, or some similar expression of the concept of *Jus Sanguinus*, or right of blood. This is contrary to the practice in the United States, Canada, and other nations of the new world, where nationalism is expressed more as a set of common values, and the population is made up of a host of different ethnicities, the descendants of settlers and immigrants. Likewise, the nations of Europe, in their inception, were largely based not on ethnocentrism but on religious affiliation. The 1555 Peace of Augsburg, as well as the 1648 Peace of Westphalia, both institutionalized and legitimated the territorialization of religion as a means of promoting the cultural homogeneity of political units (and the cultural heterogeneity between them). This has important implications for nation-building and ethnic identity: An Australian cannot become a Korean, for example, while a Korean can, with little difficulty, become an Australian (Shipper 2010, 13; Brubaker 2012, 10).

Kurdish Identity

While many Kurds like to trace their heritage back millennia, the modern Kurdish identity, or Kurdayeti, is heavily influenced by the nation-building that took place following the fall of the Persian and Ottoman empires and the division of the region into nation-states roughly delineated along ethnic lines. It is important here that we distinguish Iraqi Kurdistan from the other unrecognized polities in the region that straddle the borders separating the Kurdish people from the homeland to which they aspire. The Democratic Federation of Northern Syria (DFNS), for example, is built upon the same cultural roots but differs greatly in political expression. Rojava, part of the DFNS, eschews nationalism—even Kurdish nationalism—in favor of a Libertarian socialist model that comes too close to anarcho-communism for the comfort of some of its allies in the ongoing fight against Daesh.

While the Arabs, Persians, and Turks obtained their nations following the dissolution of the Ottoman Empire and the geopolitical gerrymandering that ensued after World War I, the Kurds did not. Today their territory is divided by the borders separating Iran, Iraq, Turkey, and Syria. Natali (2005: xvii) describes how Kurdayeti became ethnicized, and how this is important, "given the repertoire of an ethnic group's identities, politics affects how national identity becomes institutionalized and the various forms nationalism may assume." This quote could just as easily be used to describe the Taiwanese identity or *Taiwan Rentong*, and the way it is expressed politically.

In Kurdistan, the political shift from an empire to a modern nation-state opened the door to a new kind of political space that had a distinct impact on Kurdish identity. For one thing, identity no longer had to be predicated on religion but could find expression in conceptions of ethnicity. This is not to say that the Kurds did not have such a conception of themselves prior to the end of the imperial era: rather, the ruling elite of the Ottoman and Persian empires conceived of their minority populations strictly in terms of religious affiliation (Natali, 2005).

Taiwanese Identity

In Taiwan, the concept of Taiwanese ethnic identity as separate from Chinese began to emerge during the Japanese Colonial Period (1895–1945) and only grew after the island was taken over by the Republic of China in 1949. Different languages and, after a half-century of separation, different customs, practices, and belief systems between the two populations only served to highlight the distinctiveness of the Taiwanese identity, despite heavy-handed government efforts to stamp it out through draconian Sinicization campaigns. During the White Terror period, the political expression of this distinct identity was met with harsh reprisals, but under the surface, society continued to become more ethnicized.

The end of the Martial Law era imposed under the regime of Chiang Kai-shek unleashed the population and freed them to openly embrace their Taiwanese identity, and further democratization allowed for the opening of a new channel through which to express and explore that identity in the political realm. Under the Kuomintang (KMT) regime (and indeed: in the eyes of the Chinese Communist Party, which seeks to rule over Taiwan), the Taiwanese ethnicity did not exist *per se*, because they considered the Taiwanese people to be a mere sub-group of Han Chinese ethnicity, indistinguishable from their counterparts on the mainland: all fellow descendants of the Yan and Yellow Emperors. Under Zhongnanhai today, as under the Ottoman and Persian empires, ethnicity is a tool of psychological and sociological control.

GEOPOLITICAL HISTORY

Thus, the Taiwanese, like the Kurds, are acutely aware that they are not just outsiders, but outsiders under constant threat of being subsumed by the tyranny of a regional majority. Kurdish history is replete with reminders of this dynamic, not the least of which is the Anfal Genocide, the most infamous incident of which was the gassing of Iraqi Kurds in the city of Halabja, perpetrated by Saddam Hussein's brutal Baathist regime.

Development of a Political Identity in Kurdistan

Historian Sharaf al-Din Bitlisi (1543–1599) may have been the first writer to explicitly associate the term "Kurd" with a particular land area. According to Bitlisi, Kurdish territory stretched from the Persian Gulf to southern Turkey. The geographical boundaries that such a state would entail were famously unveiled at the Versailles Peace Conference where, after the destruction wrought by the First World War, Sherif Pasha, a Kurdish general in the Ottoman Empire, made a plea for Kurdish independence in 1919 conference, where he introduced a map outlining the boundaries of the aspirant state. This was the opportune moment to push for an independent state, as the prevailing scholarly opinion at the time was that, to the degree that it is possible, all ethnic nationalities should have their states to prevent a repeat of the geopolitical conditions that led inexorably to the outbreak of hostilities in WWI. It was widely acknowledged by the thinkers of the day that the multicultural makeup of the German, Ottoman, and Austro-Hungarian empires contributed to the inevitability of war and that to avoid a repeat of this, political sovereignty should be conferred upon monocultural populations. When the Treaty of

Sèvres was signed in 1920, Article 62 of that document outlined the boundaries of the newly formed Kurdistan state as follows:

> for the predominantly Kurdish areas lying east of the Euphrates, south of the southern boundary of Armenia as it may be hereafter determined, and north of the frontier of Turkey with Syria and Mesopotamia (History Learning Site 2015).

This legislative victory was short-lived, however. Another nationalist project, this one on the part of the Turks, engulfed the land that is modern-day Turkey, partly spurred on by the loss of Turkish territory that would have been incurred through the implementation of the Treaty of Sèvres, This Turkish nationalist movement led to the 1919–1923 Turkish War of Independence, the 1922 dismantling of the Ottoman sultanate, and the 1923 establishment of the Republic of Turkey. The Treaty of Lausanne that put an end to the conflict superseded and nullified the Treaty of Sèvres, dashing all hopes for an independent Kurdistan (Novak 2006, 4; Rafaat 2012, 26).

Nevertheless, the question remains to what degree the Kurdish state has enjoyed the status of being its own political entity. Throughout much of history, Kurdistan has been politically separate from Iraq and Turkey, with a history of resisting foreign rule going back to the Abbasid Revolution and the overthrow of the Umayyad Caliphate (661–750 AD). Sharaf al-Din Bitlisi refers to the political unit as Welati Kurdistan, or the country of Kurdistan, and writes that Kurdish chiefs are mentioned in Friday khutbah, or prayers. Official documents dating from the sixteenth to the eighteenth centuries show that an administrative unit referred to as "Kurdistan" had Diyarbakir (now in modern-day Turkey) as its capital and that the Kurdish provinces of Mosul and Shehrizor were administered not by Baghdad or Istanbul, but by Diyarbakir. Despite Kurdish semi-autonomy, and being governed separately from the Arabs, much of the sovereignty of the Kurdish emirates was gradually being eroded by the central administration of the Ottoman Empire. The Ottomans for example would name replacements for Kurdish leaders—often chosen from within the same loyal clan—whenever they felt it was necessary, and though these emirates were nominally autonomous, they were generally responsive to demands from Istanbul and had conferred formal suzerainty to the Ottoman sultan. Indeed, until it was annexed to Iraq in 1926, Kurdistan enjoyed centuries of at least nominal semi-independence, reinforcing the growth and development of its own unique political culture (Özoğlu 2005, 59; van Bruinessen 1999, 6; Rafaat 2012, 26).

Development of a Political Identity in Taiwan

As an island, the boundaries of Taiwan have always been well-defined, though just how much of that island was under its control in any given period is a subject open to interpretation. An incident occurred in 1871 that not only involved the island's aboriginal residents but had international repercussions, and which illustrated the reticence of the Qing Dynasty (1644–1911) to claim effective governance over the entire island. A vessel out of Ryuku, Japan became shipwrecked near the southern point of Taiwan, after which the fifty-four crewmembers who survived the wreck were decapitated by the area's Paiwan indigenous people. The Japanese government, seeking to use the so-called Mudan Incident as a pretext to test the Qing court's level of commitment to the island, demanded compensation. The Chinese government refused, pointing out that the area where the incident occurred was outside their effective jurisdictional control. The Japanese seized upon this opportunity to send a military mission to pacify the area in 1874. The venture was deadly for the Paiwan, and the Japanese as well. The event was interpreted as a case of Japan testing the waters before possible colonization. At this point, Japan was in the throes of the rapid modernization period that accompanied the Meiji Restoration, and it was keen to follow the Western example and become a colonial power. Taiwan's geostrategic position would have facilitated Japanese access to points farther southward and westward. In view of this obvious interest on the part of the Japanese, Peking began to reevaluate Taiwan's importance to the dynasty's maritime defense. This is when the island's administration was raised from a single prefecture to two prefectures in 1875. A similar test of the Qing government's dedication to Taiwan took place a decade later, this time with a French blockade of Keelung Harbor, after which the island has finally declared a province in 1887, and some attempts were made to modernize. These modernization efforts included carrying out a land survey and launching infrastructure projects like the island's first railroad: sixty kilometers of track connecting Keelung with Hsinchu (Wang 1990, 45; Cauquelin 2004, 14; Li 1956, 120; Brown 2004, 52).

It should be noted that, despite two hundred years of nominal Qing sovereignty over the island and its late designation as a full province, by the time of the outbreak of the First Sino-Japanese War, only roughly 45 percent of Taiwan was under the effective Qing administration. The remainder, though remote, mountainous, and underpopulated, remained under the control of the aboriginal people who lived there. The island's status as a Qing province lasted less than ten years: until 1895 when it was ceded to Japan as a spoil of war. It was in that year that the short-lived Republic of Taiwan was declared, following the Qing retreat from the island and until Japanese troops took control of the Republic's capital, Tainan, on 21 October 1895. Some historians hold that the republic was established in a genuine effort to achieve sovereignty for the island, pointing to efforts by the island's gentry to have the UK government make the island a British protectorate, rather than let it fall into Japanese hands. Others claim it was an attempt to remain within China's sphere of influence, being nominally independent while giving suzerainty to the Middle Kingdom. These latter scholars point to the republic's flag, which depicted a large yellow tiger on a navy-blue background—the tiger being lower in stature than the dragon that symbolized China (Befu & Guichard-Anguis 2001, 224; Alsford 2017; Lamley 1968).

In many ways, the First Sino-Japanese War was a quest for ideological dominance in East Asia. Japan's victory in this conflict surprised many observers and vindicated the country's colonial ambitions. Japan's interest in acquiring Taiwan for its strategic and economic significance became a reality with the Treaty of Shimonoseki. The new colonial rulers exploited their new territory for the benefit of the home islands. They made Japanese the official language and embarked on a remarkably efficient modernization and industrialization campaign, building a self-sufficient economy on the island, constructing railroads, schools, and hospitals, and expanding Taiwan's larger cities (Huffman 1997, 202; Ka 1995, 58).

Taiwanese people were being assimilated into Japanese culture by the policies of the day, and there was an ever-present cognition of the distinction between the ruled and the rulers. Identifying themselves in opposition to their oppressors, the Taiwanese people could have chosen to embrace the notion of Chinese identity, but it was also well known that their predicament of being under Japanese control was a direct result of having been cast aside by China when the Qing Court handed the island over to Tokyo. This, plus the distinct cultural differences that had evolved over the centuries of their separation from China, led to a sense of *Taiwan Rentong* being forged in the fire of Japanese occupation. Even after the war, when the island fell into the hands of the ROC, the people of Taiwan continued to see themselves as ethnically distinct from the wave of Chinese refugees who, fleeing the communists four years later, moved to Taiwan *en masse* and established the ROC capital in Taipei.

IMAGINED COMMUNITIES

The road to nationhood in Iraq and Kurdistan represented a source of conflict between these two projects. The Kurds saw themselves as a nation with the inherent right to build a *bona fide* nation-state in their ancestral homeland, with several principles underpinning Kurdayeti and its nation-building effort—an effort that stood in opposition to the similar project being undertaken in Iraq.

Likewise, the nationhood project in Taiwan stands in stark opposition to that undertaken in China, and in the People's Republic of China (PRC), which culminated in the burning of temples and the purging of any remnants of traditional Chinese society to be replaced with Mao Zedong Thought.

Central to understanding the Kurdish and Taiwanese nationhood projects is the concept of imagined communities. The groundbreaking work of Benedict Anderson (2006) offered a new paradigm on nationalism as a way that a population imagines—and in imagining, creates—a community, regardless of the preexisting historical or cultural factors mitigating against such a union. The nation, Anderson writes, "is imagined as a community, because, regardless of the actual inequality and exploitation that may prevail in each, the nation is always conceived as a deep, horizontal comradeship." In other words, even though a member of a community may never meet or even hear of most of the other members of his nationality, they nevertheless share an identity by virtue of their common membership (Anderson 2006, 6).

Imagined Community: Kurdistan

In terms of nation-building, the imagined community of Kurdistan is unique and separate from that of Iraq. As an ethnic group, the Kurds are believed to have tribal and social roots that go back more than two thousand years. This pre-Islamic heritage has been revived and leveraged to support the modern nation of Kurdistan as it seeks to differentiate itself from the Iraqi state. The Kurdistan flag, for example, places the Mithraic sun at its center, whose twenty-one points represent rebirth in Yazdanism, or the Cult of Angels: considered the original religion of the Kurdish people. Other aspects of modern Kurdish culture focus on liberation from tyranny, such as the New Year celebration of Newroz, which recalls the myth of the people's liberation from a despotic Assyrian king, Zuhak. Mythological as well as historical stories of struggle and glory dating to the pre-Islamic civilization of the Kurds contribute to the imagined community shared by all Kurds, and their culture that is separate from that of Iraq (Sana *et al.* 2010).

Imagined Community: Taiwan

The case of Taiwan is similar to that of Kurdistan in that it likewise has its own national symbols and celebrations that serve to distinguish it from the PRC, but many of these are yet once more removed under the island's unique history concerning the ROC. Thus, when we speak of an imagined community that contributes to the project of Taiwan independence, it sets the Taiwanese apart from the Chinese across the Taiwan Strait, to be sure, but it also sets them apart from the so-called Mainlanders: the refugee population that arrived in large numbers in 1949 and established the ROC capital in Taipei, taking over the government and other positions of social power. They, too, consider themselves Chinese, and hence for this reason, the Taiwanese nationhood project competes with the Mainlander worldview, which (put simply) sees Taiwan as part of China (albeit the *Republic* of China).

Indeed, it is a testament to the utility of Anderson's concept of imagined communities that it can be used to conceptualize how several actors imagine the community of Taiwan to be. Moreover, Anderson addresses how modern nation-building projects have succeeded in making newly constructed traditions feel primordial, and how new cultural identities can rally feelings of loyalty and patriotism. Though they could be criticized as being mere false consciousness, on the contrary, they operate as a potent political force. Mainlanders, for example, may see their nation (the ROC) as the one created in 1912 after the fall of the Qing Dynasty and hence the inheritor of the Mandate of Heaven, and yet due to the vagaries of history, the heirs to this ancient and august birthright are consigned to suffer a marginal existence on a remote island far away from the Middle Kingdom's rightful seat of power in Peking.

On the other hand, advocates of Taiwan independence, uninterested in writing themselves into the annals of Chinese lore and who simply desire recognition of the *de facto* reality that theirs is already an independent country, must content themselves with an imagined community as there are no others who recognize them as a country (even Taipei's few remaining diplomatic allies recognize the ROC, not Taiwan). Indeed: even those, on either side of the Taiwan Strait, who yearn for unification are engaged in flights of imagination, for no matter how many international corporations are browbeaten into listing Taiwan as a "Province of China" on their websites, it is simply not so (Calhoun 2017; Wang 2000, 94; Ching 2001, 70).

The emergence of a Taiwanese consciousness stands in contradistinction to the view—once officially promulgated by the KMT authorities—of the Taiwanese as a subset of the Han Chinese ethnonational consciousness. Indeed, it would be impossible for the Taiwanese to have been able to share in the imagined community that assisted in the creation of the ROC nationhood project, as the island and its people were governed by Imperial Japan during the ROC's formative years. It was not until 1945 that they passed into the hands of the KMT regime. Moreover, the Taiwanese were at the time being subjected to the Japanese effort to inculcate in them a Japanese identity (albeit as members of the Japanese Empire, not the Japanese ethnicity itself), adding further complications. Thus, the imagined community being constructed by the Taiwanese sets them apart from both the Japanese and the Chinese and hence creates something new.

NATIONALIST LITERATURE

In any nation-making project of the sort described by Anderson, a common identity is required, and so common stories and beliefs must be promulgated to and embraced by the entire population, hence the psychological and sociological importance of a grand narrative, and therefore a nation's need to have its literature.

Kurdish Literature

In Kurdistan, there have been many nationalists whose writing continues to be studied and whose works have entered the canon of Kurdish literature and contributed to the Kurdish national identity. Prime among these is the Sharafnama by Sharaf al-Din Bitlisi (1543–1599), which presents a history of the Kurdish people from their pre-Islamic ancestors and including the Ayyubid dynasty of Saladin and the principalities of the Medieval Middle East. The 1597 book provides an origin story for the distinct Kurdish ethnicity and puts them in opposition to their neighboring "others," including the Arabs, Persians, and Turks. In the late seventeenth century, poet Ahmad Khani (1651–1707) wrote his seminal work, *Mam and Zin*, which tells the true story of star-crossed lovers who, like Romeo and Juliet, are tragically fated to have their love frustrated by powers intent on keeping them apart—even in death. The story is one that had been told for generations as an oral ballad, and it has been used as an analogy by Kurdish nationalists in the modern era to illustrate how the two lovers—one of whom represents the Kurdish homeland, and the other the Kurdish people—must continue to struggle for unity amid a sea of oppressors. Carrying on in the tradition of Khani, nineteenth-century poet Haji Qadir Koyi promoted not just military might as a means of independence, but literacy and learning as well, and he targeted the message of his nationalist poems to all the Kurdish people, not just the ruling class. As a well-traveled and highly educated man, he was familiar with the struggle for statehood in other parts of the world and knew that independence would not come by the sword alone, but by the pen. He urged his compatriots to learn to immortalize the stories in their oral tradition by committing them to paper, as well as promoting the publication of Kurdish-language newspapers and magazines. Even though he was a mullah, he sought a future for the Kurdish people in which they could rise above what he perceived as backwardness deriving from religious fanaticism (Rafaat 2012, 25).

Taiwanese Literature

The effort to establish a truly Taiwanese literary tradition has been a recurring theme that goes hand in hand with the emergence and growth of the *Taiwan Rentong*, as it grew out of the necessity to push back against the assimilation efforts of first the Japanese and later the Chinese Nationalists. The Taiwanese New Literature Movement of the 1920s was an effort to explore this new identity; not Japanese yet not quite Chinese. Writers like Huang Cheng Cong began to advocate for a new culture based on local realities rather than importing one from a country (China) that no longer represented these realities. The culture and society in Taiwan had undergone hundreds of years of development, in addition to the decades of Japanese colonial rule, and had diverged so significantly from China that a new nativist culture had emerged, and this culture demanded recognition. These efforts were underway both in Taiwan as well as among Taiwanese intellectuals studying in the home islands of Japan. It was in Tokyo, for example, that intellectuals including Huiru Cai began publishing *Taiwan Youth*, the magazine of the Xin Min Society they founded in 1920. Their compatriots back home founded the Taiwanese Cultural Association in 1921, which was a springboard to the Taiwanese People's Party and an important stepping stone in the anti-colonial movement against Japan. Co-founder Chiang Wei-Shui penned an influential short story called "Clinical Lecture," in which a diagnosis is provided to a sick patient—the patient representing Taiwan itself—who is determined to be suffering from a form of cultural malnutrition.

Likewise, the Taiwanese literature movement of the 1970s and 1980s was a reaction to the loss of identity through the assimilationist policies of the KMT regime. As Taiwan was the only remaining territory of the ROC, schoolchildren were taught Chinese history and had access only to Chinese literature, and the island's myths, songs, and stories were being lost. To remedy this, writers such as Lin Yang-min and Li Kuei-Hsien found eager audiences for their nativist writing, and there was a renewed interest in local literary traditions. Not only did this trend serve to distinguish the nativist identity among the Taiwanese as distinct from their Nationalist leaders, even today it continues to distinguish the Taiwanese experience from the life patterns to be found in China (Hsiau 2004; Hillenbrand 2007).

CLASSICAL LIBERAL VALUES

In both nations, the writers and intellectuals who ushered in a new era of localized literature were cognizant of the world outside their borders: they had witnessed or at least studied independence movements in other parts of the world and had presumably been exposed to different political philosophies and cultural values. There is little surprise, then, that as both Taiwan and Kurdistan set about the project of crafting their own unique cultural identities, there should be evidence of the influence of what in the West is known as classical liberal values. Primary among these values are the advances made toward freedom as evidenced by their respective periods of democratization in the late 1980s and early 1990s. In Taiwan, Martial Law was repealed in 1987, and just nine years later the country held its first democratic presidential election, with Lee Teng-hui emerging victorious despite Chinese attempts to intimidate the electorate by launching missiles and conducting military exercises in the Taiwan Strait. In 1992, Iraqi Kurdistan held its first democratic elections, in which Massoud Barzani's Kurdistan Democratic Party (KDP) and Jalal Talabani's Patriotic Union of Kurdistan (PUK) formed a power-sharing agreement. This commitment to compromise was unexpected given the antagonistic relationship between the two parties and showed a great deal of maturity and willingness to take whatever steps are necessary for the success of the fledgling democracy.

Liberal Values in Kurdistan

It may be that, far from stamping out the distinct ethnic identities that have arisen in Kurdistan and Taiwan, the threat posed by outside cultural actors only aids in feeding them and pushing them to grow in ways that distinguish themselves from the oppressive majority. In both cases, this appears to be expressed in the adoption of values and practices that are normally associated with Western notions of classical liberalism. In the words of poet and historian Arif Qurbany (2018), the Kurdish nation "has been well ahead of the Turkish and Arab nations in terms of society, customs, behavior, respect for human values, equality, and tolerance of other religions." This is evidenced by Erbil's banning of forced marriages and female genital mutilation, restrictions placed on polygamy, and amendments made to the Iraqi Personal Status Law that resulted in a marked decline in honor killings. The Kurdistan Regional Government has been largely successful in its efforts to protect members of the nation's Christian, Jewish, and Yezidi minorities from persecution—groups that widely suffer from ethnic-based violence elsewhere in Iraq, and throughout the Middle East region. More recently, speaking on the periphery of an event to mark the International Day for Eliminating Violence Against Women, the Head of the European Union's Liaison Office in Erbil, Clarisse Pásztory, remarked on 25 November 2018, that Iraqi Kurdistan has a great reputation of inclusivity in all aspects of society, ranging from ethnicity to religion (Frantzman 2018).

Liberal Values in Taiwan

Many theories endeavor to explain why a country such as Taiwan should adopt democracy and political liberalism. In the post-war years, and until well into the 1970s, Taiwan was ruled by a dictatorial regime under Chiang Kai-shek. This regime received a great degree of support from the West—primarily the United States—by virtue of the context of the times. It was the height of the Cold War, and the global imperative was to stop the spread of communism. An ardent anti-communist with designs of retaking the mainland, Chiang made an ideal ally in that fight. Later, as the threat of global communism begin to wane, and then all but extinguished with the fall of the Berlin Wall, leaders in Taipei needed to find another means of securing continued US support. Shared values fit the bill, and the ruling elite slowly began top-down democratization of the island, which was already experiencing bottom-up pressure towards democratization from the various civil society movements that had grown in intensity and begun demanding greater freedoms.

Taiwan continues to face the constant threat of military annexation by China. That country leverages its considerable economic clout to erase the Taiwanese identity from the consciousness of the international community and to normalize the idea that Taiwan is a part of China. It does this through such means as listing Taiwan as "Taiwan, China" on multinational firms' websites; forcing Taiwan to compete in the Olympics as "Chinese Taipei"; and bullying other countries into dealing with Taiwan simply as a "Separate Customs Territory" and not a country in its own right.

Taiwan is likewise ahead of its regional neighbors in terms of legislation and practices predicated upon such concepts as gender equality, freedom of speech, and respect for human rights. Democratization, along with the nation's impressive economic growth (known as the Taiwan Miracle) served to create the conditions wherein rapid changes to the social structure and society's values would take place. In the wake of the lifting of Martial Law, Taiwan saw enormous changes in almost all aspects of civic life, including the growth of a middle class (and hence a civil society), the widespread acceptance of Western liberal values, a thriving political environment wherein leaders vie for votes to represent their constituencies, and most recently, a deep belief among young people in justice to the point where they are willing to take to the streets to protest unconstitutional actions on the part of government representatives. In March 2002, the government passed the Gender Equality Labor Law. This law institutes equal pay for work of equal value, makes sexual harassment and discrimination in the workplace chargeable offenses, and allows women to take up to two years of maternity leave. Moreover, Taiwan as a nation is remarkably tolerant of homosexuality—especially in comparison with its East Asian neighbors. By connecting with the media, popular culture, and postmodernism, gay/lesbian/queer movements on the island have succeeded in presenting their community as avant-garde, trendy, and the most progressive on the cultural front (Liou 2006: 143).

Referenda in Kurdistan

Like their shared experience with democratization, the two countries also have a fraught relationship with public plebiscites. In September 2017, fresh off a string of Kurdish battlefield victories against Daesh, the Barzani government was emboldened to hold an independence referendum. The result was a Pyrrhic victory: the population voted overwhelmingly (at 92.7 percent) for formal independence from Iraq. Unfortunately, the government was not in a position to deliver on that dream, and the results scared and angered the region's other stakeholders: Capitals from Washington to Istanbul expressed their displeasure, and Baghdad shut down air travel in and out of the area and took over the lucrative oil-producing region of Kirkuk, robbing Erbil of much-needed petro revenue. The best that can be said of the referendum is that it was the right idea, but at the wrong time.

Referenda in Taiwan

Taiwan, too, is suffering a hangover from too many recent plebiscites, the results of which left the island's progressives deeply disappointed. Like the referendum in Kurdistan, the questions in Taiwan seem to have been the right ideas, just at the wrong time. While Taiwan's Referendum Act explicitly bars any plebiscites on matters pertaining to the ROC Constitution (which a question on independence would certainly do), independence-minded activists and politicians have had to make do with tangential issues serving as proxies for localization, such as same-sex marriage and the name rectification of Taiwan's Olympic team (from "Chinese Taipei" to "Taiwan"), both of which failed to earn public support in the polls in late 2018.

CONCLUSION

For the time being, it suits the needs of global powerholders to keep Taiwan and Kurdistan's status indeterminate, largely for geopolitical considerations. Iraqi Kurdistan is the central pivot point around which all of the region's players (Iran, Iraq, Syria, and Turkey) rotate. It sits on Iran's doorstep; encompasses the trade (primarily oil) route to and from Turkey; serves as a link to US forces fighting in Syria; and exerts some measure of influence in government coalitions in Baghdad. Likewise, Taiwan occupies a key position in the First Island Chain that is so pivotal for America to maintain its security guarantee in the entire Asia Pacific, and its economy is deeply integrated with those of the West as well as that of China. In other words: the stability of both states is needed in order to maintain the balance of power in their respective regions. And just as the security of the global order needs a strong Kurdistan region, it likewise needs a strong Taiwan—one that is at least strong enough to maintain its *de facto* independence from China.

The experience of Taiwan and Kurdistan share not only the similarities enunciated in this chapter, but they provide a degree of inspiration as well: that with determination and hard work, and a belief in the nation-building project, even an underdog can prevail against the geopolitical powerholders that would mitigate against their success. At the beginning of this chapter, the crucial difference between the concepts of nation-building and state-building was noted. It is worth examining whether success in the former translates into success in the latter. In the two cases under scrutiny, the prognosis is not heartening.

The undercurrents of statehood and independence can be boiled down to four distinct qualifications that must be met. These were promulgated in the 1933 Montevideo Convention on the Rights and Duties of States, and even today remain the benchmarks ostensibly employed by the United Nations when determining whether to admit a new member. They are 1) a permanent population; 2) a defined territory; 3) a government; and 4) the capacity to enter into relations with other states. As discussed in this chapter, both Taiwan and Kurdistan would seem to meet all of these basic requirements. And yet in both cases, international recognition of their *de facto* statehood remains unforthcoming. This says less about the efforts made in their respective nation-building projects than it does about the weaknesses of the international system.

Of the two, Taiwan arguably has the stronger case for UN membership. Indeed, the ROC was a founding member of the United Nations, signing the Charter on 26 June 1945 and ratifying it on 28 September 1945. The fact that the country is now excluded from representation is a consequence of the recalcitrance of Chiang Kai-shek in the days before democratization, combined with modern-day diplomatic obstruction on the part of the PRC. Though Taiwan manifestly meets the prerequisite conditions for statehood under the rules as laid out in the Montevideo Convention, it is China's influence within the UN system that is preventing any such recognition. It is for this reason that the case of Taiwan, and equally that of Iraqi Kurdistan, are so inspiring in their unyielding work toward nation-building: in both cases, the global power holders have made it clear that they will be frustrated in any attempt at official recognition, yet the two nations have persisted in their efforts, nevertheless.

Despite their disparate conditions and the distance that separates them, Taiwan and Kurdistan share remarkable similarities in how they conducted their respective nation-building projects. Kurdayeti became a potent political force after the fall of the Persian and Ottoman empires, and while the Arabs, Persians, and Turks obtained their nations following the dissolution of the Ottoman Empire when the region was divided into nation-states along ethnic lines, the Kurds were left out. In Taiwan, on the other hand, centuries of colonization led rise to the emergence of a distinct Taiwanese consciousness with different customs, practices, and belief systems from those in China. Moreover, whether these imagined communities can trace their genesis back several thousand years or several dozen matters little, as the national symbols, celebrations, and a rich localized tradition of literature all contribute to making newly constructed traditions feel primordial and creating a narrative that inspires the loyalty and patriotism so necessary to building a nation. This is especially true when, as both Kurdistan and Taiwan are, the imagined community is under intense existential threat from hostile external forces, and risks being subsumed by the tyranny of a foreign other. Far from collapsing, both cultures have responded to this pressure by thriving and honing their respective constructed identities in such a way that they have incorporated into their belief systems a deep and abiding respect for human rights, freedom, and the dignity of the individual.

REFERENCES

Alsford, Niki J.P. *Transitions to Modernity in Taiwan: The spirit of 1895 and the cession of Formosa to Japan* (London: Routledge, 2017).

Anderson, Benedict. *Imagined Communities: Reflections on The Origin And Spread Of Nationalism.* Verso Books, 2006.

Befu, Harumi, and Sylvie Guichard-Anguis, eds. *Globalizing Japan: Ethnography of the Japanese Presence in Asia, Europe, and America.* London: Routledge, 2001.

Blundell, David. "A Century of Research: Austronesian Taiwan, 1897–1997," *Austronesian Taiwan: Linguistics, History, Ethnology, and Prehistory.* David Blundell, ed. Berkeley, CA: Phoebe A. Hearst Museum, University of California, 2000, pp. 3–44.

Brown, Melissa J. *Is Taiwan Chinese? The Impact of Culture, Power, and Migration on Changing Identities*. Berkeley, CA: University of California Press, 2004.

Brubaker, Rogers. Religion and Nationalism: Four Approaches. *Nations and Nationalism,* Volume 18, Issue 1, January 2012, pp. 2–20

Calhoun, Craig. Nation and Imagination: How Benedict Anderson Revolutionized Political Theory. ABC *Religion and Ethics*. 9 May 2017.

Cauquelin, Josiane. *The Aborigines of Taiwan: The Puyuma—From Headhunting to the Modern World.* New York: RoutledgeCurzon, 2004.

Ching, L. T. (2001). *Becoming" Japanese": Colonial Taiwan and The Politics Of Identity Formation.* Univ of California Press.

Dobbins, James. (2003). "Nation-Building: The Inescapable Responsibility of the World's Only Superpower." *RAND Review,* Summer 2003.

Frantzman, Seth. A Strong Kurdistan Region Is Good for US In Iraq. The Hill. 16 October 2018. Available online at: https://thehill.com/opinion/international/411243-a-strong-kurdistan-region-is-good-for-us-in-iraq. Accessed 26 June 2019.

Hillenbrand, Margaret. (2007) *Literature, Modernity, and the Practice of Resistance: Japanese and Taiwanese Fiction, 1960–1990.* Leiden and Boston: Brill, 357.

History Learning Site. (2019). The Treaty of Sevres—History Learning Site. [online] Available at: http://www.historylearningsite.co.uk/modern-world-history-1918-to-1980/the-treaty-of-sevres/ [Accessed 24 Jun. 2019].

Hsiau, A-Chin. *Contemporary Taiwanese Cultural Nationalism.* (Routledge Studies in the Modern History of Asia). Taylor & Francis, 2004.

Huffman, James L. *Creating a Public: People and Press in Meiji Japan.* Honolulu: University of Hawaii Press, 1997.

Ka, Chih-Ming. *Japanese Colonialism in Taiwan: Land Tenure, Development, and Dependency, 1895–1945.* Boulder, CO: Westview Press, 1995.

Lamley, H. (1968). The 1895 Taiwan Republic: A Significant Episode in Modern Chinese History. *Journal of Asian Studies*, 27(4), 739–62. Doi:10.2307/2051577.

Li, Chien-Nung. *The Political History of China, 1840–1928.* Trans. Ssu-Yu Teng and Jeremy Ingalls. Princeton, NJ: D. Van Nostrand, 1956.

Liou, Liang-ya. "Queer Theory and Politics in Taiwan: The Cultural Translation and (Re)Production of Queerness in and beyond Taiwan Lesbian/Gay/Queer Activism." *NTU Studies in Language & Literature* 14 (2006): 123–54.

Natali, Denise. *The Kurds and the state: Evolving national identity in Iraq, Turkey, and Iran.* Syracuse University Press, 2005.

Novak, Erik, Lament of Ahmad Khani: A Study of the Historical Struggle of the Kurds for an Independent Kurdistan, Concept: *An Interdisciplinary Journal of Graduate Studies*, Vol 29 (2006).

Özoğlu, Hakan. (2005) *Kurdish Notables and the Ottoman State: Evolving Identities, Competing Loyalties, and Shifting Boundaries.* Albany: SUNY Press, ISBN-10: 0791459934

Qurbany, Arif. Kurds can't rely on regional rivalries to further their cause. Rudaw, 5 April 2018. Available online at: http://www.rudaw.net/mobile/english/opinion/05042018. Accessed 27 June 2019.

Rafaat, Aram. (2012) The Kurdish and Iraqi Counter-Quests for Nationhood and the Transformation of Iraqi Kurdistan into a Quasi-state (Doctoral dissertation). Retrieved from http://hdl.handle.net/2440/82074.

Rokkan, S. (1971). Nation-building: A review of models and approaches. *Current Sociology*, 19(3), 7–38.

Sana D. Jalal, Nasir A.S. Al-Allawi, Nooshin Bayat, Hasham Imanian, Hossein Najmabadi & Azad Faraj (2010) β-Thalassemia Mutations in the Kurdish Population of Northeastern Iraq, Hemoglobin, 34:5, 469–76, DOI: 10.3109/01676830.2010.513591.

Shipper, Apichai, Politics of Citizenship and Transnational Gendered Migration in East and Southeast Asia, *Pacific Affairs*: Volume 83, No. 1 Spring 2010 pp. 11–29.

Stephenson, C. (2005). Nation building." Beyond intractability. Burgess, G., & Burgess, H. (Eds.). Conflict Information Consortium, University of Colorado, Boulder.

van Bruinessen, Martin, (1999). "The Kurds and Islam." Working Paper no. 13, *Islamic Area Studies Project*, Tokyo, Japan.

Wang, Yu-San, ed. "*The Republic of China and Japan." Foreign Policy of the Republic of China on Taiwan: An Unorthodox Approach.* New York: Praeger Publishers, 1990, 45–59.

Wang, Horng-luen. (2000). Rethinking the Global and the National: Reflections on National Imaginations in Taiwan. *Theory, Culture & Society* 2000 (SAGE, London, Thousand Oaks and New Delhi), Vol. 17(4): 93–117 [0263–2764(200008)17:4;93–117;013704].

Weber, M. (1946). *Politics as a Vocation. From Max Weber: Essays in Sociology.* Trans. HH Gerth and C. Wright Mills. Oxford: Oxford UP, 77–128.

9

Taiwan in United States' Domestic Politics and Foreign Policy Agenda

Felix Kumah-Abiwu

INTRODUCTION

The relations between the United States (U.S.) and Taiwan did not only change in 1979 after the diplomatic recognition of mainland China or the People's Republic of China (PRC) by the U.S., but the geopolitics of the Cross-Strait region and the Taiwan sovereignty question has been part of U.S. domestic politics and foreign policy agenda for several decades. Following the establishment of formal diplomatic ties with the PRC in 1979, the U.S. severed its diplomatic relations with Taiwan, also known as the Republic of China (ROC). Notwithstanding the formal diplomatic recognition of the PRC, the U.S. has continued to maintain a robust unofficial relationship with Taiwan ever since (Kan and Morrison, 2014; Maizland, 2022). One of the central issues of the Cross-Strait region deals with the "one-China policy," where China maintains the principle of one China with Taiwan as part of its territory, while Taiwan also seeks to gain full independence as a sovereign country (Rich, 2009; Kan and Morrison, 2014; Maizland, 2022). As the preceding discussion has revealed, U.S.-Taiwan relations can therefore be considered as complex and systematically ambiguous. It is no wonder that the foreign/security policy of the U.S. toward Taiwan is often described as a policy of "strategic ambiguity" (Zhongqi, 2003; Haass and Sacks, 2020; Clarke and Sussex, 2021).

As several scholarly works in the fields of international relations and international law have underscored, sovereignty, territorial integrity, geographical space, permanent resident population, effective government, organized economy, recognition, and the capacity to enter diplomatic relations, among other determinants, constitute the fundamental elements for statehood (Knight, 1992; Mellor, 1989; Kan and Morrison, 2014). We have well-known examples of places such as Taiwan and other contested territories such as Palestine and Western Sahara that may fall within the conceptual definition of states in certain categories but are faced with decades of contested status and geopolitical dynamics regarding their quest for full political independence. While some of these disputed territories are less likely to attract the attention of great powers such as the U.S. in domestic politics and foreign policy engagement, this has not been the case with Taiwan. In essence, Taiwan appears to be different from other contested places. The chapter is therefore guided by two central questions in an attempt to better understand why Taiwan is different.

1. What explains the robust unofficial relations and close cooperation (i.e., economic, trade, cultural, technology, military/weapon sales) between the U.S. and Taiwan?
2. What are changing trends in the relationship between the U.S. and Taiwan concerning the policy of strategic ambiguity?

To explore these questions, the chapter starts by systematically engaging with the scholarly literature on the evolution and changing trends in U.S.-Taiwan relations. This discussion is grounded on further discussion of U.S. domestic politics and foreign policy agenda or engagement with Taiwan and the region. The chapter argues that a likely conflict-related deteriorating situation between China and Taiwan will shape the response or behavior of the U.S. toward the region. In terms of organization, the chapter is divided into three parts. The first part provides an overview of the history of U.S.-Taiwan relations with a focus on various eras or phases. The second part explores the U.S. foreign/security policy toward Taiwan with a critical discussion of the policy of strategic ambiguity. The third or final part looks at the rise of China and its implications for U.S.-Taiwan relations. This final section also discusses the ongoing debates on the relevance of the U.S. policy of strategic ambiguity toward Taiwan and the broader region in terms of policy change or continuity.

OVERVIEW OF U.S.–TAIWAN RELATIONS

To better understand U.S.-Taiwan relations, a brief history of Taiwan's complicated history and its global status will be useful. In their work titled "U.S.-Taiwan Relationship: Overview of Policy Issues," Shirley Kan and

Wayne Morrison note that Taiwan traces its political lineage to the 1911 revolution in China (Kan and Morrison, 2014). Prior to this period, as also captured by the World Factbook, the territory of Taiwan was first inhabited by Austronesian people. Over time, Taiwan became the home of Han immigrants beginning in the late Ming Dynasty of the seventeenth century (World Factbook, 2022). Following the communist victory in the Chinese civil war in 1949, the Nationalist-controlled government and about two million Nationalists fled to the island of Taiwan and have since continued to claim the legitimate government of representing Taiwan and mainland China (World Factbook, 2022; Kan and Morrison, 2014; Yu, 1963).

Taiwan or ROC's claim of being the legitimate government representing all of China is not without a challenge from PRC. The ROC's claim of being the legitimate government representing all of China and the counterclaim from the PRC have been at the center of the contentious relationship between the ROC and PRC for several decades (Rich and Vasabjit, 2015; Harold et al. 2019). Critical to the contentious relationship, as earlier noted, is the Taiwan sovereignty question with the "one-China policy," where China maintains the principle of one China with Taiwan as part of its territory, while Taiwan also seeks to gain full independence as a sovereign country with diplomatic recognition from other countries in the comity of nations (Rich, 2009; Kan and Morrison, 2014; Maizland, 2022). It could therefore be argued that this geopolitical issue between ROC and PRC is not only complex and complicated, but it is one of the potentially explosive global concerns in world politics in our contemporary era (Blanchard and Hickey, 2014). This could, perhaps, explain the attention of great powers such as the U.S. to Taiwan and the Cross-Strait region. It also offers some explanations for the robust unofficial relations and other close cooperation in the areas of economic, trade, culture, technology, and military between the U.S. and Taiwan.

For other scholars of the region, Taiwan seems to have successfully captured the attention of the political class and policymakers in the U.S. on these critical issues for three reasons. First, because of the volatile nature of the Taiwan sovereignty question between mainland China and Taiwan. Second, the U.S. foreign/security policy goal of maintaining peace and stability in Asia where it has vital interests. Third, the strong economic ties between the U.S. and Taiwan and the U.S. support Taiwan's democratic practices and values in a region that has limited democracies (Kan and Morrison, 2014; Maizland, 2022). For other observers, the rise of China in recent decades to a global powerhouse in the military and economic spheres and its assertive behavior in the Cross-Strait region as well as the South China Sea has continued to elevate Taiwan's strategic role/standing as a democratic ally of the U.S. in the region (Rich, 2009; Kan and Morrison, 2014; Maizland, 2022).

On the changing trends in the relationship between the U.S. and Taiwan, the chapter draws on relevant works on U.S.-Taiwan relations, especially the work of Vincent Wei-cheng Wang for the analysis. Wang's (1996) work is important to underscore for two reasons. First, it provides a comprehensive evolutionary history of U.S.-Taiwan relations over time and space. Second, the categorization of the eras into six periods (1949–1995) is not only useful as a relevant starting point, but this categorization provides the flexibility to extend the period beyond the sixth period to cover the contemporary era (from 1995 to the present) of U.S.-Taiwan relations. I draw on Wang's (1996) ideas/categorization in discussing the evolutionary history of the U.S. and Taiwan but prefer to discuss them in phases.

Phase I (1949–1950)

As earlier stated, the communist victory in the Chinese civil war in 1949 led to the move of the Nationalist-controlled government and millions of Nationalists to the island of Taiwan (Kan and Morrison, 2014; Yu, 1963). The communist victory not only sent a strong message to the U.S. as the Nationalist-controlled government moved to Taiwan but U.S. policy bearing during the period under review (the Truman administration) was generally described as a "wait until the dust settled" strategy as regards the outcome of the Chinese civil war (Wang, 1996).

Phase II (1950–1969)

The Truman administration's policy strategy of "wait until the dust settled" contained white papers or government official reports that were issued in the1950s following the outbreak of the Korean War. As a great power with a strategic interest to protect Asia, the U.S. had to quickly re-assess the security situation in East Asia following the outbreak of the Korean War. The outcome was a change in policy position of the "wait until the dust settled" position toward Taiwan (Wang, 1996; Rich and Vasabjit, 2015). The dispatch of the Seventh Fleet to the Taiwan Strait by the Truman administration as a response to the altered security situation not only prevented the Communist attack on Taiwan but also reinserted the U.S. into the "unfinished Chinese civil war" by bringing the U.S. and China into an extended proxy war in the region. This occurred as China offered its support to North Korea as the U.S. also offered its support to South Korea (Wang, 1996, p. 157). From an interpretation standpoint, one could argue that the security situation that emerged after the outbreak of the Korean War pushed the U.S. to elevate the status of Taiwan as a vital strategic partner whose loss to Communist forces would imperil the U.S. position in Japan and the Philippines (Wang, 1996; see also Clough,

1978). Taiwan became a strategic partner of the U.S., which led to a defense treaty that was signed in 1954 under the Eisenhower administration as part of the broader security efforts to complete the so-called frontiers along the Sino-Soviet bloc (Wang, 1996).

Phase III (1972–1978)

The likelihood of potential conflict between U.S. involvement in the region with China and the Soviet Union could also explain the strategic policy of détente that marked the third phase of the evolutionary period in the relationship between the U.S. and Taiwan. President Nixon's historic trip to China in 1972 and the signing of the Shanghai Communique created the framework for U.S. China policy for several years (Wang, 1996; Harding, 1992). This third phase of the evolutionary period was also important from two standpoints. First, Nixon's visit created the opportunity for the U.S. and China to discuss pertinent regional issues relating to the Korean Peninsula, Indochina, and Southwestern Asia among other security issues facing the region. Second, both countries (U.S. and China) were able to avoid the Taiwan issue as part of the conditions for normalizing relations. Wang's (1996) analysis of the U.S.-China engagement is quite revealing to reiterate at this point.

According to Wang (1996, p. 157), the U.S.-China engagement through Nixon's visit led the U.S. to concede to the three main demands of China on Taiwan. They included a) severance of diplomatic ties with Taiwan, b) the abrogation of the U.S.-R.O.C. mutual defense treaty, and c) the withdrawal of U.S. forces from Taiwan. These steps culminated on December 15, 1978, when the Carter administration established diplomatic relations with China and severed formal diplomatic ties with Taiwan (Wang, 1996, p. 157). Glaser et al. (2020) have articulated similar ideas in their discussions on the major shift in U.S. foreign policy following the establishment of diplomatic relations with China. To these scholars, the Carter administration's normalization of diplomatic relations with China or PRC in 1979 led to the decision of the U.S. Congress to re-assert its commitments to the people of Taiwan through the Taiwan Relations Act (TRC).

Phase IV (1979–1987)

The fourth phase of the evolutionary era of U.S.-Taiwan relations could be described as the dualistic era of U.S. policy goals. For example, Wang (1996) describes U.S.-China engagement as an unusual and mostly uneasy dual-track framework where the U.S. engaged with China on a diplomatic level whereas the relations between Taiwan and U.S. were handled through the Taiwan Relations Act (TRA). TRA underscored the commitment of the U.S. to

Taiwan's security by providing it with defensive weapons while insisting on a peaceful settlement of Taiwan's future. In other words, the U.S. was committed to supporting Taiwan's security by providing Taiwan with defense weapons while at the same time making sure China is committed to settling the Taiwan sovereignty question through a peaceful resolution. China's peace overtures toward Taiwan during the period under view with Deng Xiaoping's "one country, two systems" framework is another good case in point regarding the fourth phase (Wang, 1996).

Providing further details on the Taiwan Relations Act (April 1979) and its significance to U.S.-Taiwan relations, Chang (2001) argues that many Americans were not too comfortable that the U.S. was breaking off official ties with Taiwan, which has been a longstanding ally of the U.S. in the region. This prompted the unprecedented display of bipartisan cooperation/support that led to the passage of the TRA, which was signed into law by President Carter on April 10, 1979. TRA establishes itself as the basis for U.S. foreign/security relations with Taiwan. It involves the following:

1. To preserve and promote extensive, close, and friendly commercial, cultural, and other relations between the people of the U.S. and the people of Taiwan;
2. To declare that peace and stability in the area are in the political, security, and economic interests of the U.S., and are matters of international concern;
3. To make clear that the U.S. rests upon the expectation that the future of Taiwan will be determined by peaceful means;
4. To consider that any effort to determine the future of Taiwan other than peaceful means, including by boycotts, or embargoes, to be a threat to the peace and security of the Western Pacific area and of grave concern to the U.S.;
5. To provide Taiwan with defensive arms; and (6) To assert the right to resist any resort to force or other forms of coercion that would jeopardize the security or social and economic systems of the people of Taiwan (Chang, 2001, p. 4).

In a similar work on U.S.-Taiwan relations titled "Does Taiwan Matter to the United States? Policy Debates on Taiwan Abandonment and Beyond," Gang Lin and Wenxing Zhou argued that the dramatic geopolitical changes that occurred in the late 1980s and the early 1990s within the former Soviet Union and Eastern Europe have also shaped U.S. policy posture in the region. The era (post-Cold War), as Lin and Zhou (2018) have observed, created a strategic situation where the U.S. no longer took China's fundamental interest seriously, including the national unification with Taiwan as was in the past.

Phase V (1987–1995)

The fifth era in U.S.-Taiwan relations experienced other changes. Drawing on relevant work on the period, I address these changes from two standpoints. First, issues connected to the Shanghai II Communiqué (August 17, 1982). This era saw a formal note of protest from China to the U.S. Ambassador, Leonard Woodcock in Beijing after President Carter signed the TRA into law in April 1979 (Chang, 2001). The Act was seen as a serious obstacle to the development of meaningful PRC and U.S. relations. It was also perceived and interpreted by China as a legal framework for creating two Chinas (Chang, 2001). Second, the political situation in Taiwan in the 1980s with respect to their rapid democratization process was another major event that occurred. In 1987, for example, President Chiang Ching-kuo lifted the ban on the registration of newspapers and political parties, and allowed Taiwanese citizens to visit their relatives on the mainland. In addition to the political liberalization, trade and investment between PRC and ROC also increased during the period under review (Wang, 1996).

Phase VI (1995 to present)

Like the other phases, the sixth phase witnessed further changes in Taiwan, which also shaped U.S. relations with China, Taiwan, and the broader region. One of the changes occurred when the 1947 Constitution of Taiwan was amended to allow all parliamentarians to be directly elected by the people as regards major executive heads, including the President of the R.O.C., the governor of the Taiwan Province, and the mayors of Taipei and Kaohsiung (Wang, 1996). The political liberalization and improved relations in trade and investment between PRC and ROC were good signs of enhanced relations between the PRC and ROC, but these developments were also interpreted differently by China and Taiwan. Taipei's approach was functionalist in nature with emphasis on what Wang (1996) describes as "practical" and "peripheral" matters on issues of fishing disputes, document verification, and crime prevention that can serve as a foundation for the eventual discussion of "core" political negotiations on the future status of Taiwan. On the other hand, China was more interested in talking about political negotiations toward reunification.

Another important point to underscore in U.S.-Taiwan relations during the sixth phase was the deepening of Taiwan's democratization process that helped institutionalized its "de facto, if not de jure, independence" (Wang, 1996, p. 160). Similarly, the period from 1995 onward witnessed what some experts have described as the era of Taiwan's assertive foreign policy approach, also known as "pragmatic diplomacy" or "substantive diplomacy"

(Wang, 1996; Wong, 2000). Wong's (2000) analysis of Taiwan's changing foreign policy and relations during the era would be useful to reiterate at this point of our discussion. According to Wong (2000), Taiwan's foreign relations experienced various levels and stages of change since 1949. From an era of their uncompromising adherence to the "one-China" policy to a "practical diplomacy" of greater involvement in nongovernmental organizations to a "pragmatic diplomacy" of accepting dual recognition of the two Chinas, and finally to the "pragmatic diplomacy" of pursuing sovereign status under the principle of 'divided nation'" (Wong, 2000, p. 6; also see Kumah-Abiwu, 2022).

We should note that Taiwan's foreign policy changes in the 1980s, as Wong (2000) has argued, were particularly important, especially in the country's "pragmatic diplomacy" posture. Wong (2000) describes Taiwan's "pragmatic diplomacy" as consisting of three elements. First, Taiwan not only relaxed the ideological principle of no-coexistence with the PRC, but it also sets to attain membership and participation in international organizations as well as the willingness to engage in diplomatic relations with countries that have already established diplomatic relations with China (Chen, 1988; Wong, 2000; Kumah-Abiwu, 2022). Second, "pragmatic diplomacy" emphasizes softening attitude on critical issues concerning ROC and its name representation in international organizations. Third, Taiwan also engaged in efforts to improve relations with other communist countries besides the PRC (Wong, 2000).

The preceding discussions/analyses have underscored two important points worth noting. First, Taiwan, although a contested country, has occupied an important place in domestic politics and the foreign/security agenda of the U.S. with bipartisan support for several decades. Second, the U.S. policy of strategic ambiguity is still the core guiding policy choice for the region, although there are emerging debates among scholars and policy experts on the need to redefine or revise the U.S. policy of strategic ambiguity toward Taiwan and the greater region. The next section looks at the policy of strategic ambiguity and the ongoing debates on its relevance.

U.S. POLICY OF STRATEGIC AMBIGUITY

As previously stated, U.S.-Taiwan relations have not only been several decades old, but the outbreak of the Korean War in 1950 changed the dynamics of the relationship by creating the incentives for a broadened scope of the U.S. containment policy against the spread of communism in Asia. At the same time, as others have suggested, the U.S. engagement with Taiwan marked an important moment in how nations that might be of marginal strategic importance to great powers could suddenly assume that significant role (Hickey, 1986). This is where Taiwan stands out, especially on the U.S. policy of strategic ambiguity. The U.S. policy of *strategic ambiguity* rests on the equivocal post-1979 policy that ensures that neither China nor Taiwan can be certain of the involvement of the U.S. in the event of a conflict in the Cross-Strait region (Zhongqi, 2003; Clarke and Sussex, 2020). The policy, as Clarke and Sussex (2021) have captured it, has guided the Taiwan Relations Act that was passed by the U.S. Congress following the normalization of Sino-U.S. relations in 1979. The Act underscores Washington's recognition of mainland China as well as the following about the island of Taiwan:

- To preserve and promote extensive relations with the people of Taiwan.
- Peace and stability in the area are in the political, security, and economic interests of the U.S.
- That the establishment of relations with the PRC rests upon the expectation that the future of Taiwan will be determined by peaceful means.
- That any effort to determine the future of Taiwan by other than peaceful means would constitute a threat to the peace and security of the Western Pacific area and be of grave concern to the U.S. (Clarke and Sussex, 2021, p. 1; Zhongqi, 2003)

The Act also highlights U.S. support for Taiwan through various means, including arms sales to help them defend their country if attacked by China. Providing further details on the U.S. strategic ambiguity policy, Zhongqi (2003) argues that the three Joint Communiques, which were signed in 1972, 1979, and 1982, together with the TRA constitute the fundamental basis on which the formal Sino–US relations and America's Taiwan policies rest. Like other works on Sino–US relations that have interpreted the Sino–US relations and the strategic ambiguity policy in many ways, Zhongqi's (2003) analysis of the policy of strategic ambiguity might be of interest here. To Zhongqi (2003), the strategic ambiguity policy consists of three core elements. They include:

1. Commitment to Taiwan's Defense

This is one of the core aspects of the strategic ambiguity policy. As outlined in the TRA, Zhongqi (2003) observes that the U.S. has never stated its obvious position on defending Taiwan, and neither has the U.S. been clear in its commitment to protecting Taiwan from an attack from China. To put it differently, the U.S., as stated in the TRA, is not crystal clear about its commitment to Taiwan's defense in terms of the set conditions that will allow it to come to the aid of Taiwan in the event of an attack. A case in point occurred during the Taiwan Strait crisis between 1995–1996. Former U.S. Assistant

Defense Secretary, Joseph Nye, noted that "Americans do not want to give Taiwan a 100 percent guarantee that no matter what Taiwan does, Americans will come to its defense, because that would encourage Taiwan to take actions that would be risky" (cited in Zhongqi, 2003, 388–89). Former U.S. Secretary of State, James Baker, made a similar statement when he noted: "If we said we would come to the defense of Taiwan under all circumstances, she would declare independence and China would move—no doubt about that in my mind. If we said we wouldn't, China would move. And so we shouldn't say under what circumstances and to what extent we will aid Taiwan, but we should make it clear that we would view with the gravest concern any resort to the use of force" (cited in Zhongqi, 2003, p. 389).

2. Arms sales to Taiwan

The second element of the U.S. strategic ambiguity policy deals with arms sales to Taiwan. This aspect of the strategic ambiguity policy is key to the TRA, which underscores the commitment of the U.S. to "provide Taiwan with arms of a defensive character," to "make available to Taiwan such defense articles and defense services in such quantity as may be necessary to enable Taiwan to maintain a sufficient self-defense capability" (cited in Zhongqi, 2003, p. 389). Zhongqi (2003) observes that the arms sale policy of the U.S. on Taiwan is not only misleading but also complex since the provision is not well-defined with a clear language. For example, what does the statement, "the defense articles and defense services in such quantity as may be necessary to enable Taiwan to maintain a sufficient self-defense capability" mean? Also, how would the so-called quantity be determined? And what does the phrase "as may be necessary" mean? This is where Zhongqi's (2003, p. 389) criticisms of the vague language become important to highlight. In his work titled "U.S. Arms Sales to Taiwan: Implications for the Future of the Sino-U.S. Relationship," John McClaran notes that the U.S. has become the sole source of imported arms for Taiwan's military following the systematic strategy of mainland China to isolate Taiwan on the international stage, which has been quite successful in reducing the number of countries that have been engaged in arms sales to Taiwan (McClaran, 2000; Clarke and Sussex, 2021).

3. "One China" and Taiwan's Future Status

Another element of the U.S. strategic ambiguity policy deals with the "one China" principle. As earlier noted, the "one China" principle recognizes China or PRC as "the sole legal Government of China," but the principle, as Zhongqi (2003) notes, does not provide a further definition of what "China" is—PRC, ROC, or something other than both PRC and ROC. Zhongqi (2003) highlights the problematic nature of the U.S. policy choice, especially the "one China" policy. This is where the U.S. has expressed its commitment not to infringe on China's territorial integrity by not pursuing a policy of "two Chinas'" or "one China, one Taiwan" (Zhongqi, 2003). The "one China" policy, as earlier noted, is the recognition of China's policy position that there is only one Chinese government, and under the policy, the U.S. has formal relations with China rather than the island of Taiwan, which China considers as a breakaway province to be reunified with the mainland one day (BBC, 2020; Zhongqi, 2003). In sum, the "one China" policy not only serves as the basis of Sino-U.S. relations, but it also represents the bedrock of China's foreign engagement with the U.S. and on the Taiwan issue (BBC, 2020).

This might explain why the U.S. takes an ambiguous policy approach to the Taiwan question. At the same time, the U.S. appears to take a clear policy position on these two issues. First, the U.S. opposes Taiwan's declaration of independence which is consistent with its broad policy goals for the region. Second, the U.S., as part of its policy of strategic ambiguity opposes the use of force by China in the resolution of the Taiwan issue (Zhongqi, 2003; McClaran, 2000). In other words, the centrality of the U.S. policy of strategic ambiguity underscores a peaceful settlement of the Taiwan issue (Zhongqi, 2003). It could be argued, based on the preceding analysis, that the U.S. policy toward Taiwan and the region is systematically/intentionally ambiguous to provide U.S. policymakers/political actors with the flexibility to respond to any likely security threats in the region (Zhongqi, 2003; Clarke and Sussex, 2021; Maizland, 2022).

DEBATES ON POLICY CHANGE OR CONTINUITY (STRATEGIC AMBIGUITY)

China's rise and growing influence in crucial areas of the global economy, military capabilities, and technological advancement has continued to worry scholars and policy experts on a likely conflict between China-Taiwan that could also impact the U.S. In their recent piece on why China-Taiwan relations are becoming so tense with rising potential conflicts, Maizland (2022) argues that a likely conflict between China and Taiwan has the potential to become a major flash point in U.S.-China relations as well. According to Maizland (2022), as other scholars of the region have argued, tensions between China and Taiwan have been escalating in recent years, especially since the election of the Taiwanese President, Tsai Ing-wen in 2016. One of the reasons for the rising tensions is the refusal of President Tsai to accept a formula of her predecessor, Ma Ying-jeou, that has accepted Cross-Strait relations with China (Maizland, 2022). As a result, PRC has taken some aggressive actions of what could be described as intimidation tactics by flying military fighter jets near Taiwan. For others, the recent development is part of China's goal of promoting the framework of the "one country, two systems" idea (Maizland, 2022, p. 1). President Xi Jinping, for example, delivered a speech in 2019 and reiterated China's long-standing goal of incorporating Taiwan into mainland China under the framework of "one country, two systems" (Maizland, 2022, p. 1). This was the same formula that has been pursued in Hong Kong where their political and economic systems were to be "preserved" with "a high degree of autonomy." But the ongoing political situation in Hong Kong raises further questions about the viability of the formula of "one country, two systems" (Maizland, 2022, p. 1).

Given these rising tensions in the region with the growing military capabilities of China, some scholars/security experts have been raising critical questions and debating the significance of the U.S. policy of strategic ambiguity. The chapter draws on Maizland's (2022) analyses of the various viewpoints or schools of thought on these issues. One of the issues centers on whether war could erupt over Taiwan given the current developments in the region. The first school of thought states that China's growing military capabilities and its assertiveness could ignite major conflicts that could potentially lead to U.S.-China military confrontation as well. This is particularly significant because China has not ruled out using force to achieve Taiwan's "reunification." At the same time, the U.S. has also not ruled out helping Taiwan to defend itself if attacked by China through its policy of strategic ambiguity. The two scenarios present a murky/complex geopolitical and fragile situation for the region (Maizland, 2022).

Another school of thought that has been advanced by other experts who the idea of a likely outbreak of a major conflict in the region. For these scholars/experts, the debates on China's "readiness" to attack Taiwan might not be likely. David Sacks is one of the experts who has advanced this argument. According to Sacks (2021), while Cross-Strait relations should be worrying for everyone, a major conflict is unlikely because China will remain more preoccupied in the next few years with its pressing challenges while Taiwan will do whatever is necessary not to provoke China to escalate the tension. Sacks (2021) further contends that the Taiwan question might be one of the incentives for China's military modernization. Moreover, Taiwan does not seem to have the robust military capacities to defend itself against a likely China attack without external support, especially from the U.S. While the current government of Taiwan under President Tsai has increased defense spending with a record budget of about $17 billion for 2022, China's military spending is estimated to be around twenty-two times more than Taiwan. In this case, it becomes clear that Taiwan will be extra cautious not to provoke each other into a major conflict situation (Maizland, 2022; Sacks, 2021).

Other experts have also raised the issue of Russia's invasion of Ukraine in February 2022 as a case in point for China to emulate in Taiwan. This argument rests on the logic that Russia's invasion of Ukraine has emboldened China to strategize on the Taiwan question (Maizland, 2022). On the above argument, Sacks (2021) posits that China might be emboldened but would also be cautious given the tactical/operational failures of the Russian military in Ukraine. In essence, as this chapter concurs, China is not likely to follow Russia's example given the U.S. is a strong factor in Taiwan's case. For other observers, as Maizland (2022) has very well captured, 2049 is the critical year when China's "unification" efforts might occur with Taiwan since President Xi has emphasized the year 2049 as the year when China's dream of restoring itself as a great power is said to be achieved (Maizland, 2022).

These ongoing geopolitical dynamics, especially on China's rise to great power status, as discussed in the preceding, provide some persuasive explanations for the ongoing debates on U.S. foreign policy toward Taiwan. For some, it is time for the U.S. to revise its existing policy toward what some scholars/security experts have described as *strategic clarity* from the existing policy of *strategic ambiguity*. I draw on Clarke and Sussex's (2021) ideas to advance the argument on the ongoing debates on policy change or continuity. In a "town hall" event in Baltimore in October 2021, for example, President Joe Biden was asked whether the U.S. would defend Taiwan if it was attacked by China and the president was emphatic and stated: "Yes, we commit to doing that" (cited in Clarke and Sussex, 2021, p. 21). President Biden's statement, for many experts, seems to contradict America's longstanding foreign policy objective of strategic ambiguity. Clarke and Sussex (2021) note that Biden made a similar statement in the past, only to have the White House say that the longstanding policy of the U.S. toward Taiwan had not changed. The U.S., as previously noted, provides Taiwan with defensive weapons to defend its territory in case of an attack from China. At the same time, the U.S. has remained intentionally ambiguous on whether it would directly intervene militarily when China attacks Taiwan, which is the cornerstone of the strategic ambiguity policy toward Taiwan and the greater region (Clarke and Sussex, 2021).

As part of the policy debates on change or continuity, others have advanced the argument that the U.S. needs to consider revising its policy of strategic ambiguity. In their recent piece on the issue, Richard Haass and David Sacks have advanced the idea of a policy change toward a more policy of *strategic clarity*. To them, American support for Taiwan must not be characterized by ambiguity. The policy needs to be clear to send a strong message to China of the commitment of the U.S. to help defend Taiwan if attacked. They also argued that the policy of strategic clarity will help maintain peace and security in the region since China may not be willing to be engaged in a major conflict with the U.S. (Haass and Sacks, 2020). This line of thinking, as this chapter concurs, could be plausible given how integrated the economies of both the U.S. and China have become and a likely war will not serve the interests of the U.S., China, and Taiwan. At the same, we need to be reminded that geopolitics and the issues of national interest relating to sovereignty issues, as history teaches us with great power politics, could eclipse decisions by states on economic interests. This is why this chapter argues, or better put recommends the need for the key actors/players to continue to pursue the pathway of diplomacy for a peaceful resolution and settlement of the Taiwan question.

The preceding statement could help us to better understand why successive Republican and Democratic administrations have always tried to avoid answering the question of whether the U.S. would directly defend Taiwan if attacked by China. This deliberate policy of strategic ambiguity has not only helped to deter China from any attempt to "reunify" Taiwan with the mainland, but the policy of strategic ambiguity makes China not to be sure that the U.S. would remain on the sidelines and not support Taiwan (Haass and Sacks, 2020; Clarke and Sussex, 2021; Maizland, 2022). At the same time, the strategic ambiguity policy has also dissuaded Taiwan from declaring independence—a step that would have prompted a cross-strait crisis—because its leaders could not be sure of unequivocal U.S. support (Haass and Sacks, 2020; Clarke and Sussex, 2021).

The emerging idea that is being advanced by some scholars/experts as a redefined policy of *strategic clarity* from *strategic ambiguity* has been met with skepticism. In his piece titled "'Strategic Clarity' on Taiwan Is Clearly Mad," Daniel Larison, offers a fierce criticism of the proposed idea by Richard Haass and David Sacks on the policy of strategic clarity. Larison (2020) describes the idea as unnecessarily provocative to China since it would create a security guarantee over a territory that China views as an "integral" part of its territory. Larison (2020) added that the proposed idea of strategic clarity and the security guarantee it will create for Taiwan could create a further incentive for Taiwan to declare its full independence, which will end up triggering a major regional crisis that might also involve the U.S. (Larison, 2020; Clarke and Sussex, 2021). Moreover, there seems to be less American public support for the U.S. to fully commit itself to fighting a full-scale war in defense of Taiwan (Larison, 2020). A survey conducted by the Chicago Council for Global Affairs in 2019 shows that just about 35 percent of Americans are in favor of the U.S. responding to an attack on Taiwan from China. About 59 percent of Americans are opposed to such action (Larison, 2020).

CONCLUSION

The relationship between the U.S. and Taiwan has not only been characterized by many complexities for decades, but the U.S.-Taiwan relations can also be described as systematically ambiguous for various reasons as we have examined in this chapter. It is therefore not out of place that the U.S. foreign/security policy toward Taiwan has often been described as a strategic ambiguity (Maizland, 2022; Sacks, 2021). The volatile nature of the region in relation to the Taiwan question and the security interest of the U.S. in the region provide a further explanation of why Taiwan occupies a special place in U.S. domestic politics and foreign policy agenda although Taiwan is still a contested territory. To enhance our understanding of the robust unofficial relations between Taiwan and the U.S. and as part of this chapter's contribution to this important and timely book on contested territories, the chapter examined the evolution and changing trends in U.S.-Taiwan relations over time and space. Discussions in the chapter also focused on how a likely deteriorating change in China-Taiwan relations might shape U.S. response and behavior in the region. The debates on whether there is a need for a policy change or continuity on the U.S. policy of strategic ambiguity toward Taiwan and the broader impact on the region have also been examined in the chapter with supporting examples.

Given the volatile nature of the region coupled with the growing global influence of China in terms of its military capabilities, this chapter argues that a likely war between China and Taiwan with the involvement of the U.S. is always a possibility. At the same time, as this chapter suggests, all the key players such as China, Taiwan, and the U.S. need to continue to pursue the pathway of engaged diplomacy and active dialogue for a peaceful settlement of the Taiwan question. A continuous commitment by all the actors or players of the region to a peaceful settlement will serve the interest of maintaining the regional/global peace and security architecture for the region's human development.

REFERENCES

Blanchard, J. and Hickey, D. (2014). Introduction. In J.M., and Dennis V. Hickey (eds). *New Thinking about the Taiwan Issue: Theoretical insights into its origins, dynamics, and prospects.* New York: Routledge.

British Broadcasting Corporation (BBC). (2020). What is the "one China policy?" 2017. Accessed December 16, 2020. https://www.bbc.com/news/world-asia-china-38285354.

Chen, M. (1988). Taiwan at the crossroads: Human rights, political development, and social change on the beautiful island. *Asia Resource Center* (1988).

Chang, J. (2001) U.S. policy toward Taiwan. Weatherhead Center for International Affairs. (Weatherhead Scholars Program). Retrieved on July 23, 2022. https://scholarsprogram.wcfia.harvard.edu/publications/us-policy-toward-taiwan.

Clarke, M and Sussex, M. (2021). Why 'strategic ambiguity' trumps 'strategic clarity' on Taiwan. *RUSI.* Retrieved on July 24, 2022, from https://rusi.org/explore-our-research/publications/commentary/why-strategic-ambiguity-trumps-strategic-clarity-taiwan.

Clough, R. N. (1978). *Island China.* Cambridge: Harvard University Press.

Glaser, B. S, Bush, R.C., Green, M.J. (2020). Toward a stronger U.S.-Taiwan Relationship. *A Report of the Center for Strategic and International Studies* (CSIS).

Harold, S. Morris, L. and Logan M. (2019). *Countering China's Efforts to Isolate Taiwan Diplomatically in Latin America and the Caribbean the Role of Development Assistance and Disaster Relief.* Santa Monica. California. RAND Corporation, 2019.

Harding, H. A. (1992). *Fragile relationship: The United States and China since 1972.* Washington, DC: Brookings.

Haass, R and Sacks, D. (2020). American support for Taiwan must be unambiguous. *Foreign Affairs.* Retrieved on July 24, 2022, from https://www.foreignaffairs.com/articles/united-states/american-support-taiwan-must-be-unambiguous.

Hickey, D. Van V. (1986). U.S. arms sales to Taiwan: Institutionalized ambiguity. *Asian Survey* 26 (12) 1324–36.

Kan, S.A., and Morrison, W. M. (2014). U.S.-Taiwan Relationship: Overview and policy issues. CRS Report, Washington D.C.: Congressional Research Service.

Knight, D.B. (1992). Statehood: A politico-geographic and legal perspective. *GeoJournal* 28, 311–18.

Kumah-Abiwu, F. (2023). Taiwan-Africa relations: Exploring the changing trends. In S. Abidde. (Ed). *China and Taiwan in Africa: The Struggle for Diplomatic Recognition and Hegemony. New York: Lexington Books (Roman & Littlefield Group, Inc), pp. 25–44.*

Larison, D. (2020). Strategic clarity on Taiwan is clearly mad. *The American Conservative*. Retrieved on July 24, 2022, from https://www.theamericanconservative.com/strategic-clarity-on-taiwan-is-clearly-mad/.

Lin, G. and Zhou. W. (2018). Does Taiwan matter to the United States? Policy debates on Taiwan abandonment and beyond. *China Review* 18(3), 177–206.

Maizland, L. (2022). Why China-Taiwan relations are so tense. Council of Foreign Relations. Retrieved on July 23, 2022, from https://www.cfr.org/backgrounder/china-taiwan-relations-tension-us-policy-biden.

Mellor, R. E. (1989). *Nation, state, and territory*. Routledge, London.

McClaran, J.P. (2000). U.S. Arms sales to Taiwan: Implications for the future of the Sino-U.S. relationship. Asian Survey 40(4), 622–40.

Rich, T. and Vasabjit, B. (2015). Running out of time? The evolution of Taiwan's relations in Africa. *Journal of Current Chinese Affairs* 44 (1), 141–61.

Rich, T. (2009). Status for sale: Taiwan and the competition for diplomatic recognition. *Issues & Studies* 45 (4), 159–88.

Sacks, D. (2021). Why a cross-strait crisis will be averted in 2021. *Council on Foreign Relations.*Retrieved on July 22, 2022, from https://www.cfr.org/blog/why-cross-strait-crisis-will-be-averted-2021.

Yu, G. (1963). Peking versus Taipei in the world arena: Chinese competition in Africa.*Asian Survey* 3(9), 439–53.

Wang, V. W.-C. (1996). Rethinking US-Taiwan relations after the cold war: creative ambiguity vs. assertive democratization. *American Asian Review* 14 (3), 151–79.

Wong, T. (2000). Changing Taiwan's foreign policy: From one China to two States. *Asian Perspective* 24 (1), 5–46.

World Fact Book (2022). Retrieved on July 24, 2022, from https://www.cia.gov/the-world-factbook/countries/taiwan/.

Zhongqi, P. (2003). US Taiwan policy of strategic ambiguity: A dilemma of deterrence. *Journal of Contemporary China*. 12 (35), 387–407.

IV

Western Sahara and the Decolonization Process

10

The Sahrawi Arab Democratic Republic

A State That Never Was?

Gino Naldi and Cristiano d'Orsi

INTRODUCTION AND BACKGROUND

The conflict between Morocco and the Sahrawi national liberation movement, the Polisario Front, regarding sovereignty over Western Sahara remains "intractable" after nearly fifty years (Mundy, 2009, 115–16). The status of the former Spanish African colony, or protectorate, of Western Sahara, remains undecided to this day. Colonized by Spain in the 1880s Western Sahara has been the subject of a longstanding territorial claim by Morocco. In the 1960s the United Nations (UN) began calls for its decolonization (UN General Assembly [UNGA] Resolution 2229 (XXI), 20 December 1966) and was listed as a Non-Self-Governing Territory under Chapter XI of the UN Charter (UNSC, 2002, para. 5). In 1974 Spain announced that it would hold a referendum in Western Sahara under UN auspices.

However, in what with hindsight may be considered a blunder, the UNGA, rather than pursue the referendum, asked Spain to postpone it and instead requested an Advisory Opinion from the International Court of Justice (ICJ) on whether Western Sahara was, at the time of colonization by Spain, *terra nullius* and, if not, to determine the nature of the legal ties that existed between the Western Sahara and Morocco and the Mauritanian entity. The ICJ found that Western Sahara had not been *terra nullius* and that the legal ties with Morocco and the Mauritanian entity did not amount to ties of territorial sovereignty. The ICJ additionally found that the principle of self-determination applied to Western Sahara and its people (*Western Sahara Case* 1975 ICJ

Rep. 12). Morocco's response was to organize a "peaceful" Green March to occupy the territory, a fact that was "deplored" by the UN Security Council (UNSC) in Resolution 380 (1975) and that further demanded the immediate withdrawal of the Green March. However, the Green March was successful in that it persuaded Spain to terminate its administration of Western Sahara. In November 1975, the Madrid Accords were agreed upon by Spain, Morocco, and Mauritania according to which administrative power in Western Sahara would be transferred to a temporary tripartite administration. In February 1976, Spain informed the UN secretary-general (UNSG) that it was withdrawing from Western Sahara and that it no longer accepted international responsibility for the territory. In April 1976, Morocco and Mauritania concluded an agreement dividing up Western Sahara. Meanwhile, in 1975 the Polisario Front, the Sahrawi national liberation movement, commenced an armed struggle for the independence of Western Sahara.

Even though much of the territory has been occupied by Morocco since 1975 the independent State of the Sahrawi Arab Democratic Republic (SADR) was proclaimed in February 1976 by the Polisario Front, recognized as the legitimate representative of the Sahrawi people by the UN (UNGA Resolutions 34/37, 21 November 1979, and 35/19, 11 November 1980) and acknowledged by the courts of the European Union (EU) (T-279/19 *Front Polisario v Council*, ECLI:EU: T:2021:639, paras. 92, 93). The General Court of the EU has found that the Polisario Front is "recognized internationally as the representative of the people of Western Sahara, even if, as the Council, the French Republic, the Commission . . . contend, that recognition is confined to the limited framework of the self-determination process for that territory. In addition, its participation in that process implies that it has the necessary autonomy and responsibility to act in that context" (T-279/19 *Front Polisario v Council*, para. 96). As such the Polisario Front enjoys "basic elements of legal personality," which, however, are not to be compared to the rights and obligations of States or international organizations (IO) (T-279/19 *Front Polisario v Council*, para. 97). At the same time the Polisario Front embarked on a guerrilla war of national liberation.

In September 1988, the United Nations (UN) proposed a settlement plan for the region, including a cease-fire that would allow the holding of a referendum, which eventually led to the cease-fire formally taking effect in September 1991. The ceasefire was in effect for thirty years but in November 2020 the SADR denounced it and announced a return to the armed struggle (International Institute for Strategic Studies, 2021), a fact that was noted with "deep concern" by the UNSC (UNSC Resolution 2602 [2021]). The ostensible cause was a dispute over the buffer zone at Guerguerat, a border checkpoint between Moroccan-occupied Western Sahara and northern Mauritania which Morocco occupied in 2016 (UNSC, UN Doc S/2019/787, paras. 4–5).

In fact, the Polisario Front's presence in Guerguerat was condemned by the UNSC, which called for its "immediate withdrawal" (UNSC Resolution 2414 [2018], para. 7). However, the Polisario Front's decision may have been primarily motivated by the lack of progress on the referendum. Thirty years after a broad agreement in principle the referendum has still to take place as the parties quarrel over the modalities of the referendum, particularly over identifying and registering qualified voters.

The current UN position favors a political solution based on compromise providing for self-determination. However, international efforts at a peaceful resolution of the conflict were undermined in 2020 when the Trump Administration issued a proclamation recognizing Moroccan sovereignty over Western Sahara. The proclamation affirmed US support "[f]or Morocco's serious, credible, and realistic autonomy proposal as the only basis for a just and lasting solution to the dispute over the Western Sahara territory" (Proclamation No. 10126). This recognition was made in exchange for Rabat's normalization of relations with Israel (Eichensehr, 2021, 321).

The focal point of the Western Sahara conflict remains the right of the Sahrawi people to self-determination, whether that right has been validly exercised through the founding of the SADR, and whether the SADR is a State member of the international community. The Polisario Front is adamant that the status of Western Sahara must be determined by its people in a referendum that meets international standards. By contrast, Morocco insists that its proposal for autonomous status within the framework of its sovereignty and territorial integrity forms the only basis of negotiations. At present, the SADR remains listed as a non-self-governing territory by the UN Special Committee of 24. Although many Western States and institutions regard the status of Western Sahara as undetermined (T-512/12, *Front Polisario v Council* ECLI:EU: T:2015:953, para. 56) there is near universal agreement that the Sahrawi people are entitled to the right to self-determination, a right which had been explicitly recognized by the ICJ in the *Western Sahara Case* 1975 ICJ Rep. 14, and the courts of the European Union (C-104/16 P, *Council v Front Polisario* ECLI:EU: C:2016:973; C-266/16, *Western Sahara Campaign UK* ECLI:EU: C:2018:118; T-279/19, *Front Polisario v Council* ECLI:EU: T:2021:639). In an article by one of the present authors (Naldi, 1985), it was argued that the SADR should be considered a State. This was a view shared by eminent jurists, such as Shaw who nevertheless conceded that such a conclusion was controversial (Shaw, 2017, 185).

The Polisario Front's proclamation of independence could be considered to have constituted a valid exercise of the right to self-determination. International law does not insist that the right be exercised in any particular manner, although a referendum may seem the most suitable means of so doing, as long as a free and genuine expression of the will of the people has taken place. But the choice of independence does not seem to be conditional on a prior referendum (Cassese, 1995, 73). In the *Western Sahara Case* 1975 ICJ Rep. 33, the ICJ asserted that "consultations" with the local inhabitants were not always necessary because of "special circumstances." In addition, the ICJ stated the UNGA had a measure of discretion regarding the form and procedures by which the right to self-determination is to be realized (*Western Sahara Case* 1975 ICJ Rep. 36–37). It must be recalled that the Special UN Visiting Mission to Spanish Sahara had found overwhelming support among the people of Western Sahara for independence and the goals of the Polisario Front (United Nations Visiting Mission to Spanish Sahara, 1975, para. 18).

In light of Morocco's obstructive approach to holding a referendum recognition of the SADR's independence would have seemed like natural justice. Although the SADR did not meet fully the criteria of statehood, principally because it did not exercise complete and exclusive control over its territory, the fact that Western Sahara was under foreign occupation and being forcibly denied its right to self-determination meant that strict compliance with the criteria of statehood was not required; self-determination offset any deficiencies in satisfying the conditions which should accordingly be liberally construed. Furthermore, a Polisario victory in the conflict seemed plausible and imminent at the time. In August 1979 Mauritania was compelled to sign a peace agreement with the Polisario Front and renounce its claim to the southern part of the Western Sahara, which was then promptly annexed by Morocco. The peace agreement was welcomed by the UNGA (Resolution 34/37). In 1982 the SADR was admitted to the Organization of African Unity (OAU). Membership of the OAU was conditional on the applicant being an "independent sovereign" State (*Charter of the Organization of African Unity*, opened for signature 25 May 1963, 479 UNTS 39 (entered into force 13 September 1963) art XXVIII, para. 1). Shaw has expressed the view that the SADR's admission to the OAU "can be taken as OAU recognition of statehood and, as such, of evidential significance" (Shaw, 2017, 185). The SADR went on to be recognized by over eighty States ("International recognition of the Sahrawi Arab Democratic Republic," 2022; SADR Recognitions), including Mauritania. Recognition and membership in a regional organization can play a decisive role where the question of statehood is open to question. Admission to membership of an IO, especially the UN, may constitute evidence of statehood. It has been said that "admission raises a very strong presumption that the new Member is a State" (Aust, 2010, 187), that membership may constitute *prima facie* evidence of statehood (Brownlie, 2008, 94), or that it "establishes a strong presumption that an entity is a state" (Klabbers, 2009, 94). Such events may perform a quasi-constitutive function, that of consolidating statehood (Shaw, 2017, 332). But then the tide of fortune began to turn against the SADR.

Yet in another article by the same author twenty years later (Naldi, 2005), doubts were expressed regarding whether the SADR could still be said to meet the requirements of statehood. What accounted for this reversal of opinion? Several reasons were behind this turnaround. The passage of time seemed to be undermining the SADR's claim to statehood. Morocco has been able to establish effective control over most of the territory in question, a situation that has persisted for some thirty years. The SADR, therefore, fails to satisfy one of the primary requirements of sovereign statehood, that of exercising exclusive authority over the bulk of its territory. Even though the SADR is an original member of the African Union (AU) (*Constitutive Act of the African Union*, opened for signature on 11 July 2000, 2158 UNTS 3 (entered into force 26 May 2001), the OAU's successor, its capacity to conduct foreign relations has diminished. The SADR has failed to convince the wider international community of its claim to statehood. The relevant events that led to this change of opinion are considered in greater detail.

In the 1980s, Morocco began to build a series of long fortified defensive sand walls known as berms which neutralized the Polisario Front's guerrilla tactics and allowed it to extend the areas under its control; a stalemate ensued. The UN, in association with the OAU, then embarked on a proactive policy in an attempt to find common ground for a settlement. In 1988 the then UN Secretary-General (UNSG) put forward a plan, which complied with UNGA Resolution 1514 (XV), for a cease-fire and a subsequent referendum under UN supervision. The so-called Settlement Plan, which was accepted in principle by both parties, made provision for a transitional period during which a cease-fire would be implemented in 1991, to be followed in January 1992 by a referendum held under UN auspices in which the Sahrawis would be able to vote for independence or integration with Morocco (UN Doc S/21360, UN Doc S/22464). The Settlement Plan was endorsed by the UNSC in Resolution 658 (1990) and a detailed plan was subsequently adopted by the UNSC under Resolution 690 (1991), which formally established the UN Mission for the Referendum in Western Sahara (MINURSO), an integrated group of UN civilian, military and police personnel. MINURSO was mandated with, inter alia, monitoring the cease-fire, supervising the return of Sahrawi refugees, identifying and registering qualified voters, and organizing and ensuring a free and fair referendum (its mandate has been extended to 31 October 2023, UNSC Resolution 254 [2022]). Its current role is limited to monitoring the cease-fire.

The Settlement Plan was soon to run into difficulties over the referendum process, however, chiefly concerning the criteria for voter eligibility. In 1997 the former US Secretary of State, James Baker III, was appointed as the UNSG's envoy with the task of determining whether the Settlement Plan could be implemented (UN Doc S/2003/565, para. 23). Baker's mediation resulted in the Houston Accords, because of which the parties reached agreement on several contentious issues, including the identification of voters (UN Doc S/1997/742, annex I, annex II, and annex III). Significantly, the UN would have sole and exclusive authority over the referendum, including its organization and conduct. Morocco soon raised objections to the proposals on voter registration. In an attempt to keep the Settlement Plan afloat, in 1998 the UNSG put forward a compromise proposal which was accepted by both parties (UN Doc S/1998/997). Nevertheless, further progress has stalled as the parties have proved unable to resolve their differences despite the continued mediation of the UNSG's Special Representatives.

Subsequent efforts by the UNSG's personal envoys have not made it possible to break the impasse. Various possible political solutions have been advanced which have come to naught. A proposed framework agreement drafted in 2001 "would take account of Morocco's sovereignty and territorial integrity, and the specifics of the region, in compliance with . . . democratic and decentralization principles that Morocco wished to develop and apply" (UN Doc S/2002/178, para. 35). Western Sahara would be offered a devolved autonomous status within Morocco, corresponding to international standards, its final status to be determined by a referendum (UN Doc S/2001/613, annex I). This proposal failed to garner the necessary support but in 2003 Baker tabled his final effort, a Peace Plan for the Self-determination of the People of Western Sahara (UN Doc S/2003/565, annex II), which the UNSC, in resolution 1495 (2003), described as an optimum political solution. The Plan proposed a referendum under UN auspices after an interim period of up to five years with three options: integration with Morocco, autonomy under Moroccan jurisdiction, or independence. The Plan also contained further proposals on voter eligibility. However, the Plan failed to obtain Moroccan support. In April 2007 Morocco submitted a further proposal to the UN entailing a plan for a "Saharan Autonomous Region" based on "autonomy within the sovereignty and territorial integrity of Morocco" which included augmented decentralization ("Western Sahara Autonomy Proposal", 2021,") which received the backing of France and the United States (Mundy, 2009, 118–20). In a diplomatic coup for Morocco, Spain announced in 2022 that it, too, supported its autonomy plan (Peregil & González, 2022; Minder, 2022).

The UNSC, in Resolution 1754 (2007), requested the UNSG to renew negotiations. His new Personal Envoy launched a series of direct talks in 2007 and 2008, the so-called Manhasset Process, but these also proved unsuccessful. Despite further negotiations, there has been little movement of any substance since, with both Parties entrenched in their positions. Morocco will not compromise on its "sovereignty," in 2020 Morocco claimed sovereignty over the waters of Western Sahara ("Morocco adds Western Sahara waters to its maritime borders," 2020), insisting that autonomy is the only basis for negotiations, while the Polisario Front insists on the implementation of the right to self-determination in line with international standards which requires a referendum with independence an option. Nevertheless, the negotiating process has again been relaunched by the UNSG with the endorsement of the UNSC, which has emphasized the importance of a commitment by the parties to continue the process of negotiations through UN-sponsored talks. Pursuant to UNSC Resolution 2440 (2018) the UNSG's Personal Envoy arranged an initial round-table discussion between Morocco, the Polisario Front, Algeria, and Mauritania in December 2018 for the first time in six years. Talks are ongoing.

THE CURRENT STATUS OF WESTERN SAHARA

Arguments in Support of Statehood

The SADR naturally continues to assert its statehood. It was a founding member of the AU, membership of which is open to "[A]ny African State" (*Constitutive Act*, art 29[1]), and remains so. It has ratified several AU treaties (Periodic Report of the SADR, 18–19), although to the authors' knowledge, the SADR has not signed nor ratified any global treaties, except for Additional Protocol I to the Geneva Conventions, opened for signature 8 June 1977, 1125 UNTS 3 (entered into force 7 December 1978). On 23 June 2015, the Swiss Federal Department of Foreign Affairs issued a notice declaring that on 23 June the Polisario Front, as opposed to the SADR, had deposited a unilateral declaration acceding to Additional Protocol I (Notification aux Gouvernements des Etats parties aux Conventions de Genève du 12 aoÛt 1949 pour la protection des victimes de la guerre, June 26, 2015). It must be assumed that the noun "State" in such a text must denote the ordinary meaning of the word and signify "State for the purposes of international law" (Crawford, 2006, 179), lending weight to the SADR's claims. The SADR is subject to the supervisory and reporting mechanism of the African Commission on Human and Peoples' Rights, including the submission of State Reports (African Commission on Human and Peoples' Rights, State Reports and Concluding Observations), which again implies that the SADR is considered a State for the AU. However, to the authors' knowledge, the SADR has not joined any other regional or universal IO, except for the New Asian-African Strategic Partnership which is properly a forum for cooperation rather than an IO. However, in 2021 the SADR announced its intention to apply for membership in the UN (SADR claims full membership to the UN as a member State, 2021). This application is unlikely to be successful; the SADR lacks the support of a sufficient number of States, including crucially, most of those of the Permanent Members of the UNSC. The SADR continues to be recognized by a not insignificant number of States with which it has diplomatic relations at the ambassadorial level, over eighty at one time.

The SADR continues to have the trappings of a State. It has a constitution, last amended in 2007, providing for executive, legislative, and judicial functions and offices, as well as other organs of the State (Periodic Report of the SADR, 14–16, 20–23). It, therefore, purports to have an effective government.

It is possible to regard Morocco's presence in Western Sahara as one of belligerent occupation. This proposition has been advanced by the Polisario Front which has described Morocco as an occupying power according to international humanitarian law (T-512/12, *Front Polisario v Council*, para. 76). An EU Advocate General has asserted that it is one of "military occupation" (Opinion of Advocate General Wathelet, *Western Sahara Campaign UK*, C-266/16 ECLI:EU: C:2018:1, paras. 245–250). The UNGA has described the situation in the past as one of "occupation" (UNGA Resolutions 34/37, and 35/19), a view shared by several States, Sweden for instance (Sweden, Summary of review of Sweden's Western Sahara policy, 2016). As such, the annexation of occupied territory pending a final settlement is prohibited and *de jure* sovereignty would continue to reside with the SADR and not the occupier (*Cobb v United States*, 191 F.2d 604 (9th Cir. 1951); Bledsoe & Boczek, 1987, 352–53; Shaw, 2017, 899). *Strictu sensu* the international legal status of Western Sahara remains unaffected by the Moroccan occupation. Significantly, the legal status of the territory is immaterial (*Legal Consequences of the Construction of a Wall in the Occupied Palestinian Territory* 2004 ICJ Rep. 136, 177). The Eritrea–Ethiopia Claims Commission has expressed a similar opinion, stating that the role of international humanitarian law "should not be cast into doubt because the belligerents dispute the status of territory . . . respecting international protections in such situations does not prejudice the status of the territory." It added that there was nothing in international humanitarian law to suggest that "only territory the title of which is clear and uncontested can be occupied territory" (Eritrea–Ethiopia Claims Commission, Partial Award, Ethiopia's Claim 2, XXVI RIAA 155 [2004], para. 28).

Arguments Opposed to Statehood

But several factors continue to weaken the SADR's claims to statehood. As just narrated, the completion of the berm has gradually allowed Morocco to establish effective control over most of the territory in question, some 80 percent it would appear, including the main habitations, a situation that has persisted for many years, with the Polisario Front controlling a sparsely populated area in the east of the territory. The SADR, therefore, fails to satisfy one of the primary requirements of sovereign statehood, that of exercising exclusive authority over the bulk of its territory. This is a specific reason why Sweden asserts the SADR does not meet the criteria of statehood (Sweden, Summary of review of Sweden's Western Sahara policy, 2016). By way of contrast, however, Guinea-Bissau's independence was acknowledged by the UNGA under Resolution 3061 (XXVIII) on 2 November 1973 despite the fact parts of the territory were still controlled by the Portuguese colonial forces (Shaw, 2008, 205–06). Similarly, with the collapse of Yugoslavia, Croatia and Bosnia-Herzegovina were recognized as independent States and admitted to the UN notwithstanding the fact that sizeable parts of their territories were not under government control (Shaw, 2017, 159–60). Such a situation does not appear to have influenced negatively the European Community's Arbitration Commission when it considered these States' requests for recognition (Arbitration Commission Opinion No. 4, 31 ILM 1503 [1992]; Arbitration Commission Opinion No. 5, 31 ILM 1501 [1992]).

It has therefore been mooted that "the criterion of effective exercise of control by a government throughout its territory" has been relaxed (Shaw, 2017, ibid.). If so, this boosts the SADR's case. It could further be argued that the SADR is a victim of unlawful occupation and annexation such as that experienced by the Baltic States and others in the inter-war years, the *de jure* statehood of which remained unaffected and was not extinguished (Crawford, 2006, 97). However, this thesis would be plausible only if the SADR had indisputably existed as a State before the Moroccan occupation, the actuality of which is mired in controversy. Doubts may exist over another criterion of statehood, that of the capacity to enter into relations with other States, in that the ability of the SADR to conduct foreign relations also appears to have suffered setbacks since several States, almost half it has been reported ("International recognition of the Sahrawi Arab Democratic Republic," 2022), have withdrawn or suspended their recognition of the SADR (SADR Recognitions). This has also occurred in the case of Kosovo (Harris & Sivakumaran, 101–02).

In principle *de jure* recognition once given is irreversible (Montevideo Convention on Rights and Duties of States, opened for signature 26 December 1933, 165 LNTS 19 (entered into force 26 December 1934) art 6), and may not be withdrawn unless there occurs a fundamental change of circumstances, such as the extinction of a state or where an entity fails to satisfy the criteria of statehood with any degree of permanence, arguably the case with the SADR, and all semblance of authority has evaporated (Brown, 1950; Crawford, 2006, 90–91; Greig, 1976, 131). Commenting on the case of Croatia the British Government underlined that its recognition was predicated on, inter alia, its government having "a prospect of retaining control" (quoted in Harris & Sivakumaran, 142). Recognition may therefore be "provisional and transitory" (*The Gagara* [1919], 95, 104) in such uncertain circumstances. It is also politically significant that the SADR has not secured recognition from any western state or the EU (Sakthivel, 2016).

The support of the AU can no longer be taken for granted. Its role has become ambivalent, influenced it would seem by Morocco's admission in 2017 (Mohamed, 2017) and that of those Member States that support its claim ("Political status of Western Sahara", 2022,"), undermining the status of one of its founding States. This is despite the fact that membership of the AU entails legal obligations towards other Member States as set out in the *Constitutive Act*, including the sovereign equality of States, respect for borders of AU members, and the peaceful settlement of disputes (*Constitutive Act* art 4; Banerjee, 2017, 35–37). The AU had been concerned that the lack of progress in the peace process was having a destabilizing effect on the region and even threatening the functioning of the AU.

In its Plan of Action adopted at its Special Session on the Consideration and Resolution of Conflicts in Africa (Special Session of the Assembly of the Union on the Consideration and Resolution of Conflicts in Africa, SP/ASSEMBLY/PS/RPT[I] 30–31 August 2009), the AU Assembly resolved to support the UN efforts to surmount the stalemate on Western Sahara. To this end, the Special Session called for the intensification of efforts for the holding of a referendum to enable the Sahrawi people to choose between the options of independence and integration with Morocco. In 2013 the AU Executive Council requested that all necessary measures be taken for the organization of a referendum in compliance with the relevant OAU decisions and UN resolutions (Decision EX.CL. Dec.758 [XXII]). In 2017 the AU reaffirmed its support for the UN efforts at a negotiated solution (Decision on the Issue of Western Sahara, Assembly/AU/Dec.653[XXIX]Rev.1, 3–4 July 2017). The following year the AU renewed "its call on the two Member States, to engage, without pre-conditions, in direct and serious talks facilitated by the AU and the UN for the holding of a free and fair referendum for the people of Western Sahara" (Decision on the Report of the Peace and Security Council on its Activities and the State of Peace and Security in Africa, Assembly/AU/Dec.677[XXX], 28–29 January 2018, para. 17).

Pursuant to Assembly/AU/Dec.653 the Chairperson of the Commission on Western Sahara submitted a Report (Report of the Chairperson of the Commission on Western Sahara, 2018) in which it was recommended, inter alia, that the AU actively contribute to the search for a solution, support the UN efforts more effectively, and that all Member States, including neighboring countries, contribute actively to a solution. The AU took account of these recommendations and decided to establish an African mechanism comprising an AU Troika to provide effective support for the UN efforts by encouraging the parties to the conflict to demonstrate flexibility and mobilizing as widespread support as possible for them (Decision on the Report of the Chairperson of the Commission of the African Union on Western Sahara, Assembly/AU /Dec.693[XXXI], 1–2 July 2018).

But the cause of the SADR and the Polisario Front received a severe setback in 2020 when the Trump Administration recognized Moroccan sovereignty over Western Sahara (Eichensehr, 2021, 321), the first State to have done so officially, a decision that has not been reversed by the Biden Administration (Zunes, 2022). Indeed, the Biden Administration has gone on to endorse Morocco's autonomy plan (US Department of State, 2022). The Trump policy was justified on the grounds that "an independent Sahrawi State is not a realistic option for resolving the conflict and that genuine autonomy under Moroccan sovereignty is the only feasible solution," which did not rule out further negotiations to that end (Eichensehr, ibid.). The announcement attracted both domestic and international criticism, including from James Baker (Baker, 2020), some observing the policy's incompatibility with international law (Drury, 2020), in particular the right of self-determination, the prohibition on the forcible annexation of territory, and the principle of *uti possidetis*, with both the UN and EU reiterating that their policies on the conflict would remain unchanged (Eichensehr, 2021, 321–22; Zunes, 2022).

A NON-SELF-GOVERNING TERRITORY?

For the UN the status of Western Sahara remains unchanged; it considers the situation as a question of decolonization which has yet to be brought to fruition and Western Sahara continues the UN list of non-self-governing territories, as it has done since the UN embarked on its decolonization policy in the 1960s. The UN Legal Counsel has made clear that in his opinion the international status of Western Sahara is that of a non-self-governing territory. In his view the "Madrid Agreement did not transfer sovereignty over the Territory, nor did it confer upon any of the signatories the status of an administering Power, a status which Spain alone could not have unilaterally transferred. The transfer of administrative authority over the Territory to Morocco and Mauritania . . . did not affect the international status of Western Sahara as a Non-Self-Governing Territory" (UNSC, 2002, para. 6). However, over the years a subtle shift in the attitude of the UN political organs becomes discernible. Once the UNSC assumed responsibility for the Western Sahara conflict the priority shifted from the more robust stance of the UNGA to a more consensual approach. This attitude is typified by the UNSC which initially expressed its disapproval of Morocco's actions in Resolution 380 (1975), but which in more recent times has called upon the parties to the dispute to re-engage with the proposals for a mutually acceptable political solution compatible with the Sahrawis' right to self-determination "in a spirit of realism and compromise."

While it has recognized that "the status quo is not acceptable," the UNSC has stressed "the need to make progress toward a realistic, practicable and enduring political solution to the question of Western Sahara based on compromise" and has repeated its calls on the parties to resume negotiations under the UNSG's auspices "without preconditions and in good faith," "with a view to achieving a just, lasting, and mutually acceptable political solution, which will provide for the self-determination of the people of Western Sahara in the context of arrangements consistent with the principles and purposes of the Charter" (UNSC Resolutions 2351 [2017], 2414 [2018], and 2440 [2018]). An article by one of the present authors some years ago was critical of the UN's handling of the situation as pusillanimous and called for a more resolute response to Morocco's obstructionism (Naldi, 1994), indeed, it seems Baker may have resigned in frustration at the UNSC's hesitant handling of the issue (Mundy, 2009, 116), but it is now accepted that such an approach was never likely. A Resolution in accordance with Chapter VII UN Charter would have attracted a veto but even if such a Resolution had been adopted would the international community have been willing to impose a solution on an unwilling Morocco and even further endanger the incendiary state of affairs in the region? By way of contrast, the UNSC's role in overseeing East Timor's transition to independence was facilitated because of prior Portuguese and Indonesian agreements and was not an imposed solution (Shaw, 2017, 183).

But it is also interesting to contrast UNGA resolutions adopted years apart. Resolution 35/19, for instance, is strongly worded, expressing deep concern at Morocco's "occupation" of the Western Sahara. In 1990, the UNGA reiterated that the question of Western Sahara was one of decolonization which remained to be completed by the people of Western Sahara, reaffirming that they had an inalienable right to self-determination and independence (UNGA Resolution 45/21). Thirty years later specific mention of the Sahrawis' inalienable right to self-determination and independence had been omitted. Instead, the UNGA was asserting its support for a mutually acceptable political solution to the dispute which will provide for the self-determination of the people of Western Sahara, and that all available options for self-determination of Western Sahara were valid if they were in accordance with the freely expressed wishes of the people concerned (UNGA Resolutions 75/106, 76/89). Independence, therefore, is no longer necessarily the goal. While it is strictly speaking true that self-determination does not automatically equate to independence but that it makes provision for a variety of different outcomes, including integration with another State (UNGA Resolution 1541 [XV], 15 December 1960, Principle VI; UNGA Declaration on Principles of International Law, 24 October 1970), the fundamental and indispensable requirement, as the ICJ highlighted in the *Western Sahara Case* 1975 ICJ Rep. 31–33, and *Legal Consequences of the Separation of the Chagos Archipelago from Mauritius in 1965* 2019 ICJ Rep 95, paras. 156–57, is that account must be taken of the freely expressed wishes of the people concerned. This is a mandatory requirement as made clear by UNGA Resolution 1541 (XV) Principle VII (Cassese, 1995, 73). But progress on the referendum remains at a standstill as Morocco continues to dispute its terms.

The UN's stance is supported by the EU, which also considers the Western Sahara to be a non-self-governing territory (Opinion of Advocate General Wathelet, C-104/16 P, *Council v Front Polisario* ECLI:EU:C:2016:677, para. 80; C-104/16 P, *Council v Front Polisario* para. 92). According to the European Parliament the EU's consolidated position on the Western Sahara "is based on full respect for international law in accordance with UN Security Council resolutions and the UN-led political process of achieving a just, lasting, peaceful and mutually acceptable negotiated solution by both parties" (Texts adopted, 2021, para. 5). The EU does not recognize the SADR (T-512/12, *Front Polisario v Council*, para. 80) but neither does it recognize Moroccan claims over the Western Sahara (C-104/16 P, *Council v Front Polisario*, para. 95; T-279/19, *Front Polisario v Council*, para. 202) although the position of some Member States, and even of its institutions, is somewhat ambiguous (Sakthivel, 2016; Barigazzi, 2020; Cavanagh, 2021). In T-512/12, *Front Polisario v Council*, paras. 56–57, the General Court stated that the "Western Sahara is a territory whose international status is currently undetermined. . . . As is clear from the pleadings of the Council and the Commission, both the European Union and its Member States refrain from any intervention or support for either side in that dispute and, should the case arise, will accept any solution decided under international law led by the UN."

In that connection, the Commission adds that it supports the UNSG's efforts to reach a fair, long-lasting, and mutually acceptable political solution, which allows self-determination for the people of Western Sahara. It continues by stating that "in the meantime, Western Sahara remains a non-self-governing territory administered de facto by . . . Morocco," and proceeded to describe it not only as a non-self-governing territory but also as a "disputed territory" (also T-512/12, *Front Polisario v Council*, paras. 88, 117). However, the Court of Justice (CJEU) seems to have rejected the latter designation, finding the Western Sahara to have a "separate and distinct status" in accordance with the law of decolonization and denied that it was territory over which Morocco "exercises the fullness of the powers granted to sovereign entities by international law, to the exclusion of any other territory" (C-104/16 P, *Council v Front Polisario*, para. 92; Odermatt, 2017, pp. 733–734; Odermatt, 2018, 757–58). One writer, therefore, concludes that this judgment endorses "the status of Western Sahara as a non-self-governing territory, not a part of Moroccan territory" (Odermatt, 2017, 737).

However, the possibility of implied recognition of Moroccan sovereignty over Western Sahara has been raised. The EU and Morocco have entered into various agreements relating to agricultural and similar products and the validity of the Council Decision concluding one such agreement was challenged on the ground that its territorial scope was contrary to the right of self-determination because it applied to products originating from Western Sahara. In C-104/16 P, *Council v Front Polisario*, the Advocate General observed that the Council argued that it "has not tacitly accepted. . . . Morocco's interpretation to the effect that the [Liberalisation] Agreement applies to Western Sahara as part of its territory, which could constitute evidence of indirect recognition [of its sovereignty]. It has tacitly accepted that the [Liberalisation] Agreement also applies . . . to a non-self-governing territory administered by . . . Morocco, which does not imply recognition, acquiescence, or acceptance.' . . . Its view can be briefly summarised as an 'application without recognition'" (Opinion of Advocate General Wathelet, C-104/16 P, *Council v Front Polisario*, para. 67; Rasi, 2017, 973). According to the Advocate General this policy of "applicability necessarily and inevitably implies recognition" (Opinion of Advocate General Wathelet, C-104/16 P, *Council v Front Polisario*, para. 85).

However, the CJEU managed to sidestep this hazard by holding that the EU could not implement the agreement in a manner incompatible with the principle of self-determination, thereby acknowledging its peremptory status (C-104/16 P, *Council v Front Polisario*, para. 123; Rasi, 2017, pp. 974). The CJEU held further it would be contrary to the principle on the relative effect of treaties to consider Western Sahara coming within the scope of the agreement (C-104/16 P, *Council v Front Polisario*, paras. 105–07; Odermatt, 2017, 734–35, 736–37).

Morocco has sometimes been described as the administering power or the *de facto* administering power in Western Sahara. For instance, the stance of the different EU institutions seems contradictory, asserting that Morocco is not accepted as the *de facto* administering power but on other occasions describing it as the administering power (Opinion of Advocate General Wathelet, C-104/16 P, *Council v Front Polisario*, paras. 67, 97). But as has already been seen earlier, the UN Legal Counsel has stated that the Madrid Agreement did not transfer sovereignty or the status of an administering power over Western Sahara to Morocco. Moreover, Morocco is not listed as the administering Power in the UN list of Non-Self-Governing Territories. Certainly, Morocco is not the *de jure* administering power. Nevertheless, the UN Legal Counsel does refer to "Moroccan administration" which may in context be a term of convenience rather than a legal term of art (UNSC, 2002, paras. 6–7). Morocco is not in a position comparable to that of, for example, the United Kingdom in relation to the British Overseas Territories.

THE RELEVANCE OF SELF-DETERMINATION

Western Sahara is a case of incomplete or frustrated decolonization and a victim of a forcible denial of the right of its people to self-determination. Unquestionably, the right of self-determination continues to apply to the people of Western Sahara. This is the formal position of the UN, the EU, and the international community as a whole. It has been upheld on separate occasions by the courts of the EU (C-104/16 P, *Council v Front Polisario*, paras. 88–89; T-279/19, *Front Polisario v Council*, para. 92; C-266/16, *Western Sahara Campaign UK*, para. 63). It needs to be recalled that respect for the right to colonial self-determination is an obligation *erga omnes* (*East Timor Case (Portugal v Australia)* 1995 ICJ Rep 90, 102; *Legal Consequences of the Construction of a Wall in the Occupied Palestinian Territory* 2004 ICJ Rep. 136, 199; *Chagos Case*, 139), amounting to "a legally enforceable right *erga omnes*" (C-104/16 P, *Council v Front Polisario*, para. 88).

Although the ICJ has thus far avoided classifying self-determination as a norm *jus cogens*, instead describing it as an essential principle of international law (*East Timor Case*, 102; C-104/16 P, *Council v Front Polisario*, para. 88), arguably it does have that status as several ICJ judges have observed (*East Timor Case*, 131, Separate Opinion of Judge Ranjeva; *East Timor Case*, 266, Dissenting Opinion of Judge Skubiszewski; *Chagos Case*, 193–202, Separate Opinion of Judge Cançado Trindade; *Chagos Case*, 316–24, Separate Opinion of Judge Robinson; *Chagos Case*, 277, Separate Opinion of Judge Sebutinde), as well as other authorities to that effect (*Delimitation of Maritime Boundary between Guinea-Bissau and Senegal* [1989] 20 RIAA 119, 135; Commentary on Article 40, 2001, 113; Brownlie, 2008, 513; Cassese, 1995, 133–40). All parties are therefore under an obligation to ensure the right of the Sahrawi people is exercised in accordance with international standards (*Chagos Case* para. 180). Moreover, States are under a duty not to act in a manner that denies that right or impairs its exercise (*East Timor Case*, 204, 221, Dissenting Opinion of Judge Weeramantry). While it is the case that international law does not impose any particular method by which the inhabitants of non-self-governing territories exercise their right to self-determination whichever mode employed must reflect the freely expressed will of the people (*Chagos Case* para. 158). The indispensable feature remains the basic need to take account of the wishes of the people concerned through informed and democratic processes. To acquire international legitimacy a free and fair referendum, open to all indigenous Sahrawi people, seems the most reasonable option. The UN was able to organize a successful referendum in East Timor and there is no reason in principle why that should not be the case in Western Sahara. There is nothing unreasonable in the Polisario Front insisting on this basic right being met or on the option of independence being on the ballot. Likewise, it is legitimate for autonomy under Moroccan sovereignty to be an alternative option. If the Sahrawi people were to choose the latter option in a free and fair vote so be it.

Morocco's continued presence in Western Sahara, whether as *de facto* administering power or occupying power, raise issues of international responsibility. The ICJ's findings in the *Chagos Case* seem apposite. There it was determined that the United Kingdom's continued administration of the Chagos Archipelago, being inconsistent with the right to self-determination, "an unlawful act of a continuous character" according to the ICJ, amounted to a wrongful act of a continuing nature entailing its international responsibility (*Chagos Case* para. 177). The ICJ proceeded to call for a prompt end to the United Kingdom's administration of the Chagos Archipelago (*Chagos Case* para. 182; Draft Articles on State Responsibility, 2001, art 30[a]). These findings seem equally applicable to Western Sahara.

CONCLUSION

The dispute over Western Sahara remains at an impasse because of the entrenched and polarized positions of the parties, Sahrawi independence versus Moroccan sovereignty, which has only been exacerbated in more recent times because of Morocco's insistence that its proposal for autonomy is the only basis of negotiations. The UN bears its share of responsibility for this state of affairs as it has "monumentally mishandled" it since the very beginning (Franck, 1976) and subsequently (Naldi, 1994). Spain's offer of a referendum in 1974 should have been accepted with alacrity by the UNGA. The UNSC should not have treated Moroccan intransigence with such indulgence, but a resolute approach was never likely with Moroccan allies as Permanent Members.

As reviewed above, it seems unlikely that the SADR's claims to statehood are sustainable; there may have been a basis for an optimistic assessment in its early days but those grounds have been whittled away by subsequent events. And realpolitik continues to undermine the Sahrawi cause, with one UNSG Personal Envoy having expressed the view that independence was "unrealistic" (Mundy, 2009, 121).

No member of the international community, apart from the United States, presently recognizes formally Morocco's claims to sovereignty over the Western Sahara, which remains committed to the UN efforts to secure a negotiated solution based on respect for the principle of self-determination. However, in reality, many influential States are sympathetic toward Morocco's autonomy plan. The support of France and the United States for the autonomy plan has been referred to above, indeed the United States has recently reaffirmed its backing for it ("US reiterates support for Morocco 'autonomy plan' in Western Sahara," 2021; US Department of State, 2022) while Germany has recently also expressed its support ("Alemania ofrece nuevas señales de acercamiento a Marruecos," 2022). Crucially, Spain has also come out in favor of the autonomy plan. This has been described as "the autonomy consensus," which is gaining ground with influential members of the international community (Chitty, 2010). But the Moroccan annexation, because that is what it is, should not be recognized as per the Stimson Doctrine and as a result of the application of the principle *ex injuria non jus oritur*, that is, that an unlawful act cannot be a source of benefits or rights for the wrongdoer.

The better view, therefore, is that Western Sahara remains a non-self-governing territory. International law requires that the resolution of the Western Sahara conflict must respect the right of self-determination but while Western Sahara remains a low priority for the international community the prospects of such an outcome seem to recede. As has already been observed, "the ideal situation is obvious enough . . . the will to achieve it will probably never coalesce so long as Morocco remains a steadfast ally of the United States and France" (Mundy, 2009, 122).

REFERENCES

African Commission on Human and Peoples' Rights, State Reports and Concluding Observations. https://www.achpr.org/statereportsandconcludingobservations.

Alemania ofrece nuevas señales de acercamiento a Marruecos. (2026, January 6). *El Pais.* https://elpais.com/internacional/2022-01-06/alemania-ofrece-nuevas-senales-de-acercamiento-a-marruecos.html.

Arbitration Commission Opinion No. 4 on the Recognition of the Socialist Republic of Bosnia-Herzecegovina by the European Community and its Member States, 31 ILM 1501 (1992).

Arbitration Commission Opinion No. 5 on the Recognition of the Republic of Croatia by the European Community and its Member States, 31 ILM 1503 (1992).

Aust, A. (2010). *Handbook of International Law* (2nd ed.). Cambridge University Press.

Baker, J. (2020, December 17). Trump's recognition of Western Sahara is a serious blow to diplomacy and international law. *Washington Post.* https://www.washingtonpost.com/opinions/2020/12/17/james-baker-trump-morocco-western-sahara-abraham-accords/.

Banerjee, A. (2017). Moroccan Entry to the African Union and the Revival of the Western Sahara Dispute. *Harvard International Law Journal, Online Journal, 59*, 33–37.

Barigazzi, J. (2020, December 10). EU stresses UN peace process after US U-turn on Western Sahara. *Politico.* https://www.politico.eu/article/eu-stresses-un-peace-process-after-us-u-turn-on-western-sahara/.

Bledsoe, R. & Boczek, B. (1987). *International Law Dictionary*. ABC-Clio.

Brown, P. (1950). The Legal Effects of Recognition. *American Journal of International Law, 44(4)*, 617–40.

Brownlie, I. (2008). *Principles of Public International Law* (7th ed.). Oxford University Press.

Cassese, A. (1995). *Self-Determination of Peoples: A Legal Reappraisal*. Cambridge University Press.

Cavanagh, M. (2021, May 4). The EU's confused Western Sahara position—a foreign policy failure, or an opportunity? https://blogs.lse.ac.uk/internationalrelations/2021/05/04/eu-western-sahara/.

Charter of the Organization of African Unity, opened for signature 25 May 1963, 479 UNTS 39 (entered into force 13 September 1963).

Chitty, A. (2010, June 5). Western Sahara—Territorial dispute, self-determination, and the UN. https://exploringgeopolitics.org/publication_chitty_alex_western_sahara_territorial_dispute_self_determination_un_polisario_sahrawi_plebiscite_minurso_morocco_rio_de_oro_terrritory_algeria_mauritania/.

Cobb v United States, 191 F.2d 604 (9th Cir. 1951).

Commentary on Article 40, Draft Articles on Responsibility of States for Internationally Wrongful Acts, with commentaries. (2001). *Yearbook of the International Law Commission*, vol. II, Part Two.

Constitutive Act of the African Union, opened for signature 11 July 2000, 2158 UNTS 3 (entered into force 26 May 2001).

Council v Front Polisario, C-104/16 P, ECLI:EU:C:2016:677. Opinion of Advocate General Wathelet.

Council v Front Polisario, C-104/16 P ECLI:EU:C:2016:973.

Crawford, J. (2006). *The Creation of States in International Law* (2nd ed.). Oxford University Press.

Département fédéral des affaires étrangères. (June 26, 2015). Notification aux Gouvernements des Etats parties aux Conventions de Genève du 12 aoÛt 1949 pour la protection des victimes de la guerre, https://www.eda.admin.ch/dam/eda/fr/documents/aussenpolitik/voelkerrecht/geneve/150626-GENEVE_fr.pdf.

Draft Articles on Responsibility of States for Internationally Wrongful Acts. (2001). UN Doc A/56/10.

Drury, M. (December 22, 2020). Sahrawi Self-Determination, Trump's Tweet and the Politics of Recognition in Western Sahara. Middle East Report Online. https://merip.org/2020/12/sahrawi-self-determination-trumps-tweet-and-the-politics-of-recognition-in-western-sahara/.

Eichensehr, K. (2021). Contemporary Practice of the United States. *American Journal of International Law, 115(2)*, 318–23.

Eritrea–Ethiopia Claims Commission, Partial Award, Ethiopia's Claim 2, XXVI RIAA 155 (2004).

European Parliament. (June 10, 2021). Texts adopted, P9_TA (2021)0289.

Franck, T. (1976). The Stealing of the Sahara. *American Journal of International Law, 70(4)*, 694–721.

Front Polisario v Council, T-512/12 ECLI:EU:T:2015:953.

Front Polisario v Council, T-279/19 ECLI:EU:T:2021:639.

The Gagara [1919] P 95.

Greig, D. (1976). *International Law* (2nd ed.). Butterworths.

Harris, D. & Sivakumaran, S. (2020). *Cases and Materials on International Law* (9th ed.). Sweet & Maxwell.

International Institute for Strategic Studies (2021, November). *The end of the ceasefire in Western Sahara.* https://www.iiss.org/Home/Publications/Strategic%20Comments/2021/The-end-of-the-ceasefire-in-Western-Sahara#:~:text=In%20November%202020%2C%20the%20Polisario%20Front%20%E2%80%93%20a,protestors%20blocking%20a%20strategic%20road%20leading%20to%20Mauritania.

International recognition of the Sahrawi Arab Democratic Republic. (2022, January 10). In *Wikipedia.* https://en.wikipedia.org/wiki/International_recognition_of_the_Sahrawi_Arab_Democratic_Republic#:~:text=States%20that%20have%20recognized%20SADR%20%20%20,People%27s%20Repu%20...%20%2024%20more%20rows%20.

Klabbers, J. (2009). *An Introduction to International Institutional Law* (2nd ed.). Cambridge University Press.

Legal Consequences of the Construction of a Wall in the Occupied Palestinian Territory 2004 ICJ Rep. 136.

Minder, R. (2022, March 19). Spain, seeking better ties with Morocco, shifts stance on Western Sahara. *New York Times.* https://www.nytimes.com/2022/03/19/world/europe/spain-morocco-western-sahara.html.

Mohamed, H. (2017, January 31). Morocco rejoins the African Union after 33 years. *Aljazeera.*

Morocco adds Western Sahara waters to its maritime borders. (2020, January 26). *Arab Weekly.*

Mundy, J. (2009). Out with the Old, in with the New: Western Sahara back to Square One? *Mediterranean Politics, 14(1)*, 115–22.

Naldi, G. (1985). The Statehood of the Saharan Arab Democratic Republic. *Indian Journal of International Law, 25(3–4)*, 448–481.

Naldi, G. (1994). The UN Buries its Head in the Desert Sands -The Saga of Western Sahara. *African Journal of International & Comparative Law*, *6(3)*, 653–60.

Naldi, G. (2005). The Western Sahara: Suspended Statehood or Frustrated Self-Determination? *African Yearbook of International Law, 13*, 11–41.

Odermatt, J. (2017). Council of the European Union v. Front Populaire. *American Journal of International Law, 111(3)*, 731–38.

Odermatt, J. (2018). Fishing in Troubled Waters. *European Constitutional Law Review, 14(4)*, 751–66.

Peregil, F., & González, M. (2022, March 18). España toma partido por Marruecos en el conflicto del Sáhara. *El País.* https://elpais.com/espana/2022-03-18/sanchez-considera-la-autonomia-del-sahara-como-la-base-mas-seria-realista-y-creible-para-resolver-el-conflicto.html.

Periodic Report of the Sahrawi Arab Democratic Republic to the African Commission on Human and Peoples Rights Containing All the Outstanding Reports in accordance with Article 62 of the Charter. https://www.achpr.org/public/Document/file/English/periodic_report_sahrawi_eng.pdf.

Political status of Western Sahara. (2022, January 17). In WikiMili. https://wikimili.com/en/Political_status_of_Western_Sahara.

Rasi, A. (2017). Front Polisario: A Step Forward in Judicial Review of International Agreements by the Court of Justice? *European Papers, 2(3)*, 967–75.

Report of the Chairperson of the Commission on the Issue of Western Sahara, Assembly/AU/4(XXXI), 1–2 July 2018.

"SADR claims full membership to UN as member State" (April 5, 2021). https://www.spsrasd.info/news/en/articles/2021/04/05/32476.html.

Sakthivel, V. (June 10, 2016). The EU, Morocco, and the Western Sahara: a chance for justice. https://ecfr.eu/article/commentary_the_eu_morocco_and_the_western_sahara_a_chance_for_justice_7041/.

Shaw, M. (2017). *International Law* (8th ed.). Cambridge University Press.

Sweden, Ministry for Foreign Affairs. Summary of review of Sweden's Western Sahara policy. https://www.government.se/48e908/contentassets/504adc5e222e4518bf01281cdc149271/sammanfattning_engelska.pdf.

UN General Assembly. Declaration on Principles of International Law concerning Friendly Relations and cooperation among States in accordance with the Charter of the United Nations. (1970). Resolution 2625 (XXV).

UN General Assembly, United Nations Visiting Mission to Spanish Sahara. (1975). UN Doc A/10023/Add. 5.

UN Security Council, Letter dated 29 January 2002 from the Under-Secretary-General for Legal Affairs, the Legal Counsel, addressed to the President of the Security Council. (2002). UN Doc S/2002/161.

UN Security Council, Report of the Secretary General. (1990). *The Situation Concerning Western Sahara*. UN Doc S/21360.

UN Security Council, Report of the Secretary General. (1991). *The Situation Concerning Western Sahara*. UN Doc S/22464.

UN Security Council, Report of the Secretary General. (1997). *The Situation Concerning Western Sahara*. UN Doc S/1997/742, annex I, annex II, and annex III.

UN Security Council, Report of the Secretary General. (1998). *The Situation Concerning Western Sahara*. UN Doc S/1998/997.

UN Security Council, Report of the Secretary General. (2001). *The Situation Concerning Western Sahara*. UN Doc S/2001/613, annex I.

UN Security Council, Report of the Secretary General. (2002). *The Situation Concerning Western Sahara*. UN Doc S/2002/178.

UN Security Council, Report of the Secretary-General. (2003). *The Situation Concerning Western Sahara*. UN Doc. S/2003/565.

UN Security Council, Report of the Secretary General. (2019). *The Situation Concerning Western Sahara*. UN Doc S/2019/787.

Universidade de Santiago de Compostela. SADR Recognitions. https://www.usc.gal/en/institutos/ceso/RASD_Reconocimientos.html.

U.S. Department of State. *Joint Communiqué on the Morocco-US Strategic Dialogue Dialogue on Regional Political Issues.* (March 8, 2022). https://www.state.gov/joint-communique-on-the-morocco-u-s-strategic-dialogue-on-regional-political-issues/.

US reiterates support for Morocco 'autonomy plan' in Western Sahara. (November 24, 2021). *Middle East Monitor.* https://www.middleeastmonitor.com/20211124-us-reiterates-support-for-morocco-autonomy-plan-in-western-sahara/.

Western Sahara, Advisory Opinion, 1975 ICJ Rep 12.

Western Sahara Autonomy Proposal. (2021, October 11). In *Wikipedia*. https://en.wikipedia.org/wiki/Western_Sahara_Autonomy_Proposal#:~:text=Moroccan%20backed%20advisory%20council%20on%20Western%20Sahara%20%28CORCAS%29,that%20Morocco%20will%20control%20defense%20and%20foreign%20affairs.

Western Sahara Campaign UK, C-266/16 ECLI:EU: C:2018:1. Opinion of Advocate General Wathelet.

Western Sahara Campaign UK, C-266/16 ECLI:EU: C:2018:118.

Zunes, S. (January 21, 2022). Biden's Dangerous Refusal to Reverse Trump's Western Sahara Policy. Foreign Policy in Focus. https://fpif.org/bidens-dangerous-refusal-to-reverse-trumps-western-sahara-policy/.

11

The Case for Independence

J.J.P. Smith

INTRODUCTION

In post-colonial Africa, the case for Western Sahara's statehood is a straightforward matter to argue. The territory's original inhabitants, the Sahrawi people, have the benefit of civil society and democratic governing institutions comparable to established nation-states elsewhere, not least those in Africa. Uniquely, the Sahrawi people enjoy a combination of a regional organization, the African Union, which accepts their statehood, the commitment of the United Nations organization to their self-determination, and established law underpinning their right to choose an international status. And yet the political and legal circumstances of the Sahrawi people remain unresolved—in stasis—even as their project of nation-building continues. The incomplete or, more accurately, *unrealized* statehood of the Sahrawi people marks a continuing failure of the international order for human rights and decolonization with a basis in the *UN Charter*. The case of the Sahrawi people is brought into relief by Russia's attempted destruction of Ukraine, a comparable example of aggression and violation of territorial integrity, although with a different response from the organized international community including Global North states.[1]

Despite widespread practice of decolonization after 1945, supported by a continuing consensus of states—particularly in the setting of the United Nations General Assembly—and not least the well-defined right of non-self-governing peoples to choose their international legal status (or "personality"), for the Sahrawi people such an elective choice has remained out of reach. The assurance to them under article 2 of the *UN Charter* of sufficient political independence to be able to determine their status as a former colony of Spain continues to be denied them. Yet in the face of such circumstances, a Sahrawi statehood in legal-formal and functional dimensions emerged and became substantial.[2] The question today is properly about what is needed to *complete* Sahrawi's independence. Inquiring into Sahrawi statehood is about what lies ahead for civil society and the governing institutions of a policy toward a universally recognized independence in the organized international community. East Timor (Timor-Leste) reminds us that such a descriptor of completing statehood—the choice and effort needed to create a sovereign entity—is insufficient: The statehood of the Sahrawi people seems less about justifying a political project than the processes and measures for its completion.[3]

A preliminary appraisal reveals numerous features of statehood inherent to the Sahrawi entity, the Saharawi Arab Democratic Republic (SADR).[4] Indeed, analysis of this presumptive statehood risks being superficial because of the considerable evidence. The facts on the ground pointing to an established entity are considerable. In colonialism's hold over Africa, the final case of Western Sahara, therefore, seems inexorable in its result, needing only the imprimatur of ratification-by-referendum. However, such contention for states in the ordinary sense as well as non-self-governing territories can never be absolute. Arguments and apologies for a status contrary to statehood must always be contemplated. If nothing else, states and peoples have the opportunity when they exercise their political independence to choose forms of international personality other than a nation-state.

This chapter contends with the viability and apparent necessity of creating a Sahrawi state. The analytical task lies on a continuum from discernment to justification. The former is exegesis, a matter of locating the essential facts of a present statehood and identifying what few matters remain after Sahrawi self-determination and an end to the occupation of Western Sahara are accomplished.[5] At the opposite end of the continuum, a counter-point of justification requires an explanation of the rationale for a Sahrawi state without preconception. Justification includes elements of law (the right to self-determination), of the organized international community's explicit assurances to the Sahrawi people that they may choose their identity by an expression of political status, and, not least of all, of what appears to be an undiminished Sahrawi desire for statehood.

With such a continuum in mind, the Sahrawi people's journey to an emergent statehood is first canvassed, with reference to related chapters in this volume. Sahrawi *political independence* is arguably established, needing culmination only by popular ratification through an act of self-determination followed by universal recognition among states.[6] Here, a leading area of inquiry is the *internal*, namely, the right of the Sahrawi people to elect their status including how they would assume an international legal personality. The analysis considers the political landscape, starting with the Sahrawi aspiration to create for themselves a nation-state before turning to its viability. The conditions for a democratic, capably governed, and economically successful state are explored. The second area of inquiry is what can be called the *external associative*, reviewing the utility and apparent necessity for the organized international community to accept and even support the creation of a Sahrawi state. Here, the role and implications for the African Union are of interest. A third area of inquiry is the importance of realizing the goals of the post-colonial order to ensure sufficient political independence of non-self-governing peoples so that they may choose Westphalian statehood.[7] This is about assuring the rule of law, especially a right to self-determination which stands at the apex of the international human rights order. However, for a Western Sahara in Africa, the significance of such a vindication is greater. Achieving a Sahrawi state marks a new beginning for an African polity.

ORIGINS

The starting place to examine the emergence of the SADR and thereby what remains for its presumed completion is the Sahrawi unilateral declaration of independence (UDI) of 27 February 1976. The circumstances are easily recalled: Faced with a colonial Spain's imminent withdrawal following the November 1975 *Madrid Accords*—which purported to share responsibility for Sahrawi self-determination with a then-invading Mauritania and Morocco—a proclamation of statehood was something symbolic and formal, an assertion of an entity with sovereign legal personality.[8] In the history of decolonization cases, such a step was hardly unique. East Timor's first-post colonial government had done so in November 1975 when faced with an invasion by Indonesia. However, the Sahrawi UDI attracted continuing recognition by states and tended to reinforce the perception of what can be called an *achieved statehood* in the circumstances of considerable autonomy of the Sahrawi people in refugee camps inside Algeria.[9] Sahrawi conceptions of civil society organization and the government built on each other out of a persistent desire for statehood to result. A later formalistic process of self-determination, including ratification of the popular will through an UN-administered plebiscite, would be understood by the Sahrawi people as something procedural in nature, a necessary step toward an assured result after Morocco had come to occupy three-quarters of Western Sahara by the mid-1980s (Omar 2008).[10]

The ready achievement of an *emergent statehood* has been useful for Sahrawi's self-determination. It fostered a polity that could credibly engage with other states, especially those of the region. It underscores powerfully the need to allow the Sahrawi people to choose, even if only formally and after the fact as ratification, an identity, and international legal form. Statehood would bring participation as a sovereign equal in the African Union and with it, until recently, the confounding of Morocco's membership in the organization.[11] In addition, although not often considered by the organized international community, this path to statehood demonstrates a Sahrawi entity with considerable readiness for the tasks of government. Sahrawi institutions and activities of legislating and providing functional courts (civil, administrative, criminal, and military) are arguably more evolved than any other non-self-governing people with a right to self-determination in the post-1945 age of the *UN Charter* (Wilson 2016).

THE MONTEVIDEO INDICIA

The criteria of the 1933 *Montevideo Convention* to define a state's formal (and threshold) features of existence, now part of customary international law, are abundantly displayed by the Sahrawi Arab Democratic Republic. The first characteristic is that of a defined territory. The presence of the Sahrawi people in a particular setting was established early in the Spanish colonial period and has remained unchanged since. Marked out by colonial boundaries drawn in 1900 and completed in 1912, Western Sahara's territory has been consistently accepted by the organized international community.[12] This is especially true of African Union states with their collective position to maintain sometimes inconvenient, even artificial, boundaries that are the legacy of colonialism.[13] While the SADR is not in control of Western Sahara as a whole, it exclusively governs the territory's inland area including the presence of its armed forces and a small civilian population.[14] The SADR government seeks to act throughout the entire territory, for example with legislation to claim maritime zones from a coastline that remains mostly beyond its possession and control (Maritime Zones Law No 3 of 2009).[15]

Turning to the second Montevideo criterion, Western Sahara's population is also readily identifiable. After Spain's colonial control over Western Sahara began in 1884, the Sahrawi people as a semi-nomadic indigenous population retained a distinct Arab language dialect and cultural precepts. Western Sahara's colonial frontiers may have been artificially drawn, without consultation of the Sahrawi, but they resulted in the only limited division of ethnic groups from the Spanish colony. The territory's population remained unitary in part because it was small, counted at just under seventy-four thousand in a 1974 Spanish census.[16] However, the passage of time since 1999 when the UN completed the identification of Sahrawi people to vote in a referendum promised them under the 1991 Settlement Plan has confounded the identity of the population.[17] But what continues to be done unlawfully in pursuit of annexation cannot diminish this aspect of statehood.

The third Montevideo indicum of statehood is also extensively manifest. Sahrawi government control was reinforced by the 1991 Settlement Plan and Western Sahara's physical partition, ensuring a territorial space of exclusivity, *i.e.*, freedom of action. That Western Sahara is occupied in part by a foreign power does not diminish the capacity to deliver government.[18] The activities of the Sahrawi state range from ordinary regulatory matters such as veterinary measures for livestock, to issuing of passports, and the direction of modest public works in town sites.[19] This Montevideo criterion is reinforced and made credible by the Sahrawi government acting—and being democratically constituted—with unimpeded (*i.e.*, exclusive) autonomy in the refugee camps in Algeria (Wilson 2016).[20] Here the institutional presence of government compares to other African states, with only a large-scale formal economy and tertiary education being absent. Education, health care, policing, courts, and defense as public goods are maintained (San Martín 2010).[21] Democratic norms, meanwhile, underpin the legitimacy of a government operating partly in exile, for example, the occasional amending of the Sahrawi constitution by representative assemblies elected in four-year cycles (Fernandez-Molina & Ojeda Garcia 2019). The Sahrawi government also has a demonstrated capacity (although limited financially) to act externally, such as participation in African Union bodies and asserting sovereignty over natural resources.[22]

The fourth Montevideo characteristic of the existence of a state—the capacity to engage other states and international institutions—is perhaps SADR's most constrained feature. But not by much: The Sahrawi state engages in bilateral and multilateral relationships with apparent effectiveness, for example in consular affairs. The extent of engagement with the organized international community can be measured by observing activities (including in the name of the Frente Polisario) to involve others in Sahrawi self-determination. The UN is a particular counterparty to Sahrawi institutions in this regard. Treaty activity is another example, from multilateral African agreements joined by the SADR and the 2015 accession of the Frente Polisario (a national liberation movement) to the 1949 Geneva Conventions.[23] The context of Sahrawi diplomacy is important: The SADR operates in partial exile, territorially displaced, with limited financial resources, and, since November 2020, in a resumed armed conflict.[24]

RECOGNITION

Merely identifying the degree to which the SADR fulfills the Montevideo criteria does not complete the argument (or justification) for Sahrawi statehood.

The political element of acceptance of the SADR's existence in the organized international community—recognition—is far from complete.[25] It is recognition as the discretionary act of states, namely, of governments at a moment in time, that marks the emergence of a non-self-governing people into the organized international community. A widely anticipated emergence of statehood overcomes concerns about the viability or the joining of the organized international community by a new, sovereign and equal entity. So, we must necessarily consider the question of recognition.

The question of the existence of a Sahrawi state suggests the theoretical framework of constitutive and declaratory recognition under international law is worth revisiting.[26] That is because in the decades since the framework was articulated the recognition of states has been concerned with diplomatic relations with them and their admission to international organizations. And, for non-self-governing peoples, the right to create (more accurately, elect) a state has become an inherent right. Their choice, in other words, arguably results in statehood and is not something that must somehow fulfill any condition precedent of recognition. Such an evolved understanding of the law enjoyed by non-self-governing peoples is consistent with the obligation of *non-recognition* where would-be states emerge in unlawful circumstances, for example after the occupation by others. States emerging from cases of dissolution and secession can expectedly be subject to the framework because the central question of sovereignty for them would remain. International law has progressed to the point of assuring the original exclusive sovereign rights of non-self-governing peoples to their territory. The *UN Charter* basis for this is, again, Articles 2 and 73.

In practical terms, recognition of a Sahrawi state is stalled in part because of the obligations which result from recognition and in part from the understood operation of the 1991 Settlement Plan. Recognition of the Sahrawi state means dealing with it (and its citizens) under the rules of international law, including matters such as the protection of human rights and export trade in natural resources. Recognition is the highest refutation of an occupying Morocco's claim. Diplomatic consequences are expected to result from such a step. In addition, recognition is at odds with the Settlement Plan: The organized international community has committed, if through the UN, to an externally administered process of self-determination. This explains why most state recognitions of the SADR occurred before 1991. However, as will be discussed, the UN has not fulfilled its controlling role. That, together with Morocco's increasing annexation of Western Sahara, suggests a new consideration of recognition.[27]

STATEHOOD AND THE RIGHT TO SELF-DETERMINATION

A precept of the Westphalian order holds that statehood, if not at first coming out of an act of popular will, is at least maintained in discrete geographic entities by continuing social consensus. After 1945 the right of non-self-governing peoples to choose for themselves their political and legal status became significantly more defined, evolving into a peremptory norm of international law within decades.[28] The right to choose status can be understood as having two characteristics: The first is the externally conferred right, whether by operation of law, the directing consensus of the organized international community, or, as has often been the case, a combination of both.[29] Both feature in the case of Western Sahara. The second (and complementary) aspect is the choice of non-self-governing people to exercise their political independence as a matter of the agency they have, again prescribed by the combination of Articles 2 and 73 of the *UN Charter*. In other words, this second feature moves the right to exercise choice in self-determination to something more fundamental and therefore with a greater normative obligation on the organized international community, namely, a sufficiency of political independence in the circumstances of (as described by Article 73) "alien domination" to be able to make a self-determination decision. The maintenance of the Westphalian order has more than territorial definition and integrity as outcomes. What such requirements assure is the foundation of human security and political independence. The collective response of the organized international community to colonialism in the second half of the twentieth century could only succeed if non-self-governing peoples were assured their agency, choosing their place in that community. Anything less would be to perpetuate colonialism.

Of course, in the considerable majority of decolonization cases, the formal step of a decided choice of a non-self-governing people was not considered necessary. It was enough for a clear wish of a colonized people to be manifest. Only in the difficult cases involving competing for internal factions or colonization by a neighboring state (*e.g.*, East Timor) was outside intervention necessary to assure elective choice. The relatively few cases where non-self-governing people elected a status other than statehood illustrate the point. For them and also remaining (and long-persisting) cases of decolonization, a credibly assured choice as an act of political independence is needed. An example is the Cook Islands, its people choosing an autonomous arrangement with New Zealand.[30] In the same neighborhood of the Pacific Ocean, New Caledonia is another example, its circumstances of a population divided on the question of international status to be tested by multiple plebiscites.[31]

The Sahrawi people are hardly unique in their aspiration for statehood. More remarkable is this desire having persisted over five decades, undiminished from an original near-total expression. It is arguably this that most justify an acceptance of the factual circumstances of statehood, the goal of a *UN Charter*-prescribed political independence. The origins of this elective desire and how it has withstood the problems of refugee exile, armed conflict, and failure of the UN organization to deliver a means to its realization are important to consider. A Sahrawi aspiration to statehood will always demand fresh assessment. Moreover, the present stalled circumstances in delivering a self-determination referendum suggest a search for something new, a remedial shortcut.[32]

The origins of Sahrawi nationalism (perhaps more accurately, *statehood aspiration*) must be understood if the strength and apparent unanimity of the desire for independence are to be understood. This nationalism emerged in three historic phases, with features in common to those of other peoples in colonial Africa. And they have tended to be reinforced in Sahrawi social-political discourse since 1975 and with what appears to be greater amplification following the return of armed conflict in 2020.

As a first phase, the Spanish colonial period until 1975 fostered a Sahrawi identity in response to an alien governing presence—even as it was minimally intrusive during the first decades of the twentieth century. Territorial enclosure is also relevant: Imposing land frontiers was less a matter of colonial control and more something that reinforced different governing presences and distinctions between indigenous peoples in the vast area surrounding Western Sahara; Algeria, Mauritania, and Morocco today. By the 1960s, the factors of a small Sahrawi elite and educated cadre, coupled with the global anti-colonial movement (with a legal foundation in the 1960 UN General Assembly self-determination resolutions) and a particular identification of Western Sahara as a place requiring decolonization reinforced this nationalism.[33] Such a political identity could be understood as possible, leading to its acceptance in part because of a relatively small Sahrawi population in a setting a great distance from other peoples.[34] A social and political identity took hold after 1970:

> It was at its second congress [in] 1974, that the [Polisario Front] came out unambiguously in favor of full independence. . . . A manifesto adopted by the congress declared that "the Saharawi people have no alternative but to struggle until wresting independence, their wealth and their full sovereignty over their land." (Hodges 1983, 163 [citation omitted])[35]

By 1975, a palpable Sahrawi insistence for independence could be discerned. Three events are notable for reinforcing a collective understanding of what self-determination could entail. The first was the visit of the UN General Assembly's mission to discern the wishes of the territory's population, in May 1975. It should be remembered that during this era the General Assembly had the leading role in decolonization in the United Nation organization. The Polisario Front effectively arranged for mass demonstrations of Sahrawi, the visiting mission concluding that "the majority of the population within the Spanish Sahara was manifestly in favor of independence."[36] The mission's report was presented to the General Assembly within days of the International Court of Justice's advisory opinion on Western Sahara. In this second event of the time, the Court unequivocally upheld the Sahrawi right to self-determination and that Mauritania and Morocco did not have "any" claim to the territory of Western Sahara (*Western Sahara Advisory Opinion*). Among the many decolonization cases considered by the ICJ, the result has been arguably the clearest about the status of a non-self-governing territory and the right of its people to exercise their political independence. Only in 2019 when the Court considered the separation of the Chagos Islands from Mauritius during that country's 1960s decolonization would there be an equally unambiguous outcome (*Separation of the Chagos Advisory Opinion*). What can be called the *legalization* of Sahrawi status has persisted as a result of an ongoing reinforcement of the wish for independence.

The third event of this period was the time between Western Sahara's incipient invasion by Mauritania and Morocco in the last days of October 1975, Morocco's Green March into the territory, Spain's treaty agreement (the Madrid Accords) to confer administration of Western Sahara (and, ostensibly, shared responsibility for some act of self-determination) until the Sahrawi UDI in February 1976. The creation of a state has meant a continuing basis for the conception of Sahrawi identity. Moreover, the state has been able to comport itself in a governing fashion for Sahrawis in exile at the Tindouf refugee camps, adding to legitimacy and popular subscription to the "project" of independence.

> Set up in an inhospitable environment where there was nothing, and everything had to be done, the camps were a blank slate on which to write a new historical narrative based on the desire for an independent nation-state. If, on the one hand, the camps represent the ultimate possibility of the present, on the other, it is that very impossibility (of a territory, of a 'normal state,' of peace, private property, material wealth, et cetera) that generates a radical desire for the better future incarnated by the Saharawi state. The camps, although connected in some ways with (narratives of) the past, are basically a projection for the future. (San Martin 2010: 118)[37]

The elements of a desire for statehood today are undiminished. A manifestation of the sentiment can be seen in the unanimity among Sahrawis in the Tindouf camps and in the occupied part of Western Sahara to recover the foundational strands for independence, starting with an end to occupation and exercising the right to self-determination. Meanwhile, a "popular instruction" to the Sahrawi government to function as a state continues. This can be seen in activities as diverse as elections (in the camps) for governing bodies, the pluralism of numerous civil society organizations, and the conduct of government toward ultimate liberation, something taking on a different character with a return to armed conflict in 2020.

No further justification (or apology) for a Sahrawi state appears needed. If self-determination as a universal norm is to include acts of political independence appears to have chosen such a result.[38] The importance of that agency and preserving the legal order from which it would be realized is undeniable. A manifested wish for statehood, surpassing threshold considerations of democratic legitimacy and popular credibility, is something in the circumstances of a non-self-governing territory to be given effect.[39]

VIABILITY

In the era of decolonization after 1945, people proposing to create for themselves new states have been evaluated, often with bias, on the viability of their projects. This has been apparent in the hard cases of non-self-governing peoples of small states (population, geographic circumstances), who, on the journey to self-determination, were annexed by neighboring states. Namibia, East Timor, and Western Sahara are prominent examples. Often this question of capacity or prospects reduces to asking whether the would-be state can "succeed." Success in statehood is routinely defined from a Global North perspective, as necessarily extending to economic feasibility, democratic institutions, and the absence of problematic behaviors for neighboring states and the organized international community.[40] What is central to identifying success in the case of Western Sahara are Sahrawi perceptions of it.

Viability can be thought of as an *assured capacity*, in other words, the sustained ordering and function of governing institutions for a state's activities and those of civil society. The Sahrawi capacity ledger weighs heavily toward sufficiency. Indeed, it may be more expedient to consider and then discard the few things that impede successful statehood. We can usefully take the two in turn.

An arguably objective measure of state viability is the capacity to maintain the Montevideo criteria. Can a state persist, for example, in the identification, securing and control of its territory? Does it presently have a population that identifies in some way with the state, that is, is not transient and accepts (if not prefers) citizenship? Such things are clearly established for the Sahrawi people. The reinforcing of their identity, in partial exile and as subjects of occupation, contributes to an ambition to result in the basic activities of the state. Viability is also prospective, the potential for an organized and functioning state to be gauged.

The essential future grounds for success seem to be available. Of course, as in other decolonized territories whose people have experienced conflict and occupation (Namibia, East Timor) the adverse, sometimes traumatic, impacts of the journey to statehood must be provided for. Matters ranging from the return of Sahrawi in exile (including those in the Tindouf camps who number more than 160,000) to reconciliation, and the social position of Moroccan settlers and others in a new civil society will present initial problems.[41] The foundations of success include a now-pronounced democratic governing tradition, the related characteristic of the unity of Sahrawi society, and a base of natural resources.[42] The composition of Sahrawi society, with a relatively small diaspora—mostly in Mauritania and Spain—with what has become a singular ethnic makeup and language tradition are features of this unity. In social terms and through the development of their governing institutions the Sahrawi have the advantage, relative to others in Africa's twentieth-century decolonization, of decades of refining society and government.

A Sahrawi state is also demonstrably economically possible. Again, a relatively small population is helpful, although it should not be so small that governing and economic services cannot be provided by it. Natural resources will be a crucial part of the national economy, principally from the coastal fishery and export of phosphate mineral rock, each at annual market values (2022–2023) of approximately € 200 million.[43] In addition, the acquisition and extension of solar electrical generating facilities assure large-scale electrification for domestic uses and industry, with the possibility of export.[44] The extraction of petroleum, meanwhile, remains an open question given development costs.[45] Western Sahara is rich in minerals, and the iron ore potential of the southern half of the territory is now understood. The long-term success of relying on primary resources for a Sahrawi economy will mean local processing (*e.g.*, seafood products) and addition of value (*e.g.*, fertilizer manufacturing with the use of locally mined phosphate), together with regulatory and financial services operating under a transparent rule of law.[46]

THE EXTERNAL-ASSOCIATIVE: SUPPORTING THE CREATION OF A SAHARAWI STATE

Undeniably, the organized international community has an obligation to ensure the Sahrawi people have undiminished self-determination. But does that duty extend to recognition of either an existing Sahrawi state or, in the future, a choice of independence? The basic precepts of the modern (and Westphalian) international order contain the answer, found in Articles 2 and 73 of the *UN Charter*: It is a threshold political independence of the Sahrawi people—their agency in a post-colonial order—which must be assured for them so that their right to self-determination is realized. (This is why the illegal resettlement of Moroccan citizens into Western Sahara is a concern, properly labeled the international crime that it is: Nothing impedes the agency of choosing status like the presence of those who would deny it.) The threshold is a narrow one: The obligation is to ensure the Sahrawi people the ability to exercise elective choice. If their decision is independence, then, the organized international community must respect the sovereign equality of their state. That is different from the discretionary act of recognition of a Sahrawi state, or its admission to international organizations such as the UN General Assembly. Recognition, of course, has no compulsion as a matter of law. However, the support for a consistent Sahrawi demand for what can be called a *fulfilled statehood* does.

This is the first extrinsic basis for the assurance of Sahrawi statehood. More accurately (and as noted at the start of this chapter), in the circumstances of a Sahrawi people who repeatedly choose institutions through which to govern themselves as a state, the *completion* of statehood.[47] In support of this contention, three precepts that apply to the "question" of Western Sahara can be recalled. The first is the right of non-self-governing people to self-determination. The second is the commitment of the Frente Polisario, Morocco, and the United Nations to the exercise of self-determination set out in the 1991 Settlement Plan. While Morocco has increasingly avoided its commitment after 2007, and the UN has failed to administer an act of self-determination, the obligation is no less compelling for such things. Third, the organized international community (and notably the AU) has persistently required Sahrawi self-determination. Even after the United States declared in 2020 that it recognized Morocco's territorial claim in Western Sahara and Spain asserted in March 2022 its support for Morocco's autonomy plan, the international community has maintained its (admittedly tacit) stance (Minder 2022).

A second external basis for Sahrawi statehood is the continuing African consensus that statehood has resulted. This is hardly a monolith. The SADR is recognized only by a majority of the continent's states and not universally among them. But all have been content for the SADR to be a member of the AU and for Union institutions to engage the question of Western Sahara in critical terms (African Union Report 2015). Such a regional consensus has been held for four decades. It is difficult to contemplate a reversal without a clear choice being expressed by the Sahrawi people. Such an act would be contrary to the AU's founding principles and the experience of most states in bringing colonialism in them to an end. Moreover, the relativism that might inform such a withdrawal of support for the exercise of a fundamental right would have to be in light of Western Sahara's legal status, more accurately, the settled understanding that Morocco has no territorial claim to it. Like everywhere else, although uniquely as a matter of the *AU Charter,* African states have an interest in territorial integrity. In the circumstances of the continent's decolonization during the twentieth century, this precept has been held with remarkable durability. African states have reliably looked to international law to maintain and resolve colonially prescribed frontiers, as well as maritime boundaries following the 1982 *UN Convention on the Law of the Sea*.[48]

VINDICATING THE POST-COLONIAL

In contemplating an independent Western Sahara, the goals of the post-colonial order can be recalled. They are directed significantly to the ending of "alien domination" by securing the equality of peoples in sovereign polities enjoying assured political independence. This, of course, is the intended result of Article 2 of the *UN Charter*. Where it is compromised or reduced in its application, the necessary universality of its application in new cases of self-determination and where existing policies have their political independence threatened is correspondingly weakened. Reciprocity and the consistent application of what is a fundamental norm of the international order matter, both symbolically and transactionally.

In addition, the decision of the United Nations organization to singularly administer a ratifying act of Sahrawi self-determination underscores the responsibility delegated to it by its member states in a fundamental matter of human rights. This responsibility extends to the remaining cases of decolonization and by extension to instances of unlawful occupation where "alien domination" persists. An equal ethical burden would seem to fall upon the African Union organization, if not in law responsible to assure an act of self-determination. The AU's responsibility would, however, be to recognize the circumstances of one of its member states being occupied, thereby responding to universal principles of the protection of a Sahrawi civil population in the circumstances and confronting aggression now manifested as annexation. These matters are the responsibility of the entire organized international community, of course, obscured (as noted earlier) by the singular characterization of Western Sahara as a question of self-determination.

Because a people can reverse a choice of statehood, for example in the 1990s era dissolution of Yugoslavia, and because the Sahrawi people have persistently sought statehood as the sole outcome of self-determination, a vindication of the post-colonial and rule of law orders now seems necessary through expedited statehood. There are two elements to this. The first is the practical aspects or instrumentalization of statehood, something which turns on ending the occupation of Western Sahara. A realized statehood depends on territorial integrity. The second element is recognition. A Sahrawi entity is less to be presented as viable or meeting threshold Montevideo criteria, and more one that has overcome—sidestepped—what was long understood to be the legitimating act of an UN-administered referendum. Locating a fresh basis to proceed means understanding the relationship between occupation and the international community's implied requirement of a validating choice, *i.e.*, an act of self-determination as overcoming the status quo. The problem is that, so long as the occupation persists, a validating act that entails international acceptance (recognition) will be denied. Is there some new event or phenomenon to be found that overcomes this iteratively reinforcing impasse that would be attractive to the organized international community?

The first answer is in the work and representations of the African Union. This may be exercised both directly and indirectly. The direct would be an insistence on resolving the status of the Sahrawi people, by representations to the parties involved and African governments in general. Since 2015 the AU Commission and the AU Peace & Security Council have demonstrated an outspoken approach to the question of Western Sahara. By indirect activity the AU as a whole can usefully assert its position with the United Nations and, if to a lesser extent, European Union institutions (Parliament, Council, Commission), thereby acquiring greater influence. The objective would be to shift or dismantle the UN's central requirement of an exclusively administered self-determination referendum. This seems a radical proposition. After all, if the resolution of the question of Western Sahara turns into a credible validating act of self-determination, a UN-delivered referendum is an act *par excellence*. For an African Union as an institution that accepts Sahrawi statehood that is not the case, of course. The 1991 Settlement Plan referendum ratifies less the choice of status and more the resolution of a conflict between the Sahrawi people and Morocco.

For the African Union, therefore, if it is to pursue a more active role, this means the promotion of a referendum—perhaps now involving the Union alongside the UN—or in the alternative proceeding to recognize statehood for a Sahrawi entity. The latter suggests a remedial approach that because the UN administration of self-determination has stalled (to a point of failure), an expedient means of assuring self-determination is needed. The self-determination of non-self-governing peoples is itself remedial, of course. And the practice of decolonization allows for a range of processes, from colonial administering state withdrawal, to internationally supervised plebiscites. A change of mechanism, therefore, is hardly remedial. It simply needs to deliver an assured result to the organized international community. Apart from a regional diplomatic consensus among African states coupled with a wider promotion of AU initiatives, some legal cover could be useful, recalling the advice sought by the UN General Assembly from the International Court of Justice following Kosovo's unilateral declaration of independence in 2008 (*Kosovo Advisory Opinion*). Provocatively, the question for referral to the Court could be whether the SADR is an existing state. More to the AU's involvement, the indicated questions seem to be whether the UN has exclusivity in administering Sahrawi self-determination and, if not, what modes or processes of the act are permissible under the law.[49]

Much is made in completing the decolonization of Africa of the legitimacy of the process. It is important, the reasoning would have it, to implement established methods of confirming a non-self-governing people's decision about their international status. In this, the 1991 Settlement Plan presents the most credible means of assuring Sahrawi's self-determination. And it, therefore, follows that decolonizing Africa should maintain an accepted process. But perhaps not. Discarding a process after three decades is not precipitous. Moreover, the question of Western Sahara remains captive to states and organizations outside the continent. A capacity and willingness for an African community of states to act is a necessary shrugging off of external imperatives.

In the end, Sahrawi statehood is a matter of the expressed will of a people locating and establishing for themselves an international legal personality. Aspects of the factual, recalling the fulfillment of the Montevideo criteria discussed above, and of the legal must always be the framework for identifying a Sahrawi state. Viability, meanwhile, is a proper concern of the organized international community. But none should serve as conditions precedent or impediments, including mechanistic referendum processes serving to ratify popular will. In asking what the factual preconditions are to identify the Sahrawi people and their eligibility for statehood, the answer has been before us.[50] The final act of decolonizing Africa is no more conceptually challenging than acceptance of a long-understood choice of political independence.

REFERENCES

Books

Cassese, A (2005), *International Law,* 2nd ed. Oxford: Oxford University Press.

Clark, J & Brooks, N (eds) (2018), *The archeology of Western Sahara: A synthesis of fieldwork, 2002 to 2009.* Oxford: Oxbow Books.

Dumienski, Z (2019), "Shared Citizenship and Sovereignty: The Case of the Cook Islands' and Niue's Relationship with New Zealand," in Ratuva, S (ed), *The Palgrave Handbook of Ethnicity*. London: Palgrave, 221–46.

Fernández-Molina, I & Porges M (2020), "Western Sahara," in Visoka, G, Doyle, J and Newman, E (eds), *Routledge Handbook of State Recognition*. Abingdon: Routledge, 376–90.

Harzl, BC and Petrov, R (2022), *Unrecognized entities: Perspectives in International, European and Constitutional Law.* Leiden: Brill Nijhoff.

Hodges, T (1983), *Western Sahara: The Roots of a Desert War*. Westport: Lawrence Hill & Company.

Nascimento, D (2020), "Trials and Tribulations: The challenges of building a sustainable state in South Sudan," in Santi, RH, Polese, A and Kevlihan, R (eds), *Limited Statehood and Informal Governance in the Middle East and Africa*. Abingdon: Routledge, 85–99.

Prelz Oltramonti, G (2020), "The Viability of De Facto States: Cases from the Caucasus and the Horn of Africa," in Riegl M and Dobos, B (eds), *Perspectives on Secession: Theory and Case Studies*. Berlin: Springer, 93–108.

San Martín, P (2010), *Western Sahara: The Refugee Nation*. Cardiff: University of Wales Press.

Shaw, MN (2017), *International Law*, 8th ed. Cambridge: Cambridge University Press.

Simpson, G (2012), "International law in diplomatic history," in Crawford, J & Koskenniemi, M (eds), *The Cambridge Companion to International Law*. Cambridge: Cambridge University Press, 25–46.

Smith, JJ (2018), "Plunder Intercepted: The legal case to seize globally traded phosphate from occupied Western Sahara," in Hagen, E & Pfeifer M (eds), *Profit over Peace in Western Sahara: How commercial interests undermine self-determination in the last colony in Africa*. Berlin: Sternberg Press, 128–47.

Soroeta Liceras, J (2014), *International Law and the Western Sahara Conflict*. Chicago: Wolf Legal Publishers.

Vrancken, PHG and Tsamenyi, M (2017), *The Law of the Sea: The African Union and Its Member States.* Claremont, South Africa: Juta and Company.

Wilson, A (2016), *Sovereignty in Exile: A Saharan Liberation Movement Governs*. Philadelphia: University of Pennsylvania Press.

Wilson, A (2020), "Everyday Sovereignty in Exile: People, Territory, and Resources among Sahrawi Refugees," in Bryant R and Reeves M (eds), *The Everyday Lives of Sovereignty*. Ithaca, NY: Cornell University Press, 134–53.

Zunes, S and Mundy, J (2010), *Western Sahara: War, Nationalism, and Conflict Irresolution*. Syracuse, NY: Syracuse University Press.

Journal Articles

Fernandez-Molina, I & Ojeda Garcia, R (2019), "Western Sahara as a Hybrid of a Parastate and a State-in-exile: (Extra)territoriality and the Small Print of Sovereignty in a Context of Frozen Conflict," *Nationalities Papers,* Vol 48, pp 83–99.

Leblic, I (2022), "Sovereignty and Coloniality in French-Speaking Pacific: A Reflection on the Case of New Caledonia, 1980–2021," *Oceania,* Vol 92, 107–32.

Kamal, F (2015), "The role of natural resources in the building of an independent Western Sahara," *Global Change, Peace and Security*, Vol 27, 345–60.

Mundy, J (2012), "Moroccan Settlers in Western Sahara: Colonists or Fifth Column?" *Arab World Geographer*, Vol 15, 95–126.

Smith, JJ (2020), "A Four-Fold Evil? The Crime of Aggression and the Case of Western Sahara," *International Criminal Law Review*, Vol 20, 492–550.

Omar, SM (2008), "The Right to Self-determination and the Indigenous People of Western Sahara," *Cambridge Review of International Affairs*, Vol 21, 41–57.

Omar, S (2018), "The African Union policies towards the Western Sahara," *Africana Studia*, Vol 29, 91–102.

Visoka, G (2021), "Statehood and recognition in world politics: Towards a critical research agenda," *Cooperation and Conflict*, Vol 57, 133–51.

Caselaw

Accordance with International Law of the Unilateral Declaration of Independence in Respect of Kosovo, Advisory Opinion, ICJ Reports 2010, 403 (*Kosovo Advisory Opinion*).

Legal Consequences of the Construction of a Wall in the Occupied Palestinian Territory, Advisory Opinion, ICJ Reports 2004, 136 (*Palestine Wall Advisory Opinion*).

Legal Consequences of the Separation of the Chagos Archipelago from Mauritius in 1965, Advisory Opinion, ICJ Reports *2019*, 65 (*Separation of the Chagos Advisory Opinion*).

Saharawi Arab Democratic Republic and Another v Owner and Charterers of MV 'NM Cherry Blossom' [2017] ZAECPEHC 31.

Western Sahara Advisory Opinion, ICJ Reports 1975, 12.

Treaties and Treaty Materials, and African Union, European Union, and United Nations Documents

African Union, "Report of the Chairperson of the Commission on the Evolution of the Peace Process in Western Sahara and Other Related Issues" (27 March 2015),

Peace and Security council document PSC/PR/2.(CDXCVI) (African Union Report 2015).

European Commission Staff Working Document, "2021 Report on the benefits for the people of Western Sahara on extending tariff preferences to products from Western Sahara" (22 December 2021), Document SWD (2021) 431 final.

Constitutive Act of the African Union (11 July 2000), OAU Doc. CAB/Leg/23.15 (2001).

Convention on the Rights and Duties of States (26 December 1933) 165 LNTS 19 (in force 26 December 1934) (*Montevideo Convention*).

Declaration of Principles on Western Sahara by Spain, Morocco and Western Sahara (14 November 1975) (1976) *Revue Générale de Droit Public*, Vol 80, 380 (*Madrid Accords*).

Swiss Federal Department of Foreign Affairs, Letter, "Notification to Governments of the States parties to the Geneva Conventions of 12 August 1949 for the Protection of War Victims" (26 June 2015) (Available at: <https://www.eda.admin.ch/dam/eda/fr/documents/aussenpolitik/voelkerrecht/geneve/15026-GENEVE_en.pdf>, accessed 31 May 2022).

UN General Assembly Resolutions 1514 "Declaration on the Granting of Independence to Colonial Countries and Peoples" (10 December 1960).

UN General Assembly Resolution 1541 "Principles which should guide members in determining whether or not an obligation exists to transmit the information called for under article 73e of the Charter" (10 December 1960).

UN General Assembly Resolution 2072 "Question of Ifni and Spanish Sahara" (16 December 1965).

UN Security Council Resolution 2602 (2021), "Question of Western Sahara" (29 October 2021).

United Nations Visiting Mission to Spanish Sahara, 1975, General Assembly, 30th Session, Supplemental 23, UN Document A/10023/Rev. (Report of the UN Visiting Mission to Western Sahara, 1975).

Saharawi Arab Democratic Republic Legislation and UNFCCC NDC Instruments

Maritime Zones Law No. 3 of 2009 (21 January 2009).

Mining Law No. 2 of 2014 (26 May 2014).

Sahrawi Arab Democratic Republic, "First Indicative Nationally Determined Contribution" (November 2021), (Available at: <https://research-portal.uea.ac.uk/en/publications/sahrawi-arab-democratic-republic-first-indicative-nationally-dete>, accessed 31 May 2022).

Non-Governmental Organization Research Reports, Media Articles, and Wikipedia Entries

Minder, R (19 March 2022). "Spain, Seeking Better Ties With Morocco, Shifts Stance on Western Sahara. *New York Times* (Available at: <https://www.nytimes.com/2022/03/19/world/europe/spain-morocco-western-sahara.html>, accessed 31 May 2022.)

Western Sahara Resource Watch, "P for Plunder 2021" (April 2022). Brussels.

Western Sahara Resource Watch, "Greenwashing Occupation: How Morocco's renewable energy projects in occupied Western Sahara prolong the conflict over the last colony in Africa" (October 2021). Brussels.

Wikipedia, "International recognition of the Sahrawi Arab Democratic Republic" (Available at: <https://en.wikipedia.org/wiki/International_recognition_of_the_Sahrawi_Arab_Democratic_Republic>, accessed 31 May 2022).

NOTES

1. The decolonization of Western Sahara differs from all other cases except *apartheid* South Africa in South West Africa/Namibia, because its territorial integrity and the right of its people to self-determination were judicially confirmed during a colonial period before invasion by neighboring states. In October 1975, the International Court of Justice concluded Mauritania and Morocco did not have "any" territorial claim to a then Spanish Sahara. See *Western Sahara Advisory Opinion* at para 162.

2. *Sahrawi,* as the anglicized descriptor of people (*Ahel es-Sahel*) and territory is employed in this chapter. Where an original context requires it, Saharawi is used. The Sahrawi national liberation movement founded 10 May 1973, Frente Popular para la liberacion de Saguia el-Hamra y Río de Oro, is referred to as the Frente Polisario.

3. Both Timorese and Sahrawi people refer to their international legal status—statehood—as being *restored*, with less emphasis as achieved.

4. The Saharawi Arab Democratic Republic (SADR) was declared in a meeting of civil society leaders on 27 February 1976. Given Spain's withdrawal after legislation enacted in November 1975 to end responsibility for its Spanish Sahara colony, the declared creation of a Saharawi state—as with East Timor in November 1975—occurred in a vacuum, without the colonial state's direct or tacit consent. See Hodges 1983: 229–40.

5. For a discussion of the circumstances and legal implications of Western Sahara under occupation, see Smith 2020.

6. Political independence is meant in the context of the organizing principles defined in Article 2 of the *UN Charter*, for an international community governed by the norms of territorial integrity, sovereign equality, and peaceful coexistence to assure the political independence of peoples organized as states.

7. The Westphalian order, European by conception and significantly in its character, is the international community composed of states as sovereign equals. Non-state entities and persons have subordinate juridical status although this has changed

to allow regional organizations and some international organizations to acquire state-like personalities in the twentieth century, *e.g.*, the African Union. The treaties resulting from the Peace of Westphalia in 1648 "contain early examples of what came to be called the (legal) principles of non-intervention and self-determination." Simpson 2012: 31.

8. For a discussion of the *Madrid Accords*, see Naïli this volume. The Accords were unlawful as a means of transferring responsibility for self-determination in Western Sahara. See Soroeta Liceras (2014): 126–55.

9. "After the founding of the SADR, the [Polisario] front's bodies tended to overlap, in function and composition, with those of the new republic. This was inevitable, in conditions of war and partial exile. . . . Such measures did not, in an of themselves deny the validity of the SADR's claim to statehood—for, despite its inability to administer the principal towns of Western Sahara, the SADR had such state attributes as the control of a large and well-equipped army and a functioning system of civil administration in exile. . . . However, it was Polisario, as much as the SADR, which possessed these attributes of statehood." Hodges 1983: 340.

10. See also Wilson 2020. A Saharawi identity toward statehood—nationalism—has been reinforced in the circumstances of an isolated refugee community that is not politically dependent on a host state (or other benefactors) for its conceptions of civil society.

11. Morocco withdrew from the OAU in 1984 on the Organization's acceptance of the SADR as a member state. Morocco rejoined the African Union in 2017.

12. Morocco contends that Western Sahara is part of an historic "greater Morocco" polity. Mauritania renounced a similar claim in a 1979 peace agreement with the Frente Polisario. For discussion and documents about both state's claims see the materials considered by the International Court of Justice in the *Western Sahara Advisory Opinion* case. In November 2020 the outgoing United States presidential administration recognized Morocco's claim to Western Sahara, contrary to international law.

13. The *Charter of the African Union* is usefully read alongside the *UN Charter* Article 2 principle for the territorial integrity of states, Article 4(b) requiring that: "The Union shall function in accordance with the following principles . . . respect of borders existing on achievement of independence."

14. The UN secretary-general routinely reports to the UN Security Council about "Frente Polisario" activities in the "liberated zone."

15. The SADR detailed its claimed exclusive economic zone along with a map in a letter to the UN secretary-general dated 5 March 2016.

16. In August 1974, Spain informed the United Nations that it would allow a self-determination referendum in the territory in the first half of 1975. See Hodges 1983: 170.

17. See Mundy 2012, and see also Naïli this volume.

18. The governing authority responsible for a non-self-governing territory can be permissibly absent from part or all of a territory, as the example of the UN Council for Namibia demonstrates.

19. The SADR also legislates for mining exploration, with iron ore in the south of the liberated zone offering promise of commercial development. See *Mining Law No 2 of 2014.*

20. See also San Martín 2010.

21. See also Wilson 2016.

22. In 2017 the SADR (and Frente Polisario) brought civil claims in courts in Panama and South Africa to recover ownership of cargos of phosphate exported from Western Sahara aboard ships that had stopped in those countries. See *Saharawi Arab Democratic Republic and Another v Owner and Charterers of MV 'NM Cherry Blossom.* For a discussion of the case see Smith 2018.

23. See the Status Lists at African Union, "OAU/AU Treaties, Conventions, Protocols & Charters." See Letter, Swiss Federal Department of Foreign Affairs, "Notification to Governments of the States parties to the Geneva Conventions of 12 August 1949 for the Protection of War Victims" (26 June 2015).

24. For useful discussions of these mixed characteristics see Fernandez-Molina & Ojeda Garcia 2019.

25. Eighty-four states have recognized the SADR, 75 during the period 1976–1990, almost all in the Global South. Forty-three states have variously suspended or withdrawn recognition, contrary to customary international law, for which see article 6 of the Montevideo Convention. See Wikipedia, "International recognition of the Sahrawi Arab Democratic Republic."

26. For a discussion of these theories of recognition, see Shaw 2017: 73.

27. On changes in the understanding and application of recognition, see Visoka 2021 and see Harzl and Petrov 2022. See also Fernández-Molina & Porges 2020.

28. "Both State practice and *opinio juris* at the relevant time [1965] confirm the customary law character of the right to territorial integrity of a non-self-governing territory as a corollary of the right to self-determination." *Separation of the Chagos Advisory Opinion*, para 160. "Since respect for the right to self-determination is an obligation *erga omnes*, all States have a legal interest in protecting that right," ibid at para 180 (citations omitted).

29. Articles 2 (territorial integrity) and 73 (self-determination) are the principal constitutive requirements of international law which apply to decolonization, arguably followed by common articles 1 (self-determination of non-self-governing peoples) of the *International Covenant on Civil and Political Rights* and the *International Covenant on Economic, Social and Cultural Rights*. The particular legal obligation to ensure for a non-self-governing people the choice of independence flows from UN General Assembly Resolutions 1514 "Declaration on the Granting of Independence to Colonial Countries and Peoples" and 1541 "Principles which should guide members in determining whether or not an obligation exists to transmit the information called for under article 73e of the Charter," both of 10 December 1960.

30. For a discussion, see Dumienski 2019.

31. For a discussion, see Leblic 2022.

32. The process of self-determination in Western Sahara, notwithstanding the 1991 Settlement Plan, is open to be revisited by the UN General Assembly. "The General Assembly assumed [oversight of the application of the right to self-determination]

in order to supervise the implementation of obligations incumbent upon administering Powers under the Charter. . . . The General Assembly also monitors the means by which the free and genuine will of the people of a non-self-government territory is expressed, including the formulation of questions submitted for popular consultation." *Separation of the Chagos Advisory Opinion*, para 167.

33. UN General Assembly Resolutions 1514 and 1541. Spanish Sahara was first identified for decolonization in UN General Assembly Resolution 2072 "Question of Ifni and Spanish Sahara" (16 December 1965). For a discussion of the evolution of UN General Assembly and Security Council resolutions, see Naïli this volume.

34. This suggests Western Sahara's colonial geography defined by 1900–1912 Franco-Spanish frontiers were somehow appropriate to the people within them. This may be arguably true in comparison to more obvious cases of artificial division and joining of peoples into colonial entities elsewhere in Africa. The familial, linguistic and nomadic distinction of the Sahrawi people with those of Morocco to the north is the clearest distinction.

35. Hodges observes that, although the colonial frontiers set for Western Sahara did not account for the entire range of traditional Sahrawi migration, the Polisario Front "pledged to respect them [during its 1974 congress] in order to avoid transgressing the established OAU doctrine on African frontiers and to summon as wide diplomatic support as possible." Ibid (citation omitted).

36. "At every place visited, the Mission was met by mass political demonstrations and had numerous private meetings with representatives of every section of the Saharan community. From all these, it became evident to the Mission that there was an overwhelming consensus among Saharans within the Territory in favour of independence and opposing integration with any neighbouring country. . . . " Report of the UN Visiting Mission to Spanish Sahara, 1975.

37. Algeria's obligation toward the Sahrawi people as refugees under international law is sometimes cited for the necessity of its protection of their human rights. Arguably, the greater protection accorded them is the assurance they may govern themselves in exile.

38. "[T]he right of peoples to self-determination is today a right *erga omnes*." *Palestine Wall Advisory Opinion*, para 88 (citation omitted).

39. This is certainly a settled rule of customary international law. A large number of states have been accepted as coming into existence with expression of the political independence of their peoples.

40. The experience of post-colonial states has sometimes shown concerns about their viability to be misplaced. Consider Singapore (given its geographic size) and Palestine (given its governance and security). On one level, therefore, recognition of a state functions as a marker of anticipated "success."

On the viability of *de facto* states—which can be defined as ones awaiting formal statehood (or accepted independence)—see Prelz Oltramonti 2020. See also Nascimento 2020.

41. The Frente Polisario has continued after 2007 in its position that Moroccan settlers in Western Sahara would be permitted to remain should independence result from self-determination. "Polisario officials have long maintained that their state will

be viable only with the continued presence of Moroccan settlers as a part of the labor force." Zunes and Mundy 2010: 232.

42. Saharawi civil society may not expectedly be homogenous at independence, given a divided population since 1975 and some possibility of Moroccan settlers to remain.

43. These figures are the author's, on analysis of market activity and fishing vessels present. For a Sahrawi perspective, see Kamal (2015). And see European Commission Staff Working Document, "2021 Report on the benefits for the people of Western Sahara on extending tariff preferences to products from Western Sahara."

44. See Western Sahara Resource Watch, "Greenwashing Occupation: How Morocco's renewable energy projects in occupied Western Sahara prolong the conflict over the last colony in Africa."

45. See Sahrawi Arab Democratic Republic, "First Indicative Nationally Determined Contribution" (November 2021).

46. A territorially restored SADR will experience initiation costs of new institutions, resettlement of its people from the Tindouf camps and the clearing of munitions along the 2,700 kilometre length of the berm.

47. The UN organization employs phrasing differently than a full spectrum choice which includes the option of independence. See the UN Security Council resolutions after 2007, *e.g.*, UN Security Council Resolution 2602 (2021), "Question of Western Sahara," the Council "reaffirming its commitment to assist the parties to achieve a just, lasting, and mutually acceptable political solution."

48. "The Union shall function in accordance with the following principles . . . (b) respect of borders existing on achievement of independence." *Constitutive Act of the African Union*. See also Omar 2018. And see Vrancken and Tsamenyi 2017.

49. Other questions could usefully examine the supervising role of the UN General Assembly in the circumstances. What could the General Assembly require of the Security Council and of the parties?

50. The question is Judge Antônio Cançado Trindade's from the *Kosovo Advisory Opinion* case, separate opinion, 612 at para 225: "And what are the factual preconditions for the configurations of a 'people,' and of its eligibility into statehood, under international law?"

12

Western Sahara Peace Process, 1975–2008

An Overview

Meriem Naili

INTRODUCTION

The impasse reached in Western Sahara is the result of a self-determination conflict that has become "frozen" over the past few decades (Fernandez-Molina & Ojeda-Garcia 2019, 86). A former Spanish colony, it has been listed since 1963 as one of the seventeen non-self-governing territories (NSGTs) by the UN but remains the only such territory without a designated administrating power.[1] Despite having openly stated its support for self-determination between 1966 through 1974, the Kingdom of Morocco, since becoming independent from France in 1956, has claimed sovereignty over Western Sahara. It has, since the official departure of Spain on 26 February 1976, formally annexed around 80 percent of its territory, over which it exercises de facto control contrary to the conclusions reached by the ICJ in its 1975 advisory opinion.[2] Through the self-proclaimed Sahrawi Arab Democratic Republic (SADR), the Frente Polisario has been campaigning since its creation in May 1973 in favor of independence through a referendum on self-determination.

The UN Mission for the Referendum in Western Sahara (MINURSO) was created by Security Council Resolution 690 in 1991 to put an end to the sixteen-year-long war that broke out in November 1975 following Morocco's 'Green March' commanded by King Hassan II. The resolution provided for the declaration of a cease-fire and the organization of a self-determination referendum on the final status of the territory, which has yet to take place. The conflict, therefore, remains unresolved to this day and the territory of

Western Sahara has become "the last colony in Africa." Since the late 1970s, that part of the territory occupied by Morocco has remained under its military control. The General Court and the Court of Justice of the European Union, as well as the High Court of South Africa and the African Court on Human and Peoples' Rights, have recently reaffirmed the status of Western Sahara as an NSGT, so identified by the UN in 1963 following the last transmission of information on Spanish Sahara by Spain under Article 73 of the UN Charter. All three Courts have rejected any claims of sovereignty by Morocco by restating the distinct status of the territory.[3] Morocco's presence has been defined as an occupation by the UN General Assembly (UNGA), the African Union, the High Court of South Africa, and the CJEU (through its press release services).[4]

In October 2021, a fifth personal envoy to the UN secretary-general for Western Sahara (PE) was appointed to relaunch the talks between Morocco and Frente Polisario, at a time when the people of Western Sahara have yet to exercise their right to self-determination. Staffan de Mistura, an Italian/Swedish diplomat, is responsible for finding a way to ensure this right is implemented following international law and relevant UN resolutions. MINURSO initially tasked with organizing the referendum and monitoring the cease-fire, has failed to fulfill its mandate. The mission arguably stands as an exception in modern peacekeeping given its absence of explicit human rights monitoring components. All documents and utterances bear witness to the deadlock that the negotiation process has reached. The diverging interpretations by the parties to its mandate are unambiguous, including in the most recent reports by the Secretary-General (UNSG) about Western Sahara, and are regarded as a continuous impediment to the UN's commitment to administer the process of self-determination.[5]

The sovereignty over the territory of Western Sahara has been and remains the primary issue of this protracted conflict for which the international system has failed to provide a solution. This chapter discusses the various phases in the peace process from 1975 and the ICJ advisory opinion until the four rounds of negotiations that took place in Manhasset, New York, between 2007 and 2008. The first phase of the peace process points to a stronger involvement from the international community in the 1980s in the context of armed conflict, reaching a peak when the Settlement Plan was agreed upon in 1988 and MINURSO was deployed in 1991. The next phase saw a voter identification process dragging out, causing delays in the holding of the referendum and the appointment of the former US secretary of state James Baker as the first PE in 1997 and the parties' signature of the Houston Agreements the same year. This apparent progress in the peace process was eroded, a last phase starting with Baker's resignation in 2004 following the rejection of two consecutive plans for Saharawi self-determination and the crystallization of the process from 2007 onward with the Moroccan proposal for Autonomy.

PHASE I: THE ROLE OF THE ORGANISED INTERNATIONAL COMMUNITY AND THE DEPLOYMENT OF MINURSO: 1975–1991

The year 1975 was a turning point in the conflict over Western Sahara. That October 16, the ICJ rendered its Advisory Opinion requested by the UNGA, joined by the Kingdom of Morocco and the Mauritanian entity (with Spain as a participating state by a memorial and in the hearing). The Court was requested to assess whether the territory of Western Sahara was considered *terra nullius* before Spanish colonization in 1884, i.e., whether a population was in some way present at the time of colonial acquisition. The Court unanimously concluded that, at the time of colonization by Spain, the territory was not *terra nullius.* On the second question referred to it, the ICJ did not find "any legal ties of such a nature as might affect the application of resolution 1514 (XV) in the decolonization of Western Sahara and, in particular, of the principle of self-determination through the free and genuine expression of the will of the peoples of the Territory" (paras. 129, 162).[6] Consequently, Spain—with the support of the UN—was required under international law to proceed with the decolonization process of the Spanish Sahara. The advisory opinion did not, however, prevent the Kingdom of Morocco from launching its "Green March" that November, which reportedly saw between 100,000 (Hodges) and 350,000 (Zunes & Mundy) Moroccan subjects to the King invaded the territory to "regain its southern provinces." This event was precipitated by the worsening health of Spain's head of state, Francisco Franco, with the result that a few days later, Spain agreed to transfer administrative power to Morocco and Mauritania. On 14 November 1975, the Madrid Accords—formally the Declaration of Principles on Western Sahara—were signed between Spain, Morocco, and Mauritania setting the conditions under which Spain would withdraw from the territory and divide its administration between the two African states. Its paragraph two reads that "Spain shall immediately proceed to establish a temporary administration in the territory, in which Morocco and Mauritania shall participate in collaboration with the Jemâa,[7] and to which the responsibilities and powers referred to in the preceding paragraph shall be transferred."[8] Although it was never published on the *Boletin Oficial del Estado,* the accord was executed and Mauritania and Morocco subsequently partitioned the territory in April 1976. Protocols to the Madrid Accords allowed for the transfer of the Bou Craa phosphate mine and its infrastructure and for Spain to continue its involvement in the coastal fisheries (Thompson 1980, 175).

The protocols were only made known or came to light, many years later, although the fisheries arrangements were clear enough. Spain held a 35 percent ownership share in Phosboucraa until 2002 when the Moroccan Office Chérifien des Phosphates acquired the entirety of the shares.[9] Akin to the request for an advisory opinion sent to the ICJ in late 1974, it seems that the initial purpose of the Madrid Accords was to clarify the situation over the status of the territory. However, the administrative arrangements for the NSGT of Western Sahara were discussed without consultation or consent of any representatives of the Sahrawi people.[10] Furthermore, as will be discussed below, in a legal opinion by Hans Corell, UN under-secretary-general for legal affairs, the agreement 'did not transfer sovereignty over the Territory, nor did it confer upon any of the signatories the status of an administering Power, a status which Spain alone could not have unilaterally transferred.'[11] On 26 February 1976, Spain formalized its withdrawal from Western Sahara in a letter addressed to the UNSG, and, the next day, Frente Polisario and an assembly of Sahrawi people unilaterally proclaimed the creation of an independent state.

Over an ensuing four-month period, the armed conflict between Morocco, Mauritania, and the Frente Polisario intensified in the territory of Western Sahara. In 1979, three years after it engaged in an armed conflict, Mauritania signed an armistice agreement in Algiers with Frente Polisario and formally renounced all claims on the territory of Western Sahara. This decision has caused the immediate takeover by Morocco of the portion previously under Mauritania's control.

Even though hostilities were ongoing in the territory, there was not much of a peace process *per se* between 1975 and 1986. There were indeed some efforts through the UNGA in the early years following the withdrawal from Spain to try and prevent the conflict from escalating further. Only when there was a will to have the African Unity (AU) intervene—to provide 'good offices'—was there movement toward a ceasefire and dealing with self-determination. The aim of any process or initiative at the time was first to put an end to hostilities on the ground. The hostilities attracted the interest of the organized international community in a context where the ongoing Cold War made the rules on the international diplomatic stage. Like many battlegrounds around the world, each of the parties was supported diplomatically, financially, and militarily by competing powers and superpowers. Morocco was the West and the USA's *protégé*, while Frente Polisario remained very much under the guardianship of Algeria, on the other side of the international political spectrum. Yet, the Soviet Union did not directly support the Frente Polisario (Zoubir, 1987). Not only did states individually attempt to affirm their spheres of influence, the organized international community through international and regional organizations, offered the parties the space to pursue their conflict in diplomatic terms. The UN, the AU, and the EU have all been, in one way or another, actors in the peace process.

The United Nations

The UN, which was dealing at the time with a large decolonization process throughout the world, was seized early with the "question of Western Sahara" as the UNGA had issued resolutions since December 1965. A review of the relevant UN documents on Western Sahara from the UN Security Council, Secretary-General, and General Assembly shows various levels of involvement by each since the inclusion of the territory on the list of NSGT in 1963. While the UNSC passed no resolution on the subject between 1975 (after S/RES 380) and 1988 (with S/RES 621), the UNSG did not issue any reports until June 1990 (S/21360). The UNGA adopted 16 resolutions between 1975 and the deployment of MINURSO, including two resolutions requesting the withdrawal of Morocco from the territory, "[urging] Morocco to join in the peace process and to terminate its occupation of the territory of Western Sahara" (34/37). The Assembly has also annually considered the question of "Spanish Sahara" from 1965 (later the question of "Western Sahara"), signaling the Assembly's primary role, which has been seized of the oversight and direction of decolonization worldwide from 1946 onward. The UNGA pursued its traditional and prescribed work regarding matters of decolonization. But this was overtaken in 1986 and decidedly by 1990 through UNSG and UNSC-led initiatives as evidenced by an increasing number of applicable resolutions. Given the ICJ advisory opinion and an armed conflict, the initial demurring of the Western Sahara question by the UNSG and UNSC from 1975 highlights the existing gap between the international legal and political mechanisms and the inability of the UN, as a political organization, to apply or compel international law. Yet, it is during this 1975–1991 period that the UN used the strongest language in a peace process narrative aimed at stopping violence.

The African Union

At the more regional level, the role of the African Union—and its predecessor (the Organization of African Unity OAU)—was more pronounced during the period prior to the deployment of MINURSO. In 1984, the SADR was admitted as a full member of the AU, resulting in Morocco's decision to withdraw the same year in protest. Morocco would only join the African Union in 2017. The admission of the SADR to the AU consolidated the movement in favor of its recognition internationally, with up to eighty-four UN member states officially recognizing the SADR. In the meantime, to strengthen its colonization of the territory, Morocco had begun building what it later called "le mur de défense" (the defense wall). In August 1980, following the withdrawal of Mauritanian troops the previous year, Morocco sought to "secure" a part of the territory that Mauritania had occupied. Construction of the wall—or "berm"—was completed in 1987 with an eventual overall length of just under 2,500 kilometers (Zunes & Mundy 2010, 21). A "coordination mission" was established in 1985 by the UN and the AU with representatives dispatched to find a solution to the conflict between the two parties. After consultations, the joint AU-UN mission drew up a proposal for settlement accepted by the two parties on 30 August 1988 and would later be detailed in the UNSG report S/21360 of 18 June 1990 and the UNSC resolution establishing MINURSO. The fact that the AU was part of the peace process and negotiations leading up to the Settlement Plan being agreed upon is not inadvertent. The continent was facing a similar decolonization challenge at a time the war in Western Sahara was ongoing. Namibia—formerly known as South West Africa—was also a case of decolonization preceded or interrupted by an episode of occupation by a neighboring *apartheid* South Africa. In contrast to Western Sahara, the UN laid the groundwork for human rights protection and conflict resolution long before the popular consultations organized in 1989 leading to its independence, notably through the creation of the UN Council for South West Africa in 1967[12] (later renamed Namibia in 1968).[13]

The European Union

Finally, the role of the European Union (EU) and that of the two-member states ought to be mentioned. The general position of the EU in the conflict in Western Sahara is a prime example of the primacy of its economic and political interests over the promotion of democracy and human rights. The European Economic Community (EEC), later the EU, was never much involved in the post-1975 phase of a peace process for Western Sahara. At the time when the war started, Spain, the former colonial power, was dealing with its inner political turmoil and evolution to democracy. It only joined the EU in 1986. Subsequently, the EU assumed responsibility for fisheries arrangements from Spain, with the first treaty signed with Morocco in 1988 (Smith 2013, 275). France's support of King Hassan II's expansionist plans was reaffirmed in its views against the "multiplication of micro-states" and materialized in arms shipments sent to Morocco during the war (Naylor 1987, 12). France certainly had to revise its policy and could not risk reaching a political and economic crisis with a newly independent Algeria, a former colony, and a privileged commercial partner with a deep historical, economic, and cultural connection. Following the end of its direct intervention in the territory in July 1978 and a visit by the Minister of Foreign Affairs in Algiers in March 1979, France's official position toward Western Sahara has been described as "impartial" (Naylor 1987, 14). However, as the peace process evolved into the next phases of the conflict, this apparent impartiality proved illusionary.

In the EU, the European Parliament was the first of its institutions to have mentioned the conflict in its work. Its first resolution on Western Sahara was adopted on 12 March 1981[14] when Spain had not yet joined the EEC. It mentioned "the end of Spanish administrative authority in Western Sahara" in its English version, which seems to have caused some confusion over Spain's status. Following its second resolution on the issue dated 17 December 1987,[15] the EU Parliament began to take the situation on the ground and the human rights conditions in Western Sahara into account in the resolutions approved in the following years.[16] All were adopted before the UNSC approved the Settlement Plan for Western Sahara in April 1991.

The momentum which followed the issuance of UNGA resolutions 34/37 and 35/19 of 1979 and 1980, the admission of the SADR to the AU in 1984, and the waterfall effect of international recognition of the new Sahrawi state in the late 1980s undeniably created leverage or sympathy in favor of Frente Polisario. At this stage of the peace process and given the disengagement of both Mauritania and France in the armed conflict as well as the impossibility for Spain to take a strong stand or an active role in the conflict due to internal disorder, it seemed that Frente Polisario had the upper hand diplomatically. Arguably, if Morocco was ascendant in the war, it would have never agreed to the Settlement Plan. The political background in which the armed conflict was taking place seemed, therefore, to be strengthening Frente Polisario's position in the international fora. These elements constitute the premises of a shift towards a 'war by other means' (Zunes & Munday 2010) - at least until the resumption of armed conflict in November 2020 - which materialized in 1991 with the deployment of MINURSO, discussed next.

TOWARD THE IMPASSE AND THE APPOINTMENT OF THE FIRST PERSONAL ENVOY: 1991–1997

The Settlement Plan agreed to in principle between Morocco and Frente Polisario in August 1988 was submitted to the UNSC on 12 July 1989 and approved in 1990 (resolution S/21360). On 29 April 1991, the UNSC established MINURSO in resolution 690, the terms of reference for it being set out in the UNSG's report of 19 April 1991. The operating mandate of MINURSO is routinely described in reports of the UNSG to the UNSC in 1990 (S/21360) and 1991 (S/22464). The plan provided for a cease-fire, followed by the organization of a referendum of self-determination for which the people of Western Sahara had to choose between two options: integration with Morocco or plain and simple independence.[17] In this regard, it provided for the creation of an Identification Commission to resolve the issue of the eligibility of Sahrawi voters for the referendum, an issue which has since generated a great deal of tension between the two parties. A Technical Commission was created by mid-1989 to implement the Plan, with a schedule based on several phases and a deployment of UN observers following the proclamation of a ceasefire (Jensen 2005, 132). Talks quickly began to draw up a voters list amid great differences between the parties. Frente Polisario maintained that the Spanish census of 1974 was the only valid basis, with 66,925 eligible adult electors (Díaz Hernández et al. 2014, 5), while Morocco demanded inclusion of all the inhabitants who, as settlers, continued to populate the occupied part of the territory as well as people from southern Morocco. It was decided that the 1974 Spanish census would serve as a basis, and the parties were to propose voters for inclusion because they were omitted from the 1974 census (Zunes & Mundy 2010, 186). In 1991, the first list was published with around eighty-six thousand voters. However, the process of identifying voters would be obstructed in later years, mainly by Morocco which attempted to include as many Moroccan settlers as possible. The criteria for eligibility had sometimes been modified to accommodate Morocco's demands and concerns (Zoubir & Pazzanita 1995). Up to 180,000 applications had been filed on the part of the Kingdom, the majority of which had been rejected by the UN Commission as they did not satisfy the criteria for eligibility (Zunes & Mundy 2010, 214). Consequently, the proclamation of "D-Day," which was in 1991 or 1992 to mark the beginning of a twelve-week transition period following the cease-fire leading to the referendum on self-determination, kept being postponed and eventually never declared.

The Deterioration of the Peace Process and the Reasons for the Emergence of a Deadlock

The impasse is, therefore, the result of the disagreements around the identification of eligible voters as well as what elective choice accepted voters are to have. Yet, King Hassan II, before the UNGA, made a solemn "commitment . . . to accept the holding of a referendum in Western Sahara to enable the people of that territory to exercise their right to self-determination," as recalled in UNGA resolution A/RES/38/40 of 7 December 1983. The frustration of the right to self-determination via referendum agreed upon by both parties in 1991 (and later in 1997 with the Houston Agreements) has become the crux of every discussion between the parties in the peace process[18] given the "winner-take-all" nature of the Settlement Plan. Arguably, MINURSO is meant to ensure the implementation of the peace agreement. Therefore, how has an agreement (and what has become a peacekeeping mission) aimed at ending a dispute become the ground for further disagreement? Several factors can explain the failure to implement the plan and organize the referendum, and thus, the deterioration of the peace process.

Firstly, the process with which the parties came to "agree in principle" on the Settlement Plan—and the difficulty to conform with AU Resolution 104 (XIX) of June 1983—has been questioned. Indeed, the latter called on both parties to negotiate directly[19] but the document which was later referred to as the Settlement Plan was presented to them separately. Marrack Goulding, the then–UN under-secretary-general for special political affairs noted there were no signatures on the settlement proposals and that there were times during the negotiations when he "even wondered whether the two sides had been shown the same document" (Goulding 2002, 201). The parties had never previously held formal direct talks (although there were informal, secret talks in 1978 and the presence of Hassan II in 1989), and therefore substantial issues were not addressed in the settlement proposals and implementation plan. Nevertheless, the enforceability of the plan is based on three factors. Firstly, its existence and endorsement by the UNSC arguably superseded all earlier directions and mutual commitments of the parties. Secondly, and despite that there is conceivably no agreement for Western Sahara comparable to other settlements directly signed by all the contending factions and therefore, clearly binding them, such as the 1991 Cambodia settlement,[20] the parties had solemnly pledged their cooperation and support for the Settlement Plan and their performance of the Plan demonstrated their contract-like acceptance of it. Thirdly, one can also argue that the Plan has, by its long operation, become a part of customary international law through the fulfillment of two constitutive elements required under Art. 38 of the ICJ statute: general and widespread practice and the belief that this practice is obligatory.[21] The International Law Commission has, more recently, issued its Draft Conclusions on Identification of Customary International Law. The Conclusions concern how the existence and content of rules of customary international law are to be determined.[22] Given the recent and ongoing debates around the capacity of international organizations to create custom independently from that of States, it would be however difficult to establish that a norm exists.

Secondly, the voter identification process was derailed at an early stage and, according to some observers, was doomed from the outset. The UN, indeed, arguably made the mistake of allowing the parties to put forward the candidates they wished to see take part in the referendum. The main mistake that was made on the part of the UN was to grant the parties a margin of maneuver concerning the identification of voters. All of the names that came to the Identification Commission had to be processed through the two parties.

More disturbingly, the procedure allowed an occupying Morocco to bring forward candidates to file petitions to be elected as voters.

Thirdly, MINURSO has, in most recent years, been described as unfit for that purpose, with an inadequate mandate, repartition of resources and even inadequate question to be asked at the prospective referendum (Sola-Martin, 2006; Theophilopoulou, 2006; Rousselier, 2019). This can be perceived as being the result of uncoordinated efforts from the three main UN organs. For instance, the political component of the mission was deemed disproportionate by the UNSG given the purpose of the mission *vis à vis* the military element (Sola-Martin 2006). As far as the mission's cost is concerned, it had been originally budgeted at $260 million in 1991 for an initial thirty-six-week operation. As a comparison, the total planned cost for organizing the referendum in Namibia fell just under US$370 million for over seven hundred thousand registered voters,[23] or nearly ten times as many voters as for a referendum in Western Sahara.[24]

Finally, the way the UNSC resolutions related to MINURSO were worded and the conflict, in general, illustrated the extent of UN involvement and revealed a certain latitude from the organization at this stage of the peace process (1991–1997). In contrast, in 1966, the UN, through a UNGA resolution, placed the territory of South West Africa under the direct responsibility of the organization. Following the creation of the United Nations Council for South West Africa mentioned previously, the Council went so far as to enact a Decree for the Protection of the Natural Resources of Namibia, in 1974. In UNSC resolution 435 of 29 September 1978 establishing the UN Transition Assistance Group in Namibia (UNTAG), delegates agreed to incorporate in the text strongly worded legal provisions including the "*legal responsibility* of the United Nations over Namibia," a reference to South Africa's "*illegal* administration" and the "early *independence* of Namibia through free elections under the supervision and control of the United Nations." These provisions, though without actionable legal implications for the UN as an organization, set a specific tone and a message geared toward more significant pressure to put on the main stakeholders—including the UN itself—to resolve the conflict. In the case of MINURSO, the language of the Settlement Plan does not include terms such as "legal responsibility," "illegal administration," or "occupation" and mostly refers to the conflict as a "question." This is a typical reflection of the background and political context occurring in the case of Western Sahara since the start of UN involvement in the political process. The conflict remains one of both legal and political discussions in various degrees. The legal battles initiated at European and national levels in the past decade about the trade in natural resources from the territory are prime examples of this duality.[25]

This status quo evident in the mid-1990s was mirrored at the EU level. At the time the UN Settlement Plan was issued, the EU Parliament approved a resolution in support of the Plan, and shortly afterward reiterated its demands for respect of human rights in different resolutions (12 September 1991, 29 October 1992, 27 May 1993, 10 February 1994, 16 March 1995, 13 July 1995). Yet, this did not prevent the EU from entering into an association agreement on 26 February 1996, which came into force in 2000. Henceforth, EU Parliament resolutions became less demanding about respect for human rights, instead inviting Morocco to a "broad and permanent dialogue aimed at promoting respect for human rights," as stated in Parliament's resolution of 6 June 1996.[26] Thus, the EU, through its foreign trade policy, embarked on the perpetuation of the status quo.

The Appointment of the First Personal Envoy of the UNSG for Western Sahara

In the face of the challenges caused by the identification of voters and the derailment of the peace process, then UNSG Kofi Annan appointed the first Personal Envoy for Western Sahara in 1997. The role had been created following an internal UN review based on developments on the ground and the emergence of a political stalemate (Whitfield 2007, 179–80; Zunes & Mundy 2010, 142; Theofilopoulou 2017, 40–41). On the one hand, the role of the PE must be distinguished from the role of the Special Representative of the UNSG (SRSG), who, according to the Settlement Plan, during the transitional period, was to exclusively lead the mission in the territory and perform organizational and supervisory functions in relation to the conduct of a referendum. On the other hand, the PE was to act as the lead UN negotiator (Zunes & Mundy 2010, 143; 207) and the first appointee was to answer three fundamental questions raised by the UNSG:

a. Can the settlement plan be implemented in its present form?
b. If not, are there adjustments to the settlement plan, acceptable to both parties, which would make it implementable?
c. If not, are there other ways by which the international community could help the parties resolve their conflict?[27]

It is clear from the UNSG report of February 1997 that the creation of this post was to bring the parties together and remedy the impasse to which the organization of the referendum has led.[28] Subsequently, negotiations between the parties were to be held "under the auspices of the PE." This has displaced the role of the SRSG further into the background, now a mere *fonctionnaire.* Indeed, the impasse, consolidated by the fact that the transitional period never officially began, already meant that the SRSG would never be able to perform the referendum-related duties he or she was required to under the Settlement Plan. From having a highly central role in the Settlement Plan detailed in 1990 and 1991 UNSC resolutions, the UN secretariat (via the SRSG) has slowly lost the authority it had been initially equipped with. By the 1997 appointment of James Baker and then the signing of the Houston Accords, the UN and the international community hoped to end the continuing disagreements stalling a referendum agreed upon at the start of the decade. Yet, a long stalemate was going to occur, partly due to the accession of Mohammed VI to the Moroccan throne in July 1999.

THE CRYSTALLISATION OF THE STALEMATE AND THE MOROCCAN PROPOSAL FOR AUTONOMY: 1997–2007

The year 1997 was marked by a series of direct talks conducted between the parties under the auspices of the newly appointed James A. Baker as PE. The protagonists met in Lisbon (on June 23), London (July 19 and 20), and back in Lisbon (August 29 and 30). The parties discussed voter identification as well as questions of troop withdrawal and confinement, political prisoners, prisoners of war, and a code of conduct for a referendum (Zunes & Mundy 2010, 208; Zoubir & Benabdallah 2004). As a result of these direct talks, the Houston Accords were signed in September 1997 and intended to clarify all outstanding issues.[29] The voter identification process was completed in 2000 when the final list of voters was published; however, Morocco rejected the list by appealing the decision to reject 135,431 of the candidates, which it sought to have enfranchised as voters (Zunes & Mundy 2010, 214). This rejection marked the crystallization of this next phase in the peace process.

A Shift in Morocco's Approach to Conflict Resolution in Western Sahara

The catalyst for change in the dynamics of the negotiation has certainly come from King Hassan II's death. The accession of his son, Mohamed VI, marked a significant shift in Morocco's stance on the peace process. Less permissive than his father in the face of what was presumed or expected from his reign, the new sovereign has attempted to focus his regime's efforts on legitimizing the occupation. He started offering attractive trade deals to foreign corporations, including from the EU. Attracting investors in Western Sahara has become the cornerstone of Morocco's strategy to legitimize its military presence in the territory and its annexation project by developing and growing the area economically and attracting more settlers (Naili 2021, 4). Beyond the exploitation of natural resources, events aimed at attracting new investors to these sectors under the monarch's patronage in the occupied area of the territory have perpetuated and legitimated an illegal military occupation, undermining the peace process. Nevertheless, the controversy around the first oil and gas exploration permits issued in 2001 by the Moroccan authorities to the American company Kerr-McGee and the French enterprise TotalFinaElf (currently Groupe Total, S.A.) attracted attention from the media, civil society, and the UNSC itself. The permits resulted in the UNSC requesting a legal opinion from the UN's senior jurist, Under-Secretary-General for Legal Affairs Hans Corell. Corell concluded that "if further exploration and exploitation activities were to proceed in disregard of the interests and wishes of the people of Western Sahara, they would violate the principles of international law applicable to mineral resource activities in Non-Self-Governing Territories."[30] Both companies eventually ended their exploration projects, but the exploitation of natural resources has become a new contentious issue between the parties and a new impediment to peace negotiations.

Mohamed VI found, within the UNSC itself, fertile ground for his enterprise. The UNSC persuaded in part by the "Group of Friends of Western Sahara" started to play into a strategy for the status quo influenced by Morocco's position regarding counterterrorism and immigration. The Group, whose best interest is or should be the resolution of the conflict, was formed in 1993, at a time when the creation of other groups proved effective (in El Salvador, Guatemala, or East Timor for instance). The Group is composed of France, Russia, Spain, the United Kingdom, and the United States, whose national interests seem to lack an evident coherence (Whitfield 2007, 165), mainly because most of them are favorable to Morocco. They place more emphasis on their relationships with Morocco—and Algeria—than on the implementation of the Settlement Plan (Whitfield 2005, 4), which eventually allowed Morocco to be rewarded—and the referendum on self-determination to be postponed—by its allies for services both in the war against communism and later in the "global war on terror" (Zoubir 2007, 159).

A direct consequence was the inclusion of the phrase "mutually acceptable political solution" in UNSC resolution 1309 of 25 July 2000, and the term "referendum" last mentioned in UNSC resolution 1359 of 29 June 2001. These certainly signaled a shift toward resolving the conflict based on a new approach. The contents of UNSG reports to the UNSC also shifted towards the search for an alternative resolution of the dispute during Kofi Annan's tenure. Up until September 1995, the UNSG limited himself to making observations in the last paragraph of reports to the UNSC. It is only when difficulties started to arise on the ground that secretaries-general began to include "recommendations." Indeed, in his report for 1995, Boutros Boutros Ghali suggested the possibility of MINURSO's withdrawal if "the conditions necessary for the start of the transitional period are not in place" before the end of the proposed extension.[31] However, in his report dated 22 May 2000, Kofi Annan highlighted "the fact that no enforcement mechanism was envisaged in the settlement plan" and that "it would be essential that the parties now offer specific and concrete solutions to the multiple problems relating to the implementation of the plan that can be agreed to."[32] The UNSC asked James Baker in 1997 to "explore all ways and means to achieve an early, durable and agreed resolution,"[33] and Kofi Annan even evoked for the first time in his report of October 2000 the idea of "alternative ways for self-determination."[34]

The Failure of Baker Plans I and II and the Moroccan Proposal for Autonomy

In this context—and following the failure in ensuring the implementation of the 1991 Settlement Plan and abandonment of the 1997 Houston Accords—Baker put forward two successive plans for consideration by the parties. After a tour of the region from 8 April to 11 April 2001, and several rounds of talks between the parties in April, May, June, and September, the Framework Agreement (or Baker Plan I) was put forward for consideration that June, but never submitted to the UNSC. Under the Agreement, an autonomous government of Western Sahara was to be responsible for internal affairs while the Moroccan government would have control over foreign relations and defense (Zunes & Mundy 2010, 223). A final status referendum—for which no option for independence was explicitly included—would take place within five years of the plan's implementation with voters "a full-time resident of Western Sahara for the preceding year."[35] Because the plan allowed for the establishment of an electorate largely favorable to Morocco, it was rejected by Frente Polisario, without comment. Baker Plan I was a clear departure from the Houston Accords (Zoubir & Benabdallah-Gambier 2004).

The Peace Plan for Self-Determination of the People of Western Sahara of 2003 (or Baker Plan II) was based on the Framework Agreement (Baker Plan I) and envisioned the holding of a referendum after a four or five-year transitional power-sharing between an autonomous Western Sahara Authority and the Moroccan state. The entire population of the territory could vote for the status of the territory, which included the option of independence. Although the UNSC 'supported' Baker Plan II in resolution S/RES/1495 which Frente Polisario reluctantly accepted, the option for independence caused Morocco to reject the plan altogether (Fernandez Molina 2016, 55) as largely explained in its letter annexed to the UNSC resolution S/2003/565 of May 2003.[36] Two months later, the UNSC affirmed for the first time that it was "acting under

Chapter VI of the Charter," suggesting that no decision could be forced upon the parties, unlike those taken under Chapter VII.[37]

Following Morocco's rejection of Baker Plan II and a complete suspension of referendum activities in 2003, Morocco's 2007 proposal for the autonomy of the territory under its sovereignty would perpetuate the stalemate following Baker's resignation in June 2004. Independence was not on offer. The proposal did not contemplate a shared or mutual sovereignty but rather offers control of local affairs through legislative, executive, and judicial bodies. The monarch would retain exclusive competencies regarding defense and external relations.[38] In April 2007, the UNSC called on the parties to "enter into negotiations without preconditions in good faith, taking into account the development of the last months," namely, Morocco's new proposal for autonomy (Fernandez Molina 2016, 64). The resolution was adopted despite the submission by the parties of two different and irreconcilable peace plans (Theofilopoulou 2010). This confirmed a break with Baker's view and ensured a stalled political process in the longer term, evidenced by the subsequent resolutions from the Council[39] and despite the appointments of Peter Van Walsum in 2005 as a new personal envoy.

CONCLUSION: THE PEACE PROCESS TODAY: 2007–2022

This chapter provides a rather brief account of events regarding the peace process in Western Sahara since the territory was first put on the 1963 list of territories to be decolonized. It offers an overview of the steps taken by both parties as well as the international community between 1975 and 2008 and the implications in terms of conflict (ir)resolution. The peace process in the conflict over Western Sahara seems to have, therefore, occurred in a cycle. Each time the parties reached an agreement, Morocco created obstacles to continuing the status quo. The 1991 Settlement Plan paved the way for a war "by other means" and a voter identification process held hostage by those hoping to not lose such a war. Following the 1997 Houston Agreement, the succession of Mohammed VI marked the beginning of a clear abandonment of the referendum to which the two parties agreed in 1991 and the start of the war "on other grounds" for Morocco, i.e., moving from discussing how the referendum would take place and to if it would be held at all.

The most recent fifteen resolutions adopted by the UNGA on the question of Western Sahara are characterized by both their extraordinary similarity and corresponding inertia. First, from resolution A/RES/62/116 of December 2007 onward, all documents presented the same number of paragraphs (seven), when the average between 1965 and 2006 was greater (over nine paragraphs). Secondly, references made to the Settlement Plan have completely disappeared. These trends would be repeated in the UNGA's annual resolutions without exception. Four years earlier, UNGA resolution A/RES/58/109 of December 2003 revealed several tendencies. All mention of the "referendum on self-determination" was removed. In a similar vein, "recalling the agreement in principle given on 30 August 1988" has disappeared from recitals. Lastly, the "presence of neighboring countries" in meetings and discussions also began to be highlighted from 2003 onward.

As far as the UNSC is concerned, the fact that MINURSO's mandate has started to be extended for one year since April 2008 rather than the maximum of six months in place since 1991 has deprived the resolution of the conflict of any sense of urgency. This confirms the growing detachment of the UNSC from the prospects of ensuring the organization of a referendum on self-determination. In this regard, since November 2001, the word "referendum" has not been used in any UNSC resolution on MINURSO (other than referring to the acronym of the mission itself) as mentioned earlier in this chapter. However, the notion of "self-determination" has been referred to multiple times since July 2003.[40] This is illustrative of the diminishing prospect holding of the referendum while maintaining the desire to implement some form of self-determination. Almost inadvertently, when the UNSC reaffirmed on one occasion "the provisions contained in paragraph 2 of Article 1 of the Charter of the United Nations" on self-determination (resolution 1359 of 29 June 2001),[41] it was the last time the word "referendum" was used in UNSC resolutions regarding MINURSO. It seems that Morocco's initial position of agreeing to a referendum on self-determination was driven by its fear of being diplomatically isolated in the African continent rather than by a genuine commitment to implement all the resolutions on the matter (Aguirre 1991). The content of UN resolutions bears witness to this approach. Subsequently, from the moment Morocco managed to subtly introduce the idea of an "autonomy plan" instead of a referendum, which would include an option for independence, resolutions had become lengthier and scarcer.

In addition, the role of PE has had two different forms. The role of the first Envoy—James Baker—was, in conjunction with the secretariat, to implement the 1991 Settlement Plan by conducting negotiations with the parties. However, his role was different from his successors in the sense that he created the proposals, the initiative was his and he pursued their negotiation. In addition, Baker had been appointed without the parties being consulted. For Baker's successors, their role was to facilitate direct negotiations between Morocco and Frente Polisario and they had no flexibility to introduce proposals of their own. Their role was to convene meetings and encourage negotiations. This distinction in the roles of PEs was made possible with the introduction of the "negotiations without preconditions" following Morocco's proposal as evoked in this chapter.

Despite a clear deterioration of the peace process over the decades, several factors have signaled a renewed interest in this protracted conflict among key actors and observers from the international community. A Special Envoy of the AU Council Chairperson for Western Sahara (Joaquim Alberto Chissano from Mozambique) was appointed by the Peace and Security Council of the African Union in June 2014. This was followed by Morocco becoming a member of the AU in January 2017. More recently, major events have begun to de-crystalize the status quo. The war resumed on 13 November 2020 following almost 30 years of ceasefire. Additionally, for the first time, a UN member state—the United States—recognized Morocco's claim to sovereignty over the territory. Former US President Trump's declaration of 10 December 2020—made less than a month after the resumption of armed conflict—has not been renounced by the current Biden administration as this recognition secured Morocco's support for Israel as per the Abrahamic Accords. Yet, in September 2021, the General Court of the European Union issued decisions invalidating fisheries and trade agreements between Morocco and the EU insofar as they extended to Western Sahara, disapproving Morocco's sovereignty.[42] Although these events have not directly impacted MINURSO's continuing mandate or facilitated a resolution, the changes in conflict dynamics have kept alive the prospect of ensuring the right of self-determination, leaving Western Sahara on the list of NSGTs. The conflict is indeed not resolved. But is it resolvable?

REFERENCES

Aguirre, J.R.D., Guerra en el Sáhara. Ediciones Istmo, 1991.

Dias Hernandez., R., Domingez Mujica., J., & Parreño Castellano., J., M., 'Gestión de la población y desarrollo urbano en el Sahara Occidental: un análisis comparado de la colonización española (1950–1975) y de la ocupación marroquí (1975–2013).' *Revista Electrónica de Geografía y Ciencias Sociales,* Vol. 18 (2014).

Fernandez-Molina, I., *Moroccan Foreign Policy under Mohammed VI*, 1999–2014. Routledge, 2016.

Fernandez-Molina, I., & Ojeda-Garcia, R. "Western Sahara as a Hybrid of a Parastate and a State-in-Exile: (Extra)territoriality and the Small Print of Sovereignty in a Context of Frozen Conflict." *Nationalities Papers- The Journal of Nationalism and Ethnicity*, 48: 1 (2019): 83–99. DOI 10.1017/nps.2019.34

Goulding, M. 2002. *Peacemonger*. John Murray Press.

Hodges, T. *Western Sahara: The Roots of a Desert War*, Lawrence Hill Books, 1983.

Hultman, T., 'The Struggle for Western Sahara.' *Issue: A Journal of Opinion*, Vol. 7, No. 1 (Spring, 1977), 27–32.

Jensen, E. *Western Sahara: Anatomy Of A Stalemate*. Lynne Rienner Publishers, 2005.

Naili, M. 'Defeating Illegal Trade in Western Sahara: Corporations under Pressure from NGOs,' *Journal of North African Studies* (April 2021), DOI: 10.1080/13629387.2021.1917124

Naylor, P., C., 'Spain and France and the Decolonization of Western Sahara: Parity and Paradox, 1975–87,' *Africa Today*, Vol.34, No. 3, Western Sahara: Africa's Forgotten War (3rd Qtr., 1987), 7–16.

Smith, J., 'Fishing for Self-determination: European Fisheries and Western Sahara—The Case of Ocean Resources in Africa's Last Colony,' *Ocean Yearbook*, Vol. 27, No.1 (January 2013), 267–90.

Solà-Martín, A. "Lessons from MINURSO: A contribution to new thinking." *International Peacekeeping*, Vol.13, No.3, (2006): 366–380. DOI:10.1080/13533310600824066.

Theofilopoulou, A. "Western Sahara: The failure of 'negotiations without preconditions,'" Peacebrief for the United States Institute of Peace, 2010.

Theofilopoulou, A. "The United Nations' Change in Approach to Resolving the Western Sahara Conflict since the turn of the Twenty-First Century," in Ojeda Garcia, R. Fernandez-Molina, I., & Veguilla, V. *Global, Regional and Local Dimensions of Western Sahara's Protracted Decolonization*. Palgrave Macmillan, 2017.

Whitefield, T. *Friends Indeed: The United Nations, Group of Friends and the Resolution of Conflicts*. United States Institute of Peace Press, 2007.

Zoubir, Y. H. "Soviet Policy toward the Western Sahara Conflict," *Africa Today* Vol. 34, No. 3, (1987), 17–32.

Zoubir, Y.H. "Stalemate in Western Sahara: Ending International Legality." *Middle East Policy*, Vol. 14, No.4. (2007): 158–77.

Zoubir, Y.H. & Benabdallah, K.G. (2004). "Morocco, Western Sahara and the Future of the Maghrib" (with Karima Benabdallah-Gambier, doctoral candidate), *Journal of North African Studies* [Commissioned/refereed], Vol. 9, No. 1, 49–77.

Zoubir, Y.H. & Benabdallah, K. (2003). "Western Saharan Deadlock" (co-authored with Karima Benabdallah-Gambier, doctoral candidate), *Middle East Report* [MERIP] [Commissioned/refereed], 227, 8–11.

Zoubir, Y.H. & Pazzanita, A.G. (1995). "The United Nations' Failure in Resolving the Western Sahara Conflict," *Middle East Journal*, Vol. 49, No. 4, Fall 1995, 614–28.

Zunes, S. & Mundy, J. *Western Sahara: War, Nationalism and Conflict Irresolution*. Syracuse University Press, 2010.

NOTES

1. Spain unilaterally rejected any international responsibility towards the territory in a letter dated 26 February 1976 from the Permanent Representative of Spain to the United Nations addressed to the secretary-general (A 31/56, S/11997). The declaration has been archived amongst UN Secretariat Working Papers on Non-Self-Governing Territories (NSGTs).

2. Western Sahara, Advisory Opinion, I.C.J. Reports 1975, p.12 para. 129, 162.

3. General Assembly "Report of the Committee on Information from Non-Self-Governing Territories" A/5514–Annex III of August 1963, available from https://www.undocs.org/A/5514(Supp).

4. Only the UNGA, the African Union (Peace and Security Council, Commission) and the High Court of South Africa have employed the descriptor 'occupied.' The UK High Court in its 2015 WSCUK first instance decision implied that Western Sahara was occupied. But the International Court of Justice did not use such a label or declared that Western Sahara is occupied as it was not when the opinion was published.

5. Report of the Secretary General S/2019/282, Situation concerning Western Sahara, para. 54, available from https://minurso.unmissions.org/sites/default/files/unsg_report_s.282.english.pdf.

6. *Western Sahara* (1975), Advisory Opinion, I.C.J. Reports 1975, p.12 §129, §162 available from https://www.icj-cij.org/public/files/case-related/61/061-19751016-ADV-01-00-EN.pdf.

7. The tribal assembly established by Spain in May 1967 was to serve as a local consultative link with the colonial administration (Hultman 1977, 27).

8. https://peacemaker.un.org/sites/peacemaker.un.org/files/MA-MR-ES_751114_DeclarationPrinciplesOnWesternSahara%28fr%29.pdf.

9. OCP Group no longer has a corporate style or name. The company discontinued its former government agency name, Office Chérifien des Phosphates (which was later incorporated as OCP, SA) to signal a clear break from being a state agency. However, it is still a parastatal corporation.

10. Spain also legislated the end of its responsibilities in the Cortes on November 19th, 1975. See the *Law on Decolonization of the Sahara*, Ley 40/1975 de 19 de noviembre sobre descolonizacion del Sahara, available from https://www.boe.es/boe/dias/1975/11/20/pdfs/A24234-24234.pdf.

11. UN Security Council resolution S/2002/161 of 12 February 2002, §6.

12. UN General Assembly resolution A/RES/2248 of 19 May 1967, Question of South West Africa, available at https://www.refworld.org/docid/3b00f048c.html.

13. UN General Assembly resolution A/RES/2372(XXII) of 12 June 1968, Question of South West Africa, available at https://digitallibrary.un.org/record/203084/usage?ln=fr.

14. European Parliament resolution on the Western Sahara, OJ C 77 (6-IV-1981) of 12 March 1981, available at https://www.usc.es/export9/sites/webinstitucional/gl/institutos/ceso/descargas/PE_res_120381_en.pdf.

15. European Parliament resolution on the Western Sahara, OJ C 13 (18-I-1988) of 17 December 1987, available at https://www.usc.es/export9/sites/webinstitucional/gl/institutos/ceso/descargas/PE_res_171287_en.pdf.

16. Resolution dated 15 March 1989, 15 February 1990 and 11 October 1990 respectively published in the Official Journal of the European Union on 17 April 1989, C 96, 59–61; 19 March 1990, C 68, p. 143–144; 12 November 1990, C 284, 131–32.

17. UN Secretary General report S/21360 on "The Situation Concerning Western Sahara," (18 June 1990), §1, available from https://digitallibrary.un.org/record/94688?ln=en.

18. The Houston Accords remains the last document which both parties had signed in an attempt to resolve all outstanding issues regarding the identification of voters (Zunes & Mundy 2010, 208–09).

19. AU resolution AHG/Res. 104 (XIX) on Western Sahara, §2, available at https://www.peaceau.org/uploads/ahg-res-104-xix-e.pdf.

20. Final Act of the Paris Conference on Cambodia, UNGA Letter dated 30 October 1991, from the Permanent Representatives of France and Indonesia to the United Nations addressed to the Secretary General, A146/608, October 30, 1991, Annex, 2–57.

21. The North Sea Continental Shelf cases of 1969 confirmed the necessity for widespread and representative participation, uniform practice, and general recognition of the rule of law. The Court also held that the passage of a considerable period of time was unnecessary for the formation of a norm of customary international law.

22. U.N. Doc. A/RES/73/203 (2018); see also ILC, "Draft conclusions on identification of customary international law and commentaries thereto," Report of the International Law Commission, Seventieth Session (30 April-1 June and 2 July–10 August 2018), U.N. Doc. A/73/10 (2018), 119–56.

23. UNTAG facts and figures webpage, available from https://peacekeeping.un.org/sites/default/files/past/untagF.htm.

24. Although Namibia never had a referendum as such. The elected constituent assembly simply moved to independence.

25. See, for reference, Council v Front Populaire pour la libération de la Saguia-el-Hamra et du Rio de Oro (Front POLISARIO), [2016], C-104/16 P; Order issued in the High Court of South Africa (Eastern Cape Local Division, Port Elizabeth) on Friday, 23rd February 2018 in the Case No. 1487/2017; and The Queen(on application of WSCUK) v Commissioners for Her Majesty's Revenue and Customs and Secretary of State for Environment, Food and Rural Affairs, [2018], C-266/16.

26. Official Journal of the European Union, 24 June 1996, C 181, 15–16.

27. UN Security Council, Report of the Secretary-General on the Situation Concerning Western Sahara, 5 May 1997, S/1997/358, available at: https://www.refworld.org/docid/3ae6aecd18.html, §17.

28. UN Security Council resolution S/1997/166 of 27 February 1997, available from https://digitallibrary.un.org/record/231541, §16.

29. (UN doc S/1997/742, paragraphs 4 to 13).

30. UN Security Council Resolution S/2002/161 of 12 February 2002.

31. UN Secretary General report S/1995/779, 8 September 1995, §52, available from https://digitallibrary.un.org/record/186203?ln=fr.

32. UN Secretary General report S/2000/461, 22 May 2000, available from https://digitallibrary.un.org/record/414738?ln=fr.

33. UN Security Council Resolution S/RES/1301.

34. UN Secretary General Report S/2000/1029.

35. UN Secretary General Document S/2001/613, Annex I:§5.

36. UN Secretary General report S/2003/565, 23 May 2003, available from https://minurso.unmissions.org/sites/default/files/unsg_report_23_may_2003.pdf.

37. UN Security Council resolution S/RES/1495, (31 July 2003), available from https://digitallibrary.un.org/record/499978?ln=fr.

38. Full text of the Moroccan initiative for an Autonomy Plan, submitted to the UN on 11 April 2007, available from http://www.moroccoembassy.org.au/?q=full-text-moroccan-initiative-autonomy-plan.

39. Thc content of UN Security Council Resolutions S/RES/1783 of 31 October 2007, S/RES/1813 of 30 April 2008, S/RES/1871 of 30 April 2009 and S/RES/1920 of 30 April 2010 are almost all identical. The following UN Security Council resolution (S/RES/1979) will refer to the term "human rights" for the first time.

40. UN Security Council resolution S/RES/1495, (31 July 2003), available from https://digitallibrary.un.org/record/499978?ln=fr.

41. UN Security Council resolution S/RES/1359, 29 June 2001, available from https://www.un.org/en/ga/search/view_doc.asp?symbol=S/RES/1359(2001).

42. See judgment of the EU General Court dated 29 September 2021 in joint case T-344/19 and T-356/19, available at https://curia.europa.eu/juris/document/document.jsf;jsessionid=F0B113BC90ABD496149454C39AD55EA0?text=&docid=246702&pageIndex=0&doclang=EN&mode=lst&dir=&occ=first&part=1&cid=360243.

Conclusion

General Comments on Statehood and Collective Aspirations

Sabella Ogbobode Abidde

In May 1998, the then-secretary-general of the United Nations, Kofi Annan, speaking on the broad issue of *independence, for self-rule*, asserted that "Ultimately, the struggle for independence, for self-rule—for the right of a people to be a master of its own destiny—is the struggle for human rights" (UN, 1998). While self-government connotes political independence and freedom from external forces and the ability to freely carry out all the functions of governance; statehood or nation-state, on the hand connotes the ability to have and to function as a sovereign entity with all the rights and responsibilities conferred on it by international law and at once function as a full member of the United Nations. In other words, to achieve international legal personality as a nation-state.

However, because of the convoluted nature of the international system, domestic and regional considerations; and because of the nature of realpolitik, some political entities are unable to gain statehood (become nation-states) even after meeting all the conditions outlined in Article 1 of the Montevideo Convention of 1933 viz: "the state as a person of international law should possess the following qualifications (a) a permanent population; (b) a defined territory; (c) government; and (d) Capacity to enter into relations with the other states (Avalon Project)." The entities at the center of this volume—the States of Palestine, Taiwan, and Western Sahara—have met the forested requirement, but are not considered nation-states.

Of the entities under discussion, the State of Palestine has made the most progress toward statehood. As of the spring of 2022, Palestine is recognized by 138 of the 193 UN member states and has a status of a non-member observer state in the United Nations (Charbonneau, 2012). However, despite the global goodwill toward Palestinian statehood, the State of Israel has consistently opposed the Palestinians; and the United States, a member of the UN Security Council, is determined to veto statehood unless Tel-Aviv signs off and or a complete peace treaty is achieved. Long before the United States became the major stumbling block, some scholars blamed the British and other colonial powers for the predicaments of modern Palestine, while others point to the duplicity of the parties involved in the numerous peace accords. While the State of Israel declared independence in 1948 and became a member of the UN in 1949; the Palestinians continue to live in a state of flux and uncertainty.

Much of the tension and hostilities in the Middle East and many other parts of the world are attributable to the Israeli-Palestinian brouhaha. As we approach the third decade of the twenty-first century, there is no justification for denying the Palestinians their sovereign state. Unless this issue is resolved, the State of Israel will continue to "live in fear" no matter her level of military superiority, technological advancement, and economic and political growth. A free and freed Palestine is also likely to hasten the acceptance of Israel by the people and governments in the Arab world. And indeed, in much of Africa, Israel is viewed with suspicion because of how they have and continue to treat the Palestinians.

The case of the Republic of China (ROC/Taiwan) seemed complicated, but not as complicated as that of the Palestinians. While the People's Republic of China (PRC/mainland China) claims Taiwan as one of its provinces; Taiwan and some scholars argue that Taiwan, in its current or original state, was never controlled or subject to the laws of the PRC. Essentially, they argued, Taiwan was not and is not part of China and is therefore deserving of statehood (Lin, Wu, and Yeh, 2022). Even if it were, they argued, it has been more than seven decades since the end of the Chinese Civil War; therefore, Taiwan ought to be able to conduct its domestic and foreign affairs independently.

But does China need Taiwan to be a part of it to continue on its match toward global hegemony? China's economy, going into the third decade of the twenty-first century is second only to that of the United States. Its military and technological reach is likely to surpass that of the United States within this or the next decade. All these and more she has achieved without Taiwan. So, what's the point of wanting Taiwan at all costs? Except, perhaps, on the grounds of nationalism. Or perhaps to say they brought the Kuomintang (KMT) to its knees and then formally declare an emotional victory which was never declared after the Chinese Civil War "ended" in 1949.

Unless the people and government of Taiwan agree to a confederation or some sort of "alignment" with China, talks of military annexation seem feasible at this or any point in the near future. Not minding the prevailing "One-China" policy and the absence of a formal defense treaty, the United States and her allies within and outside of the region are not likely to stand by and watch the invasion go on. Some countries would be happy to see China brought to its knees. So, an invasion would be militarily exorbitant for the Chinese. And of course, it would be financially costly to the Chinese and global economy. Especially to the Chinese economy! Third, it would have a politically destabilizing effect regionally. These negatives would severely impact China's place and standing in the world. Her goal and rise to global dominance would be curtailed by, say, three decades. And the leadership under which the ill-advised adventure took place would be replaced by contenting powerhouses within the Chinese Communist Party (CCP) and the People's Liberation Army (PLA).

Furthermore, a failed invasion would simply lead to a global clamor and fervor for "Independence Now for Taiwan." Within a year of the military misadventure, Taiwan will achieve its aspiration. So, what's the solution? Simple! Acquiesce to and promote the aspiration of the people and government of Taiwan. By so doing, the two states may—may—gradually move toward unification or at the very least a mutually beneficial confederation. Or a "one-state, two systems" that are interconnected at almost every level (except perhaps in terms of political culture and economic liberalization).

It's been more than seven decades since the Civil War ended. That's long enough for the PRC to give up military invasion or forceful unification of both countries. The Taiwanese should be allowed to decide their future, their destiny. It is also time for the international community—member states of the UN to realize that the status quo is unmanageable and indefensible. Statehood should be debated and granted this decade. Nothing else would do; anything else would be contrary to the idea of a people being the "master of their own destiny."

Western Sahara is an anomaly insofar as colonialism and decolonization in Africa are concerned. For much of its history, Spain used it as a port during the Transatlantic Slave Trade, but after the Berlin Conference of 1884/85, it became a colony. Thereafter, an agreement between Spain and Morocco allowed for its takeover by Morocco. Even as the wind of decolonization swept through the continent, Western Sahara's independence remained a complicated and protracted issue. Beginning with the International Court of Justice Advisory Opinion on Western Sahara in 1975, to the Baker Plan (2000) and the Manhasset negotiations (2007–2008), the international community has not been able to resolve this decades-old issue. Ironically, even the African Union (AU) seems powerless at ridding the continent of the last bastion of colonialism—unable to do what they did in Namibia, South Africa, and elsewhere.

The colonization of Western Sahara by Morocco is one of the waves of shame and embarrassment on the African continent. It speaks to the lack of courage, conviction, and political will on the part of the African Union and many African governments. One could and should also blame the UN, France, and the United States for the conflict and colonialism, but really, much of the blame lies with the AU and African governments for their inability to wrestle Western Sahara from Morocco. So far, it has become one of the longest conflicts on the continent and with an uncertain future. The uncertainties, hostilities, and conflicts can be ameliorated if the UN and members of the Security Council would simply "do the right things."

In chapter 1—"International Law and the Politics of State Recognition: An examination of the Cases of Western Sahara, the State of Palestine, and the Republic of China (Taiwan)"—Priye Torulagha tells us that "having examined the four conditions necessary for the attainment of statehood under the Montevideo Convention of international law and applying them to the Western Sahara/SADR, State of Palestine, and ROC (Taiwan), it is appropriate to draw some inferences. First, international law is defective in resolving disputes concerning state recognition due to the chaotic nature of international politics and state sovereignty. He then makes four interconnected assertions:

1. The three political communities are victims of ineffective international law and the structural imbalance in the Security Council system of the United Nations.
2. The UN needs to put pressure on the major actors on the Sahrawi issue so that a referendum is conducted to determine the status of SADR.
3. As Israel continues to build settlements in the West Bank and the Palestinians (Fatah and Hamas) are not in unison, a two-state solution as recommended by the UN and the Oslo Accord is eroding and incrementally being replaced by a possible one-state solution. In such a development, the notion of a purely Jewish or Palestinian state might be replaced by a binational state.
4. Fourth, since the idea of a One-China policy was originally initiated by the Republic of China and the world community agreed with the policy, Taiwan's desire for independence is compromised. Therefore, the only option left for both China and Taiwan is to continue to negotiate and find a peaceful means to resolve the matter, as recommended by the United States in the Starr Memorandum of July 12, 1971 (p. XX).

Torulagha went on to say that "in any given territorial dispute in which the indigenous population is seeking independence, it should be a codified requirement of international law that a referendum must be automatically conducted to allow people to decide whether they want independence or not in a disputed territory; (2) the global community must specify the minimum number of sovereign states an independent-seeking political community should establish relations with to gain full international recognition; and

(3) to create continental equality at the UNSC to facilitate the process of state recognition, it is time to include two states each from Africa, Asia, and Central and South America, as permanent members with veto powers in the Security Council."

Insofar as the quest for statehood is concerned, what matters is Justice. Justice! Not international relations, international law, or politics. Justice! Unless there is justice for the Palestinians, there will continue to be violent conflicts (and perhaps outright war) between the Palestinians and the Israelis. No side will know prolonged, sustainable, and enduring peace. And the UN and its member states cannot continue to look the other way vis-a-viz the hostility between China and Taiwan. The status quo is not peace, is not progress, and is not viable. There must be a final and fitting resolution that is in agreement with the aspiration of the people of Taiwan. In this case, too, it is about justice. It's been more than seven decades since the end of the Chinese Civil War. The UN and its member states must help bring the war to its logical conclusion. And who knew that some sixty years after the *year of independence*, an African country would still be colonized—and colonized by another African country for that matter? And so, the AU, along with the UN, must bring the Western Sahara (Sahrawi Arab Democratic Republic) matter to a close by forcing Morocco to leave the land they have illegally occupied for several decades. In this instance, as with the Palestinians and the Taiwanese, it is about justice and the collective aspiration of the people.

REFERENCES

Charbonneau, L. (2012, November 29). *Palestinians win implicit U.N. recognition of Sovereign State*. Reuters. Retrieved January 9, 2023, from https://www.reuters.com/article/us-palestinians-statehood-idUSBRE8AR0EG20121129.

Lin, H.-Y., Wu, C., & Yeh, Y.-Y. (2022). The Statehood of Taiwan. In S. O. Abidde (Ed.), *China and Taiwan in Africa: The Struggle for Diplomatic Recognition and Hegemony*. essay, Springer.

Treaties and other international agreements of the United States of America, 1776–1949. Avalon Project—Documents in Law, History and Diplomacy. (n.d.). Retrieved January 9, 2023, from http://avalon.law.yale.edu/20th_century/intam03.asp.

United Nations. (1998, May 22). *Struggle for independence, for self-rule is struggle for human rights, secretary-general states | UN press*. United Nations. Retrieved January 10, 2023, from https://press.un.org/en/1998/19980522.sgsm6571.html.

Appendix

Interviewees were sorted by organization, nationality, and gender. This part is just for the purpose of revision, I would rather not publish it in the final publication.

Organization	*Nationality*	*Gender*
Rabbis For Human Rights (IS1)	Israeli	Male
Rabbis For Human Rights (IS2)	Israeli	Female
Comet-ME (IS3)	Israeli	Female
All That's Left (IS4)	Israeli	Male
Centre for Jewish Non-Violence (IN1)	Israeli	Female
Ta'ayush (IS5)	Israeli	Male
Combatants for Peace (IS6)	Israeli	Male
ICAHD (Israeli Committee Against House Demolition) (IS7)	Israeli	Male
ICAHD (Israeli Committee Against House Demolition) (IS8)	Israeli	Male
The Villages Group (IS9)	Israeli	Male
Youth of Sumud (P1)	Palestinian	Male
South Hebron Hill Palestinian Popular Committee (P2)	Palestinian	Male
Operation Dove (IN2)	International	Male
AssoPace (IN3)	International	Female
Lawyer of Susyia (P3)	Palestinian origin with Israeli citizenship	Female
Susyia Popular Committee (P4)	Palestinian	Male
Ecumenical Accompaniment Programme in Palestine and Israel (P4)	Palestinian	Male
Bimkom (IS10)	Israeli	Male
Emek Shaveh (IS11)	Israeli	Male
Solidarity Sheikh Jarrah (P5)	Palestinian	Male

INDEX

About the Contributors

Sabella Ogbobode Abidde is professor of political science and a member of the graduate faculty at Alabama State University. He is the editor of two book series: Lexington Books' *African Governance, Development, and Leadership Series*; and Springer's *Africa-East Asia International Relations Series.* Dr. Abidde is an interdisciplinary scholar with a BA in international relations; an M.SC. in educational administration from Saint Cloud State University Minnesota; an MA in political science from Minnesota State University, Mankato, Minnesota; and a Ph.D. in African Studies, World Affairs, Public Policy, and Development Studies from Howard University. His scholarship includes single, edited, and co-edited volumes on Africa, Latin America, the Caribbean, and Africa-China-Taiwan relations. He is currently a MOFA Taiwan Fellow at the Center for Chinese Studies (National Central Library, Taiwan) and a Visiting Scholar at National Taiwan University, Taipei, Taiwan. Dr. Abidde is a member of the Association of Global South Studies (AGSS); the African Studies & Research Forum (ASRF); and the American Association for Chinese Studies (AACS).

Priye S. Torulagha holds a MA in Comparative Politics and Public Administration from Oklahoma State University, Stillwater, Oklahoma; an MHR in Counseling and Human Resources Management from the University of Oklahoma, Norman, Oklahoma; and a Ph.D. in Political Science from the same university. Dr. Torulagha writes regularly on Nigerian and African affairs, third-world politics, international terrorism, and democratic governance. He is the author of "Fidel Castro: His Impact on African Liberation and Governance," in Sabella O. Abidde and Charity Manyeruke (eds), *Fidel Castro and Africa's Liberation Struggle* (2020), and "China and Africa: The Beginning of a New World Order or A New Form of Colonialism," in Sabella O. Abidde and Tokunbo A. Ayoola (eds), *China in Africa* (2020).

Gbensuglo Alidu Bukari holds a Ph.D. in Development Studies (with a research focus on Political Economy of Elections); an MA in Democracy, Governance, and Law; an M.Sc. in Development Planning and Management (SPRING); a PGdp in Public Administration; a BA in Development Studies; and a Diploma in Public Administration. He is an alumnus of DAAD Centres for African Excellence and did his Post-Doctoral Research Fellowship at Merian Institute for Advanced Studies in Africa (MIASA). His research interests include political economy, the political economy of elections, the political economy of development, the political economy of governance, democracy, elections, and politics. He has been published in leading journals including *The Journal of Applied Economics and Finance*, *The Africa Journal of Public Sector Development and Governance*, *The Research in World Economy Journal*, *Legon Journal of the Humanities*, *The Social Science Journal*, and *The Journal of African Affairs*.

Stephen Zunes is professor of Politics and International Studies at the University of San Francisco, where he served as the founding director of the program in Middle Eastern Studies. He is the author of hundreds of articles for scholarly and general readership on Middle Eastern politics, U.S. foreign policy, international terrorism, nuclear nonproliferation, strategic nonviolent action, and human rights. He is the principal editor of *Nonviolent Social Movements* (Blackwell Publishers, 1999), the author of *Tinderbox: U.S. Middle East Policy and the Roots of Terrorism* (Common Courage Press, 2003), and co-author (with Jacob Mundy) of *Western Sahara: War, Nationalism and Conflict Irresolution* (Syracuse University Press, second revised expanded edition, 2022). Professor Zunes has served as a senior policy analyst for a Foreign Policy in Focus project of the Institute for Policy Studies, an associate editor of *Peace Review*, and a contributing editor of *Tikkun*.

Lawrence Mhandara is senior lecturer of Political Science in the Department of Governance and Public Management, University of Zimbabwe, Harare, Zimbabwe. He is also a visiting lecturer at the Institute of Governance, Humanities, and Social Science of the African Union's Pan-African University in Yaounde, Cameroon. Lawrence received his BSc in Politics and Administration and an MSc in International Relations at the University of Zimbabwe. He obtained his Ph.D. in Peacebuilding at the Durban University of Technology, Durban, South Africa. Lawrence is the co-editor of a published book:—*Re/membering Robert Gabriel Mugabe: Politics, Legacy, Philosophy, Life & Death*—and three forthcoming books, and he is the author of several book chapters and articles in peer-reviewed journals. His areas of specialty and research interests include international relations; international security; strategic studies; governance and politics in Zimbabwe; peace and conflict; and comparative peacebuilding.

Konstantinos D. Magliveras is attorney-at-law in Athens, Greece. Having previously taught at the University of Aberdeen, Sussex University, and the University of East Anglia, he is presently a professor in the Law of International Organizations at the University of the Aegean. He has published extensively in the areas of public international law, international criminal law, European Union law, international and regional protection of human rights, and transnational migration. His most recent book is F. Amao, M. Olivier, and K. Magliveras (eds), *The Emergent African Union Law: Conceptualization, Delimitation, and Application*, Oxford University Press, 2021.

Gino Naldi holds an LL.M. and an Ph.D. from the University of Birmingham. He is a former university senior lecturer in Law in the United Kingdom. His expertise is in the fields of public international law, human rights, and EU law. Dr. Naldi has a particular interest in international law as it relates to Africa, focusing on the organization of African unity/African union. He has published widely in learned journals, including *The African Yearbook of International Law*, *The International & Comparative Law Quarterly*, *The International Human Rights Law Review*, *The Journal of African Law*, *The Netherlands International Law Review*, *The Revue québécoise de droit international*, and *The Zeitschrift für auslandisches öffentliches Recht und Volkerrecht.* He is a co-author, with Professor Konstantinos Magliveras, of *The African Union* (Kluwer Law International 2018) and the *Association of Southeast Asian Nations (ASEAN)* (Kluwer Law International, 2022).

Federica Stagni is Ph.D. candidate in Political Science and Sociology at Scuola Normale Superiore, supervised by Donatella della Porta and Lorenzo Bosi. Her research interests include theories of political protests and social movements in Israel and Palestine. Federica holds a master's degree in European and International Studies from the School of International Studies of Trento. She worked as a research associate for ACLED and studied at the University of Lisbon and the University of Portsmouth as an exchange student. Her Ph.D. thesis deals with women's and anti-demolition movements in Israel and Palestine. In particular, she looks at these mobilizations by applying the social movement theory and a relational approach relying on a process-tracing method. She is the co-author of *The Israeli Settler Movement: Assessing and Explaining Social Movement Success*, New York: Cambridge University Press, 2021.

Idowu Johnson received his B.Sc, M.Sc, and Ph.D. degrees in Political Science at the University of Ibadan, Nigeria. He is currently a senior lecturer in the Department of Political Science, University of Ibadan, specializing in international relations. His research interests cover foreign policy, African politics, peace and conflict resolution, identity politics, Middle East politics, and strategic and development studies. He is the author of *Diplomacy, Conflicts, Bargaining and Peacebuilding in International Relations* (Gratia Associates International Press, 2015). He has contributed chapter in *Africa After Fifty Years: Retrospections and Reflections* (Africa World Press, New Jersey, 2013); *Nationalities, Identities, and Terrorism: The Nigerian Experience* (John Archers, 2013); and *Global Peace Leadership Summit 2007: Africa and the Diaspora* (Theological Seminary Press, USA, 2008). He also has published in journals at both national and international levels. He is an honorary research fellow at the French Institute for Research in Africa (IFRA), the University of Ibadan, and a member of the Nigerian Political Science Association (NPSA), the Nigerian Society for International Affairs (NSIA), and the Society for Peace Studies and Practice (SPSP).

Dean Karalekas is affiliated research fellow at the Centre of Austronesian Studies at the University of Central Lancashire, and editor-at-large of the journal *Strategic Vision*. He earned an MA in Taiwan Studies, as well as a Ph.D. from the International Doctoral Program in Asia-Pacific Studies, both at Taiwan's National Chengchi University. He also holds a B.Ed. from Canada's McGill University. He currently resides in Ottawa, Ontario, though he has lived for several years in Taiwan, and he has a particular interest in Taiwan's unique international situation—a line of inquiry that has seen him travel to several underrecognized states and potential flashpoints such as North Korea, Mindanao, Kosovo, and Transnistria. He is the author of *The Men in No Man's Land: A Journey Into Bir Tawil* and *Civil-Military Relations in Taiwan: Identity and Transformation*. Dean is also an avid ethnographic and narrative filmmaker, having produced, written, and directed several award-winning films on a diversity of subjects, from the Canadian experience in World War II to indigenous mythology.

Felix Kumah-Abiwu is associate professor at the Department of Africana Studies at Kent State University. He is also the founding director of the Center for African Studies at Kent State. He received his Ph.D. in Political Science from West Virginia University. He also studied at Ohio University and the Legon Centre for International Affairs & Diplomacy, University of Ghana. His research focuses on political leadership in Africa, elections/democratization, African security issues, foreign policy analysis, global narcotics policy, Black males/public education in the African diaspora, and African-centered theories. In addition to his published book, scholarly book reviews, encyclopedia entries, and several book chapters, Dr. Kumah-Abiwu's scholarly articles have also appeared in *The Commonwealth Journal of International Affairs (The Round Table)*, *The Journal of Pan African Studies*, *West Africa Review*, *The International Journal of Public Administration*, *Urban Education*, *The Journal of Men's Studies*, *The Journal of Economics/Sustainable Development*, *Commonwealth & Comparative Politics*, and *African Security Review*.

Cristiano D'Orsi is senior research fellow and lecturer at the South African Research Chair in International Law (SARCIL), Faculty of Law, University of Johannesburg. He holds a Laurea (BA [Hon] equivalent, International Relations, Università degli Studi di Perugia, Perugia); a master's degree (Diplomatic Studies, Italian Society for International Organization [SIOI], Rome); a two-year Diplôme d'Etudes Approfondies (Master of Advanced Studies equivalent, International Relations [International Law], Graduate Institute for International and Development Studies, Geneva); and a Ph.D. in International Relations (International Law) from the same institution. In addition, Cristiano did postdoctoral studies at the University of Michigan Law School (Hugo Grotius Fellow) and the Centre for Human Rights, University of Pretoria. Cristiano's research interests mainly focus on the legal protection of asylum-seekers, refugees, migrants, and IDPs in Africa, on African Human Rights Law, and the development of Public International Law in Africa.

J.J.P. Smith teaches law and human security at the Norman Paterson School of International Affairs at Carleton University in Ottawa. A practicing lawyer, he was counsel to the UN transitional administration in East Timor (Timor Leste) from 1999 until that country's independence in 2002. For more than fifteen years, he has served as an advisor for international law to the government of the Saharawi Arab Democratic Republic. Dr. Smith's scholarly research includes the application of international humanitarian law in decolonization, the development of oceans law in Africa, and the international order for global oceans environmental protection. His recent works about Western Sahara include "A Four-Fold Evil? The Crime of Aggression in Western Sahara," *International Criminal Law Review* (2020); "Plunder Intercepted: The legal case to seize globally trade phosphate from occupied Western Sahara," in *Profit over peace in Western Sahara Africa* (2018); and "Western Sahara Boundary Marker," in *International Law's Objects* (2018). In addition to bachelor of science, juris doctor, and master of laws degrees, he holds a doctorate from McGill University.

Meriem Naili holds a Ph.D. from the University of Exeter (United Kingdom) in Security, Conflict, and Human Rights. She obtained her master's degree in Public International Law from the University of Grenoble (France) and Amsterdam (The Netherlands). She is a member of the steering committee of the International Academic Observatory on Western Sahara (OUISO) at the University of Paris Descartes and a junior researcher at the African Research Institute of Óbudai University, Budapest. Her research focuses on the absence of human rights monitoring mechanisms within the MINURSO mandate and its impact(s) on the evolution and resolution of the conflict in Western Sahara. She is also interested in the issue of access to natural resources, and in December 2019, she published an article on the legal battle over natural resources at the EU level in the *Cahiers de L'Ouest Saharien Journal*. She is also the author of an article entitled "Defeating Illegal Trade in Western Sahara: Corporations under Pressure from NGOs," published in *The Journal of North African Studies* (April 2021). Meriem has been invited to speak in Conflict Analysis modules at the Open University of Barcelona, the University of West England, Bristol, and La Sorbonne University in Paris.

Ingram Content Group UK Ltd.
Milton Keynes UK
UKHW011413070723
424728UK00006B/68